Hermann Lange

German Composition

A Theoretical and Practical Guide to the Art of Translating English... Third Edition

Hermann Lange

German Composition
A Theoretical and Practical Guide to the Art of Translating English... Third Edition

ISBN/EAN: 9783337077822

Printed in Europe, USA, Canada, Australia, Japan

Cover: Foto ©Thomas Meinert / pixelio.de

More available books at **www.hansebooks.com**

Clarendon Press Series

GERMAN COMPOSITION

A THEORETICAL AND PRACTICAL GUIDE

TO THE ART OF TRANSLATING ENGLISH PROSE

INTO GERMAN

BY

HERMANN LANGE

LECTURER ON FRENCH AND GERMAN AT THE MANCHESTER TECHNICAL SCHOOL
AND LECTURER ON GERMAN AT THE MANCHESTER ATHENÆUM

THIRD EDITION

With the German Spelling revised to meet the requirements of the
Government Regulations of 1880

Oxford

AT THE CLARENDON PRESS

M DCCCC

Oxford
PRINTED AT THE CLARENDON PRESS
BY HORACE HART, M.A.
PRINTER TO THE UNIVERSITY

PREFACE.

'GERMAN COMPOSITION' is intended to be a Theoretical and Practical Guide to the Art of Translating English Prose into good and idiomatic German. It is arranged in such a manner that students who have reached the fiftieth Lesson of the 'German Manual' may commence and advantageously use it conjointly with that book. Being complete in itself, it is likewise adapted for the use of any other students who, possessing a knowledge of German Accidence and having had some practice in reading German Prose, wish to acquire the Art of Translating English Prose into German.

The book is calculated to serve the requirements of the B.A. Examinations of the London and Victoria Universities, the Competitive Examinations for the Civil and Military Service, the Oxford and Cambridge Local Examinations for Senior Students, the Examination of the College of Preceptors for First Class Candidates, and of similar Public Examinations—all of which require the candidates to translate English Prose into German.

I may conscientiously say that I have done all I could to make the book attractive and useful. The selection of the Extracts has been made with the greatest care directly from the works of the various authors, and is the result of many years' attentive reading and research. The pieces have been almost exclusively chosen from the works of the best modern English and American writers, and, it is hoped, will be found as interesting and instructive as they are well adapted for translation into German. They represent all the various styles of English Prose Composition, and contain a great variety of subjects, as a glance at the various pages will show; whilst the fact that the specimens, with only one or two exceptions, are no mere fragments, but complete pieces in themselves, must necessarily add to their value.

The Biographical Sketches of famous men and women, which at intervals appear in the Notes and are always given in German, form a special feature of the book. (Comp. S. 127, N. 1; S. 138, N. 12; and

S. 156, N. 1.)   They are of various lengths, according to their importance, and have been written to add to the interest of the work and at the
same time to offer the student some useful material for reading German.

With respect to the help given in the Notes, I may state that I have
proceeded with the utmost consideration and care.   The great object
I placed before me was to show, by precept and example, that a good
translation cannot be produced by the mere mechanical process of join-
ing together a number of words, as the dictionary may offer them at
first sight: but that it requires great thought and analytic power; that
every sentence, nay, almost every word, has to be weighed and considered with respect to its true bearing upon the text; and that a good
rendering is only possible when the translator has grasped the true
meaning of the passage before him.

I have endeavoured to give neither too little nor too much help, but
whenever I found a difficulty which a student of average ability could
not fairly be expected to overcome, I have stepped in to solve it.   For
this purpose I have made use of English equivalents and periphrases and
of Rules and Examples, and in cases where neither of these helps was
considered practicable I have not hesitated to give the German rendering
of the word or passage to be translated.   The last mode of procedure,
however, I have adopted only when I found that the dictionaries in
ordinary use were insufficient, as is so frequently the case, and more
especially with respect to idiomatic passages, which it is impossible to
render successfully unless the translator is well versed in both languages,
and at the same time has undergone a thorough training in the Art of
Translating English into German, which the present volume professes to
teach.   The plan of indicating the rendering of words and phrases by
means of English equivalents and periphrases must be of evident advantage to the learner, for it teaches him how to think and analyse, whilst
it leads him to render the word or phrase correctly without giving him
the translation itself.

The Notes of Sections 1 to 150 and the Appendix contain in a concise and lucid form almost all the rules relating to the German Syntax,
and in most instances these rules have been illustrated by practical
examples and models.   The Appendix gives in thirty-seven paragraphs
the Rules referring to the Construction, the use of the Indicative, Subjunctive (or Conjunctive), and Conditional Moods, which for convenient
reference have been reprinted from my 'German Grammar,' and to fa-
cilitate the student's work I have added an Index to the Grammatical
Rules and Idiomatic Renderings.

In a work containing such a great number of Extracts as the present, there are, of course, many idioms and passages which may be correctly translated in various ways, and I can therefore scarcely hope that all my renderings will meet with the approval of every German scholar. I may, however, confidently affirm here that I have devoted much thought and labour to this publication, and that I have tried with all my heart to make it acceptable to teachers and students alike.

In conclusion I respectfully tender my best thanks to the publishers—

Messrs. W. and R. Chambers, Edinburgh,

      „   Chapman and Hall,

      „   Longmans and Co.,

      „   Sampson Low and Co.,

      „   Macmillan and Co.,

Mr. Murray,   } London,

Messrs. T. Nelson and Sons,

      „   Smith, Elder, and Co., and

      „   Stanford and Co.,

and to the Editors of—

The Daily News,

    „ Daily Telegraph,

    „ Globe,   } London.

    „ Standard, and

    „ Times,

for their very kind permission to make use of the Copyright Extracts in this publication, and for the cordial manner in which they granted my request.

Page ix contains a few Hints and Directions for using the Book which I consider of great importance, and to which I beg to draw attention.

HERMANN LANGE.

HEATHFIELD HOUSE, LLOYD STREET,
GREENHEYS, MANCHESTER,
September, 1883.

PREFACE TO THE SECOND EDITION.

A second edition of this volume having been called for, I wish to express my cordial thanks to the numerous colleagues and friends who adopted it as a text-book for their classes.

As I am engaged in preparing, besides this book, a third edition of two other volumes of my 'German Course,' and, at the request of the Delegates of the University Press, also a Key to this volume, 'German Composition,' I think the present moment opportune for introducing the reformed German spelling which, by Government regulations, has been taught in German schools for the last five or six years, and is becoming more generally used from year to year in friendly intercourse, papers, periodicals, literature, and commercial correspondence. It is but fair that the students of German in this country should be taught to spell in the simplified way now universally practised by their German contemporaries. They will at least have nothing to unlearn then ; and, although the present spelling-reform may be considered but a compromise between the older and the younger schools, there being a tendency in the younger men to go even further than their older colleagues in the simplification of our orthography and to make it still more phonetic and uniform in principle, it will take a long time before the Government will be moved to make modifications of any importance in their regulations. I confidently trust that the great trouble I have bestowed upon the revision of the present edition will be appreciated by teachers and students alike. It will easily be seen that the alterations of the orthography in the various books forming this 'German Course' must have necessarily entailed a very considerable additional expense; but the publication having met with much approval on the part of the public, I was anxious to leave nothing undone in order to adapt it in every respect to the requirements of the times and to make it still more useful.

On examination it will be seen that the changes made are not so many as may be supposed, and that the principles underlying the German spelling-reform are simple and easy to understand.

At the end of the Appendix will be found a Synopsis of the principal changes the German spelling has undergone, accompanied by Examples and a few Exceptions to the general rules.

HERMANN LANGE.

HEATHFIELD HOUSE, LLOYD STREET, GREENHEYS, MANCHESTER,
December, 1886.

DIRECTIONS FOR USING THE BOOK.

Each Section should first be prepared for *viva voce* translation, *with* the assistance of the Notes in class; then translated in writing; carefully corrected; and finally practised, by comparing the English text with the corrected German version, FOR A SECOND *viva voce* TRANSLATION until the student is able to translate the English text, *without* the assistance of the Notes in class, just as readily into correct German as if he were reading from a German book.

The Grammatical Rules given in the Notes should always be carefully studied, and the reading of previously given Rules and the various paragraphs of the Appendix referred to in the text should never be omitted.

The strict and conscientious observance of these directions is earnestly requested.

THE SECOND *viva voce* TRANSLATION *without* the assistance of the Notes in class, as explained above, is especially of the greatest importance to the student's progress in the Art of Translating English into German, and is the only way of mastering all the idiomatic and syntactic difficulties contained in the Lessons and explained in the foot-notes. It commends itself likewise as the best way of committing to memory the great number of words and the various forms of construction occurring in the text, and will gradually, but surely, lead to the acquisition of a good and thorough German style of writing.

To be quite clear the Author ventures to propose the following

PLAN OF WORKING.

FIRST LESSON.

Prepare for *viva voce* translation Sections 1 and 2, WITH the assistance of the Notes in class.

SECOND LESSON.

Translate in Writing Sections 1 and 2; and prepare for *viva voce* translation Sections 3 and 4, WITH the assistance of the Notes in class.

THIRD LESSON.

PREPARE FOR FLUENT AND CORRECT *viva voce* TRANSLATION Sections 1 and 2, WITHOUT the assistance of the Notes in class, by comparing the English text with the corrected German version; translate in Writing Sections 3 and 4; and prepare for *viva voce* translations Sections 5 and 6, WITH the assistance of the Notes in class.

FOURTH LESSON.

PREPARE FOR FLUENT AND CORRECT *viva voce* TRANSLATION Sections 3 and 4, WITHOUT the assistance of the Notes in class, by comparing the English text with the corrected version; translate in Writing Sections 5 and 6; and prepare for *viva voce* translation Sections 7 and 8, WITH the assistance of the Notes in class;

Then proceed in the same way throughout the book.

It need scarcely be added that the quantity of work pointed out here may be diminished or increased according to circumstances, and that the longer sections towards the end of the book will in most cases require the former course.

The frequent attentive study of German literature will be a powerful auxiliary to this book in imparting the Art of Translating English Prose into German.

ABBREVIATIONS AND SIGNS EXPLAINED.

Acc.	Accusative.
adj.	adjective.
adv.	adverb.
App.	Appendix.
art.	article.
Comp.	compare.
comp.	compound.
conj.	conjunction.
constr.	construction.
contr.	contracted.
Dat. (*or* dat.)	Dative.
def.	definite.
d. h.	(das heißt), that is.
demonstr.	demonstrative.
e.g.	{ (exempli gratia), for example.
etc.	{ (et cetera), and so forth.
Expl.	Example.
fem., *or* (f.)	feminine.
geb.	(geboren), born.
Gen.	Genitive.
i.e.	(id est), that is.
Impf.	Imperfect.
impers.	impersonal.
indef.	indefinite.
Inf.	Infinitive.
insep.	inseparable.
intr., *or* intrans.	intransitive.
Liter.	Literally.
m., *or* (m.)	masculine.
N.	Note.

n.	noun.
neut., *or* (n.)	neuter.
Nom.	Nominative.
p. p.	Past Participle.
p. ps.	Past Participles.
pers.	person.
persnl.	personal.
posses.	possessive.
prep.	preposition.
Pres.	Present.
pres. p.	Present Participle.
pron.	pronoun.
refl.	reflective.
reg.	regular.
relat.	relative.
S.	Section.
Sing.	Singular.
str.	strong.
Subj.	Subjunctive.
tr., *or* trans.	transitive.
u. a.	{ (und andere), and others.
u. f. w.	{ (und so weiter), and so forth.
v.	verb.
viz.	{ (videlicet), namely, to wit.
w.	weak.
§	paragraph.
†	(gestorben), died.
=	is equivalent to.

CONTENTS.

CONTENTS. XV

Specimens
of
German Handwriting.

Capital Letters.

A, B, C, D, E, F, G, H,

I, J, K, L, M, N, O, P,

Q, R, S, T, U, V, W,

X, Y, Z.

Small Letters.

a b c d e f g h i j

k l m n o p q r s

Compound Consonants.

Einbildung

Ein Mann hatte die Ge-
wohnheit, oft mit sich selbst
zu sprechen. Einer seiner
Freunde hatte es bemerkt.
Warum sprechen Sie so
oft mit sich selbst? fragten
er ihn eines Tages. –
Das will ich Ihnen sagen,
war die Antwort.
Erstens mag ich gern
einen vernünftigen
Menschen sprechen hören;
und zweitens mag ich
gern mit einem vernünf-
tigen Menschen reden.

GERMAN COMPOSITION.

1. Words which, in the English text and in the periphrases of the English text, are printed in *Italics*, must not be translated.
2. When two words are separated by a dash (—) in the Notes, they represent the first and last word of a whole clause in the English text, and the rendering refers to the clause thus indicated.
3. When two or more words are separated by dots (. . .) in the Notes, the rendering refers to those words only.
4. The sign = is used in the meaning of: 'is equivalent to'.
5. As a rule, the periphrases are given in correct English construction.

Section 1.

A GOOD MAXIM[1].

My maxim is: never to begin[2] a book without finishing[3] it, never to consider[4] it finished without[5] knowing it, and to study[6] it with[7] a whole mind.—Sir Thomas Buxton. ,

1, Grundſatz, m. 2, to begin, anfangen. When the **Infinitive** is used either subjectively or objectively, it is generally preceded by the preposition zu, and is called **Supine**. Comp. S. 78, N. 14, 1. To form the **Supine Present** of compound separable verbs, like anfangen, we must place the preposition zu between the separable prefix and the verb. The Supine must be used here. See App. § 1. 3, to finish, beendigen. The **Supine** is generally used for rendering the **English Gerund** (i.e. the verbal in -ing) when the latter is governed by a preposition, though, sometimes, this form may be rendered by the help of the subordinative conjunction daß and a finite verb (i.e. one with a personal termination); as—

He judges *without understanding* anything about the matter.	Er urteilt, ohne etwas von der Sache zu verſtehen, *or* ohne daß er etwas von der Sache verſteht.

Use the Supine, which is always to be placed at the end of the clause. 4, To consider a thing finished, eine Sache als beendigt betrachten. The pronoun 'it' should begin the clause. See App. § 2. 5, without—it, ohne mit dem Inhalt deſſelben vertraut zu ſein. 6, to study, ſtudieren. 7, with—mind = with undivided attention.

Section 2.

WHAT IS ETERNITY?

The following question was[1] put in writing[2] to a boy[3] in the deaf-and-dumb school[4] at Paris: "What is eternity?" "It is the life-time of the Almighty," was the answer.—Rev. R. K. Arvine.

1, Here the verb is in the Passive Voice. Remember that the German Passive Voice is formed by the auxiliary werden. The verb is in the Passive Voice whenever the subject is suffering the action expressed by the verb; as—

The castle *was built* in the year 1609.   Das Schloß wurde im Jahre 1609 erbaut.

To put a question to a person, einem eine Frage vorlegen.   2, in writing, schriftlich, which place before the p. p. (App. § 1).   3, boy = pupil.   4, Taubstummenanstalt, f.; render 'in the' by the gen. of the def. art.; at = in.

Section 3.

THE ACTION[1] OF[2] WATER.

The action of water on[3] our food[4] is very important. There[5] would be no carrying of food into the system but for the agency of water. It dissolves everything[6] that[7] we take[8], and nothing[9] that we take as food can[10] become nutriment that[11] is not dissolved in water.—Dr. LANKESTER.

1, 'action', here = operation, Wirkung, f.   2, Use the gen. of the def. art. The definite article is always required before nouns representing the whole of a given class, and before abstract nouns taken in a general sense.   3, on = upon.   4, food = victuals, Speisen, pl.   5, This sentence must be construed in a somewhat different way; say: 'Without the agency (Vermittelung, f.) of water, no food (Nahrung, f.) would be conveyed into the body,' würde dem Körper keine Nahrung zugeführt werden.   6, everything = all.   7, 'that', here was. The indefinite relative pronoun was is the pronoun generally required after the indefinite numerals alles, etwas, manches, nichts, viel, and wenig, after the indefinite demonstrative pronoun das, and also after a superlative used substantively; as Das Schönste, was ich habe.   8, 'To take', when used of food, may be rendered by essen, trinken, or genießen, which latter verb should be used here.   9, 'nothing—food', may be briefly rendered by 'keine genossene Speise'.   10, can — nutriment = can serve as nutriment (Ernährung, f.). The verb dienen requires the prep. zu, which governs the dat. and must here be contracted with the def. art. into zur; see N. 2.   11, that—water = before (ehe, see App. § 17) the same (f.) is dissolved in water.

Section 4.

OF[1] WHAT USE IS IT?

When[2] Franklin made his discovery of the identity[3] of lightning[3] and electricity[3], it[4] was sneered at[5], and *people* asked: "Of what use is it?" To[6] which his apt reply was: "What is the use of a child? — It may[7] become a man!"— S. SMILES.

1, Of—it, Wozu nützt es?   2, 'When', referring to definite time of the Past, must always be rendered by 'als'.   3, of the identity, von der Identität, f.; see S. 3, N. 2.   4, When the agent from which the action proceeds is not mentioned, the English Passive Voice is often rendered by a reflective verb, or by the indefinite pronoun man and a verb in the Active Voice; as—

At last the book *was found.*   Endlich { fand sich / fand man } das Buch.

Say 'people (man) sneered at it.'   5, A. To sneer at something, über etwas spotten; B. 'at it' = there at, darüber.   The English pronouns 'it', 'them', 'that', and 'those', dependent on a preposition governing in German the dative or accusative, are generally to be rendered by the pronominal adverb 'ba' in combination with a corresponding preposition. This is always the case when 'it' and 'that', in connection with a preposition are used indefinitely, and frequently when either of these pronouns refers to a noun representing an inanimate object or an abstract idea. The letter r is inserted between the adverb ta and the preposition, whenever the latter begins with a vowel. **6,** To — was = Upon this (hierauf) he (inverted constr., see App. § 14) gave *the* following striking (treffent) answer. **7,** may = can; to become a man, zum Manne werten.

Section 5.

WEALTH[1].

Wealth, after all[3], is[2] but a relative thing: for he who has[4] little, and wants[5] still less, is richer than he who has much, and wants still more.—REV. C. COTTON.

1, wealth, Reichtum, m., see S. 3, N. 2. **2, When the subject, which may be preceded by its attributes, occupies the first place in a principal clause, either the copula or the verb must follow immediately.** **3,** after all ... but, ted immer nur; a—thing, etwas Relatives. **4,** to have = to possess. **5,** 'to want', here bedürfen.

Section 6.

MENDELSSOHN IN BIRMINGHAM.

When[1] Mendelssohn, on[2] the first performance of his[3] 'Elijah' in Birmingham, was about[4] to enter[5] the orchestra, he[6] said laughingly to one of his friends and critics[7]: "Stick[8] your claws into me! Don't tell[9] me what you like, but[10] what you don't like!"—ATHENÆUM.

1, See S. 4, N. 2. **2,** The preposition 'on', signifying 'on the occasion of', must be rendered by 'bei'. 'Performance', Aufführung, f. **3,** Use the gen. of the def. art.; Elijah, Elias. **4,** 'to be about', im Begriff sein. 'To be about' may also be rendered by the auxiliary verb of mood wollen and the infinitive of another verb; as—

I was just *about* to leave, when the letter arrived.	Ich war gerade im Begriff abzureisen (or Ich wollte gerade abreisen), als der Brief ankam.

5, 'to enter', betreten, see S. 1, N. 2. **6,** Since the subordinate clause precedes the principal clause, the construction of the principal clause must be inverted, see App. § 15. **7,** to—critics, say 'to a friend and critic', Regensent, m. **8,** 'Stick—me!' This metaphor must be rendered freely by: Packen Sie mich nur tüchtig an! **9,** tell = say; to like = to please, with the dat. of the person. **10,** The co-ordinative conjunction 'but' must be rendered by 'sondern', when, after a negative statement, the subsequent clause expresses an idea altogether contrary to that of its antecedent.

Section 7.

TO FORGIVE IS[1] TO FORGET.

"I can forgive, but I cannot forget," is[2] only another way of saying: "I will not forgive." A wrong *once* forgiven[3] ought[4] to be like[5] a *cancelled* note[6], torn in two and burned up, so[7] that it never can be shown against the man.—REV. H. W. BEECHER.

1, 'to be', here = to signify, heißen.   **2,** is — saying = signifies only in (mit) other words. '*Das Wort*' has two plural forms with a different meaning to each: die Wörter, single, unconnected words; die Worte, words connected into speech.   **3,** *A.* Whilst the English Perfect Participle (commonly called Past Participle) is placed both before and after the noun it qualifies, **the German Past Participle used attributively, as a rule, precedes the qualified noun**; as—

We met with a ship *bound for Bremen.*	Wir trafen **ein nach Bremen bestimmtes Schiff.**

B. Clauses containing a Perfect Participle, however, may also be rendered by the help of a **relative pronoun.** Thus rendered, the preceding sentence would read:

Wir trafen ein Schiff, **welches nach Bremen bestimmt war**;

but the first rendering is certainly more concise than the second, and it is to be preferred in all cases where the attributive construction would not be too lengthy. 'A wrong *once* forgiven', say 'A forgiven wrong', and mark that: **When Participles are used attributively, and precede the noun they qualify, they must be inflected like adjectives.**   **4,** render 'ought' by the imperfect of sollen.   **5,** like, wie.   **6,** note, Schuldschein, m.; to tear in two, zerreißen; to burn up, verbrennen. According to the rule given in N. 3, the participles of these two verbs have to be placed before the noun 'note', which they qualify.   **7,** 'so—man', say 'which never again can be used against the debtor'. According to the hint given in S. 2, N. 1, the verb is in the passive voice, and since the clause is a subordinate one, the verbs must stand at the end of the clause. Place the p. p. first, and the copula (can) last.

Section 8.

WHAT IS CAPITAL?

What is capital? Is[1] it what a man has? Is[2] it counted (App. 31) by[3] pounds and pence, stocks[4] and shares[5], by houses and lands[6]? No! Capital[7] is not what a man has, but what a man is. Character[8] is[9] capital; honour[10] is capital.—Rev. Dr. Macduff.

1, 'Is—has?' say 'Does it consist in that which (see S. 3, N. 7) we possess?' The prep. 'in' here governs the dat. Read again S. 4, N. 5, *B*, and notice that, when the **demonstrative pronouns** 'that' and 'those' are **followed by a relative pronoun**, they cannot be rendered by the adverb 'da' in combination with a preceding preposition; as—

We laughed *at that which* (*or* at what) you told us.	Wir lachten über das, was Sie uns erzählten.

2, See S. 2, N. 1; 'to count', here schätzen.   **3,** by = nach.   **4,** Wertpapiere.   **5,** Aktien.   **6,** Ländereien.   **7,** 'Capital—is'. The literal translation of this sentence would read very awkwardly in German, say 'Our capital does not consist in that which we possess, but (S. 6, N. 10) in that which we are.'   **8,** Character = A good reputation.   **9,** 'is', here ist.   **10,** Ehrenhaftigkeit, f.

Section 9.

A GOOD RULE[1].

A French minister, who was alike[2] remarkable[3] for his[4] despatch of business and *his* constant[5] attendance at places of public amusement, being [6] asked how he contrived to combine both *objects*, replied: "Simply [7] by never postponing till to-morrow what should be done [8] to-day."—S. SMILES.

1, Lebensregel, f.   2, 'alike ... and', fowohl ... wie auch.   3, to be remarkable for something, sich durch etwas auszeichnen.   4, his—business, schnelle Erledigung seiner Amtsgeschäfte.   5, constant—amusement, regelmäßiger Besuch öffentlicher Vergnügungsorte. The prep. durch, which requires the acc., must be repeated at the beginning of this clause.   6, 'being—replied'; this sentence requires an entirely different construction in German, say 'answered upon the question, how (App. § 16) he made it possible to combine both (neuter sing.)'. To combine, vereinigen. The verb 'to make' must be placed in the Present Subjunctive, since the clause contains an indirect question. Read carefully App. §§ 28 and 30.   7, Simply—to-morrow, Einfach dadurch, daß ich nie auf morgen verschiebe.   8, 'to do', here erledigen. See S. 2, N. 1, and place the verbs in the order pointed out in S. 7, N. 7.

Section 10.

ENGLAND UNDER THE RULE [1] OF [2] QUEEN VICTORIA.

The peace, the freedom, the happiness [3], and the order which Victoria's rule guarantees [4], are [5] part of my birthright as *an* Englishman, and I bless [6] God for my share [7]! Where else shall [8] I find such liberty [9] of action, thought, speech [10], or [11] laws which protect me so well [12]?—W. M. THACKERAY.

1, rule = reign.   2, Use the gen. of the def. art. The definite article is used in German before names of persons when preceded by an adjective or a common name; as—

Der arme Fritz!	Poor Fritz!
Der Kaiser Wilhelm.	Emperor William.

3, happiness = well-being, Wohlfahrt, f.   'Victoria's rule', say 'the reign of Queen Victoria'.   4, to guarantee, gewähren.   5, are part = form a part. 6, I bless = I thank.   7, share = lot.   8, shall = can.   9, Freiheit des Handelns. Repeat the article before the two following nouns. In German the articles, possessive adjective pronouns, and other determinative words must be repeated when they are used in reference to several nouns of different gender or number, whilst in English they are only required before the first noun.   10, Insert 'and' before 'speech', Rede, f., and place the verb finden immediately after that noun.   11, Substitute the words 'and where' for the word 'or'.   12, gut.

Section 11.

CONCENTRATION OF POWERS.

The weakest living creature [1], by [2] concentrating his powers on a single object, can [2] accomplish [3] something. The strongest [4], by dispersing his over many, may fail to accomplish anything [5]. The drop, by continually [6] falling [7], bores [6] its passage through the hardest rock. The hasty [9] torrent rushes [10] over it with hideous uproar, and leaves no trace behind.—T. CARLYLE.

1, creature, Wesen, n.; strengthen the superlative of the adjective by placing 'aller' before it, forming one compound expression, analogous to: Die aller-ſchönſte Blume, the finest flower (of all).   **2,** The copula 'can' must be placed immediately after the subject and its attributes, as has been pointed out in S. 5, N. 2.   **3,** 'by concentrating his powers', durch Konzentration ſeiner Kräfte; to accomplish something, etwas zuſtande bringen.   Use the adverbial expression 'at least' before 'something', which will give more force to the German rendering.   **4,** The strongest—fail, Dem Stärkſten hingegen wird es durch Zerſplitterung ſeiner Kräfte nicht gelingen.   **5,** anything, auch nur das Geringſte. **6,** to bore one's passage, ſich einen Weg bahren.   Place the verb according to S. 5, N. 2; the adverbial clause 'by continually falling' must follow it. **7,** To render 'falling', form a noun of the verb 'fallen'.   The German language makes frequent use of the **Infinitive Present** of verbs to form abstract nouns, whilst the English language uses the Verbal in -ing for that purpose.   Such nouns are always of the neuter gender; as das Gehen, going; das Eſſen und Trinken, eating and drinking.   **8,** continual, unabläſſig, adj. **9,** hasty, ungeſtüm; torrent, Strom, m.   **10,** to rush over something, über etwas hinweg ſtürzen; 'rushes—uproar', say 'rushes with hideous (entſetzlich) uproar (Getöſe) over the same.'

Section 12.

COOLNESS[1].

Of the Duke of Wellington's[2] perfect coolness on[3] the most trying occasions, Colonel Gurwood gives[4] this instance. He was[5] once in great danger of suffering[6] ship-wreck. It was bed-time[7] when (S. 4. N. 2) the captain of the vessel came to him, and said: "It will soon be *all* over[8] with us!" "Very well," answered the Duke, "then I (App. § 14) need not (App. § 12) take off[9] my boots!"—W. C. Hazlitt.

1, Kaltblütigkeit, f.   **2,** Place the genitive after the governing noun, and say: 'Of (Von) the perfect coolness of the Duke of Wellington.' Perfect = great.   **3,** 'on—occasions' = in the most dangerous (gefahrvoll) situations. **4,** to give = to relate. See App. § 14 for the construction. 'This instance' = *the* following example.   **5,** 'to be', here ſich befinden.   **6,** Construe according to S. 1, N. 3.   **7,** Schlafenszeit, f.   **8,** vorüber.   **9,** to take off, ausziehen, see S. 1, N. 2.

Section 13.

RELIGIOUS TOLERATION[1].

When[2] certain persons attempted[3] to persuade Stephen[4], King of Poland, to constrain[5] some of his subjects, who[6] were of a different religion, to embrace[7] his, he said[8] to them: "I[9] am king of men, and not of[10] consciences[11]. The[12] dominion of conscience belongs exclusively to God."—Rev. R. K. Arvine.

1, Religionsdulbung, f.   **2,** 'When', here?   **3,** attempted to = would, impf. of wollen.   **4,** say 'the king Stephen of Poland'. König Stephan von Bathori regierte von 1576-1586.   **5,** zwingen. Place the verb after the relative clause, since the relative pronoun should follow its antecedent as closely as possible.   **6,** 'who — religion', say 'who belonged to another religion'.   **7,** to embrace = to accept.   **8,** 'to say', here 'to reply', entgegnen.   **9,** I—men = I rule (herrſchen) over men.   **10,** of = over.   **11,** This noun is not used in the plural in German. See S. 3, N. 2. **12,** 'The—God', say 'God alone rules over consciences (sing.)'.

Section 14.

HOW HUGH MILLER[1] BECAME *A*[2] GEOLOGIST.

Hugh Miller's[3] curiosity[4] was[5] excited by *the* remarkable traces of extinct[6] sea-animals in[7] the Old Red Sandstone, on which he worked as *a* quarryman. He inquired[8], observed, studied, and became *a* geologist. "*It was* the necessity", said he, "which made[9] me a quarrier, *that* taught me to be a geologist."—S. SMILES.

1, Hugh Miller wurde am 10ten Oktober 1802 von armen Eltern zu Cromarty in Schottland geboren. Er arbeitete 15 Jahre als gemeiner Steinbrecher, beschäftigte sich jedoch während jener Zeit mit litterarischen und wissenschaftlichen Arbeiten, besonders mit der Geologie, der er ganz neue Bahnen eröffnete. Durch seine Werke hat er sich in der Wissenschaft einen unsterblichen Namen erworben, und als er am 24sten Dezember 1856 starb, verlor Schottland in ihm einen seiner besten Söhne, und die Geologie einen ihrer beredtesten und ergebensten Lehrer.   2, Contrary to English construction, the indefinite article is not used in German in stating the business or profession of a person; as—

He wants to be *a* soldier.   Er will Soldat werden.

Exception: When the noun denoting the business or profession is preceded by an adjective, the indefinite article is used in German, as in English:

His father was a clever physician.   Sein Vater war ein geschickter Arzt.

3, When a **Proper Name** is used in the **Genitive Case**, it is generally placed before the governing noun, as in English: Schiller's poems, Schillers Gedichte.   4, Wißbegierde, f.   5, How is the Passive Voice to be recognised? 'To excite', here lebhaft an'regen; construe accord. to S. 13, N. 5. 6, ans'gestorben.   7, in — Sandstone, in einem alten Metsandsteinlager; on which = where.   8, 'to inquire', here Nachforschungen anstellen.   9, 'to make' requires here the prep. zu contracted with the def. art.; 'that — geologist', machte mich schließlich auch zum Geologen.

Section 15.

EXTREMES MEET[1].

When Diogenes, during the famous festival[2] at Olympia[3], saw[4] some young men of Rhodes arrayed[5] most magnificently, he (App. § 15) exclaimed smiling: "This is pride!" And when, afterwards[3], he met[6] with some Lacedæmonians in *a* mean[7] *and* sordid[8] dress, he said: "And this is also pride!"—REV. R. K. ARVINE.

1, Die Extreme berühren sich.   2, the festival at Olympia, die Olympischen Feste. Diese berühmten Feste, auch Olympische Spiele genannt, wurden in jedem fünften Jahre am ersten Vollmond nach der Sommerwende (Anfang Juli) bei Olympia zu Ehren des Zeus gefeiert. Sie dauerten fünf Tage und bestanden in Wettrennen (zu Wagen, zu Pferd und zu Fuß) und in gymnastischen Spielen aller Art.   3, Contrary to English practice, the comma is, as a rule, not used in German to enclose adverbs or adverbial clauses of time, manner, and place. 4, 'to see', here erblicken, which place after 'Rhodes'; young men = youths: 'of', here aus; Rhodes, Rhodus.   5, 'arrayed — magnificently'. Turn these words into a relative clause, and say: 'which were most magnificently (aufs prächtigste) arrayed (geschmückt)', according to the rule given in S. 7, N. 5, *B.* 6, to meet with a person, einem begegnen. Place the subject immediately after 'when'. The Lacedæmonian, der Lacedämonier.   7, armselig.   8, zerlumpt

Section 16.

POOR PAY[1].

When the Duke of Marlborough, immediately after the battle of Blenheim[2], observed[3] a soldier leaning[4] pensively on the butt-end of his musket, he accosted[5] him thus : "Why so pensive[6], my friend, after so[7] glorious a victory?" "It may be glorious[8]," replied the brave fellow, " but[9] I am thinking that all *the* human blood I[10] have spilled this day[11] has only[12] earned me fourpence."—Rev. R. K. Arvine.

1, Armselige Bezahlung.   2, Die Schlacht bei Blindheim (Engl. 'Blenheim') wurde am 13ten August 1704 von dem Herzog von Marlborough in Verbindung mit dem östereichischen Prinzen Eugen gegen die Franzosen gefochten. Blindheim ist ein kleines bayerisches Dorf bei Höchstädt, an der Donau. Die Schlacht wurde zu gunsten der Verbündeten entschieden, und der Herzog von Marlborough erhielt für diesen glänzenden Sieg von der Königin Anna ein prachtvolles Schloß (Blenheim House) bei Woodstock in Oxfordshire zum Geschenk.   3, Place the verb 'observed' after the noun 'soldier'.   4, 'leaning—musket'. This passage must be changed into a relative clause, thus : 'who leant (sich stützen) pensively (gedankenvoll) upon the butt-end (Kolben, m.) of his musket', for : **Sentences containing a Present Participle which qualifies a preceding noun or pronoun, are generally turned into relative clauses; as—**

The teacher, *noticing* the boy's talent,   Der Lehrer, welcher das Talent des
    applied to the prince on his be-   Knaben bemerkte, verwendete sich
    half.   für ihn bei dem Fürsten.

5, to accost, anreden; thus, folgendermaßen.   6, here 'nachdenkend' in order to avoid the repetition of the same word.   7, so ... a, ein ... so.   8, Make the word 'glorious' emphatic by placing it at the head of the clause, and see App. § 14. Insert the adverb 'wohl' between the subject and the verb 'be', which will render the sentence more idiomatic.   9, but — thinking, aber ich bedenke.   10, Supply the relative pronoun 'which', for : **The relative pronoun can never be omitted in German;** to spill, vergießen.   11, this day = to-day.   12, This work has only earned me a shilling, diese Arbeit hat mir nur einen Schilling eingebracht.

Section 17.

THE WORLD IS A LOOKING-GLASS.

We[1] may be pretty certain that persons[2] whom all the world treat ill, deserve entirely[3] the treatment they[4] get. The world is a looking-glass, and gives[5] back to every man *the reflection* of his own face. Frown[6] at it, and[7] it will in turn look sourly upon you; laugh[8] at it and with it, and[9] it is a jolly, kind companion[10].—W. M. Thackeray.

1, We — certain. Wir können uns ziemlich sicher darauf verlassen.   2, persons — ill = those who have to suffer from everybody.   3, vollkommen.   4, they get, welche ihnen zuteil wird.   5, to give back the reflection = to reflect, zurückwerfen; every man, jeder; face = image.   6, to frown at a person, here 'einen mürrisch anblicken'; use the second pers. sing.   7, and — you, und sie wird auch auf dich verdrießlich herniederschauen.   8, 'Laugh at it' seems to be used here in the sense of: 'Smile at it'. Say: 'Smile at it, laugh with it', etc. 'To smile at a person', here 'einen freundlich anblicken'.   9, 'and — is', say: 'and it will be for thee (dir)'.   10, Gefährtin.

Section 18.

GIVE[1] THE HONOUR TO GOD ALONE.

A lady applied[2] to the worthy philanthropist[3] Richard Reynolds on behalf of a little orphan boy. After he[4] had (App. § 17) given liberally[5], she said: "When[6] he is old enough, I (App. § 15) will teach[7] him to thank his benefactor." "Stop[8]," said the good man, "thou art mistaken[9]. We do not thank the clouds for rain (S. 3, N. 2). Teach[10] him to look higher, and thank Him[11] who giveth both the clouds and the rain."— REV. R. K. ARVINE.

1, Say 'Give God alone the honour'.   2, to apply to a person *on behalf of somebody*, ſich bei einem für jemand verwenden.   3, Menſchenfreund, m. 4, To avoid ambiguity turn the pron. 'he' here by 'Reynolds'.   5, 'liberally', here reichlich.   6, The conjunction '**when**', used in the sense of '**whenever**', and referring to indefinite time, must be rendered by '**wenn**' (compare S. 4, N. 2); as—

When (whenever) my old teacher came to Hamburg, he always stayed with me.	Wenn mein alter Lehrer nach Hamburg kam, wohnte er ſtets bei mir.

7, The verb '**lehren**', to teach, requires the accusative of the person. Render the sentence 'I — benefactor' by 'I will teach him to be thankful to his benefactor'.   8, Halt!   9, to be mistaken, ſich irren.   10, Teach — higher, Lehre ihn höher blicken.   11, The pronoun 'Him' is here used as a demonstr. pron.; 'both ... and', ſowohl ... wie auch; 'to give', here = to send.

Section 19.

HOW DID CUVIER[1] BECOME *A* NATURALIST?

When young (S. 10, N. 2) Cuvier was one day[2] strolling[3] along the sands near Fiquainville, in Normandy[4], he observed a cuttle-fish lying[5] stranded on the beach. He was attracted[6] by the curious object, took it home to[7] dissect, and[8] began the study of the mollusca, which ended in his becoming one of the greatest among natural historians.—S. SMILES.

1, G. D. Cuvier, berühmter franzöſiſcher Naturforſcher (1769–1832), erhob die vergleichende Anatomie zuerſt zur Wiſſenſchaft.   2, one day, eines Tages; one morning, eines Morgens; one evening, eines Abends, etc.   3, to stroll along the sands, an der Küſte umher ſchlendern; 'near', here zu.   4, die Normandie, always used with the def. art.   5, 'lying — beach', say 'which the sea had washed (ſpülen) upon the beach. (See App. § 17.)   6, to be attracted by something, ſich durch etwas an gezogen fühlen; 'object', here 'creature'. 7, The **Supine** is used to express **purpose**, and must be employed whenever the English '**to**' is used in the meaning of '**in order to**', or '**for tho purpose of**'; clauses of this sort are generally introduced by the conjunction '**um**'; as—

I will take this animal home *to* dissect.	Ich will dies Tier mit nach Hauſe nehmen, um es zu ſezieren.

8, 'and — historian', say 'began (an fangen) to study the mollusca, and became finally (ſchließlich) one of the greatest natural historians'. Mollusca, Weichtiere or Weichtiere.

Section 20.
ON THE CHOICE OF BOOKS[1].

In literature (S. 3, N. 2) I am fond[2] of confining myself to the best company, which consists chiefly of old acquaintances[3] with whom I am desirous of becoming more intimate, and I suspect[4] that, nine[5] times out of ten, it is more profitable[6], if not more agreeable, to read an old book over again, than[7] to read a new one for the first time.—LORD DUDLEY.

1, 'of books', here ཏཿ Lektüre.   2, *A.* The verbs 'to be fond of' and 'to like' are often rendered by the auxiliary verb of mood 'mögen', either with or without the adverb 'gerne' or 'gern' (willingly), which is used to intensify its signification; as—

I am very fond of the German language.	Ich mag die deutsche Sprache sehr gern.
Are you fond of walking?	Mögen Sie gerne spazieren gehen?
I don't like this child.	Ich mag dies Kind nicht.

B. But the adverb **gerne** or **gern** in itself denotes liking and fondness, and is therefore the general translation of the verbs 'to be fond of' or 'to like' when used with the infinitive of other verbs; as—

I like to dance.	Ich tanze gern.
We are fond of confining ourselves to a few old books.	Wir beschränken uns gern auf einige wenige alte Bücher.

Construe the above clause accord. to the last example given.   3, acquaintances = friends; I am desirous of becoming = I wish to become (App. § 19). The insertion of the adverb 'noch' before the comparative will greatly improve the rendering of this clause.   4, to suspect = to believe.   5, 'nine times out of ten' may be briefly rendered by the adverbial expression meistenteils, which place immediately after the subject of the subordinate clause.   6, profitable', nützlich; 'if — agreeable', say 'if not even (gar) more agreeable; 'over again', here noch einmal.   7, 'than — time', say 'than to occupy oneself (sich beschäftigen) with a new *one*'. This periphrase is necessary to avoid a monotonous repetition in German.

Section 21.
AN APPARENTLY INSIGNIFICANT FACT[1] OFTEN[2] LEADS TO GREAT RESULTS.

When Galvani[3] discovered that a frog's leg[4] twitched when placed in contact with different metals, it[5] could scarcely have been imagined that so apparently insignificant a fact would ever lead (App. § 17) to important results. Yet therein lay the germ of[6] the Electric Telegraph, which[7] binds the intelligence of continents together, and probably before many years elapse will[8] " put[9] a girdle round the globe."— S. SMILES.

1, Thatsache, f.   2, See S. 5, N. 2, and place the adverb after the verb: 'result', Resultat, n.   3, Luigi Galvani, italienischer Anatom, entdeckte 1780 den Galvanismus. 'When — discovered', say 'When Galvani made the discovery'. 4, 'leg', here Schenfel, m.; to twitch, in Zuckungen geraten; when placed = when (S. 18, N. 6) the same was (S. 2, N. 1) brought.   5, it — imagined, hätte man sich kaum vorstellen können: 'that so apparently ... a', daß eine scheinbar so. 6, zum.   7, which — together, welcher die Geister der Kontinente mit einander verbindet; before — elapse = in *a* few years.   8, See App. § 16.   9, to put a girdle round the globe, einen Gürtel rings um die Erde ziehen. 'Rings um die Erde zieh' ich einen Gürtel in viermal zehn Minuten.' Puck, Sommernachtstraum.

Section 22.

OATS[1].

Oats are (S. 2, N. 1) chiefly used whole[2] as food for horses. Ground[3] into meal, they are used in some countries (especially in Scotland) for[4] making porridge and cakes. As[5] a plant, it is extremely hardy, and grows where neither wheat nor barley could[6] be made productive. For[7] this reason it is a favourite crop in mountainous countries and moist climates — for example in Scotland and Wales. It (S. 5, N. 2) also grows luxuriantly in Australia, Northern[8] and Central Asia, and in North America.—NELSON'S READERS.

1, Der Hafer, which noun is never used in the plural.   **2,** whole, ungemahlen; to use, benutzen; food for horses, Pferdefutter, n.   **3,** Ground — meal, zu Mehl vermahlen; they — used = one uses (gebrauchen) it (m.). See S. 4, N. 4; 'country', here Gegend.   **4,** for — cakes, um Mehlsuppe und Kuchen daraus zu machen.   **5,** 'As — hardy', say 'The plant is extremely hardy (kräftig)'.   **6,** could — productive = would thrive.   **7,** For — reason, Daher, adv., App. § 14. Render the pron. 'it' by 'der Hafer'; a favourite crop, das Hauptgetreide.   **8,** in Nord=und Mittelasien.

Section 23.

SPRING-BLOSSOMS[1].

The blossoms of Spring are as brief[2] as *they are* beautiful. For[3] *a* short time they embellish the country, spreading[4], as it were, a bridal veil over every[5] tree and hedge. It seems, indeed[6], as if Nature had given them existence only to (S. 19, N. 7) show their worth, and then to destroy them. Yet[7] they are "fair pledges of a fruitful tree," and teach us the solemn[8] lesson—that[9] everything lovely on earth is destined soon to perish, and[10] like them to glide into the grave.—REV. E. M. DAVIES.

1, Frühlingsblüten.   **2,** vergänglich.   **3,** Auf; to embellish, schmücken.   **4,** spreading = and spread; as it were, gleichsam.   **5,** 'every — hedge', say 'hedges and trees'.   **6,** wirklich; as — only, als hätte die Natur ihnen nur das Dasein verliehen.   **7,** 'Yet — tree', say 'They are however the lovely messengers (Verboten) of a fruitful (fruchtreich) tree'.   **8,** solemn lesson, ernste Wahrheit.   **9,** that — perish, daß alles Schöne auf Erden der Vergänglichkeit geweiht ist.   **10,** 'and — grave', say 'and like the blossoms must (App. § 18) glide (sinken) into an early grave'.

Section 24.

THE WINKING[1] EYELID.

The[2] object of winking is a very important one. An outside[3] window soon (S. 5, N. 2) gets soiled[4] and dirty, and a careful shopkeeper[5] cleans his windows every morning. But our eye-windows must[6] never have so much as a speck or spot upon them; and the winking eyelid[7] is the busy apprentice who, not once a day, but[8] all the day, keeps the living glass clean; so that, after all[10], we are little worse off than the fishes, who[11] bathe their eyes and wash their faces every moment.—PROF. G. WILSON.

1, Das Öffnen und Schließen der Augenlider.　　2, 'The — one', say 'The opening and closing of the eyelid (pl.) is of great importance.　　3, outside window = street window.　　4, trübe.　　5, Ladenhüter; supply the adv. 'therefore' after the verb 'cleans', and place the object last of all.　　6, 'must — them', say 'must (dürfen) never suffer (erleiden) even (selbst) the smallest speck, the least dimness (Trübung).　　7, das sich öffnende und schließende Augenlid; 'apprentice', here Ladenbursche.　　8, but — day, nein, den ganzen Tag hindurch.　　9, Augenglas.　　10, genau betrachtet; the subject should be placed immediately after the conjunction 'that'; little = not much; to be badly off, schlimm daran sein.　　11, who — moment, welche Augen und Gesicht jeden Augenblick baden und waschen.

Section 25.

A GOOD EXAMPLE.

It is reported that, one day (S. 19, N. 2), the[1] two great philosophers Aristippus[2] and Æschines had fallen at variance[3]. The[4] following day, however, Aristippus came to[5] Æschines, and said: "Shall[6] we be friends?" "Yes, with[7] all my heart!" answered Æschines. "Remember[8]," continued Aristippus, "that[9] though I am your elder, yet I sought for peace." "True[10]," replied Æschines, "and for this[11] I will always acknowledge you to be the more worthy man, for[12] I began the strife, and you the peace."— Rev. J. Burroughs.

1, Place the subject immediately after the conj. 'that'.　　2, Aristippus aus Cyrene wurde (380 v. Chr.) Stifter der cyrenaischen Philosophenschule, welche die Lehre aufstellte, daß das höchste Glück des Menschen im sinnlichen und geistigen Vergnügen zu suchen sei. Aristippus war ein Zeitgenosse des Socrates und der einzige Philosoph seiner Zeit, der sich seine Verträge mit Geld bezahlen ließ.　Äschines war ein Nebenbuhler und Gegner des Demostenes, wurde (389 v. Chr.) zu Athen geboren, lebte später zu Rhodus und siedelte endlich nach Samos über, wo er (314 v. Chr.) starb.　　3, to fall at variance, sich überwerfen.　　4, The = On the; however, jedoch, which must not be placed between commas.　　5, Use here the def. art. contracted with the prep. zu into zum, for: The def. art. is often used to mark the Gen. Dat. and Acc. of proper names.　　6, Shall = Will.　　7, von ganzem Herzen!　　8, Erinnere dich daran.　　9, Say 'that I have sought for peace, although I am the elder'; to seek for peace, um den Frieden nachsuchen. 10, Say 'That is true'.　　11, deshalb, adv. (App. § 14). He acknowledged you to be the more worthy man (of us two), Er erkannte dich als den Würdigeren von uns beiden an; construe according to this example, and supply the expletive 'auch' after the object 'you'.　　12, denn ich war der erste zum Streit, und du zum Frieden.

Section 26.

DESCRIPTION OF A GLACIER.

I must now explain to you[1] what a glacier is. You see before you[2] thirty or forty mountain-peaks, and between these peaks what[3] seem to you frozen rivers. The snow, from[4] time to time melting and dripping down the sides of the mountain, and congealing in the elevated hollows between the peaks, forms a half-fluid mass, a river of ice[5], which is called (S. 4, N. 4) *a* glacier. As[6] the whole mass lies upon a slanting surface, and is not entirely solid throughout, it[7] is continually pushing, with a gradual but imperceptible motion, down[8] into the valley below.—Mrs. Beecher Stowe.

1, Use the 2nd pers. sing. 2, Place the words 'before you' after the object. 3, glaubſt du zu (Eis erſtarrte Flüſſe zu erbliđen. 4, which (App. § 16) from time to time melts, drips down on the mountain-sides (Bergꞏ abhänge), and congeals (gefrieren), etc.; see S. 16, N. 4. Supply the adverb wieder before the verb 'congeals'. The elevated hollow, die höher gelegene Feldꞏ ſpalte. 5, (Eisſtrom, m. 6, As = Since, da (App. § 16); to be entirely solid throughout, durch und durch feſt ſein. 7, it — pushing, ſo ſenft ſie ſich fortwährend; with a ... but, mit einer zwar ... doch. 8, down — below, in das unten liegende Thal hinab.

Section 27.

WITHOUT[1] PAINS NO GAINS.

It was one of the characteristic qualities of Charles James Fox[2], that[3] he was thoroughly pains-taking in all that he did. When[4] appointed Secretary of State, being[5] piqued at some observation as to his bad writing, he actually took[6] a writing-master, and wrote copies like a schoolboy until he had sufficiently improved himself. Though[7] a corpulent man, he[8] was wonderfully active at picking up tennis-balls, and[9] when asked how he contrived to do so, he playfully replied: "Because[10] I am a very pains-taking man." The same accuracy which he bestowed upon trifling matters[11], was displayed by him in things of greater importance; and[12] he acquired his reputation by "neglecting nothing."— S. SMILES.

1, Ohne Mühe fein Gewinn. 2, Ich möchte verſchlagen zu überſetzen: 'of the famous Ch. J. Fox', weil dadurch das Verhältnis des Genitivs ganz klar ausꞏ gedrückt wird. Charles James Fox (1749–1806) ward ſchon 1768 Mitglied des Unterhauſes, 1772 Lord des Schatzes, und bildete 1783 mit Nerth und Portland ein Miniſterium, welches jedoch bald dem Miniſterium Pitt weichen mußte. Er begann darauf mit Burke und andern eine großartige parlamentariſche Oppoſition gegen Pitt und kämpfte von 1792–97 faſt allein gegen eine ſtarke Majeſtät. Im Jahre 1806, kurz vor ſeinem Tode, wurde er mit Grauville nochmals aus Staatsruder berufen. 3, daß er ſich in allem, was er that, die größte Mühe gab. 4, When he was appointed (see N. 7). The verbs machen (to make), ernennen (to appoint), and erwählen (to choose, to elect), and other **verbs denoting choosing or appointing**, require in German the prep. zu contracted with the def. art., whilst in English they govern **two** Nominatives in the Passive Voice; as—

Der Freund meines Vaters iſt zum Abꞏ My father's friend has been elected
geordneten erwählt worden.   a member of Parliament.

5, being — writing. This clause must be rendered in an altogether different form; let us say 'and hurt hurt by an observation as to (über) his bad handwriting'. To feel hurt by something, ſich durch etwas verletzt fühlen. The p. p. must be placed? 6, 'to take', here engagiren; 'actually', here faktiſch (see App. § 15); to write copies, ſich im Schönſchreiben üben; improved himself = improved his hand-writing. 7, Though he was. Grammatical distinctness, as a rule, requires that the **subject and copula**, which after certain conjunctions are so frequently omitted in English, should be clearly expressed in German. 8, When a subordinate clause, beginning with one of the conjunctions da, obgleich, weil, and wenn, precedes a principal clause, which is often done for the sake of emphasis, the **principal clause** is generally introduced by the adverbial conjunction ſo (so, thus, therefore); as—

Da es regnet, ſo können (App. § 15) wir   As it is raining, we cannot go out.
nicht ausgehen.

'He—balls', fo war er im Auffangen ber Bälle beim Tennisspiele doch merkwürtig
gewandt.   9, 'and—so', say 'and when (S. 18, N. 6) one asked him how
he did (machen) it'.   The verb machen should be used in the Pres. Subj., since
the clause contains an indirect question (App. §§ 28 and 30).   Playfully,
scherzend.   10, Weil ich mir stets bie größte Mühe gebe.   11, trifling matters,
Kleinigkeiten; 'was—importance', say 'he showed also in more important
matters' (Angelegenheiten).   12, and—nothing, unb er erwarb sich seinen Ruf
badurch, baß er nichts für zu gering erachtete.

Section 28.

THE MAGNA CHARTA[1].

The great-grandsons of[2] those who had fought under William, and
the great-grandsons of those who had fought under Harold, began to[3]
draw near to each other in friendship, and the first pledge of their recon-
ciliation was the[4] Great Charter, won[5] by their united exertions, and
framed for their common benefit.   Here commences the history of the
English nation.   The history of the preceding events[6] is the history of
wrongs inflicted[7] and sustained by various tribes, which, indeed[8], all
dwelt on English ground, but[9] which regarded each other with aversion
such as[10] has scarcely ever existed between communities separated[11] by
physical barriers.—MACAULAY, HISTORY OF ENGLAND.

1, Die 'Magna Charta' ist ber am 19ten Juni 1215 bem König Johann ohne Land
abgerungene Staatsgrundvertrag, welcher als Grundlage ber englischen Verfassung gilt.
2, 'of those—Harold'.   These two clauses are best rendered in a contracted
form, thus: 'of the men who had fought under W. and H.'   3, to draw
near to each other, sich einander nähern; in friendship, freundschaftlich, adv.
4, bie Magna Charta.   5, The two clauses containing the two p. ps. must
be turned into one contracted relative clause, as explained in S. 7, N. 3, B.
Use the verbs in the Impf. of the Passive Voice.   To frame, entwerfen.
6, Ereignis, n.   7, The two p. ps. qualifying 'wrongs' (Unbilben) should be
placed before that noun, as explained in S. 7, N. 3, A; of, von; to inflict, verü-
ben; to sustain, erleiden; by—tribes, verschiebener Volksstämme.   8, war; on =
upon; ground = soil.   9, but—aversion = but (jedoch) showed such an
aversion against one another.   **The Article**, when used in connection with
adjectives and adverbs, stands in German generally before those words: such
an aversion, einen folchen Widerwillen.   Since the clause to be translated
is in reality but a part of the preceding relative clause, which it completes, the
verb must be placed?   10, such as, wie, after which supply the pron. er, to
give more distinctness to the rendering; to exist, bestehen; communities =
nations.   11, welche burch natürliche Grenzen von einander getrennt sind.

Section 29.

HONESTY.

Mr.[1] Denham had been in business at Bristol, had failed[2], compounded,
and gone[3] to America.   There[4], by a close application to business as
a merchant, he acquired a plentiful[5] fortune in *a* few years.   Returned[6]
to England, he invited his old creditors to an entertainment, at which he
thanked them for the easy[7] terms (S. 16, N. 10) they had favoured[8] him
with, and, though the guests had expected nothing but a good treat,
every[9] man, at the first remove, found to his astonishment a cheque

under his plate for [10] the full amount of the unpaid remainder, with interest.—Dr. B. Franklin.

1, 'Mr.— Bristol', translate 'Mr. D. had had a business at (in) B.', and place the object after the adverbial circumstance of place.　2, to fail (in business) fallieren; to compound, accrediren. Verbs from the Latin with the termination iren do not admit of the prefix or augment ge in the Past Participle, but follow in all other respects the weak or modern form of conjugation. 3, say 'and was gone to America'. The verb gehen is always construed with fein, which auxiliary is especially used with Intransitive Verbs denoting a Passive State of the subject, a change from one State into another, or a Motion, if the place to which the motion is directed, or from which it proceeds, is either expressed or understood.　4, The words 'he acquired' (erlangen) should, in an inverted form (App. § 14), follow the adverb 'There'; 'by— merchant', durch unablässige kaufmännische Thätigkeit.　5, plentiful = great. For the position of the object see App. § 9.　6, Nach England zurückgekehrt; entertainment = meal; at which, wobei.　7, bequem; terms, Bedingungen. 8, to favour a person with something, einem etwas gewähren (v. tr.); nothing but, nur; treat, Schmaus, m.　9, every — plate, fand doch ein jeder nach dem ersten Gange zu seinem Erstaunen unter dem Teller einen Wechsel vor.　10, for— interest = which was issued (ausstellen) for (auf) the full amount of the remaining (rückständig) debt with (nebst) interest.

Section 30.

FORMATION OF A CORAL-ISLAND.

I.

It seems to me, that [1] when the animalcules, which form the corals at the bottom [2] of the ocean, cease to live, their [3] structures adhere to each other, by virtue either of the glutinous remains within, or of some property in salt-water. The interstices being [4] gradually filled up with sand and [5] broken pieces of coral washed by the sea, which also adhere, a mass of rock is at length formed. Future [6] races of these animalcules erect their habitations upon the rising [7] bank, and [8] die, in their turn to elevate this monument of their wonderful labours.

1, 'that when the animalcules … cease to live'. This clause may be briefly rendered by saying: 'that after the death (Absterben, n.) of the animalcules'. To translate the last noun, form a diminutive of Tier　2, Meeresteten, m. 3, 'their — salt-water'. Use the following order of words for rendering this passage: 'their little houses (dim. of Haus) either through the in them contained glutinous remains (Überreste) or through some (irgend eine) property of the salt-water held together are (Pres. of the Passive Voice)'.　4, When the **Present Participle** is used to denote a **logical cause** from which we may draw an inference, it must, by the help of the conjunction '**Da**', be changed into a finite verb, i. e. one with a personal termination, thus:—

The interstices *being gradually filled up* with sand, a mass of rock is at length formed.	Da nun die Zwischenräume allmählich mit Sand ausgefüllt werden, so wird aus dem Ganzen endlich eine Felsenmasse gebildet.

The tense in which the verb is to be used, must always be determined by the context.　5, and—sea, mit mit vom Meere herangespülten zerbröckelten Korallen; it is a matter of course that the verbs must follow this passage.　6, The following generations.　7, 'to rise', here sich erheben. Present Participles

used attributively are inflected like adjectives.　Bank = reef.　**8,** 'and
die — labours', translate 'and die to (S. 19, N. 7) contribute also in their turn
(ifrerfeits) to the elevation (Erhöhung, f.) of this monument of their admirable
work (Arbeit, f.)'.

Section 31.

FORMATION OF A CORAL-ISLAND.

II.

The[1] new bank is not long in being visited by sea-birds.　Salt-plants[2]
take root upon it (S. 4, N. 5, *B*), and[3] a soil is being formed.　A coco-
nut, or the[4] drupe of a pandanus is thrown on[5] shore.　Land-birds
visit it[6] and deposit the seeds of shrubs and trees.　Every high tide,
and still more[7] every gale, adds something to the bank.　The[8] form of
an island is gradually assumed, and last of all[9] comes man (S. 3, N. 2)
to (S. 19, N. 7) take possession.—M. FLINDERS.

1, The new coral-reef is (S. 2, N. 1) now soon visited by (von) sea-birds.
2, Sea-plants; to take = to strike.　　　**3,** und so bildet sich eine Erdschicht.
4, die Frucht einer Panane.　Die Panane (Pandanus) ist eine Art Palme und wird
auch Pandang (m.) oder Palmnußbaum genannt.　　**5,** an, contracted with the
def. art.　　　**6,** it = the same, to agree with its antecedent 'shore'; to deposit, zurücklassen; seeds, Same, m., used in the sing.　　　**7,** still more =
especially; adds — bank, trägt etwas zur Vergrößerung des Riffs bei.　　**8,** The
latter (dieses) gradually assumes (an'nehmen) the form of an island.　The adv.
'gradually' may be made emphatic; see App. § 14.　　　**9,** zuletzt; 'to —
possession' = to take possession of the same.

Section 32.

REYNARD[1] CAUGHT.

A fox observed[2] some fowls at roost, and wished to[3] gain access to
them by smooth speeches.　"I have charming news[4] to tell you," he[5]
said.　"The animals have concluded[6] an agreement of universal peace
with one another.　Come down and celebrate[7] with me this decree[8]."
An old cock, who was well on his guard, looked[9] cautiously all around,
and the fox, perceiving (S. 16, N. 4) this, inquired[10] the reason.　"I was
only observing[11] those two dogs which are coming this way[12]," replied
the cock.　Reynard prepared[13] to set off.　"What[14]," cried the cock,
"have not the animals concluded an agreement of universal peace?"
"Yes," returned the fox, "but those dogs (S. 5, N. 2) perhaps have not
yet[15] heard of it (S. 4, N. 5, *B*)."—ANONYMOUS.

1, Der überlistete Reineke (or Reinhard).　　　**2,** to observe = to see; at roost,
auf ihrer Stange sitzen.　　　**3,** to — speeches, durch glatte Worte ihrer habhaft zu
werden.　　　**4,** charming news = something pleasant.　To render 'you' use
the dat. of the persnl. pron. of the 2nd pers. pl.　For the construction see
App. § 7.　　**5,** The words indicating the speaker, **after a quotation**, must
be rendered in an **inverted form** (see App. § 13).　　　**6,** to conclude,
abschließen, str. v. tr.; the agreement of universal peace, der allgemeine Friedensvertrag: to come down, herunterkommen; supply the adv. also between the verb
and the separable particle.　　　**7,** feiern.　**8,** Beschluß, m.　　**9,** to look
all around, sich nach allen Seiten um'sehen.　　　**10,** to inquire the reason, sich nach
der Ursache erkundigen.　　　**11,** I was observing = I observed (beobachten).

Which are coming = which come. The English compound forms of the verb with the auxiliary and the present participle, and of the verb 'to do' with the infinitive (**I do come** = I come. **I did come** = I came), must be rendered by the corresponding simple forms. 12, dieſes Weges. 13, ſich zum Davenlaufen bereit machen. 14, Wie. 15, 'not yet', here noch nichts.

Section 33.

THE[1] MEANS OF CONVEYANCE IN THE TIME OF CHARLES II.

I.

Heavy articles[2] were (S. 2, N. 1) in the time of Charles II generally conveyed from place to place by waggons[3]. The[4] expense of transmitting them was[5] enormous. From London to[6] Birmingham the charge was £7 a[7] ton, and from London to Exeter £12, which[8] is a third more than was afterwards charged[9] on turnpike-roads, and fifteen times more than is now demanded by[10] railway companies. Coal[11] was seen only in districts where it was produced[12], or[13] to which it could be carried by sea, and[14] was, indeed, always known in the South of England by the name of sea-coal.

1, Die Beförderungsmittel zur Zeit Karls des Zweiten. 2, objects. 3, Laſt: wagen, which place after 'generally'. 4, 'The — them', may be briefly rendered by the compound noun 'Die Transportleuten'. It may here be pointed out that the German language lends itself more easily than any other living language to the formation of compound expressions. Many advantages result from this adaptability of the language to express in one single term which, otherwise, would require a number of words; but the greatest of these advantages seems to me to lie in the power it gives us to avoid the too frequent use of the Genitive, a power which, if rightly wielded, will impart great vigour, conciseness, and elegance to the student's style of writing. 5, were extraordinary high (groß). 6, nach; 'charge', here Fracht, f.; 'to be', here betragen; £7, ſieben Pfund Sterling. 7, **The def. art. is used in stating the price of goods,** when the English use the indef. art.; as—

Dieſer Kattun koſtet fünfzig Pfennige die   This cotton is sixpence *a* yard. (10
Elle.   pfennigs = 1¼d.)

8, The pron. '**which**' referring to a whole clause, and not to a particular word in that clause, should be rendered by the indef. rel. pron. **was**; as—

She acted without thinking about   Sie handelte, ohne über die Folgen nach:
the consequences, *which* was very   zudenken, was ſehr unrecht war.
wrong.

9, berechnen; turnpike-road, Chauſſee, f. 10, von, followed by the def. art.; to demand, beanſpruchen. 11, Steinkohlen, used in the pl. without the art. Use the active voice with man, S. 4, N. 4. 12, gewinnen. 13, or — sea, oder wohin ſie verſchifft werden könnten. 14, Say 'and it was (ſie wurden) in the South of England therefore (daher auch) only called sea-coal (Schiffskohlen)'.

Section 34.

THE MEANS OF CONVEYANCE IN THE TIME OF CHARLES II.

II.

The rich[1] (S. 5, N. 2) commonly travelled in[2] their own iron carriages with at least four horses. A[3] coach and six is in our time never seen, except as part of some procession. The frequent mention, therefore, of such equipages [4] in old books is likely to mislead us. We [5] attribute to magnificence what was really [6] the effect of [7] disagreeable necessity. People [8] in the time of Charles II travelled with six horses, because [9] with a smaller number there was danger of sticking [10] fast in the mire.— *Abridged from* MACAULAY'S HISTORY OF ENGLAND.

1, **Adjectives used as nouns** are declined as they would be if the noun, which is understood, were to follow them. They are always written with a capital initial.   **2,** in ihren eigenen mit wenigstens vier Pferden bespannten eisernen Kutschen.   **3,** 'A — seen'. This clause must be construed thus: 'Except (Außer) in processions a coach and six (eine sechsspännige Kutsche, see App. § 14) is now never seen'. Supply the words 'bei uns' before the p. p.   **4,** Staats⸗ fuhrwerke; therefore ... is likely to mislead us = can therefore easily mislead (irre führen) us. The object 'us' must be placed immediately after the copula 'can'.   **5,** Wir schreiben der Prachtliebe zu.   **6,** really = in reality; 'effect', here = consequence.   **7,** Say 'of a'.   **8,** One (S. 5, N, 2).   **9,** because ... there was danger, weil man ... Gefahr lief; 'small', here gering.   **10,** to stick fast, stecken bleiben. Use the Supine, for: When the **English Gerund** (i.e. the verbal in -ing) is governed by a noun, a verb, or an adjective, it is generally rendered by the **Supine**. Comp. S. 78, N. 14. Examples:

He possesses the *gift of speaking* well.   Er besitzt die Gabe gut zu sprechen.
Do not begin *talking!*   Fangen Sie nicht an zu sprechen!

Section 35.

SIR [1] WILLIAM HERSCHEL.

When [2] pursuing his musical avocations in the pump-room at Bath, Sir William Herschel had a small workshop close [3] at hand, and when (S. 18, N. 6) the [4] exacting loungers in the pump-room admitted of a pause in the music, he slipped off [5] to (S. 19, N. 7) complete the polishing of a speculum [6], or the grinding [7] of a lens. Scarcely, however, had he heard the signal [8], when [9] he was ready to snatch up his instrument and [10] to be the first in the orchestra. Thus [11] he gathered up the fragments of time, and this made (S. 27, N. 4) him at last the friend of monarchs [12], and the first [13] of astronomers.—REV. DR. LEITCH.

1, Friedrich Wilhelm Herschel (später **Sir William Herschel**) wurde am 15ten Nov. 1738 in Hannover geboren. Er kam als Musiker nach England, be⸗ schäftigte sich jedoch in seinen Mußestunden eingehend mit der Astronomie, welcher er sich endlich ganz widmete. Er entdeckte mit selbst verfertigten Spiegelteleskopen von bis dahin unbekannter Größe den Uranus, zwei Saturnsmonde, zahlreiche Doppelsterne, Sternhaufen und Nebelflecken, und lieferte höchst wichtige Beobachtungen über die Planeten. Diese Entdeckungen, welche der Welt durch die von der königlichen Gesellschaft der Wissenschaften veröffentlichten Journale mitgetheilt wurden, machten ihn bald zum berühmten Manne. Er wurde von dem Könige Georg III zum königlichen Astronomen ernannt und genoß Ehre, Ruhm und Wohlstand, als er am 25sten Aug. 1822 zu Slough bei Windsor starb. Es ist unmöglich, hier nicht auch zugleich seiner geliebten Schwester Karoline zu gedenken, welche mit seltener Hingebung sich den Bestrebungen und Arbeiten des älteren Bruders anschloß und so nicht wenig zu den glänzenden Erfolgen dieses großen und höchst merkwürdigen Mannes beitrug. Sie starb im Jahre 1848 in ihrer Vaterstadt Hannover. Ihre unlängst veröffentlichten Memoiren und Briefe verdienen im höchsten Grade das allgemeine Interesse, welches sie nicht allein in Deutschland, sondern auch in England hervorgerufen haben.   **2,** This passage requires a different construction in

German, thus: 'When Sir W. H. was still officiating (fungie'ren, see S. 32, N. 11) in the pump-room (Trinkhalle) at Bath as a member of the band (Kapelle), he had', etc.   3, close at hand, ganz in der Nähe, which place before the object.   4, die vielbegehrenden Müßiggänger; to admit of something, etwas gestatten, w. v. tr.   5, hinaus'schlüpfen.   6, Spiegel, m.   7, Schleifen, n.   8, das Zeichen zum Anfangen.   9, when — ready, so war er auch schon bereit: to snatch up, ergreifen, see S. 1, N. 2.   10, and — first = and as the first to take (ein'nehmen) his place.   11, Thus — time = Thus (So, adv.) he used every spare-moment; the spare-moment, der freie Augenblick.   12, 'monarch', here Fürst.   13, zum ersten Astronomen seiner Zeit.

Section 36.

THE[1] AIR-OCEAN.

I.

Enveloping[2] this solid globe of ours are two oceans, one[3] partial, and the other universal. *There is* the[4] ocean of water, which has[5] settled down into all *the* depressions[6] of the earth's surface[7], leaving[8] dry above it all the high lands, as mountain-ranges, continents, and islands; and[9] *there is* an ocean of air, which enwraps[10] the whole in one transparent mantle.

Through[11] the bosom of that ocean, like fishes with their fins (App. § 14), birds[12] and other winged creatures swim; whilst man[13] and other mamalia creep like[14] crabs at the bottom of this aerial sea[15].

1, Das Luftmeer.   2, Say 'Two oceans envelop (umgeben) our solid globe (Erdkugel).   3, the one partial (teilweise) and the other universal (ganz). The subsequent sentence is best introduced by a colon (:), which we use to direct attention to what is following. The words '*There is*' must then be omitted.   4, das Weltmeer.   5, 'which — all', say 'which fills (erfüllen) all'.   6, Vertiefung, f.   7, To render 'of the earth's surface', form a compound noun by combining the corresponding German terms of the nouns 'earth' and 'surface'.

A. When the component parts of **Compound Nouns** are substantives, we combine them often without any connecting link; as—das Lasttier, beast of burden; das Stadtviertel, the quarter of a town, ward.

B. Neither do we require a connecting link for the formation of **Compound Nouns** the first component of which is an adjective or a particle; as—die Großmutter, grandmother; das Unglück, misfortune; der Urquell, fountain-head.

C. The **Gender of Compound Nouns** (with the exception of a few compounds with Mut, m.) is determined by the last component, which is always a noun.   8, 'leaving — islands'. This passage may be rendered thus: 'so that all *the* high lands (Erhöhungen), as (wie) mountain-ranges, etc. .... rise dry above the same; to rise, sich erheben.   9, und das Luftmeer.   10, umhüllen; say 'the whole globe' (Kugel, f.); 'in', here mit.   11, In this ocean of air.   12, Since the four subsequent nouns in this passage represent a whole class, the def. art. is required before each (S. 3, N. 2).   13, Use this noun in the plural, since the noun with which it is connected by the conj. 'and' stands in the same number.   14, gleich Krebsen: to creep, unter friechen. The word 'whilst' being a subordinative conj., the verb must be placed?   15, Luftmeer.

Section 37.

THE AIR-OCEAN.

II.

The air-ocean, which everywhere [1] surrounds the earth, and feeds and maintains it, is even [2] more simple, more grand, and more majestic than the [3] 'world of waters'; more [4] varied and changeful in its moods of storm and calm, of ebb and flow, of brightness and gloom. The [5] atmosphere is, indeed, a wonderful thing, a most perfect example of the economy of nature. Deprived of [6] air, no animal would live, no plant *would* grow, no flame *would* burn, no [7] light *would* be diffused. The [8] air, too, is the sole medium of sound. Without it, mountains might [9] fall, but [10] it would be in perfect silence. Neither whisper [11] nor thunders [12] would [13] ever be heard.—MAURY, PHYSICAL GEOGRAPHY OF THE SEA.

1, Place the adverb before the verb.   2, fogar nod.   3, jene mächtige Wafferwelt, after which put a full stop and begin a new sentence.   4, This passage may be construed thus: 'It offers a greater variety (Mannigfaltigfeit) and changeableness in the transitions from storm to (3u) calm, from ebb to flow, and from light to gloom (Dunfel, n.)'. The article (which, if practicable, should be contracted with the preceding preposition) must be used with the last six nouns, see S. 3, N. 2.   5, Der Luftfreis ift in der That höchft wunderbar und gewährt ein vollendetes Beifpiel von dem haushälterifchen Wefen der Natur. 6, Without (App. § 14); would = could, Impf. Subj.   7, und fein Licht fich verbrei'ten.   8, Also (def. art.) sound can only be transmitted (fort'pflanzen) through the air.   9, might = could; to fall, ein'ftürzen.   10, Say 'and yet the prevailing silence would not be interrupted'.   11, leifes Geflüfter, acc.   12, lauten Donner, acc.   13, 'would — heard', use the active voice with the indef. pron. man.

Section 38.

CHEERFUL [1] CHURCH-MUSIC.

When the poet Carpani inquired [2] of his friend Haydn [3] how it happened [4] that his church-music was [5] always so cheerful, the great composer made [6] *the* following beautiful reply:

"I cannot make it otherwise [7]," said he, "I [8] write according to the thoughts I feel. When [9] I think of God, my heart is so full of joy that (App. § 16) the [10] notes dance and leap, as it were, from my pen; and since God has given me a cheerful heart, it [11] will be pardoned me that [12] I serve him with *a* cheerful spirit."—REV. R. K. ARVINE.

1, fröhlich.   2, inquired of = asked.   3, Jofeph Haydn (geb. ben 31ften März 1732 3u Rohrau in Öftreich, + ben 31ften Mai 1809 in Wien, bildete fich durch eigenes Studium in der Mufif aus und lebte dann namentlich als Kapellmeifter des Fürften Gfterhazy in Wien. (Er ift der Schöpfer der Symphonie und des Streich: quartetts; auch hat er fich durch die Begründung der neueren Inftrumentationsfunft ein befonderes Verdienft erworben. Seine Werfe find ebenfo zahlreich, wie mannigfaltig; durch die beiden Oratorien: 'Die Schöpfung' (1799) und 'Die Jahreszeiten' (1801) hat er jedoch feinen Namen mit ehernen Lettern in die Gefchichte der Kunft eingetragen.
4, Use the Pres. Subj. of fommen, since the clause contains an indirect question; see App. §§ 28 and 30.   5, was — cheerful, ftets einen fo fröhlichen Charafter trage.   6, to make a reply, eine Antwort geben; 'beautiful', here

finnig; for the construction see App. § 15.   7, anders; for the place of the
negation see App. § 12.   8, Translate the passage 'I write — feel' briefly
by saying: 'I write just as (so wie) I feel', since it would not be in accordance
with the genius of the German language to render the sentence in a literal
way. (Gedanken kann man nicht fühlen.)   9, Denke ich an Gott, so ist, etc.;
full of, voller.   10, Construe this clause after the following model :

The notes danced and lept, as it   Die Noten tanzten und hüpften ihm
  were, from *his* pen.   gleichsam aus der Feder.

11, so wird man mir hoffentlich verzeihen.   12, that = if.

Section 39.

OUR INDUSTRIAL[1] INDEPENDENCE DEPENDS UPON OURSELVES.

Truer[2] words were never uttered than those spoken by Mr. Dargan,
the Irish railway-contractor, at a public meeting in Dublin.

"I have[3] heard a great deal[4]," he said, "about the independence that
we are[5] to get from this or that source, yet[6] I have always been deeply
impressed with the conviction, that our industrial independence depends
upon ourselves. Simple[7] industry and careful exactness would[8] be the
making of Ireland. We have, it[9] is true, made a step in advance, but perseverance is[10] indispensably necessary for eventual success."—S. SMILES.

1, industriell.   2, A greater truth than that which Mr. D., the Irish
railway-contractor (Eisenbahn-Unternehmer), spoke (aussprechen) at (in) a public
meeting in (zu) Dublin, has never been uttered.   3, The words 'he said'
should follow here; see S. 32, N. 5.   4, a great deal = much.   5, are
to get, erlangen sollen; for the construction see App. § 16; from, aus.   6, yet
I have always had the firm conviction. Render 'to have' here by hegen.
7, schlicht; 'industry', here Fleiß, m.; careful, streng; exactness, Pflichterfüllung, f.
8, would establish (begründen) Ireland's prosperity (Wohlstand, m.).   9, it is
true, zwar; see S. 15, N. 3; 'to make', here thun; in advance, vorwärts.
10, Here follow the words 'for (zu, contracted with the def. art.) eventual
(eventuell) success'.

Section 40.

ENGLAND'S[1] TREES.

The principal native[2] trees are the[3] oak, ash, elm, poplar, aspen,
birch, larch, alder, hawthorn, hazel, and willow. The beech, maple,
horse-chestnut[4], Spanish chestnut[5], walnut[6], sycamore, acacia, weeping
willow, cedar, and Lombardy poplar have been introduced.

The moist climate of[7] England is[8] eminently suited to the growth of[9]
forest-trees, and we find that in ancient times the larger part of the
country presented one[10] vast scene of forest, as[11] the[12] uncleared districts of America do now. The[13] few scattered patches of natural wood
which remain, show[14] what was once the character of nearly the whole
country.—HEWITT, PHYSICAL GEOGRAPHY OF ENGLAND AND WALES.

1, See S. 14, N. 3.   2, einheimisch.   3, die Eiche. The article
is repeated in this passage only when the subsequent noun is of different
gender or number from the preceding one.   4, die Roßkastanie.   5, die
echte Kastanie.   6, der Wallnußbaum.   7, Englands.   8, to be suited

to a thing, einer Sache zu'träglich fein; eminently, außerordentlich, which place
before 'zuträglich'.   9, Use the gen. of the def. art.   **The definite article**
should be used in all cases where an object is individualised or singled out from
other objects.   10, one — forest = an almost uninterrupted scene of forest,
Waldlaubschaft, f.   11, as ... do now, wie noch jetzt.   12, bie ungelichteten
Waldgegenten.   13, The — remain, Die wenigen zerstreut liegenden Überreste
natürlicher Gehölze.   14, Say 'show the character which formerly belonged
almost to the whole country'.

Section 41.

THE INDIAN CHIEF[1].

I.

During the war in America, a company[2] *of* Indians attacked a small
body[3] of British troops[4], and defeated[5] them.   As[6] the Indians had[7]
greatly the advantage in swiftness of foot, and were eager in the pursuit,
very few of the English escaped; and those who[8] fell into their hands,
were treated with a cruelty of which there[9] are not many examples, even
in that country.

Two of the Indians came up[10] to a young officer, and attacked him
with great fury.   As[6] they were armed with battle-axes, he had no hope
of[11] escape.   But, just at[12] this crisis, another Indian came up[13], who
was advanced in years, and was armed with a bow and arrows.   The[14]
old man instantly drew his bow; but, after[15] having taken his aim at the
officer, he suddenly dropped his arrow, and[16] interposed between the
young soldier and his pursuers, who were about[17] to cut him to pieces.
The two Indians retired with respect.

1, Der Indianerhäuptling.   2, Haufe, m.   3, Schar, f.   4, troops =
soldiers.   5, to defeat, in die Flucht schlagen.   6, When the conjunction
'as' stands for 'since', it must be rendered by 'da'.   7, had — foot, den
Britten im Laufen bedeutend überlegen waren; and — pursuit = and eagerly pursued
the same.   For the following clause see S. 27, N. 8, and say 'only few of
the Britons succeeded to escape (davenkommen)'.   I succeed, es gelingt mir.
8, welche den Indianern in die Hände fielen.   9, there are, es giebt.   The subject 'es', which must be placed immediately after the relative pronoun, should
be followed by the adverbial clause 'even in that country'.   10, to come
up to a person, sich einem nähern.   11, auf Rettung.   12, at = in;
crisis = critical (entscheidungsvoll) moment.   13, to come up = to appear;
who — arrows = of advanced (vorgeschritten) age and armed with bow and
arrows.   14, der Alte: to draw, spannen; immediately, unverzüglich, which
may be emphasized by being placed at the head of the clause (App. § 14).
15, Say 'after he had aimed (zielen) at (auf) the officer'; to drop, fallen laßen.
16, and interposed, und stellte sich.   17, to be about, im Begriff sein; to cut
to pieces, zerstückeln; with respect = respectfully.

Section 42.

THE INDIAN CHIEF.

II.

The[1] old man then took the officer by the hand, soothed him into
confidence by caresses, and, having conducted him to his hut, treated him
with a kindness which did honour to his professions[2].   He made (S. 27,

N. 4) him less a[3] slave than a[3] companion, taught[4] him the language of the country, and instructed him in[5] the rude arts that were practised by the inhabitants. They[6] lived together in *the* most perfect harmony, and the young officer, in[7] the treatment he met with, found nothing to regret, but[8] that (App. § 16) sometimes the old man fixed his eyes upon him, regarded[9] him for some minutes with steady and silent attention, and then burst into tears.

1, Say 'Hereupon the old man seized the hand of the officer, sought by caresses to gain his (reffen) confidence, conducted him to (in) his hut, and treated', etc.   **2,** Berfprechung, f.   **3,** his.   **4,** The verb **lehren**, to teach (old German lêran, Gothic laisjan), etymologically signifies 'to cause a person to know a thing'. This is the reason that it is in German most generally used with two accusatives: that of the person and that of the thing: as—Er lehrt mich die Landessprache, he teaches me the language of the country. Lehre mich Deine Rechte! (Luther.) Wer hat dich solche Streiche gelehrt? (Uhland.)   **5,** in — arts, in den geringen Geschicklichkeiten ; to practise, üben ; by, von; 'inhabitants', here Eingebornen.   **6,** They = both; together = with one another, which place after 'harmony' (Eintracht, f.).   **7,** in — with, in der ihm zuteil werdenden Behandlung. Where must the verb be placed? Supply the word 'anderes' after · nothing'; 'to regret', here beklagen.   **8,** als. **9,** Say 'regarded him silently *for* a while (App. § 9, *A*) with steady (unverwandt) attention'.

Section 43.

THE INDIAN CHIEF.

III.

In[1] the meantime the spring returned, and the Indians again took the field. The old man, who was still vigorous, and able to bear the fatigues of war[2], set out with them, *and was* accompanied by his prisoner. They marched above[3] two hundred leagues across the forests, and came at length to[4] a plain, where the British forces[5] were encamped. The old man showed his prisoner the tents at a distance[6]: " There," said he, " are thy countrymen. There is the enemy who[7] waits to give us battle. Remember[8] that I have saved thy[9] life, that I have taught[10] thee to conduct a canoe, to arm thyself with[11] bow and arrows, and to surprise[12] the beaver in the forest. What wast thou when I first took thee to my hut? Thy hands were those of an infant. They could neither procure[13] thee sustenance nor safety. Thy soul was[14] in utter darkness. Thou wast ignorant of everything. Thou owest all things to me. Wilt thou, then[15], go over to thy nation, and take up the hatchet against us?"

1, Say 'Meanwhile it became spring'; to take the field, ins Felt ziehen. **2,** die Kriegsbeschwerden ; 'to set out', here ziehen.   **3,** more than.   **4,** to = into.   **5,** forces = troops; to encamp, sein Lager aufschlagen.   **6,** von weitem, which place before the accusative.   **7,** who waits, der darauf lauert : to give battle = to attack.   **8,** Bedenke.   **9,** *A*. The definite article is often used **instead of the possessive adjective pronoun** in cases where the possessor is clearly seen from the context ; as—

       Ich habe die Feder in der Hand.   I have the pen in *my* hand.

B. **The possessor is often indicated by a personal pronoun in the dative case**; as—

       Ich will mir die Hände waschen.   I will wash *my* hands.

The latter mode of construction must be applied in this case.   **10,** ' I have **taught thee to conduct a canoe.'** Read once more S. 42, N. 4, and mark further that: **that which is taught is often expressed in the form of a Supine,** as in this instance.   **11,** We say ' mit Pfeil und Bogen'. **12,** überfal'len.   **13,** gewäh'ren ; sustenance, Nahrung, f.   **14,** lag in Finsterniß gehüllt.   **15,** also ; nation = people ; to take up = to seize.

Section 44.

THE INDIAN CHIEF.

IV.

The officer replied that[1] he would rather lose his own life than take away that of his deliverer. The Indian, bending[2] down his (S. 43, N. 9, *A*) head, *and* covering his face with both *his* hands, stood[3] some time silent. Then, looking[4] earnestly at his prisoner, he[5] said, in a voice that was at once softened by tenderness and grief: "Hast thou a father?" "My father," said the young man, "was[6] alive when I left my country[7]." "Alas!" said[8] the Indian, "how wretched[9] must he be!" He paused[10] a moment, and then added: "Dost thou know that[11] I have been a father ? I[12] am a father no more. I saw my son fall in[13] battle. He fought at my side. I saw him expire. He was covered with wounds, when he fell[14] dead at my feet."

1, that — deliverer ═ that he would rather die than kill his deliverer. See App. §§ 28 and 30.   **2,** The two Participles in -ing are best rendered by using the Imperfect.   **3,** stood — silent, und stand so eine Weile schweigend da. **4,** Say ' Upon this (Hierauf) he looked', etc.   **5,** he — grief, und fragte mit von Zärtlichkeit und Kummer gedämpfter Stimme.   **6,** war noch am Leben. **7,** Heimat, f.   **8,** exclaimed.   **9,** unhappy.   **10,** zögern, i.e. to hesitate.   **11,** daß auch ich einst Vater war ?   **12,** Say ' But now I (App. § 14) am it no more'.   **13,** We use here the def. art.   **14,** nie'derfallen.

Section 45.

THE INDIAN CHIEF.

V.

He pronounced[1] these words with the utmost vehemence. His[2] body shook with a universal tremour. He[3] was almost stifled with sighs, which[4] he would not suffer to escape him. There[5] was a keen restlessness in the eye, but no tears flowed to[6] his relief. At[7] length he became calm by degrees : and, turning towards the east, where the sun had just risen, "Dost thou see," said he to the young officer, "the beauty of that sky, which sparkles with prevailing day ? and hast thou pleasure in the sight ?" "Yes," replied the[8] young officer, "I have pleasure in the beauty of[9] so fine a sky." "I have none!" said the Indian, and[10] his tears then found their way.

A few minutes after, he showed the young man a[11] magnolia, in full bloom. "Dost thou see that beautiful tree ?" said he, "and dost thou look[12] upon it with pleasure ?" "Yes," replied the officer, "I[13] look with pleasure upon that beautiful tree." "I have no longer any pleasure in[14] looking upon it !" said the Indian hastily[15], and[16] immediately added: "Go, return to thy father, that[17] he may still have pleasure, when (S. 18, N. 6) he sees the sun rise in[18] the morning, and the trees blossom in the spring!"—WASHINGTON IRVING.

1, spoke. Begin the clause with 'These words' (S. 7, N. 2). 2, Say 'A universal tremour shook (erſchüttern) his body'. 3, Er erſtickte faſt unter ten Seufzern. 4, Say 'which he endeavoured (bemüht ſein) to suppress'. 5, His eyes (sing.) looked restlessly about. 6, zur Linderung ſeines Schmerzes. 7, Say 'Gradually he became calmer'. The following passage requires altogether a different structure in German. Say 'He turned towards the east (ſich gen Oſten wenden), where the sun had just risen. "Dost thou see the beauty of the sky, which sparkles (erglänzen) with (von) the breaking (an'brechen) day (Tageslicht, n.)? and hast thou pleasure (Freude, f.) in (an) the sight (Anblick, m.)?" he asked the young officer'. 8, the — officer, tieſer, to avoid a useless repetition. 9, of such a (S. 28, N. 9) sky. 10, 'and his', say 'whose'; found their way, hervor'brachen. 11, eine in voller Blüte ſtehende Magnolie. 12, 'to look upon', here betrachten. 13, Say 'I rejoice in its splendour', to avoid monotony. To rejoice in a thing, ſich einer Sache freuen. 14, 'in — it', may be briefly rendered by 'in the sight'. 15, raſch. 16, 'and — Go'. Begin a new clause here, and say: '"Go," he added (fügte er dann hinzu)'. 17, auf daß (followed by the Pres. Subj. of haben). 18, des Morgens, App. § 9. The verb 'sees', being the governing verb in both clauses, takes the last place. See App. § 19.

Section 46.

RICE.

Rice forms the[1] chief subsistance of the people[2] in India, China, Japan, and other eastern[3] countries. Indeed, it supports[4] more persons than any other article of food[5]. In Asia it (S. 2, N. 1) is chiefly cultivated in India, China, and[6] Ceylon; in Europe: in Lombardy[7] (Italy) and Spain; in Africa: in Egypt; in South America: in Brazil; and in North America: in[8] the Carolines and[9] Louisiana. Its[10] cultivation requires an[11] immense quantity of moisture. It[12] grows best in[13] fields which can be inundated. Indeed[14], the fact that it is usually sown upon watery soil makes it probable that the first Verse of the eleventh Chapter in[15] Ecclesiastes refers to Rice. In Egypt, for example, it is always sown while[16] the waters of the Nile cover the land, and when the floods subside[17], (S. 27, N. 8) it is deposited[18] in the mud. A strong spirit[19], called arrack, is distilled from[20] rice, and[21] the straw is used for making plait for hats and bonnets.—NELSON'S READERS.

1, das hauptſächlichſte Nahrungsmittel. 2, Say 'of the inhabitants of India (Indiens)', etc. 3, orientaliſch. 4, ernähren. 5, Nahrungsartikel, m. 6, Supply here the prep. auf, which should always be used to render the English 'in' before names of islands. 7, in der Lombardei. 8, auf den Karolinen. 9, Supply the prep. in. 10, Der Reisbau, i.e. the cultivation of rice. 11, an — of = extraordinary much. 12, The noun 'rice' must here be repeated, since the pron. 'er' would refer to 'Reisbau'. 13, auf. 14, Ja, die Thatſache, daß, etc. 15, im Prediger Salomonis; to refer to something, ſich auf etwas beziehen. The above mentioned passage reads as follows: 'Cast thy bread upon the waters: for thou shalt find it after many days'. 16, Say 'when the land is still covered by (von) the waters of the Nile'. 17, ſich zurück'ziehen, i.e. withdraw. 18, ſich ab'lagern (see S. 4, N. 4, A); 'mud', here Schlamm, m. 19, Spiritus, m. 20, aus. 21, and — bonnets, und das Stroh gebraucht man zur Anfertigung von Männer=und Frauenhüten.

Section 47.

THE WHITE SHIP.

(A.D. 1120.)

I.

King Henry I went[1] over to Normandy with his son Prince (S. 10, N. 2) William and a great retinue, to have the prince acknowledged[2] as his successor by the Norman nobles, and to contract[3] the promised marriage between him and the daughter of the Count of Anjou. When both[4] these things had been done with great show[5] and rejoicing, the whole retinue prepared[6] *to embark* for the voyage home.

When[7] all was ready, *there* came to the king Fitz-Stephen[8], a sea-captain, and said: "My[9] liege, my father served your father all his life, upon the sea. He steered[10] the ship[11] with the gold boy upon the prow, in[12] which your father sailed[13] to conquer England. I beseech you to grant[14] me the same office. I[15] have a fair vessel in the harbour here, called the White Ship, manned by fifty sailors of renown. I pray you, Sire[16], to[17] let your servant have the honour of steering[18] you in the White Ship to England."

1, to go over, ſich begeben. The words 'to Normandy' (S. 19, N. 4) must be placed after 'retinue'.   **2,** to have acknowledged, huldigen laſſen. See S. 19, N. 7. The words 'by (von) the Norman nobles' must be placed after 'prince'. The nobles, der Adel.   **3,** to contract a promised marriage, einen verabredeten Heiratsvertrag ab'ſchließen. The pron. 'him' should be turned by 'the prince', to avoid ambiguity.   **4,** both — things = this.   **5,** Pomp, m.; rejoicing, viele Freudenbezeigungen; to be done, geſchehen.   **6,** ſich zur Heimreiſe an'ſchicken. **7,** Supply the adverb 'nun' after 'when'.   **8,** The subject and apposition must be placed immediately after the predicate. Comp. App. § 15.   **9,** Say 'My father, O prince (Fürſt), served yours (use the second pers. sing. of the posses. pron., and continue the address in the same person) his whole life long at (zur) sea'.   **10,** lenken.   **11,** das am Vorderteile mit einem goldenen Knaben verzierte Schiff.   **12,** auf.   **13,** sailed — England = sailed (ſich ein'ſchiffen) for (zu) the conquest of England.   **14,** verleihen.   **15,** Say 'I possess in this (hieſig) harbour a fair with fifty renowned (bewährt) sailors (Seeleute) manned vessel (Fahrzeug), called (App. § 1) the White Ship'. Comp. S. 7, N. 3. **16,** e Herr.   **17,** to let ... have = to grant; use the Supine.   **18,** 'to steer', here = to conduct, geleiten. See S. 1, N. 3.

Section 48.

THE WHITE SHIP.

II.

"I am sorry," replied the king, "that[1] my vessel is already chosen, and *that* I cannot therefore sail with the son of the man who served[2] my father. But[3] the prince, with all his company, shall go along with you in the fair White Ship manned by fifty sailors of renown."

An[4] hour or two afterwards, the king (App. § 15) set sail[5] in[6] the vessel he had chosen, accompanied by other vessels, and[7], sailing all night with a fair and gentle wind, arrived upon the coast of England in the morning. While[8] it was yet night, the[9] people in some of the ships heard a faint wild cry come[10] over the sea, and wondered what[11] it was.

1, Say 'that I have already chartered (gedingen) a ship'.   2, Use the **Perfect**, which is used in German to express an action or occurrence both perfect and past, without reference to any other action or occurrence. 3, Render 'but' by jedoch, which place after 'shall'; with — company, ſamt ſeinem ganzen Geſolge ; 'to go along', here fahren, to be placed at the end of the whole clause, which construe accord. to S. 48, N. 6.   4, An — afterwards = Soon after.   5, to set sail. ab'ſegeln.   6, **To place the qualifying parts before the word qualified is one of the most striking peculiarities of German Grammar.** This construction, called attributive construction, has been explained in Section 7, Note 3 with respect to the rendering of the Perfect (or Past) Participle qualifying a preceding noun; but it must here be pointed out that it may likewise be used for rendering the Present Participle qualifying a preceding noun (comp. S. 16, N. 4), and that it is sometimes even suitable for translating short relative clauses. This, as long as it is not too much indulged in, imparts to the construction great conciseness and vigour, and avoids the too frequent use of relative pronouns, which, contrary to English construction, cannot be omitted in German. (Comp. S. 16, N. 10.)

EXAMPLES.

When the fleet, *favoured* by the finest weather, was about to set sail, there arose a shout of joy, *proceeding* from many thousands of voices, and resounding mightily from the shore.

Als die von dem ſchönſten Wetter begünſtigte Flotte im Begriff war abzuſegeln, erheb ſich ein von vielen tauſend Stimmen erſchallender Jubelruf, von dem das Ufer mächtig wiederhallte.

The child, gently *sleeping* in his mother's arms, was suddenly roused by his father's noisy entrance.

Das in den Armen der Mutter ſanft ſchlafende Kind wurde plötzlich durch den lärmenden Eintritt des Vaters aufgeweckt.

The church, *which was damaged by the siege*, is now being restored.

Die durch die Belagerung beſchädigte Kirche wird jetzt wiederhergeſtellt.

The clause 'in — vessels' requires the attributive construction, since the two relative clauses, otherwise required, would make the rendering very lengthy and monotonous. To avoid a useless repetition, translate the first noun 'vessel' by Schiff and the second by Fahrzeug, and connect the two clauses by the conjunction und.   7, The passage 'and — morning' may be briefly rendered thus: and arrived, favoured (begünſtigt, App. § 1) by a gentle (mäßig) wind, the (am) next morning in England.   8, Say 'During the night'.   9, the people = one, after which supply the conj. jedoch ; in ships = upon some ships. 10, come — sea, von der See herüber, which place after 'ships'; wild cry, Angſtſchrei.   11, was dies zu bedeuten habe.

Section 49.

THE WHITE SHIP.

III.

The prince went[1] aboard the White Ship with *one* hundred and forty youthful nobles, among whom were eighteen noble ladies of the highest rank. All[2] this gay company, with their servants and the fifty sailors, made three hundred souls aboard the White Ship.

"Give three[3] casks *of* wine, Fitz-Stephen," said the prince, "to the fifty sailors of renown. My[4] father the king has sailed out of the

harbour.   What[5] time is there to make merry here, and yet reach England with the rest?"

" Prince[6]," said Fitz-Stephen, " before morning my fifty and the White
Ship shall overtake the swiftest vessel in attendance on your father the
king, if we sail at midnight."

1, to go aboard ship, ſich auf ein Schiff begeben: the young noble, ter junge
Adelige; ' to be', here ſich befinten; eighteen — rank, achtzehn tem höchſten Range
angehörige Damen.   The words ' aboard the White Ship' take the last place in
the clause.   2, This clause requires the following construction : With the
servants (Dienerſchaft, f.) and the fifty sailors consisted the whole gay company
upon the White Ship of (aus) three hundred persons.   3, Construe according to App. § 5.   4, Say ' My royal father'; has sailed out of = has
left.   Supply the adverb ſeeten after the auxiliary.   This will greatly improve
the rendering.   5, Also the two following passages require a different
construction ; say ' How long can we still make merry (ſich gütlich thun) here
(to be placed before ' still'), if we will arrive in England at the same time
(zugleich) with the others?'   The words ' in England' should stand before the
verbs, which arrange according to App. § 18.   6, Say ' " If we sail at (um)
midnight, O prince (see S. 27, N. 8), my fifty men (Leute) and the White Ship
shall nevertheless (tennech) before the coming morning overtake the swiftest
ship in the service of thy royal father," replied Fitz-Stephen'.—' The swiftest
— father' = the swiftest in the service of thy royal father standing ship.
(Comp. S. 48, N. 6.)

Section 50.

THE WHITE SHIP.
IV.

Then[1] the prince commanded to[2] make merry ; and the sailors drank
out the three casks *of* wine, and the prince and[3] all the noble[4] company
danced in the moonlight on the deck of the White Ship.

When at last she[5] shot[6] out of the harbour of Barfleur, there[7] was not[8]
a sober seaman on[9] board.   But the sails were all set[10] and[11] the oars all
going merrily, Fitz-Stephen at the helm.

The gay young nobles and the beautiful ladies talked, laughed, and
sang.   The prince encouraged[12] the fifty sailors to row harder[13] yet, for[14]
the honour of the White Ship.

1, Hereupon.   2, that they (man) should make merry.   The verb must
stand in the Present Subjunctive, as will be seen from §§ 28–30 of the App.
3, ſaＭＭ.   4, atelig; company = retinue.   5, tieſe, to be placed after
' When'.   6, shot out of = left.   7, there to be, ſich befinten.   8, not a,
auch nicht ein einziger.   9, Say ' upon the ship'.   10, geſpaＮＮt.   11, Say
' and the oars moved (ſich bewegen) merrily (luſtig), whilst F.-St. stood at the
helm'.   12, an'treiben.   13, harder = faster.   14, tem weißen Schiff
zu Ehren.

Section 51.

THE WHITE SHIP.
V.

Crash[1]!—a terrific cry broke from three hundred hearts.   It was the
cry (S. 16, N. 10) the people[2] in the distant vessels of the king had
faintly[3] heard on the water.   The White Ship had struck upon a rock,
and[4] was going down !

Fitz-Stephen hurried [5] the prince into a boat with some few nobles. "Push off," he whispered, "and row to [6] the land. It is not far, and the sea is smooth [7]. The [8] rest of us must die."

But [9], as they rowed away fast from the sinking ship, the prince heard the voice of his sister Mary calling [10] for help. He (S. 5, N. 2) never in his life had been so good as [11] he was then. He [12] cried, in an agony: "Row back at any risk! I cannot bear [13] to leave her!"

1, Krach!—es erhob sich ein aus drei hundert Kehlen erschallender fürchterlicher Angst=schrei. **2,** the people = one; in = upon. **3,** faintly on the water, unvollkommen von der See herüber. **4,** und war im Sinken begriffen! **5,** to hurry into a boat, schnell in ein Boot steigen lassen; with = and. **6,** an, contracted with the def. art. **7,** ruhig. **8,** The — us = We others. **9,** Render 'but' by jedoch, which place before the adverb 'fast' (schnell); to row away, sich ent= fernen. **10,** See S. 16, N. 4; for, um. **11,** Say 'as at (in) this moment'. **12,** The remaining passage will greatly improve by placing the clause 'Row — risk' before the words 'He — agony'. In an agony, voll Seelenangst; at any risk, koste es, was es wolle. **13,** When there is in a principal clause a transitive verb, the object of which is contained in a following objective clause, which often assumes the form of a supine (i. e. an infinitive with zu, see S. 1, N. 2), the object in the principal clause is frequently supplied by the pro- noun **es**, which then may be called the grammatical object. This is more particularly the case when special emphasis is given to the verb contained in the principal clause; as—

He *liked to hear* good music.	Er liebte es, gute Musik zu hören.
The deed proves, that she speaks the truth.	Die That beweist es, daß sie die Wahrheit spricht.

Section 52.

THE WHITE SHIP.

VI.

They rowed back. When [1] the prince held out his arms to catch [2] his sister, such [3] numbers lept in, that the boat was overset; and in the same instant the White Ship went [4] down.

Only two men floated [5]: a nobleman, Godfrey by name, and a poor butcher of Rouen. By and by [6] another man came swimming towards them, whom [7] they knew, when he had pushed aside his long wet hair, to be Fitz-Stephen.

When he heard that the prince and all his retinue had [8] gone down, Fitz-Stephen, with a ghastly face [9], cried: "Woe, woe to me!" and sank [10] to the bottom.

1, Supply here the conj. after. **2,** auf`fangen. **3,** Say 'so many persons jumped into the boat, that it capsized'. **4,** Supply the adverb auch after the verb. **5,** to float, auf dem Wasser schwimmen; of Rouen, aus Rouen. **6,** Kurz darauf; supply the adverb noch before 'another'. He comes swimming towards me, er kommt auf mich zugeschwommen. **7,** Say 'in whom they recognised Fitz-Stephen, when he', etc.; to push aside = to throw back. **8,** had gone down, den Tod erlitten. The auxiliary verb (had) may here be omitted, for: **In subordinate clauses, the auxiliary verbs (haben, sein, and werden) are often omitted for the sake of conciseness and elegance; as—**

Daß sie mir genommen (wurde), ist   That she *was* taken from me is my
mein größtes Leid.   greatest sorrow.

9, with — face, totenbleich, adv.   How must the words be arranged here?
10, to sink to the bottom, in die Tiefe hinab'sinken. Supply the adv. dann after
the verb, which will establish a closer connection between this clause and the
preceding one.

Section 53.

THE WHITE SHIP.

VII.

The other two clung[1] to the yard for some hours. At length (App.
§ 14) the young noble said faintly[2]: " I am exhausted, *and* benumbed[3]
with cold, and can hold[4] no longer. Farewell, good friend. God preserve (App. § 34) you!"

So[5] he dropped and sank, and of all the brilliant crowd[6], the poor
butcher of Rouen alone was saved. In[7] the morning, some fishermen
saw him floating in his sheep-skin coat[8], and got[9] him into their boat,—
the sole relater of the dismal tale.

For[1] three days no one dared to carry[10] the intelligence to the king; at
length they[11] sent into his presence a little boy, who, weeping[12] bitterly,
and kneeling at his feet, told him that the White Ship was[13] lost, with all
on board.

The king fell to the ground like[14] a dead man, and[15] never afterwards
was seen to smile.—C. DICKENS, A CHILD'S HISTORY OF ENGLAND.

1, to cling to the yard, sich an eine Segelstange an'flammern: for some hours,
einige Stunden lang; for three days, drei Tage lang.   2, kraftlos.   3, vor
Kälte erstarrt.   4, ' to hold', here sich halten.   5, Say ' Upon this (Hereupon) he fell into the water and sank to the bottom (in die Tiefe hinab'sinken)'.
6, crowd = company.   7, In the morning, am Morgen.   8, sheep-skin
coat, Schafpelz, m.   9, nehmen; the appositional clause ' the sole relater
(Überbringer) of the dismal (traurig) tale (Kunde)' must be placed immediately
after the pronoun ' him', to which it belongs ; and mark that : **The apposition
must always agree in number, gender, and case with the noun or pronoun to which it belongs.**   10, to carry an intelligence to a person,
Einem eine Botschaft verkünden. See App. § 5.   11, man; into his presence
= to (zu) him, which place after ' boy'.   12, **The Present Participle
may be used adverbially, as in English, to denote manner or state.**
Say ' who told him kneeling and weeping bitterly, that', etc.   13, was
— board, mit Mann und Maus gesunken sei.   14, like — man = as if dead
(wie tot), which place after ' fell.'   15, Say ' and never has one seen him
smile again '.

Section 54.

BARLEY (S. 3, N. 2).

Barley is (S. 2, N. 1) now principally used[6] to make[1] malt for[2] brewing
beer and distilling spirits. It serves, however[3], as food[4] in *the* form of
pearl barley, used[5] for thickening soups. It is also used[6] as food for
poultry. Barley[7] meal is used for fattening pigs and turkeys. Barley
straw furnishes us fodder[8] for cattle and horses. Barley is chiefly produced[9] in the northern regions of Europe, in Central Asia, and in North

America. It is much hardier [10] than wheat, resists [11] *both* heat and drought better, and [12] may therefore be raised from poorer soils. It [13] is said to be the most ancient food [4] of (S. 3, N. 2) man.—NELSON'S READERS.

1, bereiten, see S. 19, N. 7. 2, for — spirits, zur Bierbrauerei und Branntweinbrennerei, after which supply daraus. 3, indessen. 4, Nahrungs= mittel, n. 5, Say 'which one uses for thickening soups', zur Verdickung der Suppen. 6, benutzen and gebrauchen, which use alternately; as — poultry, als Hühnerfutter. 7, Say 'With barley meal one fattens (mästen) pigs and turkeys (türkische Hühner)'. 8, Vieh=und Pferdefutter. 9, gebaut. Where must the p. p. be placed here? 10, kräftig. 11, 'to resist' here = to bear, vertragen. Use the def. art. before the first noun. 12, Say 'and can therefore be cultivated (au'bauen) upon poorer soil'. Supply the adverb auch after 'therefore'. 13, It is said to be, sie soll ... sein. The verb sollen is frequently used to express an assertion of another person, when it answers to the English 'it is said', 'it is reported', 'they say'.

Section 55.

THE SOLDIER AND HIS FLAG (Fahne).

On seeing [1] a young Prussian soldier who was pressing his flag to his bosom in the agonies of death, Napoleon said to his officers: "Gentle- men [2], you see that a soldier has for his flag a sentiment almost ap- proaching [3] idolatry. Render [4] funeral honours at once to this young man. I regret that I do not know his name, that [5] I might write to his family. Do not take [6] *away* his flag; its silken folds will be an honourable shroud [7] for him.—GENERAL BOURRIENNE [8].

1, When the Present Participle is used in adverbial clauses of time, it must generally, by the help of one of the conjunctions als (when), nachdem (after), indem (while, whilst), and während (while, whilst), be changed into a finite verb, i.e. one with a personal termination; thus—

Hearing his opponent speak in this way, his features assumed an ex- pression of contempt.	Als er seinen Gegner so sprechen hörte, nahmen seine Züge den Ausdruck der Verachtung an.
Having given his orders, the officer rode quickly away.	Nachdem er seine Befehle erteilt hatte, ritt der Offizier schnell von dannen.
Looking at me in a suppliant manner, a tear glittered in her eye.	Indem sie mich bittend ansah, glänzte eine Thräne in ihrem Auge.
I saw it *when passing* the house this morning.	Ich sah es, als ich heute Morgen beim Hause vorüberging.

Consequently, the above passage must be rendered thus: 'When Napoleon saw (bemerken) a young Prussian soldier who was pressing his flag to (an) his (S. 43, N. 9, *A*) bosom (Herz) in the agonies of death (im Todeskampfe, which place after 'flag'), he said to his officers': etc. 2, Say 'You see, gentle- men'. 3, 'to approach' here = to border (an etwas grenzen). For the construction see S. 16, N. 4. 4, Say 'Bury this young man (Jüngling) without delay with military honours'. 5, that — write, um ... schreiten zu können. He writes *to* me once a month, Er schreibt einmal monatlich an mich. 6, Supply the pronoun ihm (from him) after the Imperative. 7, Leiden= tuch, n.; 'for him' must be rendered by the dat. of the pers. pron., which place after the copula 'will'. 8, Der General Bourrienne war Privatsekretär und späterer Biograph Napoleons des Ersten.

Section 56.

OUR CULTIVATED[1] NATIVE[2] PLANTS.

Most[3] of the fruits which grow on trees, *such* as our apples and pears, have[4] been greatly[5] improved and raised[6] above their natural state by grafting and other artificial means.

Of[7] cultivated native plants, the chief are celery[8], parsley, the cabbage, turnip, carrot, parsnips, and the hop. The onion is[9] a native of South France, the lettuce of Greece, the radish of China, and the rhubarb, now[10] so largely used in pies and puddings, of Russia. Cress comes from[11] Persia, spinach from some[12] part of Asia, and the Jerusalem artichoke[13] from Brazil.—HEWITT, PHYSICAL GEOGRAPHY OF ENGLAND AND WALES.

1, veretelt. 2, einheimisch. 3, The clause 'Most — trees' may be briefly rendered by 'Die meisten Baumfrüchte'. 4, Here follows the adverbial clause 'by grafting — means'. 5, bedeutend. 6, 'raised — state' may be elegantly rendered by the p. p. 'cultivated' (veretelt). 7, Say 'The principal cultivated native plants are', etc. 8, See S. 3, N. 2. I should recommend to repeat the art. before each of the following six nouns. 9, is a native of, stammt aus. 10, 'Now — puddings'. This elliptic clause must be completed in German. Say 'which is now so largely (much) used in pies (Pasteten) and puddings'. 11, aus. 12, 'some', here irgend ein. 13, Erdartischocke, f.

Section 57.

THE BEQUEST[1].

I.

An old avaricious English gentleman[2] had three sons, of whom one[3] was a good-natured but light-minded fellow. Whenever (S. 18, N. 6) he fell[4] into any trouble, he excused himself on[5] the ground that[6] he was seeing life. His prodigality, however, annoyed[7] his father so much[8], that he resolved to disinherit (S. 1, N. 2) him. His friends interceded[9] in his favour, but their efforts were in vain.

When the old gentleman[10] felt his end approaching, he called his sons together[11], and said to them: "I leave[12] to my son John my whole estate[13], and desire him[14] to be frugal." John[15], in a sorrowful tone, as is usual on such occasions, prayed heaven to prolong his father's life, and give him health to enjoy the gift[16] himself.

1, Das Vermächtniß. 2, Engländer. 3, Say 'the one'. 4, to fall into trouble, in Verlegenheit gerathen. 5, on the ground, damit. 6, daß er das Leben kennen lerne. Comp. App. §§ 28 and 30. 7, verdrießen. See S. 5, N. 2. 8, sehr. 9, to intercede in a person's favour, zu gunsten einer Person sprechen. He interceded in my favour, er sprach zu meinen gunsten. Supply the adverb zwar (it is true) after the verb. 10, Herr; to feel one's end approaching, sein Ende heran'nahen fühlen. 11, together, zu sich. 12, 'to leave', here = to bequeath. 13, Besitzung, f. 14, The construction of the Infinitive with an Accusative, so frequently employed in English as an imitation of the Latin and Greek, is unknown in German. Such constructions must be rendered by a subordinate clause introduced by the conjunction daß; as—

I know *him to be* an industrious man. Ich weiß, daß er ein fleißiger Mann ist.

See also App. § 34, and say 'and wish that he may be frugal (ſparſam)'.
15, This passage requires the following construction: 'As (wie) it is usual
(üblich) on (bei) such occasions, John (App. § 15) implored heaven in (mit)
a sorrowful tone to prolong', etc. The noun Himmel is always used with the
article.   16, Vermächtniſ.

Section 58.

THE BEQUEST.

II.

The father continued: "I leave to my son James my money[1],
amounting[2] to four thousand pounds[3]." "Ah, father," said[4] James, of
course in[4] great affliction, "may (App. § 34) heaven give you life and
health to enjoy the gift yourself." The[5] father, then addressing the
spendthrift, said: "As[6] for you, Dick, you[7] will never come to good;
you will never be rich. I leave you a shilling to (S. 19, N. 7) buy[8] a
halter." "Ah, father," said Dick in *a* most[9] melancholy voice, "may
heaven give you life and health to enjoy the gift yourself!"—Anonymous.

1, 'money', here = ready money, bares Geld.   2, to amount to something, ſich auf etwas belaufen. See S. 16, N. 4.   3, Das Pfund, one pound
English money, never takes the sign of the Plural in German, and the same
refers to 'die Mark', a German coin corresponding to one shilling English.
4, said = exclaimed; in = with.   5, Say 'Upon this the father addressed
himself (ſich wenden) to (an) the spendthrift and said'.   6, As — Dick, Was
dich betrifft, Richard.   7, Introduce this clause by the adverbial conjunction
je, and see App. § 15; to come to good, zu etwas Rechtem kommen.   8, The
German language, as a rule, requires that the person for whose
benefit an action is performed, is clearly indicated. When this is
not done by a noun in the dative case, it is generally done by means
of the dative of a personal pronoun; as—

I will buy a hat.   Ich will mir einen Hut kaufen.
We have built a house.   Wir haben uns ein Haus gebaut.

Supply, therefore, the necessary pronoun after the conjunction um; a halter = a
rope, Strick, m.   9, Render 'most' here by 'höchſt'.

Section 59.

WHEAT.

Wheat is the most valuable[1] of all grains, because[2] from it, chiefly, we
obtain the flour of which bread is made. In order to make[3] flour, the
grains of wheat[4] are crushed[5] between stones in a mill. The crushed
mass is then separated[6] into two parts,—bran[7] and flour. Bran is the
outer husk of the grain, which is used (S. 4. N. 4) for[8] fattening cattle,
etc.[9] It[10] does no harm, however, to mix the bran with the flour; the
mixture is more nourishing than the pure flour. The bran makes the
flour and the bread darker *in colour;* but this is no disadvantage, for
brown bread is both[11] cheaper and more nourishing than white bread.
Bread[12] is often artificially whitened by[13] the addition of alum and other
injurious substances. Wheat is[14] chiefly grown in France, Germany,
Austria, Southern Russia, (S. 46, N. 6) the British Isles, Australia, the
United States, Canada, Egypt, and Northern Africa.—Nelson's Readers.

1, wertvoll; 'grain', here Kernart, f.   **2,** Say 'because it yields (liefern) us chiefly the flour for our bread'.   **3,** bereiten.   **4,** Form a compound noun of 'wheat' and 'grains' (Körner).   **5,** zermahlen.   **6,** senden. **7,** The prep. 'in' must be repeated before this and the following noun. **8,** for — cattle, zur Viehfütterung.   **9,** u. f. w., i. e. und so weiter.   **10,** It — however, übrigens schadet es nichts.   **11,** both ... and, sowohl ... als auch. **12,** Say 'Bread receives (erhalten) often an artificial whiteness through an addition', etc.   **13,** When 'by' is equivalent to 'through', it must be rendered by **durch**.   **14,** Say 'grows chiefly', in order to make the construction more concise than it would be by using a p. p., which would have its place at the end of the whole clause, and would thus make the construction too lengthy.

Section 60.

OCCUPATION OF THE ANGLO-SAXONS.

Fishing (S. 40, N. 9) was a principal occupation, owing[1] to the frequent abstinences from flesh-meat, enjoined[2] by (S. 59, N. 13) a superstitious ritual[3]. Eels were taken[4] in immense numbers in the marsh lands of the Eastern counties; salmon in the river Dee; herrings along the shores of Suffolk, Kent, and Sussex, in[5] their annual migration; while larger species, as[6] the whale and grampus[7], were captured in the open sea. Hunting and falconry were the field-sports[8] of the great. The beasts of the forest or chase, which were protected by fines, and reserved[9] for privileged persons, were the[10] stag, roebuck, hare, and rabbit. The wolf, fox, and boar might[11] be killed by[12] any one with impunity, if (S. 27, N. 7) found without[13] the limits of the chase or forest. The wild duck and heron were the[14] common quarry.— MILNER, HISTORY OF ENGLAND.

1, Say 'in consequence of the frequent fasting'.   **2,** an'erdnen. See S. 7, N. 3, B.   **3,** Ritus, m.   **4,** 'to take', here = to catch; numbers = multitudes, Menge, f.; marsh lands, Marschgegenten.   **5,** in = upon. **6,** as = like, wie.   **7,** der Schwertfisch (Delphinus orca).   **8,** Vergnügungen.   **9,** reservieren.   **10,** I propose to use the following seven nouns in the plural and without the article, in order to avoid the frequent repetition of the same.   **11,** Use the Imperf. of dürfen.   **12,** by — impunity, von jedermann ungestraft.   **13,** without = outside, außerhalb.   **14,** Say 'the booty of all'.

Section 61.

TENDER[1], TRUSTY, AND TRUE.

I.

(Extract from a Sermon preached to a congregation of children at Chicago.)

When[2] I was in the Sunday-school, and had just begun to read about[3] David, I[4] did not feel sure he ever was a real baby, and had to be fed with a teaspoon; or that he ever was a real little boy[5] that[6] went to school as I did, and played marbles[7], and had a peg-top[8], a jack-knife[9], some slate pencils, ever[10] so many buttons, and a piece of string[11], all in one pocket; that[12] he ever had to try hard not to cry when he went to school very cold[13] mornings; or[14] that the teacher spoke sharp to him, when the little chap had tried [15] his best to get [16] his lesson, and [17] did not get it very well.

1, Zartfühlend, zuverlässig und treu.   2, Say 'When I went to the Sunday-school', and supply the adverb nach after the subject.   3, über.   4, Say 'I could scarcely imagine, that he ever really had been a little child and had to be fed with a teaspoon (und mit einem Theelöffel habe gefüttert werden müssen)'. By carefully reading §§ 29 and 30 of the Appendix, the student will see that the verbs depending on the governing verb '*imagine*' must stand in the Perfect of the Subjunctive Mood. According to S. 52, N. 8, however, the auxiliary 'sei' may be omitted in the clause 'that he ever really had been a little child'. 5, Junge. The auxiliary 'sei' may again be omitted here.   6, that = who; as I did = 'like myself', which place immediately after the relat. pron. 7, Schusser. Remember that both this and the next clause are depending on the relative clause 'that — did'; place, therefore, the verb 'played' after 'marbles', and the verb 'had' after 'peg-top'.   8, Kreisel, m.   9, Taschenmesser, n. 10, ever so many, eine Unzahl von, i.e. no end of.   11, ein Stück Bindfaden. 12, that — hard, daß er sich je habe anstrengen müssen.   13, cold mornings, an einem sehr kalten Morgen, which place after the subject. 'To go to school', zur (*or* in die) Schule gehen.   14, Say 'or that the teacher had ever scolded (schelten) the little fellow (Bursche), when he had', etc.   15, to try one's best, sich Mühe geben.   16, to get one's lesson = to learn one's lesson, seine Lektion erlernen.   17, Say 'and had not learnt it well', and supply the adverb doch (nevertheless) after the objective pronoun 'it'. For the position of the verb see App. § 17.

Section 62.

TENDER, TRUSTY, AND TRUE.

II.

But you [1] know, ministers [2] have to find out all about such men as David; and I have found out enough to [3] make me feel sure he was once a little boy, *just* like *one of* you; that he had [4] to learn verses, like you; and didn't like (S. 20, N. 2, *A*) it, like you; and that he did not like to go to bed early, or to get up early, like you.

I rather [5] fear that, in the summer, he [6] ate green apples, unripe melons, hard peaches, and sour plums, as [7] you *do*; and [8] got sick, and was very sorry, and had to take [9] medicine, as you *do*; that he said he would (App. § 28) never do it again, and that he [10] then never did *do* it again, as [11] I hope you will neither.

1, Use the 2nd pers. pl., and after the verb supply the adverb 'ja', which will be equivalent to the English 'I am sure'.   2, die Pfarrer, before which supply the conj. daß. Have to = must; to find out, ausfindig machen; all — David = all (S. 3, N. 7) that relates (sich beziehen) to (auf) such men as David. 3, Say 'to (S. 19, N. 7) be convinced, that', etc. Just — you, wie ihr.   4, The auxiliaries 'to have' and 'to be' followed by the infinitive of another verb, must generally be rendered by the auxiliary verb of mood 'müssen'; as— I have to do it, Ich muß es thun.   5, fast, adv.; see S. 5, N. 2.   6, The subject 'he' must immediately follow the conj. 'that'.   7, as you do, wie ihr.   8, that he became (werden) ill; 'and — sorry', say 'felt (empfinden) bitter repentance'.   9, 'to take', here ein'nehmen.   10, Here follows the pron. 'it'.   11, wie ihr es hoffentlich auch nicht wieder thun werdet.

Section 63.

TENDER, TRUSTY, AND TRUE.

III.

Now [1], just here I was trying to see what [2] sort of boy David was when he grew [3] bigger; and, when I shut my eyes, and *so* tried [4] to see *it* all clearly, I heard a noise right [5] under my study window. This was [6] about [7] four o'clock, Friday afternoon; the schools were out, and the children running home [8]. I turned my head to see what was the matter [9], and then (App. § 14) I saw what I want [10] to tell you. About ten boys were standing together [11]. All at once a big boy knocked [12] a little boy [13] down, and rolled him in the snow [14]. The little boy got up [15], and said: "What [16] did you do that for?" Then [17] the big boy again approached the little boy [18], and I believe [18] he would have knocked him down again [19], had not the little boy [13] walked sobbing away [20] towards home.

1, Hier wollte ich nun sehen.   2, what sort of, was für ein.   3, werden.
4, sich bemühen.   5, just under the window of my study.   6, Here
follow the words 'on Friday afternoon'.   7, Supply here the prep. 'at',
um.   8, The English '**home**', after a verb denoting motion, must be
rendered by nach Hause, and 'at home', after a verb denoting rest, by zu
Hause.   9, the matter is, es giebt, verb impers. Use the Present of
the Subj., according to App. § 32.   10, The auxiliary verb of mood
'wollen' expresses wish and want; as—

Was wollen Sie?   What do you *wish?*
Zu wem wollen Sie?   Who is it you *want?*

11, neben einander.   12, to knock down, zu Boden schlagen.   13, The
noun 'boy' need not be repeated here.   14, Supply here the adverb
'about' (umher).   15, to get up, aufstehen.   16, What ... for = Why.
Use the 2nd pers. sing.   17, Upon this, S. 44, N. 4.   18, Supply here
the conj. daß. Read carefully § 36 of the App., and construe accordingly.
Use the Pluperfect Subj. in both clauses, and observe that the verb gehen
always requires the auxiliary sein. See S. 29, N. 3.   19, noch einmal.
20, away towards home = home.

Section 64.

TENDER, TRUSTY, AND TRUE.

IV.

"There," I said, when I had seen that, "I know what David never did *do:* he (S. 5, N. 2) never struck a boy that [1] was no match for him; he never was a coward like that big boy; for he [2] is a coward to [3] strike a small boy so; and those [4] others are not the boys (S. 16, N. 10) they ought [5] to be, to [6] stand by and see it done." I saw such [7] a thing in a picture once, which was called the Wolf and the Lamb. A great, cruel boy [8] meets a small, delicate lad [9] who has lost his father, and stands over him with [10] his fist doubled, just as I saw that boy *stand* under my study window. I think [11] if [12] any [13] boy in this church were [14] to see that picture, he would instantly say [15]: "What a shame to use [16] a boy so who is not your match!"

1, that — him, ter ihm nicht gewachsen war.   2, the pron. 'he' is used demonstratively in this clause.   3, Say 'because he can strike a small boy so'.   4, those = the.   5, To render 'ought', use the Imperf. of 'follen'.   6, Say 'because they stand by (tabei stehen) and look at it (es mit ansehen)'.   7, such a thing, etwas Aehnliches. The adv. 'once' must stand immediately after the verb.   8, Bube, m.   9, lad, Bursche, m. The clause 'who — father' may be briefly rendered by the adj. 'fatherless', which place before 'lad'.   10, mit geballter Faust.   11, When the verb 'to think' is used in the meaning of 'to be of opinion', it must be rendered by 'glauben', and when it is used in the meaning of 'to be engaged in thinking', by 'denken'.   12, The conj. 'if' must always be rendered by 'wenn'.   13, any boy = any (irgend) one of you.   14, Render the words 'were to see' by the Imperf. Subj. of sehen.   15, ans'rufen.   16, to use = to abuse, miß handeln.

Section 65.

TENDER, TRUSTY, AND TRUE.

V.

Once I read in the Life [1] of Dr. Channing, who was one of the best men that ever (je) lived [2] (a [3] great deal better than David, because he lived [4] in a better time), what he once did, when he was a [5] boy and saw a [6] thing like that. Little Channing was one of the kindest [7] and most tender-hearted boys I [8] ever heard of. I will tell you a story to show you how [9] kind he was, and tender, and true. One day he found in a bush a nest full [10] of young birds just out of the shell. Children, did [11] you ever see a [12] nest full of birds just out of the shell?—little tiny [13], downy things [14], with [15] hardly more feathers than an oyster? The birds which William Channing found, were just of that kind; and when he touched them with his fingers, and felt how soft and warm they were, they all began to gape [16], very [17] much as you do when I preach [18] a very long sermon.

1, Lebensbeschreibung, f. The Genitive relation must be expressed by the Gen. of the def. art. See S. 10, N. 2. Proper names are not inflected when they are preceded by an article and a common name.—Dr. William Ellery Channing, berühmter amerikanischer Geistlicher und Schriftsteller, wurde im Jahre 1780 zu Newport auf Rhode-Island geboren und starb im Jahre 1842 zu Bennington in Bermont. Seine zahlreichen ausgezeichneten Schriften haben seinen Namen auch in europäischen Kreisen berühmt gemacht. Coleridge, dessen Bekanntschaft er machte, als er im Jahre 1822 England besuchte, war so sehr von ihm eingenommen, daß er ausrief: 'He has the love of wisdom, and the wisdom of love!'   2, Use the Perfect. See S. 48, N. 2.   3, a great deal = much.   4, lived in = belonged to, an'gehören, which governs the dat.   5, Substitute the adverb noch for the indef. art.   6, See S. 64, N. 7.   7, best and most tender-feeling.   8, Say 'of whom I have ever heard'.   9, Say 'how good, tender and true he was'.   10, voll von erst seeben aus der Schale gefrochenen Bögeln.   11, Use the Perfect.   12, To avoid repetition, turn the words 'a — shell' by 'such (je) young little birds', and render 'little birds' by forming a diminutive of Bögel.   13, zart.   14, Dingerchen.   15, Say 'almost as naked as an oyster'.   16, 'to gape', here den Schnabel auf'sperren.   17, very — do, fast wie ihr den Mund auf'sperrt.   18, to preach a sermon, eine Predigt halten.

Section 66.

TENDER, TRUSTY, AND TRUE.

VI.

Well, little (S. 10, N. 2) Channing knew[1] the birds did not gape because he preached a long sermon, but (S. 6, N. 10) because they were hungry. So[2] what did he do? He ran straight[3] home (S. 63, N. 8), got[4] some nice soft crumbs of bread, and fed the little birds with them (S. 4, N. 5, *B*); and[5] after that he fed them regularly every day after[6] having come home from school. But[7] one day (S. 19, N. 2), when he went to[8] the nest, there it lay on the ground, torn and bloody, and the little birds all dead; and the father-bird[9] was crying[10] on a wall, and the mother-bird[11] was crying on a tree. Then little Channing tried[12] to tell them that he did not kill[13] their poor young brood; that[14] he never could do such a mean, cruel thing as that, and that[15], on the contrary[16], he had tried to feed them. But it was no use; the little birds could not understand him, and[17] kept on crying; and at last he sat down, and wept bitterly.

1, Supply here the conj. baß.   2, Say 'What did he therefore (alfo) *do?*'
3, ftrachs.   4, holte fich.   5, and — that, unb ven ta an.   6, fo balt er von der Schule nach Haufe gekommen war.   7, This passage will read more elegantly by beginning with the conj. 'when', which must be followed by the subject 'he'. 'But' should then be rendered by jeboch, which takes the third place.   8, nach.   9, das Männchen.   10, jammern; on = upon.
11, das Weibchen.   12, fich bemühen.   13, Use the Perf. Subj. according to App. §§ 28 and 30.   14, baß er eine fo gemeine Graufamkeit nie begehen könne.   15, In subordinate clauses, the subject stands in most cases immediately after the conjunction or relative pronoun.   16, im Gegenteil.   See S. 15, N. 3.   17, und jammerten weiter.

Section 67.

TENDER, TRUSTY, AND TRUE.

VII.

Now[1] this was the sort of boy Channing was; and I was going[2] to tell you that (S. 66, N. 15) one day he heard of a big boy beating (S. 16, N. 4) a little one[3], like that bad boy[4] under my window. Channing was a little boy; he was a little man when he was full grown[5]; but *then* he had a big soul. I was going[2] to say he had a soul as big as a church; but indeed[6] his soul was bigger than all *the* churches in[7] the world;—and when he heard of that[8] cruel boy, who was ever[9] so much larger than himself, he went right up to him, and said: "Did[10] you strike that little boy?" "Yes, I did[11]; and what then?"—"Then," said Channing, "you are a coward, because he was no match for you; and now I am going[2] to whip[12] you for *doing* it." Because he had a big soul, and though he was a small boy, he[13] went in, and fought for the right. That was the only time he[14] ever fought in his life. But[15] I, standing in[16] this pulpit, honour him more for it than if he had (App. § 36) never[17] fought at all.

1, Say 'This was (supply here the adv. alſo = now) little Channing's character'. Comp. S. 12, N. 2.   2, The auxiliary verb of mood 'wollen' corresponds to the English 'to be going' or 'to be on the point', followed by the infinitive of another verb. Comp. S. 6, N. 4.   3, 'One' following an adjective or a pronoun, and representing a noun understood, is not to be translated; as—Which pen shall I give you,—this *one* or that *one*? Welche Feder ſoll ich Ihnen geben,—dieſe oder jene?   4, der böſe Bube.   5, full grown, ausgewachſen.   6, in der That, which place after the verb.   7, Render 'in the' by the gen. of the def. art.   8, Use the dat. of the demonstr. pron. der: 'boy', here Bube.   9, ever so much, ich weiß nicht wie viel.   10, Use the Perfect according to S. 48, N. 2.   11, I did, das habe ich gethan. 12, züchtigen.   13, 'to go in', here in den Kampf treten.   14, he — life, in ſeinem Leben, daß er ſich ſchlug.   15, Place the conj. 'but' after the subject, and, for the sake of emphasis, repeat the pron. 'I' after the rel. pron. 'der', which must introduce the next clause.   16, 'in', here auf.   17, never ... at all, nie.

Section 68.

TENDER, TRUSTY, AND TRUE.

VIII.

Boys, I like peace; I like (S. 51, N. 13) to see you play like good, true-hearted little men [1]. Never [2] fight if you can help [3] it; but [4] never strike a boy who is no match for you, and never stand [5] by quietly whilst another boy is doing (S. 32, N. 11) it. Tender, trusty, and true, boys; tender and true. King David, King Alfred, George Washington, William Channing, Theodore Parker [6], more great men than I can name, were all of that sort; and [7] they came out right, because they went in right. Brave as lions [8], true as steel, with kind [9] hearts for doves, ravens, and sparrows, they (App. § 14) would never tear [10] birds' nests, or sling stones to [11] kill birds, because they felt as Jesus *did* when he said: "Blessed are the merciful."—REV. ROBERT COLLYER, THE LIFE THAT NOW IS.

1, 'man', here Menſche.   2, The adverb cannot precede the Imperative in German. 'To fight', here ſich ſchlagen.   3, to help = to avoid. 4, Render 'but' by jedoch, which place immediately after the verb.   5, to stand by quietly, müßig dabei ſtehen.   6, Theodore Parker, berühmter amerikaniſcher Geiſtlicher und Gelehrter, wurde im Jahre 1810 zu Lexington in Maſſachuſetts geboren und ſtarb im Jahre 1860 zu Florenz, wo er ſich ſeiner Geſundheit wegen aufhielt. Durch ſeine ausgezeichnete Gelehrſamkeit, große Willenskraft und ſeltene Menſchenliebe übte er auf ſeine Zeitgenoſſen einen bedeutenden Einfluß aus, namentlich aber in Bezug auf die Befreiung der Sklaven, deren Sache er oft mit Gefahr ſeines Lebens und ſeiner Freiheit verteidigte.   7, and — right, und ſie traten als Sieger aus dem Kampfe hervor, weil ſie für das Recht in den Kampf traten.   8, Use the noun 'lions' with the def. art., but not the noun 'steel'.   9, 'kind' here — feeling. 10, zerſtören.   11, See S. 19, N. 7, and supply the prepositional adverb damit before the object.

Section 69.

DESPATCH OF BUSINESS [1].

You [2] must beware [3] of stumbling over a propensity, which easily besets [4] you from [5] the habit of not having your time fully employed [6]. I mean [7] what the women very expressively [8] call dawdling [9]. Your motto must be "Hoc age." Do instantly whatever [10] is [11] to be done, and take [12] the hours of recreation after business [13], and not before it [14]. When a regiment is [15] under march, (S. 27, N. 8) the rear is [16] often thrown into confusion, because the front do [17] not move [18] steadily [19] and without interruption. It [20] is the same thing with business. If [21] that which is first in hand is not instantly, steadily [22], and regularly despatched [23], other [24] things accumulate, till affairs [25] begin to press all at once, and no human being can [26] stand the confusion.—SIR WALTER SCOTT, LETTERS TO HIS SON.

1, Schnelle Geschäftserledigung.　　　2, Use the 2nd pers. sing. **Personal and Possessive Pronouns used in letters, and referring to the person addressed, require a capital initial in German.**　　　3, to beware of stumbling over a propensity, sich hüten, einem Hange zu verfallen. See S. 1, N. 3, and S. 34, N. 10.　　　4, beschleichen.　　　5, from the habit, wenn Du Dich daran gewöhnst.　　　6, 'to employ', here ausfüllen.　　　7, Supply here the pronominal adverb damit.　　　8, bezeichnet.　　　9, Zeitvergeudung.　　　10, was. 11, is to be done = must be done. See S. 62, N. 4, and S. 2, N. 1.　　　12, choose your hours of recreation (Erholungsstunde, f.).　　　13, business = work, which use with the def. art.　　　14, it = the same.　　　15, to be under march, auf dem Marsch begriffen sein.　　　16, to be thrown in confusion, in Unordnung geraten.　　　17, **The verb must be in the singular after a collective noun in the singular.**　　　18, 'to move', here fortmarschieren.　　　19, gleichmäßig.　　　20, Say 'And so it is likewise (auch) with business (Arbeit)'. 21, If—hand, Wenn die gerade vorliegende Arbeit.　　　22, stetig.　　　23, erledigen. 24, other—accumulate, so häufen sich inzwischen andere Sachen an.　　　25, die Arbeiten, after which place the words 'all at once', alle auf einmal. For the place of the verbs see App. § 19.　　　26, can—confusion, der Verwirrung gewachsen ist.

Section 70.

ON PERFUMERY [1].

I.

The [2] exquisite pleasure we enjoy from the smell of sweet flowers is [3] alone sufficient to account for the love of perfumery. Flowers pass away [4] so quickly that we naturally desire to preserve their sweetness [5] as [6] long as we can, and in this our perfumers succeed [7] admirably. The perfume [8] of most flowers depends upon an oil, which [9] is peculiar to the plant, almost every sweet-scented [10] plant having its own peculiar oil; and, what is of [11] more importance: these oils belong to a class called [12] essential or volatile, because they become [13] volatile when [14] heated.

1, Ueber Parfümerien.　　　2, Say 'the great enjoyment which the smell (Duft, m.) of sweet (wohlriechend) flowers affords (gewähren) us'. Place the pron. 'us' immediately after the rel. pron.　　　3, is — perfumery = explains sufficiently (zur Genüge) our love for perfumery.　　　4, to pass away, verwelken. 5, Wohlgeruch, m.　　　6, as — can, so lange wie möglich. For the position of the verbs see App. § 19.　　　7, to succeed, gelingen, v. intr. (used with sein), governs the dative of the person; as—

　　　He succeeds admirably in this.　　　Dies gelingt ihm vortrefflich. Construe the above clause accord. to the preceding example; perfumer, Parfümeur.　　　8, 'perfume', here = scent, Duft, m.　　　9, The relat. clause 'which — plant' is best rendered by the attributive construction, as explained in S. 48, N. 6; peculiar, eigentümlich.　　　10, odorous, wohlriechend; its own

particular oil, ihr befonderes Öl.   The clause 'almost — oil' must be construed accord. to S. 30, N. 4.   11, of — importance = still more important.
12, Say 'which one calls essential (ätherifch) or volatile (flüchtig) oils'.   13, to
become volatile, fich verflüchtigen.   14, when heated = when they are heated
(erwärmen). Comp. S. 27, N. 7.

Section 71.

ON PERFUMERY.

II.

The common or fixed[1] oils, on the contrary, *such* as olive[2] or linseed-
oil, do not evaporate. This[3] may be easily illustrated, thus: If a piece
of writing-paper be touched[4] with a fixed oil or grease, (S. 27, N. 8) it
leaves[5] a stain, which[6], upon being held before the fire, will not disappear.
Now[7], if any[8] plant has a peculiar smell or taste, it is[4] generally found
that its essential oil is the cause of this (S. 4, N. 5, *B*).   Consequently[9],
if we extract this, we really obtain[10] the essence.—PROF. ASCHER.

1, feft; on the contrary, hingegen. See S. 15, N. 3.   2, as olive or linseed-
oil, wie das Oliven oder Leinsamenöl.   When two **compound nouns** which have
the last component in common follow each other, the last component is
generally omitted in the first noun, which is connected with the next one by
means of hyphens. — To evaporate, fich verflüchtigen.   3, Dies läßt fich
auf folgende Weise leicht beweifen.   4, Turn the Passive Voice here into the
Active Voice by means of the pron. man, as explained in S. 4, N. 4.   5, 'to
leave', here = to leave behind; it = this.   6, The passage 'which — disappear' may be briefly rendered, thus: 'which does not disappear before the
fire'. See S. 32, N. 11.   7, Reverse the order of the first two words in
this clause.   8, any = a.   9, Consequently = therefore, alfo, which
place after the subject 'we'.   10, to obtain, gewinnen; the essence (as a
Nom.), der der Pflanze eigentümliche Wohlgeruch.

Section 72.

ON INSTINCT[1].

The[2] following most curious instance of a change of instinct is
mentioned by Darwin.   The bees carried[3] over to[4] Barbadoes and the
Western Isles ceased[5] to lay up any honey after the first year, as[6] they
found it not useful *to them.*   They found the weather so fine, and the
materials[7] for making honey so plentiful, that they quitted[8] their grave,
prudent[9], *and* mercantile[10] character, became exceedingly profligate and
debauched[11], ate[12] up their capital, resolved to work no more, and[13]
amused themselves by flying about the sugar-houses and stinging the
blacks.   The[14] fact is, that[15], by[16] putting animals in different situations[17],
you may[18] change, and even reverse, *any of* their original propensities.
Spallanzani[19] brought[20] up an eagle upon[21] bread and milk, and fed a
dove on[22] raw beef.—REV. S. SMITH.

1, Über den tierifchen Inftinkt.   2, This clause requires a different rendering; let us say 'Darwin gives the following most (höchft) curious example of a
change of the animal instinct'.   The last noun requires the def. art., as explained

in S. 3, N. 2.   **3,** to carry over, hinüberbringen. The Perfect Participle qualifies the noun 'bees'. According to S. 7, N. 3, the words 'carried — Isles' may be rendered either by the attributive construction or by forming of them a relative clause. I venture to propose the use of the attributive construction as the more elegant of the two modes of rendering, and more especially in order to avoid a repetition of subordinate clauses.   **4,** When the preposition '**to**', in connection with a verb denoting motion, stands before the names of countries, towns, islands, etc., it must be rendered by '**nach**'. **5,** Here follow the words 'after — year'; to lay up honey, einen Vorrat von Honig an'sammeln.   **6,** See S. 41, N. 6; it = this; not useful, nicht mehr von Nutzen.   **7,** materials — plentiful, Materialien zur Honigbereitung in solchem Überflusse verhanden.   **8,** auf'geben.   **9,** prudent = cautious.   **10,** ners lautlich.   **11,** unmäßig.   **12,** to eat up, auf'zehren.   **13,** und sich daran ergötzen. For rendering the passage 'by — blacks' see S. 1, N. 3. To fly about, umschwär'men, v. tr.   **14,** The — is, Es ist eine ausgemachte Thatsache. **15,** Here follows the subject 'you' (comp. S. 66, N. 15), which translate by the impers. pron. man.   **16,** by — animals, turch Wegschung der Tiere, i.e. by a removal of the animals. In = into; different = other.   **17,** Here follows the object and its attributes, 'their original (angeberen) propensities (Trieb, m.)'. **18,** may = can; reverse, in entgegengesetzte Richtungen leiten.   **19,** Lazaro Spallanzani, berühmter italienischer Anatom und Naturforscher, geb. 1729, + 1799. **20,** to bring up, groß ziehen.   **21,** bei.   **22,** mit.

Section 73.

PETER THE GREAT AND THE MONK.

Peter the Great ordered[1] many foreign books to be translated into the Russian language, and among others[2] "Puffendorf's[3] Introduction to the Knowledge of the States of Europe." A monk, to whom the translation of this book was committed[4], presented[5] it some time after[6] to the Emperor. The monarch examined[7] the translation; at[8] a certain chapter, however, he suddenly changed[9] countenance, turned indignantly to the monk, and said: "Fool, what did I order[10] thee to do? Is this a translation?" He[11] then referred to the original and showed the poor monk a paragraph in which the author had spoken with great asperity[12] of the Russians, but which had not been translated. "Go," resumed the monarch, "and instantly carry out[13] what I have bidden thee *to do*. *It is* not to (S. 19, N. 7) flatter my subjects *that* I[14] have ordered this book to be translated, but (S. 6, N. 10) to instruct[15] and reform[16] them!"— ANONYMOUS.

1, Use the auxiliary verb of mood '**lassen**' as a translation of 'to order', 'to command', and 'to cause', when these verbs are connected with the auxiliary '**to be**' and the Past Participle of another verb; as—

The emperor *ordered* the ringleaders *to be shot*.	Der Kaiser ließ die Anführer er-schießen.
The admiral *commanded* the ships *to be drawn up* in order of battle.	Der Admiral ließ die Schiffe in Schlacht-ordnung aufstellen.
He *caused* the money *to be paid* to me.	Er ließ mir das Geld auszahlen.

2, Supply here the adverb auch.   **3,** Puffendorfs Beiträge zur europäischen Staatenkunde.   **4,** an'vertrauen.   **5,** überrei'chen: it = the same, which must agree with its antecedent 'translation'.   **6,** after, darauf.   **7,** prüfen.

8, bei.   **9,** to change countenance, die Farbe wechseln.   **10,** 'to order', here befehlen.   See S. 48, N. 2.   **11,** Say 'Hereupon he opened (aufschlagen) the original'.   **12,** Schärfe, f.; had spoken . . . of = had expressed himself (sich aussprechen) . . . about.   **13,** verrichten.   **14,** Inverted construction. **15,** belehren   **16,** refermieren; the prep. zu must be repeated before this verb.

Section 74.

THE BEAUTY OF THE EYE.

I.

Look [1] how beautiful the human eye is, excelling [2] in beauty the eye of every creature! The eyes of many *of the* lower animals are doubtless very beautiful. All [3] of us must have admired the bold, fierce, bright eye of the eagle; the large, gentle, brown eye of the ox; the treacherous green eye of the cat, waxing [4] and waning [5] like the moon, as [6] the sun shines upon it (S. 4, N. 5) or [7] deserts it; the pert eye of the sparrow; the sly eye of the fox; the peering [8] little bead [9] of black enamel in [10] the mouse's head; the [11] gem-like eye which [12] redeems the toad from ugliness : and the intelligent, affectionate expression, which [13] looks out from the human-like eye of the horse and dog. There [14] are these and the eyes of many other animals full of beauty; but [15] there is a glory which excelleth in the eye of man.

1, Use the 2nd pers. sing.   **2,** Say 'and how it excelleth in (an) beauty the eye of every other creature!' The words 'in beauty' should be placed before the verb.   **3,** All of us, wir alle; all of them, sie alle; all of you, ihr (or Sie) alle.   Render the words 'must have' by 'have certainly'. The p. p. should be placed after 'eagle'.   **4,** sich vergrößern.   **5,** sich verkleinern.   **6,** as = according as, je nachdem.   **7,** or deserts it = or not. **8,** forschend.   **9,** Perlenauge.   **10,** im Mäuseköpfchen.   **11,** das einem Edelsteine gleichende Auge.   **12,** Say 'which lets us forget the ugliness of the toad'.   **13,** which — the = in the.   **14,** There are these ... full = These ... are full.   Full of, voller.   **15,** im Auge des Menschen jedoch liegt eine alles übertreffende Pracht.

Section 75.

THE BEAUTY OF THE EYE.

II.

We realise [1] this fully only when [2] we gaze into the faces of those we love. It [3] is their eyes (S. 16, N. 10) we look at [4] when we are near them, and [5] recall when we are [6] far away. The face is a [7] blank without the eye, and the eye seems to concentrate every [8] feature in itself. *It is* the eye *that* smiles, not the lips; *it is* the eye *that* listens [9], not the ear; it [10] that frowns, not the brow; it [11] that mourns, not the voice. Every sense and every faculty [12] seems to [13] flow toward it, and find expression through it [14], nay [15], to be lost in it; for all must have felt at times as [16] if a man's eye was not a part of him, but (S. 6, N. 10) the man himself; as [17] if it had not merely life, but also a [18] personality of its own :—as [19] if it was not only a living, but also a thinking being.—Prof. G. Wilson.

1, 'to realise', here = to comprehend, begreifen. The object 'this' may be emphasized by being placed at the head of the clause. Fully only, ein ganz. 2, Say 'when we look upon (betrachten) the face (Antliß, n.) of our loved ones (unferer Lieben)'.   3, Es find.   4, anbliden.   5, and which we recall (sich zurückrufen).   6, are far away, fern von ihnen weilen.   7, a blank = expressionless.   8, Supply here the adj. 'individual' (einzeln).   9, lauschen. 10, Say 'the eye frowns (zürnen, i.e. to look angry)'.   11, Say 'the eye is sad'.   12, Gemütsstimmung, f.   13, to — it, dahin zu strömen.   14, 'it', here = the same.   15, ja, darin aufzugeben.   16, as if ... was, als wäre; a man's eye = the eye of a man.   17, as if it had, als hätte es.   18, a personality of its own = a self-dependent personality.   19, as if it was, als wäre es.

Section 76.

A FUNERAL DANCE[1].

Drums were beating[2], horns blowing[3], and[4] people were seen all running in one direction. The cause was a funeral dance. I joined[5] the crowd, and soon found myself in[6] the midst of the entertainment[7]. The dancers were most (höchst) grotesquely[8] got up[9]. About a dozen huge ostrich feathers adorned their helmets. Leopard or black and white monkey-skins[10] were suspended[11] from their shoulders, and a leather, tied (S. 7, N. 3. *A*) round the waist, covered a large iron bell which was strapped[12] upon the loins of each dancer; this they rang[13] to the time of the dance. A large crowd got up in[14] this style[15] created[16] an indescribable hubbub, heightened[17] by the blowing of[18] horns and the beating of seven nogaras[19] of various notes[20]. Every dancer wore[21] an antelope's horn[22] suspended round the neck, which he blew occasionally in[23] the height of his excitement.—SIR S. BAKER, THE ALBERT N'YANZA.

1, (Ein Tanz zur Leichenfeier.   2, were beating = were being beaten. See S. 2, N. 1. To beat a drum, eine Trommel rühren.   3, horns (were) blowing = horns resounded (ertönen).   4, Say 'and one saw all (alles) people run in (nach) one direction.   5, sich anschließen, which requires the dat. 6, in the midst, inmitten, which requires the gen.   7, entertainment = festivity.   8, gretest.   9, 'to get up', here auststaffieren.   10, 'skin', here Fell, n., of which form a compound expression with the pl. of the nouns 'leopard' and 'monkey', as explained in S. 71, N. 2.   11, were suspended = hung; from = von ... herab.   12, to be strapped, mit einem Riemen befestigt sein; 'upon' here an.   13, schellen; to — dance, während des Tanzens zum Takte.   14, auf.   15, style = manner.   16, created = made.   17, Say 'which was (Passive) still heightened', according to S. 7, N. 3, *B*.   18, Use the gen. of the def. art.   19, 'nogaras'—which use in its unaltered form in German—are a kind of drum.   20, notes = sounds.   21, wore ... suspended = had ... hanging; 'round', here an.   22, To render 'antelope's horn' form a compound noun of the pl. of the noun 'antelope' and the singl. of the noun 'horn'. Comp. S. 36, N. 7, *A*, *B*, and *C*, and mark further:

A. Although the first component of **Compound Nouns** is generally in the singular, **some require the plural**; as—Kinderstube, f., nursery; Bildergalerie, f., picture-gallery.

B, 1. The first component takes sometimes one of **the genitive inflections** e, es, n, en, or ens, according to the declension it belongs to; as—Königsmantel, m., royal mantel; Tageslicht, n., day-light; Heldenmut, m., heroism; Friedensliebe, f., love of peace.

2. We find, however, the terminations **§** or **e§** used as a connecting link between the two components for the mere sake of euphony, even in cases where the first component is a feminine noun; this is more especially the case when the first component is in itself a compound expression, when it has one of the derivative suffixes heit, ing, ling, feit, schaft, tum, ung, or when it is a noun of foreign origin terminating in ien, at, and ät; as—Geburtstag, m., birthday; Hochzeitsgeschenk, n., wedding present; Weisheitslehre, f., philosophy; Religionsruldung, f., toleration; Universitätsgericht, n., university court.

C. In a few compound nouns we find one of the euphonic terminations **e, er,** and **l** used as a connecting link between the two components; as—Tages werf, n., day's work; Aschermittwoch, m., Ash-Wednesday; Heitelbeere, bilberry.

D, 1. When the first component consists of the stem of a verb, it is often joine.l to the second component without a connecting link; as—Schreib: buch, n., copy-book.

2. Sometimes a euphonic **e** is used as a connecting link; as—Zeige: finger, m., forefinger; Haltepunkt, m., place of stopping.

23, in — excitement = in the highest excitement.

Section 77.

ABSOLUTION BEFOREHAND[1].

When Tezel[2] was at Leipzig, in the sixteenth century (App. § 9), and had collected[3] a great deal of money from all ranks[4] of people, a nobleman, who suspected imposition, put[5] the question to him: "Can you[6] grant absolution for a sin which a man[7] shall intend to commit in future?" "Yes," replied the frontless commissioner, "but on[8] condition that a proper[9] sum of money be actually[10] paid down." The noble (S. 5. N. 2) instantly produced the sum demanded, and in return[11] received a diploma[12], sealed and signed by Tezel, absolving[13] him from the unexplained crime which he intended to commit. Not[14] long after, when Tezel was about (S. 6, N. 4) to leave Leipzig, the nobleman made[15] inquiry respecting the road he would probably travel[16], waited[17] for him in ambush at a convenient place, attacked and robbed him, then[18] beat him soundly with a stick, sent him back to Leipzig with[19] his chest empty, and[20] at parting said: "This is the fault[21] I intended to commit, and for which I have your absolution[22]."—Rev. R. K. Arvine.

1, Der im voraus erteilte Ablaß. **2,** Johann Tezel (eigentlich Diezel) wurde um 1460 zu Leipzig geboren, trat 1489 in den Dominikanerorden, ward 1502 vom Papst zum Ablaßprediger bestellt, später zum apostolischen Kommissar ernannt und mit dem Ablaßhandel in Sachsen betraut, zog sich jedoch, von Luther seit dem 31sten October 1517 wegen seiner unverschämten Anmaßungen bekämpft, in das Paulinerkloster zu Leipzig zurück, wo er im Jahre 1519 verstarb. **3,** einzunehmen; a great deal of, eine Masse Construe accord. to App. § 5. **4,** ranks = classes; people, Bevölkerung, f., see S. 3, N. 2. **5,** 'to put a question to somebody' here = to ask somebody. **6,** I propose to use the 2nd pers. pl. in this case, and to supply the adverb auch after the pron. **7,** a — future — which one only (ein) intends to commit. See App. § 19. **8,** unter, followed by the def. art. **9,** angemessen; to render 'sum of money' form a comp. n. of which the noun 'money' forms the first component and the noun 'sum' the last. **10,** actually = directly; to pay down, auszahlen. **11,** in return, dafür, which place after the verb. **12,** 'diploma', here Ablaßbrief, m. **13,** absolviren. See S. 16, N. 4; unexplained, ungenannt. **14,** Not — after = Soon upon that. See S. 4, N. 5, B.   15, to make inquiry respecting something, ſich nach etwas erkundigen.   16, 'to travel', here einſchlagen.   17, to wait in ambush for somebody, einen in einem Hinterhalte auf'lauern.   18, the adverb dann must be placed after the object. To beat a person soundly with a stick, einen tüchtig durch'prügeln.   19, say 'with empty chest (Kaſten, m.)', which place immediately after the object.   20, und rief ihm beim Abſchied noch zu.   21, 'fault', here = sin.   22, Supply here the adverb ſchon.

Section 78.

STAND UP[1] FOR WHATEVER IS TRUE, MANLY, AND LOVELY[2].

I.

In[3] no place in the world has individual character more[4] weight than at a public school. Remember[5] this, I beseech[6] you, all you boys who[7] are getting into the upper forms. Now[8] is the time when you may[9] have more[10] influence for good or evil in the society you live in than you ever can have[11] again. Quit[12] yourselves like men, then; speak out[13] and stand up for whatever is true, manly, and lovely. Never (S. 68, N. 2) try to be popular[13], but only do your duty, and help[14] others to do theirs; and when you leave the school (S. 27, N. 8), the[16] tone of feeling in it will be higher than you found it, and so you[16] will do good to[17] generations of your countrymen yet unborn. For boys follow one another in herds like sheep, for[18] good or evil; they[19] hate thinking, and[20] have rarely any settled[21] principles.

1, Use the 2nd pers. pl.; whatever = all that; see S. 3, N. 7.   2, ſchön. 3, In no place = Nowhere.   4, more weight = greater influence.   5, Remember this = Think (2nd pers. pl.) of it; see S. 4, N. 5, B.   6, bitten. 7, Der (m. sing.), die (f. sing.), and die (pl.) must be used as relative pronouns in reference to a personal pronoun of the first or second person of either number, and also in reference to the personal pronoun of the third person plural (Sie) used instead of the second person plural. For the sake of emphasis the personal pronoun is frequently repeated after the relative pronoun, and the verb must then agree with the personal pronoun, as the following examples will show.

Verſchmähſt du mich, die ich deine Freundin bin?	Dost thou disdain me, who am your friend?
Ich, der ich dich von deinen Feinden befreite.	I, who delivered thee from thy enemies.

Construe the clauses 'who — forms' accordingly; to get into the upper forms, in die obern Klaſſen verſetzt werden.   8, Say 'The time has [is] come'; when, re.   9, may have = exercise (aus'üben) likely.   10, Say 'more good or evil influence upon (auf) the company surrounding you (Eure Umgebung)'. 11, have = exercise.   12, Say 'Be therefore manly'.   13, 'to speak out', here gerade und frei heraus'ſprechen; 'to be popular', here ſich beliebt machen. 14, When the following verbs are used in connection with another verb governed by them, that verb stands in the Infinitive without the preposition zu (Comp. S. 34, N. 10):

A. The auxiliary verbs of mood: dürfen, können, mögen, müſſen, ſollen, wollen, and laſſen. (See Expl. 1.)

B. The verbs: bleiben, fahren, geben, finden, fühlen, heißen (to bid, to command), helfen, hören, lehren (also with zu, Comp. S. 43, N. 10), lernen, machen, sehen, and reiten. (See Expl. 2.)

C. The verb haben in phrases like Expl. 3.

D. The verb thun followed by nichts. (See Expl. 4.)

EXAMPLES.

1. Ich mag gern schreiben.   I am very fond of writing; I like to write.

2. Der Diener fand seinen Herrn tot am Boden liegen.   The servant found his master lying dead on the floor.

3. Er hat gut reden.   It is all very well for him to talk.

4. Er thut nichts als essen und trinken.   He does nothing but eat and drink.

15, the — higher = the moral tone of the same (gen.) will be a higher *one* (S. 67, N. 3).   16, Supply here the adverb noch.   17, an; remember that the p. p. 'unborn' is used as an adj. and qualifies the noun 'generations'. 18, Say 'as well in evil as in good'.   19, das Denken ist ihnen unbequem. 20, Supply here the pron. 'they'.   21, fest bestimmt.

Section 79.

STAND UP FOR WHATEVER IS TRUE, MANLY, AND LOVELY.

II.

Every school (S. 5, N. 2), indeed, has its own traditionary standard[1] of right and wrong, which cannot be transgressed with impunity, marking[2] certain things as low[3] and blackguard, and certain others as lawful and right. This standard is ever[4] varying, though *it changes* only slowly and little by little. It[5] is the leading[6] boys only, who (S. 15, N. 3), subject[7] to such standard, give, for[8] the time being, the tone to[9] all the rest, and[10] make the school either a noble institution for[11] the training of Christian Englishmen, or a place[12] where a *young* boy will get[13] more evil than if he were turned out[14] to make his[15] own way in London streets.—THOS. HUGHES, TOM BROWN'S SCHOOL DAYS.

1, Maßstab, m.; 'of', here für.   2, bezeichnen, see S. 16, N. 4, and introduce the clause with the conj. und.   3, schändlich und gemein.   4, beständig. 5, 'It is', here Es sind.   6, tonangebend.   7, diesem Maßstab unterwerfen. 8, zur Zeit.   9, to = for.   10, Supply here the rel. pron. 'who'; to make the school a noble institution, aus der Schule eine sittliche Anstalt machen.   11, to (S. 19, N. 7) educate Christian (christlichgesinnt) Englishmen. 12, Stätte, f.   13, 'to get', here sich aneignen.   14, hinausziehen; use the First Conditional.   15, his — streets = his fortune in (auf) the streets of London.

Section 80.

WORK[1] IS A GREAT COMFORTER.

Two neighbouring gardeners had the misfortune of[2] having their crop of early peas killed by frost. The one called[3] upon the other to condole[4] with him. "Ah," cried he, "how unfortunate[5] we have been, neighbour!

Do you [6] know? I have done nothing but fret ever since [7]. But it seems you have there a fine healthy [8] crop [9] coming [10] up already; what [11] is it?" "This?" cried the other gardener, "why [12], it is a crop of peas (S. 16, N. 10) I sowed (S. 48, N. 2) immediately after my loss." "What [13], coming up already?" replied the fretter [14]. "Yes, while you were fretting [15], I [16] was working." "What! don't you fret when you have a loss?" "Yes, but I always put it off [17] until *after* I have repaired [18] the mischief [19]." "Why, then you have no need to fret at all." "True [20]," replied the industrious gardener, "I [21] find working better than fretting." —ANONYMOUS.

1, Die Arbeit ist eine süße Trösterin.   2, of — frost = that (S. 1, N. 3) their young peas were (S. 2, N. 1) destroyed by (durch, followed by the def. art.) frost.   3, to call upon a person, einen besuchen.   4, to condole with a person, einem sein Beileid bezeigen.   5, I have been unfortunate, es ist mir unglücklich ergangen.   6, Use the 2nd pers. sing.   7, ever since = 'the whole time', which place after the auxiliary; 'but fret', als mich geärgert.
8, kräftig.   9, Saat, f.   10, 'to come up' here hübsch grün aufsehen.
11, Was ist's für eine?   12, ei; it — peas = they are (es sind) young peas.
13, Wie; coming up already? = and they look already so (supply hübsch) green?   14, der Trauerrede.   15, sich ärgern.   16, Say 'I have worked'.   17, aufschieben.   18, wieder gut machen.   19, Schade, m.
20, Richtig.   21, Say 'I find it better to work than to fret'.

Section 81.

PERSEVERANCE FINDS ITS REWARD.

Robert Bruce, restorer [1] of the Scottish monarchy, being [2] pursued one day by the enemy, was [3] obliged [4] to seek refuge in a barn and to spend [5] the night there. In [6] the morning, when he awoke, he saw a spider climbing up [7] the [8] beam of the roof. The spider fell [9] *down* to the ground, but immediately tried to climb up again, when it a [10] second time fell to the ground [11]. It made a third attempt, which also failed. Twelve times did (S. 32, N. 11) the little spider try to climb up the beam, and twelve times it fell down again, but the [10] thirteenth time it succeeded [12] and [13] gained the top [14] of the beam. The king (S. 5, N. 2) immediately got up [15] from his lowly [16] couch, and said: "This little spider has taught (S. 42, N. 4) me perseverance; I will follow its example. Twelve times have [17] I been beaten by the enemy. I will try my fortune once more!" He did so [18], and won the next battle. The king became the spider's scholar.—N. GOODRICH.

1, Use the noun with the def. art.   2, Construe according to S. 55, N. 1, and use the Imperf. of the Passive Voice; by, von.   3, The pron. er must be supplied here.   4, genötigt; 'to seek refuge', here sich flüchten.   5, zu bringen.
6, Say 'When he awoke in the (am) morning'.   7, hinauf kriechen . . . an; see S. 16, N. 4.   8, Use the indef. art. instead of the def. art.   9, auf den Boden fallen.   10, zum zweiten Male.   11, herunterfallen, to avoid monotony.   12, I succeed, es gelingt mir.   13, The pron. sie must be supplied here.   14, das oberste Ende.   15, sich erheben.   16, bescheiden.
17, The Active Voice will read better in German.   18, so = it.

Section 82.

THE NECESSITY OF[1] VOLCANOES.

The[2] remarkable proofs which modern geology has presented of vast accumulations of heated[3] and melted matter[4] beneath the earth's crust[5], make it evident that (S. 3, N. 2) volcanoes are essential[6] to the preservation of the globe. If (App. § 36) there[7] were no safety-valves through[8] the crust, such vast accumulations of heat would rend asunder[9] even[10] a whole continent. Volcanoes are[11] those safety-valves[12], more than two hundred of which are scattered[13] over the earth's surface. But if no such passages[14] existed (see S. 27, N. 8), nothing could prevent the[15] pent-up gases from accumulating till they had (Impf. Subj.) gained strength[16] enough to rend a whole continent, and[17] perhaps the whole globe, into fragments.—Rev. Prof. Hitchcock.

1, Use the gen. of the def. art. 2, Use the attributive construction explained in S. 48, N. 6, and say 'The by (veu, followed by the def. art.) modern geology presented (auf|ſtellen) remarkable proofs of (veu) a vast accumulation', etc. 3, erhitzt. 4, matter = masses. 5, Erdrinde, f. 6, essential = necessary; to = for. 7, 'There is' and 'there are', used in a general sense, are generally rendered by the impers. v. 'es giebt' 8, Say 'in the earth's crust'. 9, auseinan'derreißen. 10, ſegar. 11, are = form. 12, Here follow the words 'of which'. 13, vertheilen. 14, passages = openings. 15, the — accumulating = the accumulation of the pent-up (ein|ſperren) gases. 16, Kraft, f.; enough, hinreichend, adj., to be placed before the noun 'strength'. 17, 'and' here ja. The verb 'to rend into fragments' (auseinan'derreißen, of which form the Supine, S. 1, N. 2) must of course be placed at the end of the whole passage.

Section 83.

THE POWER OF BEAUTY.

In one of the worst parts of London there is[1] an institution[2] which I visited. In one room I found about[3] thirty-five men listening (S. 10, N. 4) to the teaching[4] of the daughter of a small shopkeeper[5] in[6] the neighbourhood. She was one of the prettiest women (S. 16, N. 10) I ever saw[7] in my life. I noticed that the young girl was quite alone with those rough[8] men, and said to the superintendent[9]: "Are[10] you not afraid to leave the pretty young girl alone with all those men?" He replied: "I[11] am." "Then, why don't you go to her?" "You mistake[12] my fear. I[13] am not afraid of their doing her any harm. They love her so much that they would lick[14] the ground on which[15] she walks, but I am afraid[16] that some[17] person may step in, who, not[18] knowing the manner of the place, may[19] say something impertinent[20] to her; and if he[21] did, he would not leave the place[22] alive[23]."—Lord Shaftesbury.

1, Render 'there is' by the Pres. of befinden. 2, Anſtalt, f. 3, ungefähr. 4, Unterricht, m. 5, Krämer. 6, aus. 7, saw = have seen. The auxiliary may be omitted, according to S. 52, N. 8. 8, reh. 9, This noun may be used in its unaltered form. 　10, Furcht haben. 　11, Ja, doch, which place before the words 'he replied'. 　12, mistake = misunderstand. 13, I — harm = I fear not that they will do her any harm (etwas zuleide thun). 14, 'to lick', here = to kiss. 　15, worauf. 　16, befürchten. 　17, Say 'a stranger' could (Impf. Subj.) come in. 　18, not — place, unbekannt mit den Sitten dieser Anstalt. 　19, Impf. Subj. 　20, Ungehöriges. 　21, Supply here the object 'das'. 　22, Haus. 　23, lebendig, before which supply the adverb 'wieder'.

Section 84.

THE ENGLISH CLIMATE.

The air is generally very moist, most[1] so near the western coast, and less so[2] as[3] we go eastward.

It[4] is to the abundant moisture of the air that the beautiful foliage of our trees and the rich verdure of our fields and gardens, so much praised by foreigners who visit England, are chiefly owing. Moisture is one of the two things[5] most necessary to[6] vegetation, and hence[7] our fields, trees, and woods possess during the greater part of the year a continuous richness of[8] verdure, which[9] cannot be found under[10] the sunny skies of the shores of the Mediterranean.

The weather is at[11] times liable to very sudden changes, depending (S. 16, N. 4) mainly on the changes of the wind[12].—HEWITT, PHYSICAL GEOGRAPHY OF ENGLAND AND WALES.

1, most so near, und zwar am feuchtesten an. 　2, so = moist. 　3, je mehr. 4, Say 'To the great moisture of the air owe (verdanken) our trees chiefly their beautiful foliage and our fields and gardens their rich verdure, which by foreigners, who visit England, is praised so much'. 　5, The words 'most (höchst) necessary', qualifying the noun 'things', must precede it. Things conditions. 　6, für. 　7, daher, adverbial conjunction, see App. § 24, B. 8, an. 　9, Say 'as (wie) one cannot find it (ihn)'. 　10, under — shores, an den sonnigen Küstenstrichen. 　11, mitunter. 　12, Winterwechsel, m.

Section 85.

THE LONDON DOCKS.

1.

Seemingly[1] boundless is the region of the docks, and the visitor who sets out with ever so definite an idea of the course he intends to pursue, will constantly find himself allured from the path. He passes[2] a door from[3] which issues a delicious fragrance of spice, and he turns in[4] to (S. 19, N. 7) explore[5] it. At[6] the top of a stone staircase he finds an enormous floor[7] piled[8] with bales of cinnamon and boxes of nutmeg. Here and there are great heaps which, on[9] close inspection, prove[10] to be cloves. Others, of[11] a brilliant sienna colour, he[12] finds to be heaps of mace. The[13] floor above this is stored[14] with Peruvian bark[15]. This article is used for the preparation[16] of quinine, but[17] it is imported in such quantities [18] as [19] to render it difficult to believe that [20] it can all be used medicinally.

1, Say ' The region (Bereich, m.) of the docks seems (erscheinen) almost bound-less (unbegrenzt), and even when the visitor begins his course (Wanderung, f.) with ever so (mit einem noch so) definite a plan about (über) the direction he intends to pursue (die einzuschlagende Richtung, Comp. S. 48, N. 6), (je) he will constantly find himself allured (ab'leufen) from his path'. Supply the adverb noch before the adv. ' constantly'. **2,** an etwas vorbei'gehen. **3,** aus der ihm ein festlicher Wohlgeruch von Gewürzen entgegenströmt. **4,** hinein'gehen. **5,** befichtigen; the pron. ' it' must be rendered by the persnl. pron. of the 3rd pers. pl. to agree with its antecedent ' Gewürze'. **6,** Am Ende. **7,** La-gerraum, m. **8,** an'füllen; for the constr. see S. 7, N. 3, B. **9,** bei näherer Befichtigung. **10,** Construe according to the following model: This *proves to be* false, dies erweist sich als falsch. **11,** von prächtiger Ofer-farbe. **12,** Say ' he recognises as heaps'. **13,** Der darüberliegende Lagerraum. **14,** an'füllen. **15,** Chinarinde. **16,** To render ' preparation of quinine' form a comp. n. of the corresponding German terms 'quinine' and 'preparation' (Bereitung); to use, verwenden. **17,** doch, adverbial conjunction, see App. 24, B. **18,** Menge, f., only used in the sing. **19,** as — believe, daß es sich kaum glauben läßt. **20,** that — medicinally = it (to agree with Artikel) could (Pres. Subj.) only be used (benutzen) for (zu) medical purposes (Zweck, m.).

Section 86.

THE LONDON DOCKS.

II.

On [1] another floor of the same building may [2] be found bundles of Pimento [3] sticks and Malacca [4] canes, a great store of mother-of-pearl, a heap of delicate [5], richly-tinted ear-shells [6], and a quantity *of* ivory. Here are elephants' teeth, some [7] of which are larger than bricks and weigh fourteen pounds. Passing [8] out of this building, we find [9] ourselves in an enormous shed with little black boards, hung [10] at intervals, and bearing the names of vessels. Beneath these boards are [11] goods lying ready for shipment, and these are at least as varied [12] as the imports [13]. Here are pickles [14], blacking, a [15] cartload or so *of* bricks, and scores [16] of anvils. There [17] are church-bells, a chest of drawers, a rocking-horse, a mangle, and boxes, bales, and barrels innumerable [18].—' THE GLOBE' NEWSPAPER.

1, An. **2,** Use the Active Voice with 'man', and say 'one finds'. Comp. S. 4, N. 4. For the constr. see App. § 14. **3,** Nelkenpfeffer, m. **4,** Malaffarohr. **5,** zart. **6,** Seeohrmuscheln. **7,** The clause must commence with the words 'of which'. **8,** 'To pass out' here = to leave, v. trans. Construe according to S. 55, N. 1. **9,** to find oneself, sich befinden. **10,** auf'hängen; at, in. Construe according to S. 7, N. 3, B. **11,** are — shipment, liegen zur Einschiffung bestimmte Waren. **12,** verschiedener Art. **13,** Einfuhrartikel. **14,** Use this noun in its unaltered form. **15,** Say 'one or two loads *of* bricks'. **16,** scores of, eine Unzahl von. **17,** Dort sind. Comp. S. 82, N. 7. **18,** in zahlloser Menge.

E 2

Section 87.

DR. JOHNSON ON[1] DEBT.

Dr. Johnson held[2] that[3] debt is ruin. His[4] words on the subject are weighty, and worthy of being held in remembrance. "Do not," said[5] he, "accustom[6] yourself to consider debt only as[7] an inconvenience. You will find it a calamity. Poverty takes[9] away so many means of doing good, and[10] produces so much inability to resist evil, that it[11] is by[12] all virtuous means to be avoided. Let[13] it be your first care, then, not to be in any man's debt. Resolve[14] not[15] to be poor. Whatever[16] you have, spend less. Poverty[17] is a great enemy to *human* happiness. It destroys liberty. It makes some[18] virtues impracticable[19] and others[20] extremely difficult. Frugality[21] is not only the basis of[22] quiet, but[23] of beneficence[24]. No[25] man can help others that wants himself. We must have[26] enough, before[27] we have to spare."—S. SMILES, SELF-HELP.

1, über das Schuldenmachen.   **2,** 'to hold' here = to be of opinion, der Ansicht sein.   **3,** Say 'that debt (das Schuldenmachen) leads (Pres. Subj.; Comp. App. §§ 28 and 31) to ruin'.   **4,** Say 'What he says on (über) this subject (Gegenstand, m.) is important and worthy of our notice (Beachtung, f.)'. **5,** Place the words 'said he' at the end of the whole clause.   **6, When verbs and adjectives, governing a preposition, are used in a principal clause and are followed by a subordinate clause, either in the form of a supine (i.e. an infinitive with zu, see S. 1, N. 2) or beginning with a subordinative conjunction, the adverb da, in connection with the preposition required, is generally placed in the principal clause; as—**

We will accustom ourselves to be thrifty.	Wir wollen uns daran gewöhnen, sparsam zu sein.
Do not excuse yourself with having had no time.	Entschuldigen Sie sich nicht damit, daß Sie keine Zeit gehabt haben.

The verb sich gewöhnen requires the prep. an. Construe accordingly, and use the 2nd pers. sing.   **7,** an inconvenience, als etwas Lästiges.   **8,** Say 'You will find that it leads to poverty', see S. 3, N. 2.   **9,** to take away, entziehen, after which supply the pron. uns (from us).   **10,** and — inability and makes us so often incapable.   **11,** it is...to be avoided = we must avoid it (to agree with Armut), see S. 62, N. 4.   **12,** by — means, nach bösen Kräften.   **13,** Say 'Beware therefore (sich hüten) of running into debt'. To run into debt, Schulden machen. Use the Supine according to S. 34, N. 10. **14,** sich etwas vornehmen.   **15,** not — poor = not to get (geraten) into poverty.   **16,** Say 'However little (Wie gering, after which supply the adverb auch) thy income (Einnahme, f.) may be, lay up a part of the same (je lege doch einen Teil derselben zurück)'.   **17,** Armut ist dem Glücke feind. **18,** einzelne.   **19,** impracticable = impossible.   **20,** Supply here the adverb wiederum (again).   **21,** 'frugality' here = thrift (to be used without the art.).   **22,** of quiet, des innern Friedens.   **23,** Supply here the adverb auch, and see S. 6, N. 10.   **24,** Wohltum, n., to be used with the gen. of the def. art.   **25,** Say 'He who (Wer, after which supply the pron. selbst) needs (bedürfen, requires the gen. of the def. art.) help, cannot help others'.   **26,** to have enough, zur Genüge haben.   **27,** Say 'before (ehe) we can have to spare (etwas übrig haben)'.

Section 88.

A CURIOUS[1] INSTRUMENT.

I.

A gentleman[2], just returned[3] from a journey to (S. 72, N. 4) London, was surrounded by[4] his children, eager[5], after the first salutation was over, to hear the news, and still more eager to see the contents[6] of a small portmanteau, which[7] were, one by one, carefully unfolded and displayed to view. After[8] having distributed amongst the children a few small presents, the[9] father took his seat again, saying, that[10] he must confess he[11] had brought from town[12], for his own use, something far more curious and valuable than any[13] of the little gifts (S. 16, N. 10) they had received. It was, he said[14], too good to[15] present to any of them; but he would, if[16] they pleased, first give them a brief description of it (S. 4, N. 5, *B*), and[17] then perhaps they might be allowed to inspect it.

1, merkwürdig. **2,** The noun '**gentleman**' may be used in its unaltered form in German. **3,** heimkehren; for the constr. see S. 7, N. 3, *B*. **4,** von; to surround, umringen. **5,** Say 'who after the first salutations were eager (begierig)'. **6,** der Inhalt, which has no plural. **7,** Since the antecedent of the pron. *which* (i.e. Inhalt) has no plural in German, the constr. of the passage 'which — to view' must be altered. Let us say 'from which (aus welcher, to agree with Reisetasche in the fem. sing.) then (supply the adverb auch in this place) every piece was carefully unpacked (auspacken) and shown round (umherzeigen)'. **8,** Construe accord. to S. 55, N. 1; to distribute, vertheilen; amongst, unter, with the acc. The direct object must be placed before the words 'amongst the children'. **9,** Say 'he sat down again and said'. **10,** that he must confess, er wolle es nur gestehen. **11,** This passage is best introduced by the conj. daß. Read carefully App. §§ 28 and 30. **12,** aus der Stadt, which place before the p. p. (mitgebracht). **13,** irgend eine. **14,** Say 'he continued'. **15,** See S. 19, N. 7, and supply here the pron. es: to any = to one. **16,** Say 'if they wished it'. **17,** und dann dürfen sie es sich vielleicht ansehen.

Section 89.

A CURIOUS INSTRUMENT.

II.

The children were accordingly[1] all attention, while the father thus[2] proceeded[3]: "This small instrument displays[4] the most[5] perfect ingenuity of[6] construction, and[7] exquisite nicety and beauty of workmanship. From[8] its extreme[9] delicacy[10], however, it[11] is so liable to injury, that it is always protected by a[12] sort of light curtain, adorned[13] with a beautiful fringe, and[14] so placed as to fall in a moment on the approach of the slightest danger. The[15] external appearance of the instrument is always more or less beautiful, though in this respect there[16] is a great diversity in the different sorts. The[17] internal contrivance, however, is the same in all *of them*, and is so curious, and in its power[18] so astonishing, that no one who knows it[19] can suppress his surprise and admiration."

1, natürlich die Aufmerksamkeit selbst. 2, folgendermaßen. 3, proceeded = continued. 4, displays = shows. 5, most perfect = highest.
6, Use the gen. of the def. art. 7, Say 'and is most exactly (unübertrefflich
genau) and beautifully worked'. 8, From = On account of, Wegen.
9, extreme = extraordinary. 10, Empfindlichkeit, f. 11, it — injury
= it is so easily exposed (aus'setzen) to (S. 3, N. 2) injury. 12, a sort of = a
certain. 13, Use the attributive constr., S. 7, N. 3. 14, Say 'which
is placed (angebracht) so that it falls down at (bei) the approach of the slightest
danger in a moment'. 15, The — appearance, Das Äußere. 16, Render
'there is' in this instance by 'besteht (there exists), which must be placed at the
end of the passage, on account of the preceding subordinative conj. obgleich.
17, The internal contrivance, Der Mechanismus. 18, power = efficacy,
Wirksamkeit, f. 19, it = the same (to agree with Mechanismus).

Section 90.

A CURIOUS INSTRUMENT.

III.

" By a slight *and* momentary movement, which the owner can easily
effect, he can[1] ascertain[2] with considerable accuracy the size, colour,
shape, weight (S. 10, N. 9), and value of[3] any article whatever. A[4]
person possessed of one is[5] thus saved from the necessity of asking *a*
thousand questions and[6] trying a variety of troublesome experiments,
which would otherwise be necessary; and such a slow and laborious
process[7] would, after[8] all, not succeed[9] half so well as a single application of this admirable instrument."

GEORGE. "If it is such a very useful thing[10] (S. 27, N. 8), I wonder[11]
that[12] everybody, that can at all afford it, does not have one."

1, To avoid repetition render the verb 'can' here by imstande sein.
2, bestimmen, which use in the form of a Supine and place at the end of the
whole clause. 3, of — whatever, irgend eines Gegenstandes. 4, A — one
= The possessor. 5, is — questions = needs therefore (also) not (to) ask
a thousand questions. To ask a question, eine Frage stellen. 6, and — experiments = and to make various troublesome experiments. 7, Verfahren, n.
8, after all not, doch nicht, which must not be placed between commas. Comp.
S. 15, N. 3. 9, gelingen. 10, thing = object. 11, I wonder,
es wundert mich; we wonder, es wundert uns; you wonder, es wundert Sie.
12, that — one = that not everybody, who can at all (irgend) make it possible,
possesses the same (to agree with 'object').

Section 91.

A CURIOUS INSTRUMENT.

IV.

FATHER. "These instruments are not so uncommon as you suppose;
I myself *happen to* know several individuals[1] who[2] are possessed of one
or two of[3] them."

CHARLES. "How large are they, father? Could I hold one in my
hand?"

FATHER. "You⁴ might; but⁵ I should be very sorry to trust⁶ mine to you."

GEORGE. "You must take⁷ very great care of it, then⁸?"

FATHER. "Indeed⁹ I must. I intend every night to envelop¹⁰ it in¹¹ the light curtain I mentioned; it must, besides, occasionally be washed in¹² a certain colourless liquid kept¹³ for the purpose; but this is such a delicate¹⁴ operation, that¹⁵ persons, I find, are generally reluctant to perform it. But notwithstanding the tenderness¹⁶ of this instrument, you¹⁷ will be surprised to hear that¹⁸ it may be darted to a great distance, without¹⁹ suffering the least injury, and without any danger of losing it."

1, individuals = persons.   2, who — one = who possess one.   3, of them = of the same.   4, Das könntest du wohl.   5, but — sorry = but I should be very unwilling.   6, to trust anything to a person, einem etwas anvertrauen.   7, to take great care of a thing, etwas sehr in acht nehmen. 8, then = thus, also, which place after the object.   9, Gewiß muß ich das! 10, umhüllen.   11, in — mentioned = with the above-mentioned light curtain.   12, in = with.   13, die man sich zu diesem Zwecke hält.   14, delicate = critical, bedenklich or gefährlich.   15, that — it = that one, as I have found, performs (vollziehen) the same generally but (nur) very unwillingly (ungerne).   16, Empfindlichkeit.   17, you — hear = you will hear with astonishment.   18, that — distance, daß man es in weite Fernen werfen kann. 19, Say ' without that it suffers the least injury, and without that one runs any danger of losing [to lose] it.' Comp. S. 1, N. 3.

Section 92.

A CURIOUS INSTRUMENT.

V.

CHARLES. "Indeed¹! and how high can you dart it?"

FATHER. "I² should be afraid of telling you to what a distance it will reach, lest you should think I am jesting with you."

GEORGE. "Higher than this house, I³ suppose?"

FATHER. "Much higher."

CHARLES. "Then⁴, how do you⁵ get it again?"

FATHER. "It⁶ is easily cast down by a gentle movement that does it no injury."

GEORGE. "But who can do that?"

FATHER. "The⁷ person whose business it is to take care of it."

CHARLES. "Well⁸, I cannot understand you at all; but do⁹ tell us, father, what it is chiefly used for!"

1, Das wäre!   2, Say ' I almost fear to tell you what distances it can reach, that (damit) you may not believe that I am jesting with you'.   3, 'I suppose', in interrogative sentences, may be elegantly rendered by the adverb wohl:

You have prepared your lesson well   Sie haben Ihre Lektion heute wohl gut to-day, I suppose?   studiert?

In elliptic sentences, where the verb is omitted, wohl generally occupies the first place.   4, The adv. dann must stand after the object es.   5, The pron. 'you', used in a general sense, is mostly rendered by the indef. pron. man.   6, It — down, Es senkt sich . . . leicht wieder nach unten. The place of

the words by — injury' is indicated by the three dots.   **7,** Derjenige.
8, Well = Alas, Ach.   **9,** The English 'do', in sentences of entreaty, may colloquially be rendered by the adverb **doch**; as—

Do give me the book, my child!   Gieb mir boch das Buch, mein Kind!

Section 93.

A CURIOUS INSTRUMENT.
VI.

FATHER. "Its[1] uses are so various that I know not which[2] to specify. It[3] has been found very useful in deciphering (S. 1, N. 3) old manuscripts, and[4], indeed, has its use in modern prints.   It[5] will assist us greatly in acquiring[6] all kinds of knowledge, and without it[7] some of the most sublime parts[8] of[9] creation would be matters[10] of mere conjecture.   It[11] must be confessed, however, that very much depends on a[12] proper application of it, being (S. 30, N. 4) possessed by many *persons* who appear to have no[13] adequate sense of its value, but[14] who employ it only for the most low and common purposes, without *even* thinking, apparently, of the noble uses[15] for which it is designed, or of the exquisite[16] gratification[17] (S. 16, N. 10) it is capable of affording.   It[18] is indeed in order to excite in your minds some higher sense of its value than you might otherwise have entertained, that I am giving you this previous description."

GEORGE. "Well *then*, tell us something more about it (S. 4, N. 5, *B*)."

FATHER. "It is also of[19] a very penetrating quality, and *it* can often discover secrets which can be detected by no other means.   It[20] must be owned, however, that[21] it is equally prone to reveal them[22]."

1, Its — various = It serves for (zu) such (so) various purposes (Zweck, m.). **2,** which — specify = which I shall specify (anführen).   **3,** It — useful = One has found it of great use.   **4,** and — prints = and also in (bei) our modern printing it is indeed of great use.   **5,** It — greatly = It helps us much. **6,** sich erwerben; all kinds of, allerlei.   **7,** it = the same.   **8,** 'parts' here Gebiete.   **9,** Use the gen. of the def. art.   **10,** matters = objects. **11,** It — however = I must however confess.   **12,** Use the def. art.; proper = right; of it = of the same.   **13,** no — sense = a wrong idea (Begriff, m.). **14,** und.   **15,** uses = purposes (Zweck, m.).   **16,** unvergleichlich, i.e. incomparable.   **17,** Genuß, m., i.e. enjoyment.   **18,** Say 'Only to awaken in you a higher idea of its value than you probably (vermutlich) otherwise (sonst) would have had (Pluperfect Subj.), I give you this previous (vorläufig) description'.   **19,** of — quality = very penetrative (scharfsichtig).   **20,** Say 'But (Doch) I must confess.   **21,** that — prone = that it is just as much (eben so sehr) prone; prone = disposed, geneigt.   **22,** them = the same, to agree with 'secrets'.

Section 94.

A CURIOUS INSTRUMENT.
VII.

CHARLES. "What! can it speak then?"

FATHER. "It is sometimes said (S. 54, N. 13) to[1] do so, especially when[2] it happens to meet with[3] one of its own species."

GEORGE. " What colour are⁴ these instruments?"

FATHER. "They vary⁵ considerably in this respect."

GEORGE. "Well, what colour is yours?"

FATHER. "I believe it is of *a* darkish colour; but if I shall confess the truth (S. 27, N. 8), I must say that I never saw (S. 48, N. 2) it⁶ in my life."

BOTH. "Never⁷ saw it in your life?"

FATHER. "No, nor⁸ do I wish; but I have seen a representation of it, which (S. 48, N. 6) is so exact that my curiosity is quite satisfied."

GEORGE. "But why don't you look⁹ at the thing itself?"

FATHER. "I should be in great danger¹⁰ of losing it, if I¹¹ did."

CHARLES. "Then you could buy (S. 58, N. 8) another."

FATHER. "Nay¹², I believe I could not prevail¹³ upon any one to part with such (S. 28, N. 9) a thing¹⁴."

GEORGE. "Then, how did you get yours?"

FATHER. "I am so fortunate as¹⁵ to be possessed of more than one; but¹⁶ how I got them I really cannot recollect¹⁷."

CHARLES. "Not recollect! Why¹⁸, you said you brought¹⁹ them from London to-night!"

FATHER. "So²⁰ I did; I should be sorry if I had left them behind me (see App. § 36)."

CHARLES. "Now²¹, father, *do* tell us the name of this curious instrument!"

FATHER. "It is—the Eye."—JANE TAYLOR.

1, 'to do so', referring to the preceding verb 'speak', must be rendered by the infinitive of that verb.   2, when — with = when it accidentally comes together with.   3, with — species, mit einem seinesgleichen.   4, are = have.   5, to vary considerably, sehr verschieden sein.   6, Supply the adverb noch after the object.   7, Never — life? = You have never seen it in your life?   8, ich wünsche es auch nicht.   9, to look at a thing, sich ein Ding ansehen.   10, 'to be in great danger', here Gefahr laufen.   11, Supply here the object 'es'.   12, O nein.   13, to prevail upon any one, jemand überreden.   14, 'thing', here Gegenstand, m.   15, noch mehr als eines zu besitzen.   16, but — them, aber wie ich dazu gekommen bin.   17, to recollect, sich etwas ins Gedächtnis zurückrufen.   18, The English 'why' is, in this instance, best rendered by the adverb 'ja', which place after the verb.   19, Use the Perf. Subj., according to App. §§ 28 and 30; here mitbringen.   20, Gewiß habe ich das.   21, Say 'But father, tell us at last,' and supply the adverb 'doch' after the pron. 'us'. Comp. Lange's German Manual, p. 354, L. 31, N. 4.

Section 95.

ANGLO¹-SAXON DRESS.

The dress of civilians in general consisted² of a shirt and tunic descending³ to the knee, of linen or wool, according⁴ to the season. A belt was often worn round the waist⁵, and a short cloak over the whole. Drawers, leather shoes or short boots and hose, or sandals, completed the ordinary costume. Labourers (S. 3, N. 2) are generally represented with shoes, but without hose. Females⁶ of all ranks⁷ wore long, loose garments reaching[3] to the ground, completely hiding (S. 16, N. 4) all[4] symmetry of[9] shape. Long hair, parted[10] on the forehead, and falling[11] naturally down the shoulders, with *an* ample[12] beard and moustache, distinguish the Anglo-Saxons from the closely cropped[13] Normans. Planche remarks that[14] the character of face, as delineated in illuminations, immediately designates[15] the age[16] wherein[17] the early[18] portraits of our Lord[19], which have[20] been reverently[21] copied to[22] the present day, were[23] originally fabricated.—MILNER, HISTORY OF ENGLAND.

1, Say 'The dress of the Anglo-Saxons'.   2, to consist of a thing, and etwas beſtehen.   3, to descend = to reach; to, an or auf. Use the attributive construction explained in S. 48, N. 6.   4, according to, je nach.   5, waist = body.   6, Females = Women.   7, Staub, m.   8, jede.   9, Use the gen. of the def. art.; form, Geſtalt, f.   10, geſcheitelt; on the forehead = in the middle. Use the attributive construction.   11, and falling = which fell.   12, voll.   13, kurz geſcheren.   14, that — illuminations, daß der Geſichtstypus in den Abbildungen.   15, beſtimmen.   16, Zeitalter, m., i.e. epoch.   17, wherein = in which.   18, 'early', here = first.   19, Lord = Saviour, Heiland, m.   20, Use the active voice with 'man'. Comp. S. 4, N. 4.   21, ſe pietätvoll.   22, bis auf.   23, Say 'were first (zuerſt) made (an'fertigen)'.

Section 96.

THE GLACIERS AT[1] SUNSET[2].

I.

At a distance these glaciers, as[3] I have said before, look[4] like frozen rivers (S. 26, N. 3); when[5] one approaches nearer, or when they press[6] downward[7] into the valley, they look[8] like immense crystals and pillars[9] of ice piled[10] together in every conceivable form. The effect[11] of this pile[12] of ice, lying (S. 48, N. 6) directly[13] in the lap of[14] green grass and flowers, is quite singular. Before we had entered[15] the valley, the sun had gone down; the sky behind the mountains was clear, and it[16] seemed *for* a few moments as if darkness[17] was rapidly coming on. But[18] in a few moments commenced a scene[19] of transfiguration, more[20] glorious than anything I had witnessed yet. The cold, white, dismal fields[21] of ice gradually changed[22] into hues[23] of the most beautiful rose colour[24]. A[25] bank of white clouds, which rested[26] above the mountains, kindled[27] and glared[28], as[29] if some spirit of light had entered into them.

1, bei, contracted with the dat. of the def. art.   2, Comp. S. 26.   3, Place the words 'as — before' at the head of the whole passage; 'at a distance', in der Entfernung. For the constr. see App. § 15.   4, 'to look like', here 'ähnlich ſehen', which requires the dat.   5, The clause 'when — nearer' may be briefly rendered by 'in der Nähe', i.e. 'close by'.   6, hinein'bringen.   7, abwärts.   8, 'to look' may be rendered by aus'ſehen, to avoid repetition; 'like' must then be turned by 'wie'.   9, To render 'pillars of ice' form a comp. n. analogous to 'ice-pillars'.   10, to pile together, auf'ſchichten; use the attributive constr.   11, Eindruck, m.   12, pile of ice, Eismaſſe, f.   13, unmittelbar.   14, Use the gen. of the def. art.   15, betreten, v. tr.   16, it seemed = it had the appearance. The adverbial circumstance of time '*for* a few moments' may be emphasized by being placed

immediately after the conj. 'and'. **17,** Darkness is coming on, die Dun=
felheit bricht herein. **18,** But — moments = But soon. **19,** Form a
comp. n. **20,** The passage 'more — yet' may be elegantly rendered by
'welche alles bereits Geschaute noch an Herrlichkeit übertraf'. **21,** Form a comp. n.
22, to change into something, in etwas übergehen. **23,** Farbentöne. **24,** No=
fenrot, n. **25,** A — clouds, Ein weißes Gewölf. **26,** rested = hung.
27, kindled = reddened (erröͤten). **28,** glared = glowed (erglühͤen).
29, as — them, wie von einem Lichtgeiste erfüllt.

Section 97.

THE GLACIERS AT SUNSET.

II.

You[1] did not lose your idea of the dazzling, spiritual whiteness of the
snow; yet you seemed to see it through a rosy veil, the sharp edges of
the glaciers and the hollows between the peaks reflecting wavering tints
of lilac and purple. The effect[2] was solemn and spiritual above everything I have ever seen. These[3] words, which[4] had often been in my
mind through the day, and[5] which occurred more often than any others
while I was travelling through the Alps, came into my mind with a pomp
and magnificence of meaning unknown before:—"For by (durch) Him
were all things created that are in[6] heaven and that are in earth, visible
and invisible, whether[7] they be thrones, or dominions, or principalities,
or powers[8]: all things were created by Him and for Him: and He is
before[9] all things, and by Him all things consist[10] (Col. i. 16, 17)."—
MRS. BEECHER STOWE.

1, Say 'The idea (Bild, n.) of the dazzling, spiritual (geisterhaft) whiteness of
the snow lost itself not; it seemed, however, as if one saw it (als sähe man es)
through a rosy veil, whilst the sharp edges (Zacke, f.) of the glaciers and the
hollows (Vertiefung, f.) between the peaks were beaming (erstrahlen) in wavering
(unbestimmt) colours of lilac and purple'. **2,** Say 'The impression (Ein=
druck, m.) of it (S. 4, N. 5, B) surpassed in (an) solemnity and sublimity everything (alles, S. 3, N. 7) that I had (App. § 22) ever seen'. **3,** Say 'The
following words'. **4,** which — mind, die mir ... oft vor der Seele gestanden.
5, and — before = and of (an) which I was most reminded during my Alpine
journey (Alpenreise), revealed themselves only (erst) now to my mind in their
whole splendour and magnificence. **6,** in — earth, im Himmel und auf
Erden. **7,** whether they be, seien sie. **8,** Gewalten. **9,** is before
= stands above. **10,** bestehen, which place after 'Him'.

Section 98.

THE LOST CHILD FOUND[1].

I.

A few years since, in the United States of America, a child was lost[2]
in the woods. Darkness (S. 3, N. 2) was rapidly coming on[3], and the
alarmed father, accompanied by some of his neighbours, hastened away
in[4] search of the lost child. The[5] search continued in vain till nine
o'clock in the evening. Then the alarm bell was rung[6], and the cry of

fire [7] soon resounded through the streets.   It [8] was, however, ascertained that [9] it was not fire which caused the alarm, and that the bell tolled [10] to spread the more [11] solemn tidings [12] of a child lost [13].

Every heart sympathised [14] in the sorrows of the distracted [15] parents, and multitudes [16] of the people [17] were seen (S. 4, N. 4) ascending the hill upon the declivity of which the village was situated [18], to [19] aid in the search.   The night passed away, the morning dawned, and yet no tidings came.   The sun arose.   The whole landscape glittered in the rays of the morning sun.   But the village was deserted and still; the shops were closed, and business was hushed [20].   Mothers [21] were walking [22] the streets with sympathising [23] countenances and anxious [15] hearts.   There [24] was but one thought there :—What has become of [25] the lost [13] child?

1, Das wiedergefundene Kind.   2, to be lost, sich verirren.   3, to come on, heran'rücken.   4, in — child = to seek the missed child.   5, The — evening = Till 9 o'clock in the evening (abends) their endeavours had remained without success (erfolgloß).   Remember that the verbs sein, werden, and bleiben are conjugated with the auxiliary sein.   6, ziehen.   7, Form a compound noun by combining the corresponding German terms of the nouns 'fire' and 'cry' (S. 36, N. 7, A).   8, it — ascertained, Es stellte sich jedoch heraus.   9, that — alarm = that the alarm was not caused through fire.   10, ertönen.   11, more solemn = still more dreadful.   12, tidings = message.   13, Use the p. p. of the verb vermissen.   See S. 7, N. 3, A.   14, Say 'shared the sorrow' (Kummer, m., which is only used in the Sing.).   15, angsterfüllt.   16, Scharen.   17, of the people = of country-people.   18, to be situated, liegen.   19, to — search. um mit suchen zu helfen.   20, 'to be hushed', here = to rest.   21, Say 'The women'.   22, to walk the streets, auf den Straßen umher'gehen.   23, teilnehmend.   24, Es war nur ein Gedanke, der alle erfüllte.   25, aus.

Section 99.

THE LOST CHILD FOUND.

II.

About [1] nine in [2] the morning the signal gun was fired, which announced that the child was found (S. 4, N. 4), and for [3] some time the suspense was dreadful.   Was the child found a [4] mangled corpse, or was it alive and well?   Soon (App. § 14) a joyful shout [5] proclaimed the safety of the child. A procession was formed [6] by those engaged [7] in the search.   The child was placed upon a litter, hastily constructed [8] from the boughs of trees (S. 36, N. 7, A), and borne [9] in triumph at [10] the head [11] of the procession.

When they arrived at the brow [12] of the hill, they stopped *for* a moment, and proclaimed their success with three loud *and* animated [13] cheers [14]. The mother could no longer restrain her feelings.   She rushed into [15] the street, clasped her [16] child to her bosom, and wept aloud.   Every [17] eye was suffused with tears, and *for* a moment all was silent.

But suddenly some one gave a [18] signal for [19] a shout.   One long, loud, *and* happy note of joy [20] rose from [21] the assembled multitude [22], who then dispersed to (S. 19, N. 7) return home and to resume [23] their business.— Jacob Abbott.

1, gegen. 2, in the morning, morgens. 3, for — time, eine Zeit lang. 4, a = as a = als. 5, joyful shout, Freudengeschrei (S. 76, 22, *B*). 6, Use the reflective form sich bilden; by, von. 7, welche sich bei der Auffindung des Kindes beteiligt hatten. 8, Use the attributive construction pointed out in S. 7, N. 3; constructed, zusammengefügt; from, aus. 9, einbertragen. 10, an. 11, Spitze, f. 12, brow = top. 13, animated = fiery. 14, Hurras. 15, auf. 16, her = the. 17, Say 'No eye was without tears (thränenleer)'. 18, Use the def. art. 19, zu. 20, happy — joy, form a comp. noun of the corresponding German terms 'joy' and 'cry'. 21, aus. 22, Menge, f. 23, to resume business, sich an sein Geschäft begeben.

Section 100.

PERSPIRATION.

Perspiration is the evacuation[1] of the juices of the body through the pores of the skin. It has been calculated (S. 4, N. 4) that there are[2] above three hundred millions *of* pores in the glands of the skin which covers the body of a middle-sized man. Through these pores more than one half[4] of what we eat and drink passes off[3] by[5] insensible[6] perspiration. If we consume eight pounds of food in[7] a day (App. § 9; S. 27, N. 8), five pounds of it (S. 4, N. 5, *B*) are insensibly discharged[3] by perspiration. During[9] a night of seven hours' sleep we perspire about two[10] pounds and a half. At an average we may[11] estimate the discharge[1] by[12] sensible and insensible perspiration at[13] *from* half an ounce to[14] four ounces per hour. This (Dies) is a most[15] wonderful part[16] of the animal economy, and[17] is absolutely necessary to[18] our health, and even to our *very* existence.—THE REV. DR. DICK.

1, Ausscheidung, f. 2, '(there) to be', here sich befinden. Place the reflective pron. after the conjunction daß. The words 'above — pores' come after the relative clause 'which — man', after which place the verb befinden. 3, entweichen. 4, die Hälfte. 5, mittelst. 6, unmerklich. 7, an. 8, ausscheiden. 9, Say 'During a seven hours' (siebenstündig) sleep'. 10, two pounds and a half, drittehalb Pfund. 11, may = can. 12, durch. 13, ans. 14, bis. 15, Use the superlative of the adv. hoch. 16, part — economy, Einrichtung im tierischen Organismus. 17, Substitute a relative pronoun for the conjunction 'and', which will improve the sentence very much. 18, für.

Section 101.

THE DRAMA OF THE FRENCH[1] REVOLUTION OF 1848.

I.

Our first scene is a palace; the period[2] winter; the time[3] morning, and the weather cold and miserable[4]. It is ten o'clock, and the King of France with his wife[5] and family are[6] discovered at the breakfast table. A splendid beginning! Calmness[7] is the prevailing expression of every countenance save one—the king's daughter-in-law[8], who looks anxious and disturbed. Light[9] domestic talk, *such* as[10] becomes princes and the gilded roof that[11] overhangs them, occupies[12] the moments. Hush[13]! Whilst the lacqueys, dressed (S. 7, N. 3, *A*) in gold and scarlet, move[14] noiselessly about the room, a noise is heard without[15]. It[16] becomes more[17] audible by degrees. Suddenly the door flies open, and two[18] men enter, pale as ghosts. They[19] are Ministers of State (S. 76, N. 22, *A*). They have news to communicate. Discontent prevails in the city; the[20] populace are out; the dragoons have surrendered their sabres, the soldiers their arms, within[21] sight of the apartment in which the king had just now enjoyed his meal, and his daughter-in-law had looked[22] so sad.

1, National adjectives require a small initial in German.   2, period = season.   **3,** time = day-time (S. 76, N. 22, *B*). Connect the two nouns by means of the genitive inflection *es*.   **4,** rauh.   **5,** wife, consort, Gemahlin, which term generally applies to the wife of a king, or to that of persons of the upper ranks of society.—The possessive adj. pron. is best repeated before the next noun.   **6,** Since the subject begins the sentence, the verb must be placed immediately after it. Say 'The king of France sits, etc.', and transl. the words 'at—table' briefly thus: beim Frühstückstische. **7,** Calmness—disturbed. This period is best construed thus: With *the* exception of the king's daughter-in-law (i.e. the daughter-in-law of the king), who looks anxious and disturbed, bear (App. § 14) all *the* faces the expression of (S. 3, N. 2) calmness.—Der König war Ludwig Philipp, geb. den 6. Okteb. 1773 zu Paris, ältester Sohn des Herzogs Ludwig Philipp von Orléans. Nach der Julirevolution von 1830 bestieg er kraft Kammerbeschlusses vom 7. Aug. als König der Franzosen den Thron. Durch die Februarrevolution von 1848 gestürzt, floh er nach England, wo er fortan in Claremont unter dem Titel eines Grafen von Neuilly lebte und im Jahre 1850 starb. Seine Gemahlin war Maria Amalie von Sicilien, welche ebenfalls in England starb.   **8,** Die Schwiegertochter des Königs war Helene, Herzogin von Orléans, verwittwete Gemahlin des im Jahre 1842 infolge eines Sprunges aus dem Wagen beim Durchgehen der Pferde verunglückten Herzogs Ferdinand von Orléans, des ältesten Sohnes des Königs Ludwig Philipp, welcher acht Kinder hatte.   **9,** Supply the indef. art. before the adj. 'light'; 'domestic', here = confidential; talk = conversation.   **10,** such as, wie, after which supply the pron. sie to agree with 'conversation'. It becomes princes, es paßt sich für Fürsten. **11,** '*that—them*', may be briefly turned by 'over them'.   **12,** occupies — moments, läßt die Zeit schnell dahingehen.   **13,** Herch!   **14,** to move, sich bewegen; about the room = in the room.   **15,** without = outside. **16,** Use here a demonstrative pronoun to agree with 'noise'.   **17,** more — degrees = louder and louder.   **18,** two men pale as ghosts, zwei geisterbleiche Gestalten.   **19,** They are, Es sind.   **20,** Der Pöbel ist auf den Beinen. **21,** within — meal = and this almost (fast) immediately in front of (vor) the windows of the room in which the king had just now breakfasted—Use the verb in the Imperfect, and render *just now* by soeben.   **22,** 'to look sad', here trübe einherblicken, which use likewise in the Imperfect.—**The German Imperfect is chiefly used as a historical tense and to express a past action or occurrence with reference to another.** It is, however, likewise used to denote the continuance of an action, to describe a certain state, and to express customary and habitual action. Comp. S. 48, N. 2, for the use of the Perfect.

Section 102.

THE DRAMA OF THE FRENCH REVOLUTION OF 1848.

II.

What is to be done? The king is thunderstruck[1], hesitates *for* a moment, and[2] then, urged[3] by the queen, instantly leaves the room. The[4] queen follows[5] her husband with her (S. 43, N. 9, *A*) eyes from the palace window. She sees[6] him on horseback[7] reviewing[8] the National Guards[9]. She has no fear, neither[10] has he. What[11] more? He returns, accompanied[5] by[12] the man whom[13], yesterday, to satisfy public clamour, he created Prime Minister. Has the Minister power to save his master? You (S. 92, N. 5) observe at[14] a glance that[15] he is far more anxious to save himself. He craves[16] permission to resign. Permission[17] is granted, when (S. 4, N. 2) a volley[18] is (S. 4, N. 4) heard close[19] to their ears. What does it mean? This[20] man will tell you who now enters. The King has a pen in his hand, with which he is about (S. 6, N. 4) to appoint his new Prime Minister. "Sign[21] not," shouts the[22] last comer, a[23] man of the press, with the face[24] of a student, and the spirit[25] of a soldier. "Sign rather[26] your own abdication." The situation is fine[27]. The pen drops[28] from the King's fingers; the speaker[29] takes it up, and quietly[30] replaces[31] it in the Monarch's hand (see S. 43, N. 9).

1, wie vem Donner gerührt. 2, Here place the verb 'leaves'. 3, **The Past (Perfect) Participle is often used elliptically to denote an existing state or condition;** as—

Urged by his father, he instantly left the room. Von seinem Vater gedrängt, verließ er eiligst das Zimmer.

4, Construe this period by beginning with the adverbial clause 'from the palace window', von ten Fenstern des Palastes aus. The verb must then follow immediately. To denote a starting point with respect to place, the English preposition 'from' is generally translated by von followed by the prepositional adverb aus, or by aus ... hinaus when the verb indicates a motion from one place to another. In relation to time we use von ... an, which often corresponds to the English 'beginning with', or to 'from' followed by 'forwards'; as—

Beginning with to-morrow (*From to-morrow forwards*) you must take a walk every day. Von morgen an müssen Sie jeden Tag spazieren gehen.

5, setzen requires the dative. 6, See S. 78, N. 14. 7, zu Pferde. 8, mustern. 9, the National Guards, die Nationalgarde. 10, neither has he = and he also not. 11, Was giebt's weiter? 12, by the man, von einem Manne. 13, 'whom — Minister', construe 'whom he only (erst) yesterday appointed Prime Minister, to satisfy (genügen, with the dat.) the impetuous (ungestüm) demands of the people'. To appoint, to create, ernennen. **Verbs denoting choosing and appointing,** as ernennen, machen, and erwählen, to choose, to elect, **require in German an Accusative followed by the prep. zu with the dative, when in English they govern two Accusatives in the active voice;** as—

The King *appointed* Prince Bismarck Prime Minister. Der König ernannte den Fürsten Bismarck zum Premierminister.

S. 27, N. 4 will show the construction in connection with the passive voice. 14, at a glance, augenblicklich. 15, that — anxious, daß es ihm viel mehr darum zu thun ist. 16, to crave permission to resign, um Erlaubnis bitten, sein Amt niederlegen zu dürfen. 17, Use the def. art. with this noun, and supply the dat. of the pers. pron. er after the auxiliary; the verb is in the passive voice. 18, Musketensalve, f. 19, close to their ears = in *the* immediate neighbourhood. 20, 'This — enters' may be briefly rendered: Der soeben Eintretende wird es uns zu erkennen geben. 21, unterschreiben, insep. comp. str. v., which use in the 3rd pers. pl. of the Imperative mood. As a mark of respect, the word 'Sire' may be inserted after this clause. 22, the

—comer, der Hereingetretene.   **23,** ein Journalist.   **24,** 'face', here = impudence or boldness.   **25,** spirit = courage.   **26,** lieber.   **27,** fine
= critical.   **28,** to drop from, entfallen, with the dat.   **29,** Form a noun
of the present participle of the verb sprechen. The noun Sprecher applies, as
a rule, to the Speaker in the English House of Commons. The Speaker in
the Imperial German Reichstag is styled Präsident.   **30, In German,
when the subject stands before the verb, the adverb must never
precede the latter or, in compound forms, the copula (auxiliary
verb).** Comp. App. § 9.   **31,** wieder geben.

Section 103.

THE DRAMA OF THE FRENCH REVOLUTION OF 1848.

III.

The audience[1] is already touched[2]. The poor king looks around him
for[3] advice; no[4] one offers it; even the Prime Minister of[5] yesterday
is dumb; and in[6] another instant the[7] deed is done. The King has
abdicated in[8] favour of his grandson[9]. Behind the scenes[10] you (S. 92,
N. 5) hear sounds[11] of tumult and disorder, and your[12] heart is already
beating for the issue. The King doffs[13] his robes[14], places his sword
upon the table, and[15], dressed (S. 102, N. 3) as *a* private gentleman[16], is
evidently anxious[17] to depart. The Queen would[18] fain meet the coming
danger, but his[19] Majesty has already ordered the carriages. The horses
are put[20] to, but horses and groom are shot[21] by the multitude[22]. A broad
path leads from[23] the palace garden[24], and at the end[25] of it a friendly
hand[26] has brought two hired coaches[27]. "Let[28] us go," exclaims the
Monarch, and, leaning (S. 53, N. 12) heavily[29] upon the Queen, whose[30]
head is high and erect, he hurries on. The coaches are[31] reached; the
fugitives escape[32]. They arrive at St. Cloud[33], at Versailles, but not to
(S. 19, N. 7. Supply the adv. dort) stay. On[34] they go, and at half-past
eleven o'clock at night they descend at Dreux[36].

1, Die Anwesenden.   **2,** tief ergriffen sein.   **3,** nach.   **4,** No — it,
keiner erbietet sich dazu.   **5,** of yesterday, gestern ernannt, which use attributively before the noun.   **6,** in another = in the next.   **7,** 'to do
a deed', here eine Urkunde vollziehen.   **8,** zu gunsten .   **9,** Der Enkel war
der älteste Sohn des verstorbenen Herzogs Ferdinand von Orléans und seiner Gemahlin
Helene. Dieser Sohn, welcher noch heute (Dez. 1886) in England lebt, trägt den
Namen Ludwig Philipp von Orléans und führt den Titel eines Grafen von Paris. Sein
jüngerer Bruder ist Robert Philipp von Orléans mit dem Titel Herzog von Chartres,
augenblicklich ebenfalls in England.   **10,** Use here the Sing.   **11,** sounds
— disorder = confusion and noise.   **12,** your — issue = our hearts beat already
in anxious expectation of the events to come (der Neuimenten).   **13,** von sich
werfen.   **14,** 'robes', here Staatskleider.   **15,** Here place the verb 'is'.
16, 'priv. gentl.', here Civilist.   **17,** begierig; 'to depart', here = to flee.
18, would fain = would willingly; use the Imperf. Subj. of mögen with the adv.
gern. To meet danger, der Gefahr die Stirne bieten.   **19,** Se. (for Seine)
Majestät, after which place the verb in the 3rd pers. pl., which is customary in
speaking of Sovereigns.   **20,** to put to = to put the horses to, anspannen.
21, erschießen.   **22,** Pöbel, m.   **23,** 'from', here aus ... hinaus. Comp.
S. 102, N. 4.   **24,** Form a compound of 'castle' and 'garden'.   **25,** 'end',
here Ausgang, m.   **26,** Form a comp. of 'friend' and 'hand' according to

S. 76, N. 22, *B.* 27, Mietsſutſche, f. 28, The King would address his Consort in the 2nd pers. sing. 29, to lean heavily upon, ſich ſeſt ſtützen auf (with Acc.). 30, welche mit ſtolzerhobenem Haupte einherſchreitet. 31, are reached, werden beſtiegen. 32, entlemmuen. 33, Saшet Cloud bei Verſailles war zu jener Zeit eine beliebte Reſidenz der köuiglichen Familie. 'Saшet' (abbreviated St.) comes from the Latin 'sanctus'. 34, Es geht weiter. 35, Dreur iſt ein Städtchen im Departement Eure-Leire, an der Eure, mit 7000 Eiuwehuern und enthält ein Schleß mit Grabkapelle des Hauſes Orléans, welche von der Mutter des Köuigs Ludwig Philipp gegründet wurde.

Section 104.

THE DRAMA OF THE FRENCH REVOLUTION OF 1848.

IV.

At one in the morning they are joined[1] by (von) one of the King's sons, who informs the unhappy pair that the claims[2] of the grandson had[3] been disregarded, and *that* the republic had been declared by the people of Paris. It is enough. The King shaves off his whiskers, puts on green spectacles, buries[4] his face in a handkerchief, speaks English, and calls himself Smith. The wind is[5] high, the coast[6] dangerous, embarkation[7] is out of question at the moment, and before an opportunity offers, the rank of the runaways[8] is discovered. Fortune (S. 3, N. 2), however, is[9] with them: they escape[10] capture and put to sea. Protected by Heaven, they reach in safety[11] the hospitable shores of England.

Meanwhile[12], what has happened in Paris? The whole city has given way[13] to a handful of rioters—men (S. 53, N. 9) who meditated an "emeute[14]", and effected, to their astonishment, an *actual* revolution. But[15] two individuals upon the side of the King evinced a[16] particle of courage, and these were women — his wife and his daughter-in-law already[17] mentioned. The[18] rest of the city were[19] faithless to themselves as well as to the King.

1, 'to be joined', here eingeholt werden (to be overtaken). 2, Here Threnanſprüche. 3, According to the two rules in §§ 28 and 30 of the Appendix, the Perfect of the Subjunctive Mood is to be used in this and the following clause. The two clauses, however, can be joined by omitting the second conjunction 'that' and the copula 'had been' of the first clause. Turn 'to disregard' by nicht auerfennen; the words 'by — Paris' may be briefly rendered by von den Pariſeru, which place immediately after the conjunction 'and'. 4, 'to bury', here = to veil, umhüllen; the prep. 'in' must then be rendered by mit. 5, is high = blows violently. 6, Since the copula 'is' was changed into another verb in the previous clause, it must be inserted here. 7, The literal version of this clause would not read well. I propose to use the following construction: it is (Comp. N. 19) for the moment impossible to embark. 8, runaways = fugitives. 9, is with them, iſt ihnen hold (propitious). 10, to escape capture, der Verhaſtung entgehen; to put to sea, iu die See ſtechen. 11, glücklich; 'shores', here Geſtate. 12, Iuzwiſchen, which place after the copula 'has'. The verb 'to happen' is conjugated with ſein. 13, to give way = to yield, conj. with ſein; haudtul, Häuſein. 14, Aufrubr, m.; rioter, Aufrührer. 15, but = only; individuals = perſons. 16, a particle of = a little. 17, deren wir ſchen erwähuten. 18, All the others in the city. 19, were — King = 'were juſt as faithless towards

themselves as they were towards the King', and insert the grammatical subject
es after the pronoun 'they'.—**The grammatical subject es is frequently
employed for emphasizing the real subject or to give more tone and
life to the construction;** as—Es sprach die Leidenschaft aus seinen Zügen. It is,
moreover, used with all impersonal verbs; as—es friert, es donnert, es giebt, es ist.

Section 105.

THE DRAMA OF THE FRENCH REVOLUTION OF 1848.
V.

Princes, peers[1], soldiers, and statesmen were all sneaking[2] in hiding
places whilst the capital was[3] made over to the mercy of a few dozen
incendiaries. The daughter-in-law, seeing (S. 55, N. 1) the King depart[4],
carries[5] her child to the Chamber of Deputies[6], and[7] there, with womanly
courage and queenly dignity, vindicates his rights. Her friends entreat
her to withdraw. Firm[8] in her purpose, she does not move[9] an inch.
She attempts to speak, but is interrupted; and[10] he who interrupts is
himself silenced by an armed mob that pours[11] into the hall[12]. The
Duchess is forced away[13], and in that terrible extremity *is* separated from
her son. The child is seized by (S. 106, N. 23) a rough hand, which[14]
is strong enough to strike[15], but[16] generous enough to save. The boy
is brought[17] to his mother, and mother and son pass[18] from asylum to
asylum, chased[19] by scythes, sabres, muskets, and. worse[20] than all, the[21]
bloody passions of an infuriated "canaille". For[22] four days they[23] creep
into hiding places; on the fifth day they are beyond the frontier.

1, The Peers of France were called 'Pairs', which term is used in German,
the final s being pronounced.   2, to sneak into hiding places, in den Winkel
kriechen.   3, was made over = was left (überlassen), with the dat. Construe
the sentence after the following model:—Die Festung wurde einer kleinen Anzahl
Soldaten auf Gnade oder Ungnade überlassen.   4, davon reisen. Comp. App. § 19.
5, führen, before which the subjective pronoun 'she' must be supplied.
6, Deputiertenkammer, f.   7, and — rights = where she vindicates his rights
with, etc.   8, fest ihren Zweck verfolgend.   9, zurückweichen.   10, and
— himself, und der sie Unterbrechende selbst wird.   11, to pour = to rush.
12, Saal, m.   13, gewaltsam hinwegdrängen.   14, After the rel. pron.
insert the adverb zwar (certainly, it is true, indeed), which will give more force
to the clause.   15, darein zuschlagen.   16, 'but', here doch, or aber auch.
17, 'to bring', here = to bring back.   18, 'to pass', here = to flee.
19, chased = pursued; by, von.   20, what is still worse.   21, von dem
blutgierigen Zorn eines rasenden Pöbels.   22, Vier Tage lang.   23, they —
places = they try to conceal themselves.

Section 106.

THE DRAMA OF THE FRENCH REVOLUTION OF 1848.
VI.

Everybody is escaping at[1] the same moment. There is the King's
eldest son, pale and half-naked, throwing[2] aside his tinsel and putting on
fustian, looking[3] less than a man in his fear, trembling with[4] emotion,
and finally running[5] like a madman for[6] his life. There are your[7]

ministers, of [8] European reputation and wisdom unapproachable, bounding [9] like antelopes, northwards [10], southwards, "anywhere, anywhere [11] out of the city", which they and all the rest give up [12] to indiscriminate riot. And [13] now the crowning point of our first "tableau" is near. The (S. 107, N. 13) mob, masters [14] of Paris, are sacking the Tuileries. The choicest moveables [15] are broken to atoms; a group [16] takes [17] the places which Royalty filled a moment ago at the breakfast table; others are in the wine cellar drinking [18] themselves ten times drunk; others, again [19], are in the Queen's apartments, defiling [20] that [21] domestic sanctuary. Outside the palace and on the top [22] of it a flag is waved [24] by [23] a dozen men, whose [25] shouts and shrieks invite hundreds, whom [26] you see crawling up with no earthly object but immediately to (S. 19, N. 7) slide down again.

1, at — moment = with them.   2, 'throwing — life'. The rendering of this passage according to the rule of S. 16, N. 4 would be inelegant, since there are a number of Present Participles following one another. I propose, therefore, to begin a new period here, saying: He throws aside his tinsel (here Flitterstaat, m.), puts on fustian, etc.; to put on fustian, sich in Barchent kleiden.   3, to look less than a man, kaum einem Manne ähnlich sehen.   4, ver; emotion = excitement.   5, taven'laufen.   6, um sein Leben zu retten.   7, your = the.   8, of — unapproachable = incomparable in (an) European fame and wisdom.   9, Since a relative clause follows immediately, it would be bad taste to render this clause, beginning with a Present Participle, in the same form. It will be best to commence a new period. Comp. N. 2.   10, nach Nord und Süd.   11, The second 'anywhere' is best turned by nur hinweg.   12, dem allgemeinen Aufruhr preisgeben.   13, And — near = And now we approach (sich nähern, with Dat.) the end (Schluß, m.) of our first tableau. The French 'tableau' is used with French pronunciation in the same sense in German. It is of the neuter gender and takes the inflection of an s in the Gen. Sing.   14, masters of Paris = which rules *in* Paris; to rule, beherrschen (v. tr.).   15, moveables = objects; atoms = pieces.   16, Insert the noun 'men'.   17, ein'nehmen; Royalty = the Royal family; filled = occupied (inne haben, treated like a comp. sep. v.). The adverbial clause 'at the breakfast table' is best placed after the verb 'takes'.   18, drinking themselves drunk = and drink themselves drunk (sich betrinfen).   19, wiederum anderc.   20, and defile (besudeln).   21, diese geheiligte Stätte der Häuslichkeit.   22, top = roof; of it = of the same.   23, The preposition 'by' in connection with the passive voice and establishing a relation with the noun or pronoun that denotes the doer of the action expressed by the verb, is rendered by von.   24, hin und her schwenfen.   25, To avoid a succession of relative clauses, which should always be avoided, begin again a new period here and say: The shouts and shrieks of these men invite (herbei= locfen), etc.   26, whom — but = who seem only to climb up (erflettern) the roof. The adv. 'immediately' comes after the conjunction 'to'.

Section 107.

THE DRAMA OF THE FRENCH REVOLUTION OF 1848.

VII.

There [1] is sentiment in all things. The apartments of the poor daughter-in-law are reached (S. 4, N. 4, man), but, strange [2] to say, are respected [3] in the midst of the work [4] of general destruction. Her children's toys are [5] not even touched; the hat and (S. 10, N. 9) whip of her dead [6] husband are [7] still sacred; the books (S. 16, N. 10) she had been reading lie still open [8].   It [9] is an incident that cannot fail to [10] elicit rounds of applause.   And whilst [11] anarchy and destruction prevail here, there [12] is equal confusion and danger in the Chamber of Deputies.   We have seen the [13] mob forcing their way into (ʒu) that deliberative assembly. Everybody [14] is now rushing to the tribune.   Three [15] speakers become marked from the rest; their [16] names are Lamartine [23], Crémieux [23], and Ledru Rollin [23]; they [17] gain the popular ear, and undertake (S. 51, N. 13) to establish [18] order—a superhuman responsibility!   A Provisional Government is announced, named [19], and approved on the spot.   "To (S. 72, N. 4) the Hôtel de Ville!" exclaims one [20].   "To the Hôtel de Ville!" respond a hundred; and amidst [21] yells and hootings, cries of "Vive la République!" "Vive Lamartine!" "A bas tout le monde!" *Monsieur* Lamartine [23] sets out for that celebrated building, followed by a train made [24] up of the dregs of a seething metropolis.   In the middle [26] of the shouting the curtain falls, and [26] the first act terminates.   Search [27] the dramatic annals of the world for such another.—Essays from "The Times".

1, Es findet sich jedoch überall noch eine Spur von Gefühl.   2, strange to say, sonderbarerweise.   3, are respected, werden dieselben … verschont.   4, work — destruction, allgemeines Zerstörungswerf.   5, bleiben; not touched = untouched.   6, verstorben.   7, und dem Andenken noch heilig.   8, Supply here the adverb da, which will make the sentence more emphatic.   9, It is, Es ist dies. Comp. S. 104, N. 19.   10, to = applause, den allgemeinsten Beifall hervorzurufen.—Dieser Verfall erklärt sich durch die große Popularität des verstorbenen Herzogs und seiner Gemahlin, der Herzogin Helene von Orléans.   11, Place the adv. 'here' after whilst, and use the adverb noch with it.   12, 'there is', here findet man, after which place 'in — Deputies'.   13, the — way = how the mob forces its way (sich einen Weg bahnen). In German the verb agrees in the Singular with a collective substantive in the Singular. 14, Alles; to, auf.   15, Drei Redner hört man über die andern hinaus.   16, sie heißen.   17, they = these; to gain the popular ear, sich beim Volke Gehör verschaffen.   18, wieder herstellen.   19, mit Namen benannt.   20, Say 'one voice', and afterwards 'hundred other voices'.   21, unter.   22, und unter wiederholten Ausrufen von …   23, 'to set out', here die Prozession antreten; for, nach. The verb must of course appear before the Subject Lamartine. Louis Alphonse Lamartine erregte zunächst durch seine zarten Jugenddichtungen in den zwanziger Jahren allgemeine Aufmerksamkeit. Nachdem er durch den Tod eines Oheims ein bedeutendes Vermögen ererbt hatte, bereiste er 1832 den Orient, worauf er die politische Laufbahn betrat und einer der glänzendsten Redner der Deputiertenkammer wurde. Nach der Februarrevolution von 1848 wurde er Mitglied der provisorischen Regierung und Minister des Auswärtigen, zog sich jedoch 1851 unzufrieden zurück und + am 1. März 1869 zu Passy, wo er in dürftigen Verhältnissen gelebt hatte. Isaac Adolphe Crémieux, Israelit, wurde 1830 Advokat am Kassationshofe zu Paris, bekämpfte, seit 1842 Mitglied der Kammer, heftig das Ministerium Guizot und förderte die Reformbewegung. Nach der Februarrevolution von 1848 ward er Mitglied der provisorischen Regierung und in kurze Zeit das Justizministerium bekleidete. Nach der Wahl des Prinzen Louis Napoléon zum Präsidenten trat er zur Opposition über, ward beim Staatsstreich am 2. Dez. 1851 verhaftet, jedoch bald wieder freigelassen, worauf er sich auf seine Praxis beschränkte. Im Jahre 1870, nach dem Sturze des Kaiserreichs, nochmals zum Mitglied der provisorischen Regierung gewählt, hielt er sich zu Gambetta und ward später Mitglied der Nationalversammlung.

Alexandre Auguste Ledru Rollin ward Advofat, und trat 1844 in die Kammer der Deputierten, nachdem er als Advofat in vielen politischen Prozessen plaidiert hatte. Er beteiligte sich lebhaft bei der Reformagitation von 1847, ward 1848 Mitglied der provisorischen Regierung und Minister des Innern, trat jedoch schon im Juni desselben Jahres von der Regierung zurück. Im Juni 1849 mußte er wegen politischer Intriguen nach England fliehen, ward abwesend zur Deportation verurteilt und lebte seitdem als Mitglied des dortigen Revolutionskomitees in London. Im Jahre 1857 wurde er mit Mazzini eines Komplots gegen Napoleon III. angeklagt und abermals verurteilt, und kehrte endlich am 26. März 1870 infolge der Erklärung der Republik und der Amnestie nach Paris zurück, ohne sich aber an den dortigen Ereignissen hervorragend zu beteiligen.
24, made up of, welcher sich aus . . . gebildet hat; seething, gährend. **25,** Inmitten, followed by the Gen. **26,** After 'and' supply the adv. so, which requires the constr. to be inverted. **27,** Search — another. This passage would not read well in a literal version, which may be altered thus:—Where can we find in the dramatic annals of the history of the world (comp. n.) a similar *one* (einen gleichen).

Section 108.

EXPERIENCE IS THE BEST TEACHER[1].

A French student of (S. 3, N. 2) medicine lodged[2] in the same house in London with a man in a fever. This poor man was constantly plagued by the nurse to drink, though[3] he nauseated the insipid liquids that were presented to him. At last, when she[4] grew more and more importunate, he whispered in her (S. 43. N. 9, *B*) ear:— "For[5] God's sake bring me a salt herring, and I will drink as much *as* you please[6]!"

The woman indulged[7] him in his request; he devoured the herring, drank plentifully, underwent[8] a copious perspiration, and recovered[9].

The French student inserted this aphorism[10] in his journal[11] :—" A salt herring cures[12] an Englishman in a fever."

On[13] his return to (S. 72, N. 4) France he prescribed the same remedy to the first patient in a fever[2] to whom he was called.

The patient died; on which[14] the student inserted[15] in his journal *the* following note:—"N.B. Though a salt herring cures an Englishman, it[16] kills a Frenchman."—W. C. HAZLITT, ANECDOTES.

1, Lehrerin, to agree with 'experience', which is feminine in German. **2,** Here place the words 'in London — fever'; a man in a fever, ein Fieberkranker. **3,** Construe the sentence 'though — him' after the following model: Die mir gereichten geschmacklosen Getränke wittern mich an. **4,** Here place the adv. 'at last'; more and more importunate, immer zudringlicher. **5,** Um Gotteswillen. **6,** wollen. **7,** to indulge a request, einer Bitte willfahren. **8,** to undergo a copious perspiration, in tüchtigen Schweiß geraten (str. v.). **9,** genesen, str. v. **10,** Lehrsatz. **11,** Form a comp. n. of 'day' and 'book' according to S. 76, N. 22, *C*. **12,** kurieren: in a, vom. **13,** Say 'When he had returned to France'. **14,** on which = whereupon. **15,** schreiben, after which place 'following note'. **16,** so stirbt ein Franzose daran.

Section 109.

ON[1] SELF CULTURE.

(From[2] an address delivered to an assemblage of young men at Edinburgh.)

I[3] stand before you a self-educated man. My education was[4] that which was supplied at the humble parish schools of Scotland; and *it was* only[5] when I[6] went to Edinburgh, a poor boy, *that* I devoted my evenings, after the labours of the day, to the cultivation of[7] that intellect which the Almighty has given me. From seven or eight in the morning till nine or ten at night[8], was I at[9] *my* business as *a* bookseller's apprentice[10], and[11] *it was* only during hours after these, stolen from sleep, *that* I could devote myself to study. I assure you that I did not read novels[12]; my attention was devoted[13] to physical science and other useful matters[14]. During[15] that period I taught myself French. I look back[16] to that time with great pleasure, and am almost sorry I have not to go[17] through the same troubles again. I[18] reaped more pleasure when I had not a sixpence in my pocket, studying in a garret in Edinburgh, than I now find when sitting amidst all the elegancies and comforts of a parlour. —WILLIAM CHAMBERS.

1, über Selbstbildung.   2, Aus; to deliver an address to an assemblage, vor einer Versammlung eine Rede halten; young men, junge Leute.   3, I — man. This sentence does not allow of a literal rendering; say 'You see before you a man who has educated himself' (sich selbst bilden or aus'bilden).   4, was = Scotland = was such as (it) (eine solche, wie sie) is given (erteilen) at (in) a simple Scottish village-school.   **5, The adverb 'only', when used in reference to time, is turned by 'erst', but in reference to number by 'nur'; as—**

This man has *only* (but) one coat.   Dieser Mann hat nur einen Rock.
It is *only* one o'clock.   Es ist erst ein Uhr.

6, when — boy = when I, a poor boy, came to (S. 72, N. 4) Ed.   7, Construe the clause 'of — me' according to S. 48, N. 6; intellect, Geist.   8, 'at night', here abends, since Nacht applies only to the hours between 11 P.M. and 5 A.M.   9, at = in, contracted with the Dat. of the def. art.   10, Supply here thätig (engaged).   11, Say 'and only during the later (später) hours, which I stole from sleep (dem Schlafe ab'stehlen), could I', etc.   12, Roman, m.   13, auf naturwissenschaftliche Studien ... gerichtet.   14, Gegenstand, m.   15, 'During that period' may be briefly rendered by damals; to teach oneself German, ohne Lehrer Deutsch studieren.   16, zurück blicken.   17, to go through troubles, Beschwerden durch'machen; again, noch einmal. For the constr. see App. § 19.   18, Say 'When (S. 4, N. 2) I had no sixpence (Sechspfennigstück, n.) in my pocket and studied in a garret in E., I felt (sich fühlen) happier than now, when (da) I sit in an elegant *and* comfortable (behaglich) parlour'.

Section 110.

GOETHE'S[1] DEATH.

I.

The[2] following morning—it was the 22nd March 1832—he tried to[3] walk a little up and down the room, but[4] after a turn, he found[5] himself too feeble to continue. Reseating[6] himself in the easy chair, he chatted cheerfully with Ottilie [(S. 53, N. 9) his daughter-in-law] on [7] the approaching spring, which would [8] be sure to restore him. He [9] had no idea of his end being so near. The name *of* Ottilie was frequently on his lips. She sat beside him, holding [10] his hand in both of hers. It was now observed that his thoughts began to wander [11] incoherently. " See," he exclaimed, " the lovely woman's head, with black curls, in splendid colours—a [12] dark background!" Presently [13] he saw a piece of paper on the floor, and asked *them* how [14] they could leave Schiller's letters so carelessly lying about. Then [15] he slept softly, and, on [16] awakening, asked [17] for the sketches [18] (S. 16, N. 10) he had just seen—the [19] sketches of his dream.

1, Johann Wolfgang von Göthe, geboren den 22. August 1749 zu Frankfurt a/M., gestorben den 22. März 1832 zu Weimar, kann wohl mit Recht der universalste Genius seiner Zeit genannt werden, deren Litteratur er unbestritten beherrschte. Er war Dichter, Biograph, Naturforscher, Altertumsforscher, Kritiker, Ästhetiker und Staatsmann. In fast allen poetischen Gattungen zeigte er sich als vollendeter Künstler, am bedeutendsten aber war er als Lyriker. Er hinterließ einen einzigen Sohn, dessen Frau (Ottilie) unten erwähnt wird.   2, Am nächsten Morgen.   3, im Zimmer auf und abgehen.   4, but — turn = but already after *a* few steps.   5, sich fühlen: 'to continue' may be briefly rendered by dazu.   6, After he had seated himself again, etc.   7, über.   8, would be sure = would surely (see App. §§ 28 and 30).   9, He — near = He had no idea of it (davon), that his end was so near.   10, und hielt seine Hand mit beiden Händen umschlossen.   11, umherirren.   12, a = upon a.   13, Then.   14, warum man Schillers Briefe so sorglos herumliegen lasse.   15, Hereupon.   16, beim Erwachen.   17, forterte er.   18, Bilder.   19, the — dream, seine Traumbilder.

Section 111.

GOETHE'S DEATH.

II.

In silent anguish they [1] now awaited the close now so surely approaching (S. 48, N. 6). His speech was becoming less and less distinct. The last words audible [2] were: "More Light!" The final [3] darkness [4] grew apace, and he [5] whose eternal longings had been for more light, gave a parting cry for it as he was passing under the shadow of death.

He continued to express himself by signs, drawing [6] letters [7] with his forefinger in the air, while he [8] had strength, and finally, as life (S. 3, N. 2) ebbed [9], drawing [10] figures slowly on the shawl which covered his legs. At [11] half-past twelve he composed [12] himself in the corner of the easy chair. His faithful watcher [13] placed a finger on her lips to intimate that he was asleep [14]. It was a sleep in which a life glided [15] from the world. He [16] woke no more.—G. H. LEWES, LIFE OF GOETHE.

1, they = his friends, die Seinen.   2, In ordinary prose adjectives qualifying a noun should precede it.   3, final = last.   4, Dunkel (n.) stieg hernieder.   5, he — death = he who had always longed (sich sehnen) for (nach) more light, cried still parting for it (danach) when the night of death overshadowed him.   6, The conjunction indem with a finite verb is

frequently employed for rendering the English Participle in -ing
used in adverbial clauses of manner ; as—

Supporting himself on her arm he   Inbem er fid auf ihren Arm ftüt3te,
   slowly ascended the stairs.   ftieg er langfam bie Treppe hinauf.

7, Buchftaben, which place after 'forefinger'.   8, After 'he' insert the
adverb nod.   9, tahin'ftuten.   10, drew he slowly figures (3ahlen),
etc.   11, Um halb eins.   12, to compose oneself in the corner, fid
ruhig in bie Ecfe 3urücf legen.   13, Wärterin.   14, Use the Present of the
Subj. App. § 28 and § 30.   15, fdeiben; from, aus.   16, Say 'Goethe'
instead of 'he'; woke = awoke; no more, nidt wieter.

Section 112.

ON TRAVELLING (S. 3, N. 2).

I[1] wish folks[2] in general would keep their eyes a little more open
when they travel by rail[3]. When I see young people rolling along in
a luxurious[4] carriage, absorbed (S. 102, N. 3) in a trashy[5] shilling novel[6],
and[7] never lifting up their eyes to look out of the window, unconscious[8]
of all that[9] they are passing ;—of[10] the reverend antiquities, the admirable[11]
agriculture, the rich *and* peaceful scenery[12], the[13] like of which no other
country upon earth can show (App. § 18); unconscious[14], too, *of* how
much they might[15] learn *of* botany *and* geology, by[16] simply watching
the flowers along the railway banks, and the sections[17] in the cuttings[18];
—then it grieves me to see what[19] little use people make of the eyes and
the understanding which God has given them. They complain of[20] a
dull[21] journey : but[22] it is not the journey which is dull; it[23] is they who
are dull. Eyes[24] have they, and see not; ears have they, and hear not;
mere[25] dolls in smart clothes, too many of them, like the idols of the
heathen.—CHARLES KINGSLEY, TOWN GEOLOGY.

1, Id mödte wohl.   2, Say '(the) people (bie Leute) would use (Imperf.
Subj. of braudhen, App. § 32) in general the eyes a little more', etc.   3, mit
ter Eifenbahn reifen.   4, luxurious = splendid; for the rendering of the verbs
in this passage consult S. 78, N. 14, and for their position, App. § 19; to roll
along, tahin'rollen.   5, fdledt.   6, Form comp. n. according to S. 76,
N. 22, *B.*   7, and — eyes = so that they never lift up their eyes. This
constr. is necessary to avoid a repetition of participles.   8, nidts ahneub.
9, woran fie verüberfahren.   10, Say 'nothing of'.   11, excellent.
12, landscape.   13, the — which = as, wie fie (grammatical object ; comp.
S. 51, N. 13.   14, aud nidt einmal ahneub.   15, I might learn much of
botany, id fénnte viel Botanif lernen. The subject 'they' place after 'geology'
and before the two verbs.   16, by — watching = if they would only watch
(beobadten) ; along — banks = on (an) the sides of the railway.   17, Bahn=
vrofil, n.   18, Durdftid, m. The two verbs must, of course, stand at the
end of the whole passage.   19, wie wenig, little (denoting quantity).
20, über, with Acc.   21, dull = wearisome, langweilig.   22, but — dull
= but not the journey is dull.   23, fie felbft finb es (Comp. S. 104, N. 19).
24, The inverted constr. would not read well here ; use therefore the ordinary
constr.   25, are nothing but (als) dolls in fine clothes, and like (gleid,
with Dat.) the idols (Gögenbilber) of the heathens are *there* too many of them
(finb ihrer 3u viele).

Section 113.

THE MANAGEMENT[1] OF THE BODY.

I have nothing new to say upon the management which the body requires[2]. The common rules are the best:—exercise without fatigue; generous[3] living without excess; early rising, and moderation in sleeping. These are the apothegms[4] of old women; but if they are not attended to[5], happiness[6] becomes (App. § 15) so extremely difficult that[7] very few *persons* can attain[8] to it. In[9] this point of view, the care[10] of the body becomes a[11] subject of elevation and importance. A walk in the fields, an hour's[12] less sleep, may[13] remove all these bodily vexations[14] and disquietudes which are such formidable enemies to[15] virtue; they may enable[17] the mind[16] to pursue[18] its own resolves without that constant train[19] of temptations to resist, and[20] obstacles to overcome, which[21] it always experiences from the bad organisation of its companion.—SIDNEY SMITH.

1, treatment.   2, behürfen, govern. the Gen.   3, strengthening food.   4, Lebensregeln.   5, to attend to, beobachten, v. tr.   6, the acquisition of happiness.   7, Insert the adv. 'only' after 'that'.   8, I cannot attain to it, ich kann es nicht erlangen (v. tr.).   9, In — view, Von biesem Gesichtspunkte aus betrachtet, after which follows the verb (App. § 14).   10, Pflege, f.   11, Say 'a grand (erhaben) and important subject'.   12, an hour.   13, can perhaps.   14, disturbances and troubles, Störungen und Beschwerten.   15, Use the noun with the Gen. of the def. art.   16, mind = soul.   17, befähigen, v. tr.   18, folgen, with Dat.   19, 'train', here = host, Heer, n.; of, von: to resist, widerstehen, govern. the Dat.   20, Supply here 'those'.   21, the acquaintance of which (deren) the soul always owes (verdanken, govern. the Dat.) to the defective organisation of its companion.

Section 114.

THE SOURCES[1] OF WATER.

There[2] are many sources of water. The first great source[3] is the ocean, which collects all *the* water from[4] the earth; this water contains so large a quantity *of* salt, that none[5] of us can drink it. The sun, however, bears[6] down upon the ocean's surface, and its heating[7] rays penetrating[8] the water, combine, as[9] it were, with it (S. 4, N. 5, *B*), and[10] raise it up. The atmosphere (S. 5, N. 2), like[11] a sponge, absorbs the[12] vaporous water, carrying[13] it from the Equator to[14] the Arctic and the Antartic regions; thus[15] distributing it north and south. It then condenses in the form of rain and *of* snow. When it sinks into the earth and pours down the[16] mountain sides, it forms springs and rivulets, entering[18] (S. 16, N. 4) the ocean again in[17] the form of rivers. Man catches[19] it in tubs and cisterns, draws[20] it from[21] the rivers, or digs down[22] into the earth, and catches[23] it as it passes[24] along beneath his feet. Thus[25] we have rain water, river water, and spring or well water.— DR. LANKESTER.

1, Here Urquellen.   2, The water has many sources.   3, great = chief; form a comp. n.   4, To render 'from the' use the Gen. of the def. art.   5, none of us = nobody.   6, bears down upon = shines. 7, erwärmend.   8, penetrating = penetrate, durchdrin'gen, insep. comp. str. v. 9, as it were, gleichsam.   10, and draw it upward.   11, wie.   12, das verbundete Wasser.   13, carries it.   14, nach den nördlichen und südlichen Polargegenden.   15, and distributes it north and southward. Comp. S. 71, N. 2, the principle stated there applying likewise to other compound expressions besides nouns.   16, the = on (an) the.   17, in the form of = as, which place after the rel. pron.   18, to enter again the ocean, dem Ozean wieder zuströmen.   19, auf'fangen, sep. c. str. v.   20, to draw water, Wasser schöpfen.   21, aus.   22, down = deep.   23, sammeln.   24, 'to pass along', here dahin'fließen.   25, Auf diese Weise.

Section 115.

THE ART OF ORATORY.

I[1] owe my success in life to one single fact[2], namely:—At[3] the age of twenty-seven[4] I commenced, and continued for years, the process of daily speaking (S. 34, N. 10) upon the contents of some historical or scientific book. These efforts[5] were made sometimes in a corn-field[6], at others[7] in the forest, and not unfrequently in some distant[8] barn, with[9] *the* horse and ox for my auditors. It[10] is this early practice in the *great* art of all arts that I am indebted for the primary and leading impulses that stimulated me forward, and shaped and moulded my entire subsequent[11] destiny. Improve[12], then, the superior advantages (S. 16, N. 10) you here enjoy[13]. Let not[14] a day pass[15] without exercising (S. 34, N. 10) your powers[16] of speech. There is (S. 82, N. 7) no power like[17] that of oratory. Cæsar controlled[18] men by[19] exciting their fears; Cicero[20] by[21] captivating their affection and swaying their passions. The influence of the one perished[22] with its author; that of the other continues[23] to this day.—HENRY CLAY[24].

1, To avoid beginning with the pronoun '**I**', which seldom looks well in German, and is considered bad style in letters, place the object first, and construe according to App. § 14.   2, fact = deed or action = That, f.; fact = event (as in this instance) = Thatsache, f.; the Latin Factum, pl. Facta or Facten, is, however, used in both significations.   3, At the, Im.   4, Supply 'years', and construe thus: I began the process (Verfahren, n.), which I continued for years (jahrelang) to speak daily about (über, with Acc.), etc.; some = a.   5, efforts = exercises.   6, Here place the verb.   7, zuweilen.   8, entlegen.   9, whereby horse and ox formed my audience (Zuhörer).   10, It — forward = To this early practice ... I owe the first and leading impulses (Triebfedern) which urged me forward (vor'wärtstreiben, sep. comp. str. v.).   11, subsequent = later. 12, Improve = Use, which use in the 2nd pers. pl.; then = therefore; superior = great.   13, genießen.   14, 'Not' in connection with the indef. art. must generally be rendered by 'no'.   15, vorüͤbergehen.   16, Rede= talent, n.   17, welche der der Beredsamkeit gleichkommt.   18, beherrschen. 19, durch Erregung; render 'their' by the Gen. of the def. art.   20, Supply here 'controlled them' (beherrschte sie dadurch, daß er ...). Comp. and read carefully S. 87, N. 6, and also S. 1, N. 3. The verb beherrschen requires the preposition durch.   21, by — passions = that he gained (sich gewinnen) their

love and guided (lenfen) their passions.   **22,** erſtarb; its author = the author
of the same (to agree with 'influence').   **23,** fertdauern, sep. c. w. v.; to
this day, bis auf den heutigen Tag.   **24,** Henry Clay (geb. 1777 in Virginien,
✝ 1852 in Waſhington) war ein amerikaniſcher Staatsmann, welcher ſich als Sohn
eines einfachen Landmannes bis zu den höchſten Aemtern des Staats heranſarbeitete;
1824 ward er zum Staatsſekretär des Auswärtigen ernannt und 1829 war er unter
Jackſons Präſidentſchaft im Kongreß Führer der Oppoſition, als welcher er die Schutz-
zölle und die Nationalbank verteidigte. Im Jahre 1849 brachte er den Kompromiß zuſtande, wonach dem Süden das Recht der Verfolgung flüchtiger Sklaven durch das
Gebiet der Union eingeräumt ward.

Section 116.

EARLY PRIVATIONS[1].

Admiral Jervis, Earl of St. Vincent, tells us the[1] story of his early
struggles, and, among[2] other things, of his determination (S. 1, N. 2)
to[3] keep out of debt. " My father had a very large family," said he,
" with limited means. He gave me twenty pounds (S. 58, N. 3) at[4]
starting, and that was all (S. 3, N. 7) he ever[5] gave me. After I had
been a considerable time at[6] the station at sea I[7] drew for twenty more,
but the bill came[8] back protested. I[9] was mortified[10] at this rebuke, and
made[11] a promise, which I have ever[12] kept, that[13] I would never draw
another bill without[14] a certainty of its being paid. I immediately changed
my mode of living, quitted[15] my mess[16], lived[17] alone, and[18] took up the
ship's allowance, which I found quite sufficient; washed and mended[19]
my *own* clothes; made a pair *of* trousers out *of* the ticking of my bed[20],
and, having (S. 55, N. 1) by[21] these means saved as much money as[22]
would redeem my honour, I took[23] up my bill. From (S. 102, N. 4)
that time to this I[24] have taken care to[25] keep within my means."

Jervis (S. 5, N. 2) for six years endured pinching[26] privation, but preserved his integrity, studied his profession with success, and gradually
rose[27] by merit and bravery to the highest rank.—S. SMILES, SELF-HELP.

1, Early Privations, Jugendentbehrungen; the story — struggles. This passage,
literally rendered, is not clear in German, and should be turned thus: of (von)
the struggles with privations, which he had to go through (beſtehen), when he
was a youth (als Jüngling, which place after the subject 'he').   **2,** among
other things = unter anderem.   **3,** ſich von Schulten freihalten.   **4,** at
starting, beim Beginn meiner Laufbahn; see App. § 9.   **5,** je; for the position
of the pronoun 'me' see App. § 9, and use the verb in the Perfect, omitting,
however, the auxiliary according to App. § 22.   **6,** auf meinem Poſten zur
See.   **7,** I — more = I drew another (noch ein) bill of twenty pounds. To
draw a bill, einen Wechſel ziehen.   **8,** to come back protested, mit Proteſt
wieder zurückfommen.   **9,** I felt (ſich fühlen).   **10,** mortified — humbled,
gedemütigt; at, durch.   **11,** 'to make a promise', here ein Gelübde ablegen.
12, ever = always, ſtets.   **13,** that — bill. This clause is best changed into
a shortened subordinate clause in form of a supine: never to draw a bill again.
Place 'again' after 'never'.   **14,** without — paid, ohne auch ſicher zu ſein,
daß man ihn honorieren würde.   **15,** 'To quit', here to give up.   **16,** Offi-
zierstiſch.   **17,** To live, equivalent to *reside or dwell*, is generally rendered
by **wohnen**; but equivalent to *exist* is rendered by leben.   **18,** und lnbt
mich an die Schiffsrationen; quite, durchaus.   **19,** here ſiden.   **20,** bed

= bed-covering; Comp. n. S. 36, N. 7, *A.*   21, by these means = in (auf) this manner.   22, as — honour = in order to redeem (wieber ein'löfen) my honour.   23, to take up one's bill, feinen Wechfel bezahlen.   24, Say 'I have always endeavoured'.   25, to keep within one's means, nicht über feine Mittel hinaus leben; for six years, fechs Jahre lang.   26, We would use the superlative here; pinching, brückend.   27, 'to rise', here empor'fteigen ; to, bis zu, contracted with the Dat. of the def. art.

Section 117.

THE BLESSEDNESS[1] OF FRIENDSHIP.

I.

A[2] blessed thing it is for any[3] man or (S. 10, N. 9) woman to have a friend; one human soul whom we can trust utterly; a friend who knows the best and the worst[4] of us, and who loves us, in spite of all our faults; who will[5] speak the honest[6] truth to us, while the world flatters us to[7] our face, and laughs *at us* behind our backs; who will give[8] us counsel and reproof in the days of (S. 3, N. 2) prosperity and self-conceit; but[9] who, again, will comfort and encourage us in the days of difficulty[10], and sorrow, when the world leaves[11] us alone to[12] fight our *own* battle as we can.

If we have had the *good* fortune to win such a friend, let us do anything[13] rather[14] than lose him. We must give and forgive; live and let live. If our friend have[15] faults, we must bear[16] with them (S. 4, N. 5, *B*). We must hope all *things*, believe all *things*, endure all *things*, rather[17] than lose that most precious of all earthly possessions—a trusty[18] friend.

1, Segen, m.   2, It is a blessing.   3, every.   4, Superlative of fchlimm.   5, will speak = always speaks. Use the Present likewise with the following verbs in this passage.   6, aufrichtig.   7, ins Geficht.   8, to give counsel and reproof to a person, einem mit Rat und Tabel zur Seite ftehen; self-conceit, Selbfttäufchung, f.—The adverbial clause 'in the days—conceit' stands after the rel. pron. and the Dat. 'us' (App. § 9).   9, but — again, ter uns aber auch.   10, Prüfung.   11, 'to leave a person alone', here einen imftich laffen.   12, und wir unfern Kampf, fo gut wir fönnen, allein anszufechten haben.   13, all.   14, um ihn nur nicht zu verlieren.   15, has.   16, to bear a thing, Gebuld mit etwas haben.   17, lieber, which place before the last 'all'.   18, zuverläffig.

Section 118.

THE BLESSEDNESS OF FRIENDSHIP.

II.

And a friend once won (S. 7, N. 3, *A*) need[1] never be lost, if we will only be trusty and true ourselves. Friends may[2] part, not merely in body, but in spirit, for a while. In the bustle of (S. 3, N. 2) business and the accidents of life, they may lose[3] sight of each other for years (S. 115, N. 4); and[4] more—they[5] may begin to differ in their success in life, in their opinions, in their habits, and *there* may be, for a time[6], coldness and estrangement between them: but not for ever, if each will be but trusty and true.

For then[7], according to[8] the beautiful figure of the poet, they will be like two ships which set sail[9] at morning from the same port, *and* ere[10] nightfall lose sight of each other, and[11] go each on its own course, and at its own pace, for many days, through many storms and seas; and[12] yet meet again, and[13] find themselves lying side by side in the same haven, when the long voyage is past.—CHARLES KINGSLEY, "THE WATER OF LIFE."

1, need — lost = we need (brauchen) never to lose.   2, may = can, after which place the adverbial clause 'for a while', auf furze Zeit; the verb 'part', which is equivalent to 'be separated' should stand at the end of the whole passage; 'in body', förperlich; 'in spirit', geiftig.   3, to lose sight of each other, sich aus dem Gesicht verlieren.   4, ja noch mehr.   5, Say 'it is possible that their success in life, their opinions, their habits begin to differ (differieren)'.   6, for a time, eine Zeit lang, which place after 'and'; 'may', here mag; 'be', here = exist, bestehen.   7, Here follow copula and subject according to App. § 14.   8, according to, nach; figure, Bild, n.; to be like, gleichen, which governs the Dat.   9, to set sail aus segeln.   10, ere nightfall, vor Dunkelwerden.   11, Say 'and of which each through many storms and upon many seas (Meer, n.) for days pursues its own course (Richtung, f.) and its own pace (Lauf, m.)'.   12, and — again, welche aber dennoch wieder zusammentreffen.   13, Say 'and find that they lie after the long voyage (Seefahrt, f.) side by side (neben einander) in the same haven'.

Section 119.

DO GOOD IN YOUR OWN SPHERE OF ACTION[1].

I.

"I want to be at work[2] in the world," said Tom, "and not dawdling away[3] three years at Oxford."

"What do you mean[4] by 'at work in the world?'" said the master, with[5] his lips close to his saucerful of tea, and peering at Tom over it.

"Well, I mean real work; one's[6] profession, whatever[7] one will really have to do, and make one's living by. I want to be doing some real good, feeling (S. 30. N. 4) that I am not only at play[8] in the world," answered Tom, rather[9] puzzled to find out himself what he really did mean.

"You are mixing up two very different things in your head, I[10] think, Brown," said the master, putting down[11] (S. 111, N. 6) the empty saucer, "and you ought to get clear[12] about them (S. 4, N. 5, B). You[13] talk of 'working to get your living' and 'doing some real good in the world' in the same breath."

1, Wirfungsfreis, m.: your = thy.   2, to be at work = to do something.   3, to dawdle away, vergeuten.   4, mean = understand; by, unter; use the 2nd pers. sing.   5, Die Lippen an den Mund der vollen Untertaffe fetzend: to peer at a person, auf einen blicken; over it, darüber weg.   6, jemandes.   7, whatever (das was) one must really do to make one's living (feinen Unterhalt verdienen).   8, at play = for play (zum Spielen).   9, Say 'somewhat puzzled (verlegen) at (über) the meaning (Sinn, m.) of his words'.　　10, The words 'I think, Brown' are best placed at the head of the passage; Comp. S. 64, N. 11; to mix up, vermengen.　　11, auf den Tisch stellen.　　12, to get clear about a thing, sich über etwas klar werden. I cannot get clear about that, ich kann mir darüber nicht klar werden; — ought = should.　　13, Use the 2nd pers. sing., and read carefully S. 1, N. 3, and S. 87, N. 6, which will enable you to construe this passage. The adverbial clause 'in the same breath' (= in one breath) must be placed after the predicate 'talk'; to talk of a thing, von etwas sprechen.

Section 120.

DO GOOD IN YOUR OWN SPHERE OF ACTION.

II.

Now [1], you may be getting a good living in a profession, and yet doing no good *at all* in the world, but (S. 6, N. 10) quite [2] the contrary. Keep [3] the latter before you as your one object, and you [4] will be right whether you make a living [5] or not; but [6] if you dwell on the other, you'll very likely drop [7] into mere money-making, and let [8] the world take care of itself, for good or evil. Don't be in a hurry [9] about finding your work in the world *for yourself;* you are not old enough to (S. 19, N. 7) judge for yourself yet, but just [10] look about you in the place you find yourself in, and try (S. 51, N. 13) to make things [11] a little better and honester there. You'll [12] find plenty to keep your hand in at Oxford, or wherever else you [may] go. And [13] don't be led away to think this part of the world important, and that unimportant. Every corner of the world is important. No man knows whether this *part* or that part is [14] most so, but every man may [15] do some honest work in his own corner.— THOMAS HUGHES, "TOM BROWN'S SCHOOL DAYS."

1, Now — getting, Du kannst dir nun aber vielleicht... verdienen.　　2, quite = just, gerade.　　3, Say 'Keep the last part of your sentence as your principal aim (Hauptzweck, m.) before your eyes (vor Augen)'.　　4, Say 'you will do right'.　　5, Insert dabei after 'living'.　　6, Say 'but if you have only the other (to agree with 'part') before your eyes'.　　7, to drop into mere money-making, in bloße Geldmacherei verfallen.　　8, to let the world take care of itself for good or evil, die Welt im Guten und im Bösen sich selbst überlassen.　　9, to be in a hurry, sich beeilen; about finding = to find (S. 1, N. 3).　　10, 'just', here nur, which place after verb and pronoun; in the place, an der Stelle; to find oneself, sich befinden.　　11, 'things', here = life, with def. art., after which place the adv. 'there'; honester = more virtuous.　　12, The clause 'at Oxford — go' is best placed at the head of the whole passage; to keep your hand in = to do.　　13, And — away, laß dich auch nicht dazu verleiten; to think a thing important, eine Sache für wichtig halten.　　14, is most so = is most important.— **When the superlative is used as a predicate, it is generally preceded by am** (the preposition an contracted with the definite article, dative case singular, masculine), **and takes the dative termination en**; as — This matter is not important, but that is *most important*, diese Sache ist nicht wichtig, aber jene ist am wichtigsten.　　15, may — corner = can in his own corner do *something* good.

Section 121.

THE STATE[1] OF IRELAND.

(Conclusion of a Speech delivered[2] in the House of Commons
in March 1868.)

I.

We must all endeavour to get[3] rid of passion in[4] discussing this church
question, which[5], I am sorry to say, is, of all others, the most calculated
to create passion. We are[6] all, I believe, of one religion. I do not
know (S. 51, N. 13), but I suppose there[7] will come a time in the history
of the world, when men will be astonished[8] that Catholic[9] and Protes-
tant, Churchman[10] and Nonconformist[11], had[12] so much animosity and
suspicion against each other.

I[13] *accept and* believe in a very grand passage which I once met[14] with
in the writings of the illustrious founder of the colony and (S. 10, N. 9)
state *of* Pennsylvania, that[15] " the humble[16], meek, merciful, just, pious,
and devout souls are[6] everywhere of[6] one religion ; and when death[17]
(S. 3, N. 2) has taken off the mask, they will know[18] one another, though
the diverse liveries[19] they wear make[20] them strangers."

1, Zustand, m. **2,** to deliver a speech, eine Rede halten. Construe according
to S. 7, N. 3, *A*; the House of Commons, das Haus der Gemeinen. **3,** to
get rid of passion, sich der Leidenschaftlichkeit enthalten. **4,** in discussion =
when we discuss (besprechen). **5,** welche leider mehr als jede andere dazu angethan
ist, die Leidenschaften zu erregen. **6,** are = have; of one = the same.
Commence the passage with 'I believe'. **7,** there — time, es wird einst ...
eine Zeit kommen. **8,** to be astonished at a thing, sich über etwas wundern.
Comp. S. 87, N. 6. **9,** Use the pl. with this and the three following
nouns. **10,** = members of the English Church. **11,** Nonkonformisten.
12, to have animosity, Feindschaft hegen. **13,** Say ' I believe in (an, with
Acc.) *the* following sublime utterance (Äußerung, f.) '. **14,** met with = read.
15, The passage ' that — religion ' will be much improved by substituting the
adverb ' nämlich : ' (viz.) for the conjunction ' that '. **16,** die Bescheidenen.
17, After ' death ' insert the pron. ' ihnen ', which will make the reading much
clearer ; auxiliary ' has ' may be omitted according to App. § 22. **18,** sich
einander erkennen. **19,** Use the pl. of Gewand, n. **20,** make them
strangers, sie hienieden unter einander entfremden.

Section 122.

THE STATE OF IRELAND.

II.

Let us act in this spirit, and our work is[1] easy. The noble lord (S. 5,
N. 2), towards[2] the conclusion of his speech, spoke of the cloud which is
at present hanging[3] over Ireland. It is a dark and heavy cloud, and
its darkness expands[4] over the feelings of men in all parts of the British
Empire. But[5] there is a consolation that we may all take to ourselves.
An inspired king, bard, and prophet has left[6] us words which[7] are not
only the expression of a fact, but we may take them as the utterance
of a prophecy. He says: " To[8] the upright there arises light in the
darkness."

Let us try in this matter to be upright[9].   Let us try to be just, and
that cloud will [10] be dispelled ; the dangers which we see will vanish ;
and we [11] may have the happiness of leaving[6] (S. 1, N. 3) to our children
the heritage of an honourable citizenship in a united and prosperous [12]
empire.—THE RIGHT HON. JOHN BRIGHT.

1, is easy = will be easy for us (Dat. of persn. pron.).   2, an, contr. with
the dat. of the def. art.   3, ſchweben.   4, ſich erſtreᵈen.   5, Say
' But one consolation we can all gather from it '. To gather, entnehmen; from.
aus. Read S. 4, N. 5, *B.*   6, hinterlaſſen, insep. comp. str. v.   7, Say
' which not merely designate (bezeichnen) a fact (S. 115, N. 2), but (S. 6, N. 10)
which we may (=can) also take (hin'nehmen) as a prophecy (read App. § 18)'.
8, " Für den Gerechten erhebt ſich ein Licht in der Finſternis ".   9, I think there
is but the adj. ' gerecht ' to render both ' upright ' and ' just ' in the underlying
sense.   10, wird ſich verteilen.   11, we may have = we shall perhaps
have ; happiness = joy.   12, prosperous, glücklich ; empire = state.

Section 123.

DR. GUTHRIE ON RAGGED SCHOOLS[1].

I.

The [2] interest I have been led to take in the Ragged School movement is an example of how, in Providence, a man's destiny—his course
of life, like that of a river—may be determined and affected by very
trivial circumstances.   It is rather [3] curious—at least it is interesting for
me to [4] remember—that (S. 66, N. 15) *it was* by a picture I was first [5]
led to take an interest in ragged schools—by a picture in an old, obscure[6], decaying burgh [7] that stands on the shores of the Frith of Forth,
the birth-place (S. 53, N. 9) of[8] Thomas Chalmers.   I went[9] to see
this place many years ago, and, going (S. 55, N. 1) into an inn for [10] refreshment, I found the room covered (App. § 1) with pictures of shep-
herdesses with their crooks, and   sailors in [11] holiday attire, not [12]
particularly interesting.   But above the chimney-piece there [13] was a
large print [14], more [15] respectable than its neighbours, which [16] represented
a cobbler's room.

1, Doꜩtor Guthrie über die Schulen für verwahrloſte Kinder.—Sogenannte ' Ragged
Schools ' exiſtieren in Deutſchland wohl nicht, und zwar aus dem einfachen Grunde, weil
wir ſie bisher nicht nötig hatten   2, This passage requires an altogether
different construction. Say ' The circumstances which led me (welche mich
dahin führten) to interest myself for the establishment of schools for neglected
children, are an example of (davon) how through Providence (durch die Verſe-
hung) the fate of a man (Menſch)—his course of life (S. 76, N. 22, *B*, 1) like
(gleich, with dat.) that of a river — can be determined and affected (beeinfluſt)
by very trivial (geringfügig) circumstances '. For the position of the verbs read
App. §§ 16-20.   3, ' rather ', here = not *a* little.   4, to remember,
mich daran zu erinnern.   5, zuerſt.   6, obscure = unknown.   7, ' burgh ',
here Flecken, m. ; the relat. clause ' that — Forth ' may be elegantly rendered
attributively, thus : am Uſer des Frith of Forth belegen, which last word inflect
correctly and place before the qualified noun ' burgh '.   8, ven.   9, went
to see = visited ; place, Ort, m. ; the adverbial clause of time is best placed at
the head of the passage.   10, Say ' to (= in order to) refresh myself '.

11, in holiday attire, im Feſtanzuge. **12,** Insert '*which were*'. **13,** there was = hung. **14,** print, Holzſchnitt, m.; or Kupferſtich, m. **15,** Supply 'which was'; 'respectable', here = tolerable, erträglich. **16,** Since we commenced the preceding clause with a relative pronoun, it need not be repeated here. Substitute the conj. 'and' for 'which'; a cobbler's room = the workshop of a cobbler.

Section 124.

DR. GUTHRIE ON RAGGED SCHOOLS.

II.

The[1] cobbler was there himself, spectacles[2] on nose, an old shoe between his (S. 43, N. 9) knees, the massive[3] forehead and firm mouth indicating[4] great determination of character, and, beneath his bushy eyebrows, benevolence[5] gleamed out on a number of poor ragged boys and girls who stood at their lessons round the busy cobbler. My curiosity was awakened; and in the inscription I read how this man, John Pounds, a cobbler in Portsmouth, took[6] pity on the multitude of[7] poor ragged children left[8] by ministers and magistrates, *and* ladies and gentlemen, to go to ruin in the streets—how[9], like a good shepherd, he gathered in these wretched[10] outcasts—how he had trained[11] them to God and the world—and how[12], while earning his daily bread by[13] the sweat of his brow, he had rescued[14] from misery and saved to[15] society not less than five hundred of these gentlemen[16]. I felt[17] ashamed of myself. I[18] felt reproved for the little I had done. My feelings[19] were touched. I was astonished at the man's achievements; and I[20] well remember, in[21] the enthusiasm of the moment, saying to my companion (and I have seen in my cooler and calmer moments no reason for[22] unsaying the saying): " That man is[23] an honour to humanity, and deserves the greatest monument ever[24] raised within the shores of Britain."

1, The —himself, Da ſaß der Schuhflicker, wie er lebte und lebte. **2,** spectacles, bie Brille; on, auf, with the def. art. **3,** broad. **4,** indicating = gave evidence of (zeugen ven). **5,** benevolence — cobbler = shone forth (erglanzen) a pair *of* benevolent eyes with which he looked (bliden) upon a number (Anzahl, f.) *of* poor, ragged (zerlumpt) boys and girls who learned their lessons (Aufgabe, f.) and stood around the busy (= industrious) cobbler. To stand around a person, um einen herumſtehen. **6,** to take pity on a person, ſich jemandes erbarmen, with gen. **7,** Use the gen. of the adjectives. **8,** left — streets = which ministers (Geiſtliche) and magistrates (Obrigkeit, f.) had left (überlaſſen) to their ruin in (auf) the streets. Read App. § 17. **9,** After 'how' follows the subject 'he' according to S. 66, N. 15. **10,** wretched = unfortunate; gathered in = assembled around himself, um ſich her verſammelte. **11,** to train, erziehen; to, zur. **12,** und wie er ſie, während er . . . verdiente. **13,** by — brow, im Schweiße ſeines Angeſichtes, which place after 'daily bread'. **14,** to rescue from misery, aus dem Elend ziehen. The auxiliary verb, which must be used in the Subjunctive, according to App. §§ 28 and 30. may be omitted in the intermediate clauses of this long period, and placed but once at the end of the entire passage. **15,** Use the dat. of the def. art. **16,** The word 'gentlemen' is best used in its unaltered form in this passage. It should be placed in inverted commas. **17,** to feel ashamed of oneself, ſich beſchämt fühlen. **18,** Say 'The little (was) I had done was to me (mir) a reproach'.

19, feelings = heart.   **20,** I well remember = I know yet very well.   **21,** Say 'that I said in the enthusiasm of the moment', etc.   **22,** bas Gesagte zu widerrufen.   **23,** macht ber Menschheit Ehre.   **24,** = which ever (je) has been raised within the British Isles.

Section 125.

DR. GUTHRIE ON RAGGED SCHOOLS.

III.

I[1] took up that man's history, and *I* found it animated by[2] the spirit of[3] Him who[4] had "compassion on the multitude." John Pounds was a clever man besides[5]; and, like[6] Paul, if he could not win a poor boy in (auf) any other way, he won him by art.   He[7] would be seen chasing a ragged boy along the quays, and compelling him to come to[8] school, not by (burch) the power[9] of a policeman, but by the power of a hot potato.   He knew the love an[10] Irishman has for a potato; and[11] John Pounds might be seen holding under a boy's nose a *very* hot potato, and[12] wearing a coat as ragged as the boy himself wore.   When the day comes when[13] honour shall be done to whom honour is due[14], I[15] can fancy the crowd of those whose fame poets (S. 3, N. 2) have sung[16], and to whose memory monuments have been raised, dividing[17] like a wave, and[18] passing the great, and the noble, and the mighty of the land, this poor, obscure old man stepping forward and receiving the especial notice of Him who said: "Inasmuch[19] as ye did it to one of the least of those, ye did it also to me."—DR. GUTHRIE.

1, I followed up (verfolgen) the life of this man.   **2,** ren.   **3,** of Him, bessen.   **4,** who (ber ba) had compassion with the poor.   **5,** auch, placed after the verb.   **6,** wie Paulus, which place after 'him'; by art = through cunning (List).   **7,** He — seen = One saw him often; to chase a person, einem nachlaufen.   Read S. 78, N. 14, 2.   **8,** zur Schule.   **9,** Macht, f. **10,** Say 'of an I. for a hot potato'.   **11,** and one could often see how J. P. held a hot potato under a boy's nose.—To hold a potato under one's nose, einem eine Kartoffel unter die Nase halten.   **12,** and (insert here babei) wore as ragged a coat as the boy himself.   **13,** an tem Ehre erwiesen wird. **14,** to be due, gebühren.   **15,** Say 'then I see (bann sehe ich im Geiste) how all those', etc.   **16,** besingen.   **17,** sich gleich einer Woge auseinandertheilen. **18,** and — said = see, how this poor, unknown old man steps forward (hervor= treten) and passes by (an einem vorüberschreiten) the great, noble and mighty of the land, and is received (S. 2, N. 1) with especial attention by Him (von Ihm, which place after the conj. 'and') who (insert ba) said.   **19,** Say 'What you (ihr) have done to the least (tem Geringsten) of (unter) these, that have you done to me'.

Section 126.

SHYLOCK[1] MEDITATING REVENGE.

If it will feed[2] nothing else (S. 27, N. 8), it will[3] feed my revenge. He has disgraced[4] me, and hindered[5] me of half a million! laughed[6] at my losses, mocked[7] at my gains, scorned my nation, thwarted[8] my bargains, cooled[9] my friends, heated[10] my enemies! And[11] what's his reason? I am a Jew! Has[12] not a Jew eyes? Has not a Jew hands, organs, senses, affections,[13] passions? Is (S. 2, N. 1) he not fed with[14] the same food, hurt with the same weapon, subject[15] to the same diseases, healed[16] by the same means, warmed[17] and cooled by the same summer and winter, as a Christian *is?* If[18] you stab us, do we not bleed? If you tickle us, do we not laugh? If you poison us, do we not die? and[19] if you wrong us, shall we not revenge? If we are like[20] you in the rest (S. 27, N. 8), we will resemble you in that[21]! If a Jew wrong a Christian, what[22] is his humility? Revenge[23]. If a Christian wrong a Jew, what[24] should his sufferance be by Christian example? Why[25], revenge! The villany you teach (S. 42, N. 4) me I[26] will execute; and[27] it shall go hard but[28] I will better the instruction.—WILLIAM SHAKESPEARE, "THE MERCHANT OF VENICE."

1, Styled auf Rache sinnend. 2, feed = satisfy. 3, Insert the adv. nach after the subject. 4, disgraced = insulted, beschimpft. 5, einen um etwas bringen. 6, Supply 'has' to begin this clause; at, über, with acc. 7, to mock at a thing, etwas verspotten, v. tr.; 'my gains' may be rendered by meinen Profit. 8, crossed (durchkreuzen) my enterprises. 9, cooled = made indifferent. 10, heated = incited (aufreizen). 11, And for what (aus welchem) reason? 12, As a rule the English 'not a' or 'not an' is best rendered by the indef. numeral kein. Say 'Has a Jew no eyes'? 13, feelings. 14, ren. 15, Say 'is he not subject to', etc.; to be subject to a thing, einer Sache unterwerfen sein. 16, This verb requires again the passive voice, and copula and subject must be supplied; by, durch. 17, Say 'not warmed', the auxiliary need not be repeated here. 18, Begin with the principal sentence in this and the two following passages. 'You', here ihr. 19, Say 'and we shall not revenge ourselves, if you wrong us (Unrecht zufügen)'. 20, to be like, gleichen, with dat.; in the rest, in allem übrigen. 21, in that, darin. 22, what is = in what (wherein) consists. 23, Zu ter Rache. 24, in what (wherein) shall according to the Christian example consist his sufferance (Dulten, n., or Duldung, f.)? 25, Nun, doch wohl in der Rache! 26, ich will sie anrechten. 27, and — hard, und es müßte seltsam zugehen. 28, but — instruction = if I should not even (noch, after 'not') excel ('should excel' Imperf. of the Subj. of übertreffen; App. § 33) my teachers.

Section 127.

CHARACTER[1] OF CHARLEMAGNE.

1.

In[2] analyzing the character of heroes it is hardly possible to separate altogether the[3] share of fortune from their own[4]. The epoch made[5] by Charlemagne in the history of the world, the illustrious families which[6] prided themselves in him as their progenitor, the[7] very legends of romance, which are full of his fabulous exploits, have[8] cast a lustre around his head, and testify[9] the greatness that has embodied itself in his name. None[10], indeed, of Charlemagne's wars can be compared with the Saracenic victories of Charles Martel; but[11] that was a contest for freedom, his for conquest; and[12] fame is more partial to successful aggression than to patriotic resistance.

1, Say 'The character of Charles the Great (S. 53, N. 9)'. Karl der Große, König der Franken und später römischer Kaiser, wurde am 2. April 742, wahrscheinlich zu Aachen, geboren und war der Sohn Pipins des Kleinen und der Enkel Karl Martells, dessen Siege über die Sarazenen in dieser Lektion erwähnt werden. Nach dem Tode seines königlichen Vaters (768) trat er gemeinschaftlich mit seinem Bruder Karlmann die Regierung an, ward aber schon im Jahre 771, durch den Tod seines Bruders und die Ausschließung der Söhne desselben vom Throne, Alleinherrscher über alle Franken, von den Pyrenäen bis zum Niederrhein und zum Meere, auch in Deutschland über die Bayern, Thüringer und Alamannen. Durch zahlreiche Kriege erweiterte er jedoch die Grenzen seines Reiches sehr bald, und zwar nördlich bis zur Eider, südlich bis zum Ebro und nach Unteritalien, und östlich bis zur Saale, dem Böhmerwalde und der Theiß, bis er im Jahre 800 vom Papste Leo III. im St. Peters Dom zu Rom feierlich als römischer Kaiser gekrönt wurde. Er starb am 28. Januar 814. In Karl dem Großen, wie ihn die Geschichte mit Recht benannt hat, war der Begründer der staatlichen Ordnung für die gesammte Germanenwelt erschienen. Seine Lebensaufgabe, die ihm von Anfang an feststand, war, alle deutschen Stämme in den einen fränkischen Reichsverband und in die eine christliche Kirche zusammenzufassen. Dem besten Teile nach ist sie ihm gelungen, und so hat er der nachfolgenden Zeit, dem ganzen Mittelalter, das Gepräge seines Geistes aufgedrückt. In niemand stellt sich die echt deutsche Art der alten Zeit so herrlich dar, als in ihm. Als er die Krone erhielt, zählte er erst 26 Jahre, stand also in der Kraft und Blüte der Jugend. Er war von gewaltiger Körpergröße, eine Heldengestalt, und von nicht minder gewaltiger Körperkraft, so daß er beim fröhlichen Waidwerk den Kampf mit dem wilden Auerochsen in den Ardennenwäldern wie ein Spiel annahm; überhaupt von jener Lust an Krieg und Gefahr, wie sie den abenteuernden Heerkönigen der Völkerwanderung eigen gewesen war; in den wichtigen Dingen der Welt von jener Härte und Rücksichtslosigkeit, die noch keinem großen Manne gefehlt; und ebenso im kleinen Leben des Hauses und des täglichen Verkehrs von jener Milde, Heiterkeit und Frische des Gemütes, die so gerne Gefährten echter Größe sind. Alle diese Eigenschaften hatte er mit seinem damaligen Volke gemein; was ihn aber über dasselbe erhob, das war der weitschauende Geist, der dem alten Römertum das Vorbild eines weltumfassenden Staates abgelernt hatte, und der dies Muster ohne knechtische Nachahmung dem so ganz andern germanischen Wesen anzupassen wußte. Und zwar ist dieser Geist, der sich in ihm offenbarte, um so wundervoller, weil niemand nachweisen kann, wie er sich gebildet, und wer ihn so gelehrt und erzogen hat. Aus dem Dunkel seiner Zeit geht er, im eigenen Lichte leuchtend, auf.   2, Beim Analysieren von Heldencharakteren.   3, the share (Anteil, m.) of fortune = of a happy (günstig) fate (Geschick, n.).   4, Supply 'individuality'; altogether = quite.   5, made, geschaffen; by, von. Use the attributive construction as explained in S. 7, N. 3, *A.*   6, Say 'which called him with pride their progenitor'.   7, Say 'even the romantic legends'.   8, Say 'have crowned his head with glory (Ruhm, m.)'. In elevated diction 'head' is rendered by 'Haupt', n.   9, bezeugen.   10, Say 'It is indeed (wohl) true that none of Charles's wars can be compared to (mit) the victories of Charles Martel over the Saracens'.   11, but — conquest = but these were contests for freedom (Freiheitskämpfe), whilst his (to agree with 'wars') were contests for conquest (Eroberungskämpfe).   12, Say 'and fame (S. 3, N. 2) has more partiality (Vorliebe, f.) for successful aggression (Angriff, m.)', etc.

Section 128.

CHARACTER OF CHARLEMAGNE.

II.

As *a* scholar [1], his acquisitions [2] were little superior [3] to those of his unrespected son; and in [4] several points of view the glory of Charlemagne might be [5] extenuated by an analytical dissection. But [6] rejecting a mode of judging equally uncandid and fallacious, we shall find that he possessed in everything that grandeur of [7] conception which distinguishes extraordinary minds [8]. Like Alexander, he seemed born [9] for universal innovation [10]; in a life restlessly active [11], we see him reforming (S. 78, N. 14, *B*) the coinage [12], and establishing the legal divisions of money [13]; gathering [14] about him the learned of every country, founding schools *and* collecting libraries; interfering [15], but with the tone of a King, in religious controversies; aiming [16], though prematurely, at the formation of a naval force; attempting [17], for [18] the sake of commerce, the magnificent [19] enterprise of uniting (S. 1, N. 3) the Rhine and [20] Danube; and [21] meditating to mould the [22] discordant codes of Roman and barbarian laws into one uniform system.—HALLAM, "THE STUDENT'S MIDDLE AGES."

1, Scholar = 'pupil or schoolboy' is rendered by Schüler; = 'student' by Student, and = 'learned man' by Gelehrter. The last sense is applicable here. 2, acquisitions = knowledge. 3, superior, überlegen, with dat. unrespected – unnoticed. 4, in many respects, in mancher Hinsicht, after which place 'might'. 5, be — dissection, durch eine eingehende Untersuchung geschmälert werden. 6, Say 'But if we reject an equally (eine ebenso) partial (parteiische) and (als) fallacious (trügerisch) mode of judging (Beurteilungsweise, f.)'. 7, Use the gen. of the def. art. 8, 'mind', here Geist, m. 9, born = created; 'universal', here weitumfassend. 10, innovations = reforms. 11, All parts qualifying a noun must be placed before it. 12, Münzsystem, n. 13, form a comp. according to S. 36, N. 7, *A*; both nouns are combined in the sing. 14, Complete the clause by saying: 'we see him gathering', etc.,— to gather, versammeln; about, um; of every country = of all countries. 15, interfering in religious controversies, sich mit religiösen Streitigkeiten befassen; after which place the clause 'but — King', and supply 'always' after 'but'; 'tone', here = dignity. 16, This sentence should likewise be introduced by supplying 'We see him', after which place 'though prematurely' (zu frühzeitig); to aim, streben (nach). 17, Begin this clause with 'see him'. 18, for the sake of, um . . . willen, with Gen. 19, attempt the magnificent enterprise, ten großartigen Versuch machen. 20, and = with the. 21, und daran sinnen. 22, the — laws, die sich widersprechenten römischen und sonstigen Gesetze; uniform, einheitlich; to mould, verschmelzen.

Section 129.

GOETHE'S DAILY LIFE AT WEIMAR.

I.

Passing through an ante-chamber, where, in cupboards, stand his mineralogical collections, we enter (App. § 14) the study, a low-*roofed*. narrow room (Gemach, n.), somewhat dark (S. 128, N. 11), for it is (S. 2, N. 1) lighted only through two tiny windows, and [1] furnished with a simplicity quite touching to behold.

In the centre [2] stands a plain oval table of unpolished oak [3]. No armchair is to be seen, no sofa, nothing which (S. 3. N. 7) speaks [4] of comfort. A plain hard chair has [5] beside it the basket in which he used [6] to place his handkerchief. Against [7] the wall, on the right, is a [8] long pear-tree table, with book-shelves, on which stand lexicons and manuals. Here hangs a pincushion, venerable in [9] dust, with the visiting-cards, and other trifles which[10] death had made sacred. Here[11] also a medallion of Napoleon, with this[12] circumscription : " Scilicet[13] immenso superest ex nomine multum." On the side-wall again, a book-case, with some works of poets. On the wall to the left is a long desk of soft wood, at[14] which he was wont[6] to write. A sheet of paper with notes of[15] contemporary history is fastened near[16] the door, and behind[17] this door tables[18] of music and geology.

1, and — behold = and is (ift) furnished with an almost (faft) touching simplicity.   2, middle.   3, (Eichenholz, n.; the oak = *oak-tree*, is rendered by Eiche, f., or Eichbaum, m.   4, speaks = points to; to point to a thing, auf etwas deuten.   5, has beside it = stands beside.   6, used to place, zu legen pflegte. 'To use', when employed *transitively*, is generally rendered by brauchen, gebrauchen, benutzen, anwenden, and verbrauchen, whilst *intransitively* it is rendered by pflegen or gewohnt fein, in the sense of 'to be accustomed to', 'to be in the habit of', 'to be wont to do'.   7, Against = on; on (*or* to) the right, rechts; on (*or* to) the left, links.   8, ein langer Tisch von Birnbaumholz. 9, in dust = through its age.   10, which — sacred, die durch den Tod geheiligt find.   11, Insert 'is' or 'hangs'.   12, this = the.   13, Scilicet — multum, Little honour is derived from a great name.   14, at, an. 15, über die (or aus der) Tagesgeschichte.   16, in der Nähe der Thür; to fasten, anheften.   17, an; supply 'hang' after 'door'.   18, unmusikalische und geologische Tabellen.

Section 130.

GOETHE'S DAILY LIFE AT WEIMAR.

II.

The same door leads into a bedroom; it is a[1] closet with a window. A simple bed, an arm-chair by[2] its side, and a tiny washing-table, with a small white basin *on it* and a sponge, is[3] all the furniture.

From the other side of the study we enter the library, which should[4] rather be called a lumber-room of books. Rough[5] deal shelves hold the books with[6] bits of paper, on which are written " philosophy," " history," " poetry," etc., to mark the classification. He rose at seven [o'clock], sometimes[7] earlier, after a sound *and* prolonged[8] sleep ; for like Thorwaldsen[9] he had a "talent for sleeping," only surpassed (S. 7, N. 3, *B*) by[10] his talent for[11] continuous work. Till eleven he worked without *any* interruption. A cup of chocolate was then[12] brought, and[13] he resumed work till one. At two he dined. This[14] meal was the important meal of the day. His appetite was immense. Even on *the* days when[15] he complained of not being hungry, he ate much more than most men. Puddings, sweets[16], and cakes were always welcome. He sat[17] a long while over his wine, chatting[18] gaily to some friend or other—for he never dined alone—or to one of the actors, whom he had often with[19] him, after dinner, to read over their parts, and to take[20] his instructions.

1, ein kleines Kabinett.   2, by its side = before it, davor.   3, is — furniture = form (bilden) the whole furniture (Mobiliar, n.).   4, should rather be called = could (Impf. Subj.) much rather (vielmehr) be called. The auxiliary

' could ' stands last of all, whilst ' called ' has the first place of the three verbs, which are used in the Passive Voice. 5, Say ' Upon simple (ſchlicht) deal boards stand the books '. 6, The passage ' with — classification ' may be simplified by saying: ' on (an) which (benen) bits of paper with the labels (Aufſchrift, f.) . . . indicate (bezeichnen) a certain order '. The abbreviation ' etc.' corresponds to the German ' u. ſ. w.', which is the short for ' und ſo weiter ', and so on. 7, Insert auch after ' sometimes '. 8, long. 9, Albert Bertel Thorwaldſen, berühmter bäniſcher Bildhauer, wurde im Jahre 1770 auf ber See zwiſchen Joland und Kopenhagen geboren, war ein Schüler ber Kunſtakademie zu Kopenhagen und lebte von 1796 bis 1838 in Rom, kehrte aber bann nach ſeiner Heimat zurück, wo er am 24. März 1844 ſtarb. Thorwaldſen iſt ber Schöpfer zahlreicher idealer Werke im echten klaſſiſchen Geiſte altgriechiſcher Kunſt, welche meiſtens ber antiken Mythologie, zum Teil aber auch ber chriſtlichen Religionsanſchauung entlehnt ſind. Sein Name wird unſterblich ſein, denn er lebt ber Welt in ſeinen unvergleichlichen Werken fort, bie zu Kopenhagen von ſeinen begeiſterten Landsleuten in einem beſonders bazu gebauten Muſeum, welches ben Namen bes weltberühmten Künſtlers trägt, zur Bewunderung ber Nachwelt ausgeſtellt ſind. 10, durch. 11, zur unausgeſetzten Arbeit. 12, Place the adv. ' then ' at the head of the sentence, and supply ' for him ' (ihm) after the auxiliary. **As a rule the person or persons for whose benefit an action is done must be indicated in German;** as — I will buy a hat, ich will mir einen Hut kaufen. 13, and — one = whereupon he worked again till one o'clock. 14, This — day = This was his principal meal. Form a comp. n. according to S. 36, N. 7, *A*. 15, when (wo) he complained of (über) want (Mangel, m.) of (an) appetite. 16, Süßigkeiten. 17, To sit a long while over one's wine, lange beim Wein ſitzen. 18, chatting = and chatted (plaudern); to some friend or other = to (mit) this or that friend. 19, bei ſich ; after — parts = to (= in order to) read to him their parts (Rollen) after dinner (nach Tiſche, which place after the conj. um and the dat. of the persn. pron.). To read, verʼleſen. 20, To take instructions, Anweiſungen entgeʼgennehmen.

Section 131.

GOETHE'S DAILY LIFE AT WEIMAR.

III.

He was fond of wine (S. 3, N. 2) and drank daily his two or three bottles. Lest [1] this statement should convey a false impression, I hasten to [2] recall to the reader's recollection the very different habits of our fathers in respect to drinking. It was no [3] unusual thing to be called " a three-bottle-man" in those days in England, when [4] the three bottles were *of* port or Burgundy; and Goethe, a [5] Rhinelander, accustomed from boyhood to wine, drank a wine which his English contemporaries would have called water. / The [6] amount he drank never did more than exhilarate him, and never made him unfit for work or for society. Over [7] his wine, then, he sat some hours ; no *such thing as* dessert was seen upon his table in those days ; not even the customary coffee after dinner. His mode [8] of living was extremely simple ; and even when persons [9] of very moderate circumstances burned wax [10], two [11] poor tallow candles were all that could be seen in his rooms. In the evening he often went to the theatre, and there [12] his *customary* glass of punch was brought (S. 4, N. 4, man) at six o'clock (App. § 9). If (S. 27, N. 7) not at the theatre, he received friends at [13] home. Between eight and nine a frugal supper was laid [14], but [15] he never took anything except a little salad or preserves.

By [16] ten o'clock he was usually in bed.—G. H. Lewes, "Life of Goethe."

1, Lest — impression = In order that (Damit) this observation may (Present Subj. of mögen; read App. §§ 33 and 34) not make a false impression.—For the position of the verbs see App. § 18.   **2,** to — drinking = to remind the reader of (an) the very different (ganz andern) habits of our fathers in respect of drinking.—To transl. 'drinking' form a noun of the infinitive of the verb 'to drink', and use it with the def. art., according to S. 3, N. 2, and S. 11, N. 7.   **3,** no—thing, nichts Ungewöhnliches; in those days, damals, which place with 'in England' after 'was'.   **4,** 'when', here wo.   Notice that: **The relative conjunction 'wo' is often used in reference to time as a translation of 'when' in the sense of 'at (in *or* during) which time'**; as — Es geschah zu einer Zeit, wo (zu or in welcher) Sie abwesend waren, it happened at a time *when* you were absent.   **It is also used relatively, in reference to place, instead of a relative pronoun preceded by a preposition**; as — Kennst du das Land, wo (in welchem) die Zitronen blühen? (Goethe) Know you the land *where* (in which) the citrons bloom?   Dies ist das Haus, wo (in dem) er wohnt, this is the house where (in which) he lives.   **5,** a — wine, als Rheinländer von Jugend auf an Wein gewöhnt.   **6,** The — him = What he drank had never any (=an) other effect than (als) to exhilarate him; to exhilarate, angenehm an'regen.   **7,** So he sat for hours (stundenlang) over his (beim) wine.   **8,** Lebensweise, f.   **9,** Leute; of = in.   **10,** wax = wax candles.   **11,** two — rooms = one saw in his rooms only two poor (dürftig) tallow candles.   **12,** dahin.   **13,** bei sich zu Hause.   **14,** to lay a frugal supper, ein einfaches Abendessen auftragen; to lay the table (the cloth), den Tisch decken.   **15,** Say 'but he (himself) took (essen or genießen, S. 3, N. 8.) only a little salad or preserves'.   **16,** Um.

Section 132.

THE [1] PROGRESS IN THE ART OF PRINTING.

(Conclusion [2] of a Speech delivered at the Caxton Celebration, June 30, 1877, in London.)

I now call [3] attention, in [4] a few words, to the progress of this art. I hold *up* a volume in my (S. 43, N. 9) hand, to [5] which I beg everyone to direct his eye, because I think it [6] may be called the climax and consummation of this art.   This [7] volume is bound, as you see, and stamped with the arms of the University *of* Oxford.   It is a Bible bound [8] in a manner that commends itself to the reader—I believe [9] in every sense an excellent piece of workmanship, containing more than *one* [10] thousand pages.   Well [11], you will say: "That is very [12] commonplace, why bring it before us?"   I do so [13] in order to tell [14] you that this book sixteen hours ago did not exist—it [15] was not bound, it was not folded, it was not printed.   Since the clock struck twelve last night at [16] the University Press in Oxford, the people (man) there have printed and sent us this book.   They (man) have sent several copies [17] to [18] be distributed here in the midst of your festival.   That shows what can be done, and *that is* what has been done, and [19] it shows the state to which this great art is now happily arrived.   If [20] I began with a humiliating confession as to the small share we could claim in contributing to the early history of printing, we may [21] leave off, ladies and gentlemen, in a better spirit,

because I think that such a performance as this is [22] one that will be
admitted to be a credit in any portion of the world.　Now I will trouble
you no longer, but (S. 6, N. 10) will ask [23] you to [24] drink with me to
the memory of this most distinguished name: " To [25] the memory of [26]
William Caxton, the (S. 53, N. 9) first English printer, and a native [27] of
this our beloved country [28]."—THE RIGHT HON. W. E. GLADSTONE.

1, Die Fortschritte in der Buchdruckerkunst. **The noun 'progress' is generally
rendered by the corresponding plural form in German.**　2, Schluß
einer am 30. Juni 1877 bei Gelegenheit der Cartonfeier in Londen gehaltenen Rede.
William Caxton, der erste Buchdrucker Englands, wurde im Jahre 1412 zu Weald
in Kent geboren, wohnte aber später als Bürger und Kaufmann in London, woselbst
er auch im Jahre 1492 starb.　**3, to call a person's attention to a thing,** einen
auf etwas aufmerksam machen. **Begin with the adv. 'now', and supply the personal
object** 'Sie'.　**4,** in a = with; of = in.　**5,** = which I beg you all to look
at (betrachten, v. tr.).　**8,** it — art = we may (dürfen) consider (an'sehen) it
the climax and consummation (als die höchste Stufe der Vollendung) of (= in) this
art.　**7, Say ' As you see, this volume** (here (Einband) is stamped with the
arms', etc.　**8, bound — reader** = the binding of which must commend
(App. § 18) itself at once (sich von selbst) to the reader.　**9, Here insert 'it
is**'; sense = respect, Beziehung, f.; **piece of workmanship** = 'work of art', which
render by forming a comp. n. according to S. 36, N. 7, *A*.　**10, 'One' or
'a' before 'hundred' and 'thousand' is, as a rule, not translated in
German.**　**11, Say ' But** (which place after the copula 'will') you will
perhaps say'.　12, etwas ganz Gewöhnliches, wenn es uns noch zeigen?
**13, The English 'so' in connection with a transitive verb is generally
to be rendered by 'es'. If we want to emphasize the object, however,
we use either of the demonstrative pronouns 'das' or 'dies', and
place it at the head of the clause;** as — Do you think *so?*　Glauben Sie
es? No, I do not, Nein, das glaube ich nicht.　**14,** sagen or mit'teilen.
15, Say ' it was neither bound, nor . . . nor . . .'　**16, Render 'at the' by
the gen. of the def. art.; and place the clause 'at — Oxford' after 'clock '.
Last night,** vergangene Nacht.　**17, ' Copy ' in the signification of 'specimen '
is rendered by** Exemplar, n.; pl. e (= e); Kopie, f., **is the written copy of any
book, document or MS.**　**18, Say ' in order to distribute them here during
this festival '.**　**19, and — arrived = and** it shows the high degree (Stufe, f.) of
(der) perfection which this great art has reached now-a-days (heutzutage) (App.
§ 17).　**20, If — printing = If I began with the humiliating confession that
we in respect to** (auf) our contribution to the (zur) early (früheren) history
of the art of printing can claim (beanspruchen dürfen, which comes last) only
a small (gering) share.　**21,** may = can; leave off = conclude; spirit = mood,
Stimmung, f.; performance, Leistung, f.　**22,** is — world, überall in der Welt
mit Ehren anerkannt werden wird.　**23, ' To ask ' in the signification of
'asking a question ' is rendered by** fragen or eine Frage stellen, **but in that
of 'to request' by** bitten.　**24,** to — name = to empty your glasses with
me to the (zum) memory (Andenken) of (an) this most (höchst) distinguished
name; ('**your glasses to empty ' must be placed at the end**.)　25, Zum
Gedächtnis.　**26, Use the Anglo-Saxon genitive here.**　**27,** native = son.
28, country = fatherland.

Section 133.

ROBERT DICK, THE BAKER, GEOLOGIST, AND BOTANIST.

Not long ago, Sir Roderick Murchinson discovered at Thurso, in the
far north of Scotland, a profound [1] geologist, in the person of a baker

there [2], named Robert Dick.   When (S. 4, N. 2) Sir Roderick called upon him at [3] the bakehouse in which (S. 131, N. 4) he baked and earned his bread, Robert Dick delineated [4] *to him* by [5] means of flour upon a board, the geographical features [6] and geological phenomena of his native country, pointing [7] out its imperfections in [8] the existing maps, which [9] he had ascertained by travelling over the country in his leisure hours.   On [10] further inquiry, Sir Roderick ascertained [11] that the humble [12] individual before him was not only a capital baker and geologist, but also a first-rate [13] botanist.   " I found," said the Director-General of the Geographical Society, " to my great humiliation, that this baker [14] knew infinitely more of (S. 40, N. 9) botanical science, ay, ten times more, than I *did ;* and that there were (S. 82, N. 7) only some twenty or thirty specimens [15] of flowers which he had not collected.   Some he had obtained [16] as presents, some (=others) he had purchased, but the greater portion had been accumulated [17] by his industry, in his native county *of* Caithness ; and the specimens [18] were all arranged [19] in the most beautiful order, with [20] their scientific names affixed."—S. SMILES, " SELF-HELP."

1, gründlich.   2, fertig, which use attributively before the noun 'baker': named, namens.   3, in.   4, entwerfen, insep. comp. str. v.   5, mittels eines mit Mehl bestreuten Brettes.   6, Umrisse.   7, Say 'whereby he pointed out the imperfections'.   To point out a thing, auf etwas verweisen, insep. comp. str. v.   8, Use the gen. of the def. art.   9, which — hours = of which (woven) he had convinced himself on (auf) his travels through the country in his leisure hours (Mußestunden).   10, Nach weiterer Prüfung.   11, ascertained = learnt, erfuhr, from erfahren.   12, humble = modest; individual = man.   13, first-rate = considerable, bedeutend.   14, Here follow the words 'of — science' after which transl. the adv. 'infinitely', which is followed by 'ay (ja) ten times more' and the verb 'knew'.   15, specimens of flowers, Blumenarten.   16, To obtain a thing as present, etwas geschenkt erhalten.   17, accumulated = collected.   Where, and in what order, must the verbs be placed?   Which voice must you use?—native, heimisch.   18, Exemplar, n.; pl. e.   19, zusam'menstellen, sep. comp. w. v.   20, and the scientific names everywhere (überall) affixed (hinzu fügen), sep. comp. w. v.

Section 134.

THE GOSPEL OF WORK.

I.

Work, hard [1] work, is a blessing to [2] the soul and the character [3] of the man who works.   Young men [4] may not think so.   They [5] may say : " What [6] more pleasant than to have [7] one's fortune made for one, and [8] have nothing more before one than to enjoy life ?   What [8] more pleasant than to be idle ; or, at least, to do only what one likes, and no more than one likes ?"   But they would find themselves mistaken.   They would find that idleness makes a man [9] restless, discontented, greedy, the [10] slave of his own lusts and passions, and see, too late, that no man [3] is more to be pitied than the man [11] who has nothing to do.   Yes, thank [12] God, every morning, when you get up, that you have something to do that day which must be done, whether you like it or not.   Being [13] forced to work, and forced to do your best, will breed in [14] you temperance and self-control, diligence and strength of will, cheerfulness and content, and *a* (S. 132, N. 10) hundred virtues which the idle [15] man will never know.

1, ſchwer.　　2, für.　　3, character = dignity.　Turn 'of — works' by 'of him (deſſen) who (after which insert the adv. ꞇa) works.　　4, men = people, ꞁeute.　When 'people' signifies 'persons' in the general sense of the word, it is mostly rendered by ꞁeute.　In the signification of 'nation' it is rendered by Volf, n., corresponding to the Latin 'populus' and the French 'peuple'.　In the first signification, however, we can often translate it by the indefinite pronoun 'man', which also corresponds to the English 'they', 'we', 'you', used in a general and indefinite sense.　　5, = They say perhaps.　　6, Was giebt es.　　7, to have = to see; for one = by (von) others.　　8, Say 'with no other task than to enjoy one's life'?　　9, 'Man' is here used in the signification of 'human being', when it is generally rendered by 'der Menſch'.　　10, Read S. 102, N. 13.　　11, Use the demonstrative pron. derjenige.　　12, When the Imperative of the 2nd pers. is used in a general application, we use it either in the 2nd pers. sing. or the 2nd pers. pl. Use the 2nd pers. sing. in this case.　13, Being — best = The compulsion (Zwang, m.) to work (zur Arbeit) and the necessity to do your (= thy) best.　　14, Place 'in you' (= thee) after 'virtues', immediately before the infinitive 'breed' (= awaken, erweden).　15, the idle man, der Müſſiggänger.

Section 135.

THE GOSPEL OF WORK.

II.

The monks in olden times found it so [1].　When (S. 18, N. 6) they shut [2] themselves up from the world to worship God in [3] prayers and hymns, they found that [here follows the subject "they"], without working [4], without [5] hard work either of head or of hands, they could not [6] even be good men (S. 134, N. 9).　The [7] devil came and [8] tempted them, they said, as often as they were [9] idle. An idle monk's soul was lost, they used (S. 129, N. 6) to say, and they spoke truly.　Though they gave [10] up a large portion of [11] every day, and of every night also, to [12] prayer and worship, (S. 27, N. 8) yet [13] they found [that] they could not pray aright without work.

And "working (S. 11, N. 7) is praying," said one of the holiest of them that [14] ever lived; and he spoke truth (S. 3, N. 2); if [15] a man will but do his work for the sake of duty, which is for the sake of God.—
CHARLES KINGSLEY.

1, Turn 'it so' by 'das', which place at the head of the sentence, using the inverted construction and inserting the adv. 'auch' after the verb.　　2, to shut oneself up, ſich ab ſchließen, sep. comp. str. v. rell.　　3, turd; to worship, verehren.　　4, working = work.　　5, ohne angeſtrenate Kopf= erer Handarbeit.　6, not even, nicht einmal.　　7, The words 'They said' are best placed at the head of this passage. To translate the verbs correctly, you must carefully read App. §§ 28 and 30.　　8, and tempted them = in order to tempt them.　9, wären.　　10, 'to give up', here = to devote, widmen, with dat.　　11, of — also = of the day and of the night.　　12, dem Gebet und den Andachtsübungen.　13, yet, doch, to be placed after the subject.　　14, who ever (je) has lived.

How must the verbs be placed?   15, Begin a new period here, and say:
'When a man (S. 134, N. 9) does his work for the sake of (um . . . willen,
which governs the Gen.) his duty, (S. 27, N. 8) he does it (to agree with
'duty') for God's sake'.

Section 136.

DO NOT BE ASHAMED OF YOUR ORIGIN[1].

I.

General Bau, a German (S. 101, N. 1) officer in[1] the service of Russia,
who had contributed much to the elevation of the great Catherine[2], had[3]
orders to march to Holstein with a body of troops of which he had the
command. He was a soldier of fortune, and no one knew either his
family or his native place. |One day (S. 19, N. 2), as he was encamped
near[4] Husum, he invited the principal[5] officers to dinner.   As they were
sitting down to the table, they[6] saw a plain miller and his wife brought
into the tent, whom[7] the general had sent his aide-de-camp to seek.
The poor miller and his wife approached, trembling (S. 53, N. 12) with[8]
apprehension.   The general reconciled them to[9] their situation, and
made[10] them sit down beside him to dinner, during which he asked[11]
them a number of questions about their family.

1, Origin, Herkunft, f.; in the service of Russia, in russischen Diensten.
2, Katharina I., Kaiserin von Rußland, wurde am 15. April 1684 geboren und
war die Tochter eines lithauischen Bauers, namens Samuel Stawronski. Im Jahre
1701 wurde sie die Gattin eines schwedischen Dragoners, fiel dann bei der Einnahme
Marienburgs durch die Russen (1702) in die Hände des russischen Generals Scheremetjew,
durch den sie zum Fürsten Menschikew und endlich zum Kaiser Peter dem Großen kam.
der sich in sie verliebte und sich im Jahre 1707 heimlich mit ihr vermählen ließ. Im
eigentlicher Taufname war Martha, beim Übertritt zur griechisch katholischen Kirche
erhielt sie jedoch die Namen Katharina Alexiewna. Im Jahre 1711 gelang es ihr, indem
sie sich die Gunst des Großveziers zu gewinnen wußte, am Pruth das russische Heer durch
List aus gefährlicher Lage zu befreien, worauf sie im Jahre 1712 von Peter dem Großen
öffentlich als seine rechtmäßige Gemahlin anerkannt wurde. Sie wurde endlich im Jahre
1724 als Kaiserin feierlich gekrönt, als sie jedoch nach Peters des Großen Tode im Jahre
1725 auf Betrieb des Fürsten Menschikew als regierende Kaiserin ausgerufen wurde, überließ
sie sich einer zügellosen Lebensweise und starb am 17. Mai 1727. Sie ward Mutter dreier
Töchter, Katharina, Anna (Mutter Peters III.) und Elisabeth, der nachmaligen Kaiserin.
3, Say 'had the order'; render 'to march — command,' liter. = with an under
his command standing body of troops (Truppencorps, n.) to (S. 72, N. 4) Holstein
to march.   4, near = not far from, unweit.   5, = first,   6, = they saw that
a simple miller and his wife were brought into the tent.   7, die der General
durch seinen Adjutanten hatte holen lassen.   8, vor.   9, mit.   10, made them
sit down, ließ (or hieß, bade) sie . . . platznehmen; beside him = on his side; to
dinner, beim Essen.   11, to ask a person numerous questions, einem viele
Fragen vorlegen; about, über.

Section 137.

DO NOT BE ASHAMED OF YOUR ORIGIN.

II.

The good man told him *that* he was (App. § 28) the eldest son of a
miller, and that he had two brothers in[1] a mercantile line and a sister.

" But," said the general, " had you [2] not another brother besides the two whom you have mentioned ?" The miller told him he had another [3] brother, but [4] he went to the wars very young, and as [5] they had never heard of him, they supposed he was dead. The [6] general, reading (S. 16, N. 4) in the eyes of the officers that they were surprised at his entertaining himself so long with questioning the poor man, turned to them and said : " Gentlemen, you have always been curious to know from what family I sprung [7] ; I now tell [8] you that I am not ashamed of my origin ; that I am the brother of this honest miller ; he has given you the history [9] of my family." The general, after spending [10] (S. 55, N. 1) the day with his relations, in [11] the festivity of which his officers heartily joined, took measures to better their fortune [12].—ANECDOTES.

1, in — line, im Kaufmannsstande.　　2, Translate 'you' by Ihr in this address, and use the verb in the 2nd pers. pl., which at that time was the common address for people of the lower rank of society. Say 'had you (Ihr) besides (außer) the two already mentioned brothers not yet another'?　3, noch einen.　　4, aber er sei sehr jung in den Krieg gezogen.　　5, da; read S. 27, N. 8.　　6, Say 'The general who read in the eyes of the officers their surprise (insert darüber), that he occupied himself so long with the questioning (Ausfragen, n.) of the poor man'.　　7, stammen.　　8, tell = say.　9, family-history, S. 76, N. 22, *A.*　　10, To spend a day with one's relations, einen Tag in Gesellschaft seiner Verwandten verleben.　　11, bei welcher Festlichkeit sich die Offiziere herzlich beteiligten.　　12, fortune = position.

Section 138.

NOT NEAR ENOUGH YET.

There [1] is a popular report in the Brandenburg district, where Bismarck's family has been so many centuries at home, which attributes to the Bismarcks, as the characteristic saying of the house, the phrase : " Noch lange nicht genug "—(Not near enough yet), *and* which expresses [5], we [2] suppose, the popular [3] conception of [4] their tenacity of purpose — that [6] they were not tired out of any plan they had formed by a reiterated failure or a pertinacious opposition which would have disheartened most of their compeers. There [7] is a somewhat extravagant illustration of this characteristic in Bismarck's wild, youthful days, if his biographer may be trusted. When studying [8] law at Berlin, he had been more than once disappointed [9] by a bootmaker who [10] did not send home his boots when they were promised. Accordingly [11] when this next happened, a servant of the young jurist appeared at the bootmaker's at six in the morning (App. § 9) with the simple question : " Are Herr [12] von Bismarck's boots ready ?" When he was told they were not [13], he departed [14], but *at* ten minutes past six another servant appeared, asking [15] the same question, and [16] so at precise intervals of ten minutes it went on all day, till by [17] the evening the boots were finished and [18] sent home.—EARLE, " THE PHILOLOGY OF THE ENGLISH TONGUE."

1, Say ' In the province *of* Brandenburg, where the family Bismarck for (seit) several centuries is at home (' to be at home,' here ansässig sein) there is (existiert) a popular (volkstümlich) report (Sage, f.) which, as *a* characteristic saying (Wahlſpruch, m.) attributes (zu'ſchreiben, with the dat.) to the Bismarcks the phrase (Motto, n.)'.　　　**2,** Say 'as we suppose', which place after the rel. pron.　　　**3,** populär; conception, Vorſtellung, f.　　　**4,** von ihrem zähen Feſthalten am Zwecke.　　　**5,** bezeichnet.　　　**6,** that they even (auch) through repeated failure (Fehlſchlagen) or pertinacious (hartnäckig) opposition (Widerſtand, m.), which would have discouraged (entmutigt hätte, which place at the end of this clause) most of their compeers (Standesgenoſſen), were not tired of any plan they had formed (ſich nicht von ihrem einmal gefaßten Plane abbringen ließen). **7,** A somewhat eccentric illustration (Beleg, m.) of (für) this characteristic quality we find in Bismarck's wild (ſtürmiſch) youth, if we can trust his biographer.　　　**8,** To study law, Jura ſtudieren.　　　**9,** täuſchen; by, von.　　　**10,** Say 'who had not (App. § 10) sent back his boots at the appointed (verabredet) time'. **11,** When (S. 4, N. 2) it therefore happened again (wieder geſchehen).　**12,** **Fürſt Otto von Bismarck** wurde am 1. April 1815 zu Schönhauſen, dem Stammgute der Familie Bismarck, in der Provinz Brandenburg im Königreiche Preußen geboren.　Er entſtammt der alten preußiſchen adeligen Familie von Bismarck, welche auch von Bismarck-Schönhauſen genannt wird, um dieſelbe von der ihr verwandten Familie von Bismarck-Bohlen zu unterſcheiden.　Von Bismarck trat zuerſt öffentlich auf dem Landtage von 1847 als Führer der äußerſten Rechten (extreme Conservatives) und dann als Mitglied der im Jahre 1848 tagenden zweiten preußiſchen Kammer (the Prussian House of Commons) als entſchiedener Gegner des Repräſentationsſyſtems (Representative Government) und der Reichsverfaſſung hervor.　Sein entſchiedenes Talent für die diplomatiſche Laufbahn beſtimmte die Regierung, ihn im Jahre 1851 zum Legations-ſekretär bei der preußiſchen Bundestagsgeſandtſchaft in Frankfurt a/M. zu ernennen.　Drei Monate ſpäter wurde er jedoch ſchon zum Bundestagsgeſandten erhoben, in welcher Eigen-ſchaft er vergeblich Preußens Gleichſtellung mit Öſtreich beim Bundestage erſtrebte. Nachdem er ſeit dem 1. April 1859 preußiſcher Geſandter in Petersburg und ſeit dem Frühjahr 1862 Botſchafter in Paris geweſen, trat er am 24. September deſſelben Jahres als Miniſter des Auswärtigen an die Spitze des neu ernannten Kabinetts.　Es würde zu weit führen, hier auf die Einzelheiten ſeiner großartigen Erfolge als Miniſterpräſident einzugehen, genüge es zu bemerken, daß ſein Hauptſtreben darauf gerichtet war, Preußen zur herrſchenden Macht in Deutſchland zu machen, Öſtreich daraus zu verdrängen, und ſchließlich durch Auflöſung des deutſchen Staatenbundes ein einiges Deutſchland unter dem Zepter Preußens zu ſchaffen.　Wie ihm dieſe Aufgabe gelang, iſt allgemein be-kannt.　Die ſchon lange zwiſchen Preußen und Öſtreich beſtandene Eiferſucht brach endlich im Jahre 1866 durch den Krieg in lichten Flammen aus.　Preußen ging glänzend aus demſelben als Sieger hervor.　Durch den Prager Friedensvertrag entſagte Öſtreich nicht allein ſeinen Anſprüchen als Präſidialmacht im deutſchen Staatenbunde, ſondern ſchied gänzlich aus demſelben aus und erkannte den unter Preußens Führung zu ſtiftenden Norddeutſchen Bund an.　In Anerkennung ſeiner großen Erfolge wurde Bismarck nach beendigtem Kriege in den Grafenſtand erhoben und zugleich zum Kanzler des Norddeut-ſchen Bundes ernannt, deſſen Angelegenheiten er mit ſo bedeutendem Geſchick leitete, daß bei der im Jahre 1870 von Frankreich an Preußen erfolgten Kriegserklärung auch die Südſtaaten ſich dem Norddeutſchen Bunde anſchloſſen und das ganze Deutſchland vereinigt gegen den Feind in den Kampf ziehen konnte, aus dem es mit Lorbeeren gekrönt ſiegreich hervorging.　Schon am 18. Januar 1871 ward König Wilhelm I. von Preußen unter Zuſtimmung aller deutſchen Staaten im Schloſſe zu Verſailles als deutſcher Kaiſer proklamiert.　Das große Ziel Bismarcks war erreicht.　Die Einheit des bisher zerſtückelten Vaterlandes war wiederhergeſtellt, ein mächtiges deutſches Reich unter der Führung Preu-ßens gegründet, und die demſelben drohenden Feinde waren beſiegt und geſchlagen.　Am 20. Mai 1871 wurde von dem Fürſten und Reichskanzler Bismarck zu Frankfurt a/M. der Friede mit Frankreich unterzeichnet, durch welchen die früher von dem deutſchen Reiche getrennten Herzogtümer Lothringen und Elſaß demſelben wieder einverleibt wurden und Frankreich ſich verpflichtete, an Deutſchland eine Kriegsentſchädigung von fünf Milliarden Franken zu zahlen.　Die Eröffnung des deutſchen Reichstags in Berlin, am 21. März 1871, gehört vielleicht zu den größten Triumphen dieſes höchſt ſeltſamen bewunderungswürdigen Mannes. 13, Supply 'ready', and use the Present Subjunctive. 14, fortgehen. 15, = with the same question. 16, and — day = and this was repeated (und dies wiederholte sich) all day long (den ganzen Tag lang) at (in) precise intervals of 10 minutes. 17, an, contracted with the def. art. . 18, = and were sent back.

Section 139.

A GREAT LOSS.

Mr. Thomas Carlyle had lent the Manuscript of the first volume of his "French Revolution" to a neighbour to peruse. By[1] some mischance or other, it[2] had been left lying on the parlour-floor, and[3] become forgotten. Weeks ran on[4], when at last the historian sent for[5] his manuscript, the[6] printers being loud for copy. Inquiries[7] were made, and[8] then it was found that the maid-of-all-work, finding[9] what she conceived to be a bundle of waste paper on the floor, had[10] used it to light the kitchen and parlour fires with[11]. Such[12] was the answer returned[13] to Mr. Carlyle, and his consternation and despair may be imagined (S. 4, N. 4). There[14] was, however, no help for him but to set himself resolutely to work to re-write his book; and[15] he turned to and did it. He had no draft[16], and[17] was compelled to rake up from his memory facts, ideas, and expressions, which had long since been dismissed. The composition[18] of the book in the first instance had been a *work of* real pleasure; the[19] re-writing of it, a second time, was one of pain and anguish almost beyond belief. That[20] he persevered and finished the volume under such circumstances affords[21] an instance of determination of purpose which has seldom been exceeded.—S. SMILES, " SELF-HELP."

1, By — other = Through a mischance (Mißgeschick, n.). 2, it — lying, hatte man es . . . liegen lassen. 3, and — forgotten = where it was forgotten. 4, ran on = passed away. 5, nach. 6, the — copy since the printers desired (verlangen) the same. 7, to make inquiries, Nachforschungen anstellen. 8, und nun stellte es sich heraus. 9, finding — floor = in the opinion of finding a bundle of worthless papers on the floor. 10, had used (benutzen . . . zu) the same. Read carefully S. 87, N. 6, and construe accordingly. 11, with = with it, S. 4. N. 5, B. 12, Such = that. 13, — which Mr. C. received. 14, Es blieb ihm indessen nichts anderes übrig, als. 15, und er machte sich daran und führte es aus. 16, Entwurf, m. 17, and — dismissed = and had to (= must) torture (abmartern) his memory in order to find again the from (von) him long forgotten facts, ideas, and expressions. 18, composition = work; in the first instance = at first. Supply ' for him' after 'pleasure'. 19, Say 'to write it for the (zum) second time was a painful and almost incredibly anxious (ängstlich) work. 20, Daß er sie durchführte. 21, — is; determination of purpose — strength of will, Willenskraft, f.; exceeded, übertreffen.

Section 140.

HERO WORSHIP[1].

I.

Do[2] not think it a mean thing to look up to (zu) those who are superior to yourselves[3]. On the contrary, you will find in practice[4], that *it is* only the meanest hearts, the shallowest and the basest (S. 128, N. 11) *who* feel no admiration, but (S. 6, N. 10) only envy for those who are better than themselves; who delight in[5] finding fault with them, blackening (S. 1, N. 3) their character, and showing that they are not after all so much superior to other[6] people; while[7] *it is* the noblest-hearted, the very men who are most worthy to be admired themselves, who feel[8] most the pleasure, the joy, and the strength of reverence (S. 3, N. 2); of[9] having some one whom they can look up to and admire; some one in whose company they can forget[10] themselves, their own interest, their own pleasure, their own honour and[11] glory, and cry: "Him I must hear; him I must follow; to him I must cling, whatever[12] may betide!"

1, Heldenverehrung, f.   2, Do—thing. Halte es nicht für zu gering.   3, Use the second person plural; to be superior to a person, einem weit überlegen sein.   4, in practice = always.   5, in—them = to discover weaknesses in (an, with dat.) them.   6, to other people = to others.   7, while—men, während die hochherzigsten Menschen, gerade diejenigen.   8, 'to feel', here empfinden; 'most' here = deepest, am tiefsten; pleasure, Genuß, m.   9, In order to connect this sentence more closely with the preceding, I propose to say: 'the pleasure (Genuß, m.) of having (S. 34, N. 10) some one to (zu) whom they *can* look up, and whom they can admire'. The auxiliary 'can' must be omitted in the first instance.   10, Where must you place the two verbs, and in what order?   11, It is a matter of course that the words 'their own' must be repeated here in German. Why?   12, Whatever (Was auch) may happen.

Section 141.

HERO WORSHIP.

II.

Blessed[1] and ennobling is the feeling which gathers round a wise teacher or[2] a great statesman all *the* more earnest, high-minded, pious youths of his generation[3]; the[4] feeling which makes[5] soldiers follow the general whom they trust, they know not why or whither, through danger[6], hunger, fatigue, and[7] death itself; the[4] feeling which, in its highest perfection, made[8] the Apostles forsake all and follow Christ[9], saying (S. 111, N. 6): "Lord, to[10] whom shall we go? Thou hast *the* words of eternal life," and which made them[11] ready to work[12] and to die for Him whom the world called the Son of the carpenter, but whom they, through[13] the Spirit of God bearing witness with their own pure and noble spirits, knew[14] to be the Son of the Living God.—CHARLES KINGSLEY, "THE WATER OF LIFE."

1, Beglückend.   2, Repeat here the prep. 'round', um.   3, generation = time.   4, jenes.   5, to make follow, folgen heißen, which verbs must be placed after the rel. clause; folgen requires the dat.; to trust a person, einem vertrauen.   6, Use the pl. with this noun.   7, yea, even unto death.   8, 'to make', here again heißen (to bid), str. v. tr.; which place after 'follow' according to App. § 19.   9, *Jesus Christ* has retained its Latin declension, thus: N. Jesus Christus; G. Jesu Christi; D. Jesu Christo; Acc. Jesum Christum. Use the dat. Christe, since folgen governs the dat.   10, 'to whom', here wohin (whither), which appears in the German text of the Bible.   **11,** 'to make ready', here = to enable, befähigen.   **12,** wirken is more appropriate here than arbeiten, considering the elevated style of the whole speech. **13,** through — spirits, kraft des göttlichen Geistes, der in ihren reinen, edlen Herzen Zeugniß ablegte.   **14,** knew to be, als (followed by the Acc.) ... erkannten.

Section 142.

JAMES WATT AND THE STEAM-ENGINE.

I.

James Watt was the great Improver of the steam-engine; but, in truth[1], as to all that is admirable in its structure, or vast in its utility, he should rather be described as its Inventor. *It was* by his inventions *that* its action[2] was so regulated as[3] to make it capable of being applied to the finest and most delicate manufactures, and its power so increased as to set weight and solidity at defiance. By his admirable contrivances[4] it has become a thing stupendous alike for its force and flexibility, for the prodigious power which it can exert, and the ease, precision, and ductility with which this power can be varied, distributed, and applied. The trunk of an elephant, that can pick up a pin or rend[5] an oak, is *as* nothing to it. It can engrave a seal, and crush masses of obdurate metal *before it,* draw out without[6] breaking a thread as fine as gossamer, and lift a ship of war like a bubble in the air. It can embroider[7] muslin and forge anchors, cut steel into ribbons[8], and impel[9] loaded vessels against the fury of the winds and waves.

    1, 'in truth' is better not translated here. Say 'but in regard to (in Rücksicht auf) all that (S. 3, N. 7) refers (sich beziehen) to (auf) the excellence of its construction and (wie) to (auf) the variety (Mannigfaltigkeit, f.) of its application (Nutzanwendung, f.), should he rather (eigentlich) be called the Inventor of the same'.   **2,** Wirkung, f.; in what voice is the verb? Insert the adv. erst after the auxiliary.   **3,** as — defiance = as (um) to be able to employ it in (bei) the making (Anfertigung, f.) of the finest and most delicate (zart) manufactures (Fabrikate), and its power so increased as (um) to be able to render resistance (Widerstand leisten) to every weight (Last, f.) and every solidity (Festigkeit, f.). Translate 'to be able' by können, which need be expressed but once, and must be placed at the very end of the whole period, which, along with the following, is perhaps the most difficult to translate that has yet been given.   **4,** Einrichtungen; it = the machine; thing, Werkzeug, n., after which place the verb 'become'; alike for, und zwar dies jewohl wegen ... wie auch. **5,** rend = tear down.   **6,** Say 'without tearing it', which place after 'gossamer' (Sommerfäden).   **7,** Insert the prep. auf here.   **8,** Streifen. **9,** to impel against, entgegentreiben, governing the dat.

Section 143.

JAMES WATT AND THE STEAM-ENGINE.

II.

It would be difficult to estimate the value of the benefits which these inventions have conferred upon this country. There is no branch of industry that has not been indebted[1] to them; and[2], in all the most material, they have not only widened most magnificently the field of its exertions, but[3] multiplied a thousand-fold the amount of its productions. It was our improved steam-engine, in short[4], that fought the battles of Europe and sustained and exalted, through[5] the late tremendous contest, the political greatness of our land. *It is* the same great power *which* now enables us to pay the interest of our debt, and to maintain[6] the arduous struggle *in which we are still engaged* (1819) with the skill[7] and capital of countries (S. 16, N. 10) less oppressed with (von) taxation.

But these are poor[8] and narrow views of its importance. It has increased indefinitely the mass of[9] human comforts and enjoyments, and[10] rendered cheap and accessible, all over the world, the materials of wealth and prosperity.

1, I am greatly indebted to you, ich habe Jhnen vieles zu verbanfen. 2, Say 'and in the principal branches'; most magnificently, auf bas großartigste. 3, Insert 'also' here. 4, Sturz, which place at the head of the period. 5, through = in. 6, fortießen, which rendering will make the relative clause '*in — engaged*' superfluous. 7, 'skill', here = industry. 8, poor = superficial; narrow, beschränkt; of = about. 9, of human = of our. 10, unb die Stoffe, welche fonst nur dem Reichtum unb dem Wohlstand zugänglich waren, für die ganze Welt billig unb erreichbar gemacht.

Section 144.

JAMES WATT AND THE STEAM-ENGINE.
III.

It has armed the feeble hand of (S. 3, N. 2) man, *in* short[1], with a power to which no limits can be assigned[2]; completed[3] the dominion of mind over the most refractory qualities of matter[4], and laid a sure foundation for[5] all those future miracles of mechanic power which[6] are to aid and reward the labours of after generations. It[7] is to the genius of one man, too, that all this is mainly owing! And certainly no man ever bestowed such a gift on his kind[8]. The blessing is not only universal, but[9] unbounded; and the fabled[10] inventors of the plough and the loom, who were deified by their rude[11] contemporaries, conferred less important benefits (App. § 5) on mankind than the inventor of our present steam-engine.

This will be the fame of Watt with[12] future generations, and it[13] is sufficient for his race and his country.—LORD JEFFREY.

1, Commence the period with '*In* short'. 2, to assign limits to a thing, einer Sache Grenzen stecken. 3, Say 'it has completed', etc. 4, Materie, f. 5, zu. 6, Say 'which are destined (zu etwas bestimmt fein, Comp. S. 87, N. 6) to assist and to reward the labours of (= of the) future generations. 7, It — owing = All this we owe mainly to the genius of a single man. 8, Geschlecht, n.; use the verb in the Perfect; ever, je vorher. 9, fonbern auch). 10, fagenshaft. 11, rude = inexperienced. 12, bei, with the def. art. 13, dieser.

Section 145.

MANUFACTURES OF ENGLAND[1].

The principal branches of[2] the industrial pursuits are the manufactures[3] of cotton, woollen[4], and worsted goods, iron and hardware, earthenware[5], hosiery, mining[6], and shipbuilding. The geographical distribution of the manufacturing[7] population is dependent partly on natural, partly on accidental circumstances. The proximity of a coal-field[8] decides the point[9] in many instances[10]; for, even where the raw material is bulky[11], it is generally more practicable to bring[12] it to the coal (Kohlen), than the coal to it, an[13] instance of which is furnished by the copper-ore of Cornwall being taken to Swansea to be smelted. The iron manufacture is carried on[14] generally at[15] the coal-fields, the[16] chief seats being South Wales, Staffordshire, and Derbyshire. The cotton manufacture has[17] been located in Lancashire and Cheshire for *the last* three centuries; but[18] it has attained its present dimensions very much through those counties being readily furnished with the raw material from America, as[19] well as from the abundance of coal outside those counties; Manchester, Bolton, Oldham, Stockport, and Macclesfield are the chief seats of the manufacture.—BEVAN, "THE STUDENT'S MANUAL OF MODERN GEOGRAPHY."

1, Die englische Industrie. 2, of — pursuits, der Industrie. 3, Fabrikation, f. 4, The preposition 'of' is best repeated in this enumeration; worsted, aus Kammwolle gefertigt; 'goods', here Stoffe. 5, irdenes Geschirr or Töpferwaren. 6, Berg- und Schiffbau. 7, manufacturing = industrial. 8, Kohlenlager, n. 9, the point, darüber, which place last. 10, instances = cases. 11, schwer und umfangreich. 12, hinschaffen; than — it = than the reverse, als umgekehrt. 13, It is well to begin a new period here, thus: 'An example of this (dazu) furnishes the copper-ore of Cornwall, which is taken (befördern) to (S. 72, N. 4), S.', etc. 14, betreiben, insep. c. str. v. 15, at the = in the neighbourhood of the. 16, the — being — which are mainly situated (belegen) in. 17, has been located, ist ansässig. The Present is often used in German where the English use the Perfect to express the duration of an action up to the time of speaking; as— Unsere Familie wohnt seit zwanzig Jahren (or schon zwanzig Jahre) in Manchester, our family *has been living* in Manchester *for* these last twenty years. 18, but — America. This clause containing a Gerund (being) preceded by the preposition 'through', must be construed according to S. 1, N. 3, and S. 87, N. 6 in the following way: 'but it (sie) has received its present dimension especially thereby (dadurch, read S. 87, N. 6), that these counties can easily be (S. 2, N. 1) supplied with the raw material from America'. The three verbs must, of course, be placed at the end, and in such a way that the governing verb (can) stands last, and the auxiliary of tense in the middle. 19, as — counties = as also (wie auch noch) thereby, that the coal is [use the pl. in German] to be got (zu haben sein) in abundance in the neighbouring counties.

Section 146.

MR. H. M. STANLEY'S APPEAL[1] FOR SUPPLIES.

I.

Village *of* N'sanda[2], August 4, 1877.

To[3] any Gentleman who speaks English at Embomma.

Dear[4] Sir,

    I have arrived at[5] this place from Zanzibar with 115 souls, (S. 53, N. 9) men, women, and children. We are now in[6] a state of imminent starvation. We can buy[7] nothing from the natives, for they laugh at[4] our *kinds of* cloth[9], beads, and wire. There[10] are no provisions in the country that may be purchased, except on market days, and starving people cannot afford to wait for these markets. I[11], therefore, have made bold to despatch three of my young men[12], natives[13] of Zanzibar, with (nebſt) a boy named Feruzi, of the English mission at Zanzibar, with this letter.

I do not know you, but[14] I am told there (S. 104, N. 19) is an Englishman at (in) Embomma, and as you are a Christian and a gentleman, I beg you not to disregard my request. The boy Robert will be better able to describe our lone condition than I[15] can tell you in this letter. We are in *a state of* the greatest distress; but if your supplies[16] arrive in time, I[17] may be able to reach Embomma within four days.

1, Anruf um Zuſenbung von Waren.　　2, The village of N'sanda is three days' journey from Embomma, or Boma, which is a small town on the Congo or Livingstone River at a distance of sixty-five English miles from the Atlantic, and, with regard to Stanley's position, may be considered the van of civilisation in Africa, being the first place inhabited by Europeans.—For the full understanding of this letter, it may be useful to observe that it was written at the critical period when, at their journey home from the sources of the Nile, and almost at the end of all their troubles, the heroic travellers of more than 7000 miles through Equatorial Africa found themselves face to face with the grimest of all enemies — starvation. Nearly forty men filled the sick list with dysentery, ulcers, and scurvy, and the number of victims of the latter disease was steadily increasing. For a considerable time the people had had no other food but a few ground-nuts and bananas, and were scarcely more than skin and bone. In this extremity Mr. Stanley determined to despatch four of his strongest and swiftest men with this letter to Embomma, where he was told there was one Englishman, one Frenchman, and three Portuguese. He then intended to follow these men as quickly as possible with the rest of his people, and to meet them and the expected supplies on the road to Boma, thus gaining at least one or two days, which might turn out to be of the greatest importance to his starving followers.　　3, Use the attributive construction, as explained in S. 48, N. 6.　　4, Geehrt.　　5, at this place = here.　　6, dem Verhungern nahe ſein.　　7, 'buy', here = exchange, ein'tauſchen.　　8, über, with Acc. 9, Say 'cloths, beads, and wires'.　　10, Say 'Except on (Außer an) market days there are (ſind) in the (auf dem) country no provisions to be got (zu haben) that we can buy, and if one hungers, one cannot possibly wait for (auf, with Acc.) these markets.　　11, Say 'I venture (after which use the grammatical object, as explained in S. 51, N. 13) therefore to send (abſenden)', etc. 12, Leute.　　13, welche aus Zanzibar gebürtig ſind.　　14, man ſagt mir jedoch.　　15, I can tell you — I can do.　　16, 'supplies', here = goods. 17, I may be able = I can perhaps (See App. § 15).

Section 147.

MR. H. M. STANLEY'S APPEAL FOR SUPPLIES.

II.

I want 300 cloths[1], each four yards long, of[2] such quality as you trade with, which is very different from that we have; but[3] better than all would be ten or fifteen man-loads of rice or grain to fill the pinched[4] bellies immediately, as[5] even with the cloths it would require time to purchase food, and starving people[6] cannot wait.   The supplies must arrive within two days, or[7] I may have a fearful time of it among the dying.\Of course I hold myself responsible for any[8] expense (S. 16, N. 10) you[9] may incur in the business.   What is wanted is immediate relief, and I pray you to[10] use your utmost energies to forward it at once.   If (App. § 21) you have such little luxuries[11] as tea, coffee, sugar, and biscuits by you, such[12] as one man can easily carry, I beg you on[13] my own behalf that you will send a small supply[14] and[15] add to the great debt of gratitude due to you upon the timely arrival of the supplies for my people.   Until[16] that time I beg you to believe me,

Yours sincerely,

H. M. Stanley,

Commanding[17] the Anglo-American Expedition for[18] the
Exploration of Africa.

P.S. You[19] may not know me by name, I therefore add, I[20] am the person that discovered[21] Livingstone in 1871. H. M. S.—H. M. Stanley, "Through the Dark Continent."

1, cloths = pieces *of* cloth.   2, of — have = and of that quality with which you trade, which is quite different from ours.   3, but — grain = but still better would be (Pluperf. Subj.) as much rice or grain as ten or fifteen men (Leute) can carry.   4, = hungry stomachs.   5, as — food = as (after which place the subject ' we '), even in the possession of the cloths, we should yet want time to exchange provisions for them (S. 4, N. 5, *B*).   6, die Hunger: leidenden.   7, or — dying, Liter. = if (after which place the subject '*I*') among the dying I shall (soll) not experience (durchleben) a dreadful time (App. § 18).   8, any = all.   9, die Ihnen aus dieser Angelegenheit erwachsen mögen.   10, to — once = to do the (= your) utmost *in your power* (sein Äußerstes thun) and to send us the same (to agree with relief) at once.   11, Luxusartikel; to have by oneself = to possess.   12, such = about as much.   13, on — behalf = for my own person.   14, supply = quantity.   15, and — people = and thereby still to increase (vergrößern) the great debt of (S. 3, N. 2) gratitude, to which I shall be in duty bound to you (einem verpflichtet sein) after the timely (rechtzeitig) arrival of the supplies (Warensendung).   16, Bis dahin empfehle ich mich Ihnen hochachtend und ergebenst.   17, Kommandierender der.   18, zur.   19, = Perhaps is my name unknown to you.   20, I — that = that it is I, who.   21, auffinden, of which use the Perfect.

Section 148.

ANSWER TO[1] THE PRECEDING LETTER.

English Factory, Boma, 6th August 1877, 6.30 A.M.

H. M. Stanley, Esq.

Dear Sir,

Your welcome letter came[2] to hand yesterday, *at* 7 P.M.   As[3] soon as its contents were understood, we arranged to despatch to you such articles as you requested, as much as our stock on hand would permit, and other things that we deemed would be suitable in that locality.   You will see *that* we send fifty pieces *of* cloth, each twenty-four yards long, and some sacks containing sundries for yourself; several[4] sacks *of* rice, potatoes, a few bundles *of* fish, a bundle *of* tobacco, and one demijohn[5] *of* rum. The carriers are all paid, so that you need not trouble yourself about them. That[6] is all we need say about business.⏋ We are exceedingly sorry to hear that you have arrived there in such (ſo) piteous[7] condition, but we send our warmest congratulations to you, and hope that you will soon arrive in Boma. (This[8] place is called Boma by us, though on the map it[9] is Embomma.)   Again[10] hoping that you will soon arrive, and that you are not suffering in health,

Believe[11] us to remain,

Your sincere friends,

HATTON & COOKSON.

(Signed) A. DA MOTTA VEIGA.

       J. W. HARRISON.

1, auf, with Acc.; A.M. morgens : P.M. abends.—This letter and the accompanying supplies were received by Mr. Stanley in the morning of the 6th of August, two days after he despatched his letter to Boma. Messrs. A. Da Motta Veiga and J. W. Harrison were the managers of a factory belonging to Messrs. Hatton & Cookson of Liverpool.   2, came to hand = we have . . . received.   3, As — locality = As soon as we had understood the contents of the same (to agree with letter), we (App. § 14) made arrangements (Anſtalten treffen) to send you the asked for (erbeten) articles, as far as (ſo weit) our stock (Warenlager, n., or Warenvorrat, m.) would permit us (S. 51, N. 13), and add (supply nod) some other things of which we thought they might (= could) be useful to you there.   4, several, a few = some. 5, eine große Korbflaſche.   6, Weiter haben wir nichts Geſchäftliches zu ſagen. 7, traurig.   8, Say 'We call this place (Ort, m.) B'.   9, Say 'it is called '.   10, Say 'Again (noch einmal) expressing (S. 111, N. 6), the hope'. 11, zeichnen wir in aufrichtiger Freundſchaft ergebenſt.

Section 149.

MR. STANLEY'S ACKNOWLEDGMENT[1] OF THE PRECEDING LETTER AND THE SUPPLIES[17].

I.

Banza M'Buko, August 6, 1877.

Messrs. A. Da Motta Veiga and J. W. Harrison,

    Embomma, Congo River.

   Gentlemen,

     I (S. 115, N. 1) have received your welcome letter, but better *than all*, and[2] more welcome, are your supplies. I am unable to express *just* at present how grateful I feel. At the sight of (von) the stores exposed[3] to our hungry eyes—at the sight of (von) the rice, the fish, *and* the rum, and[4] for me—wheaten bread, butter, sardines, jam, peaches. grapes, beer (ye[5] gods! just think of it—three bottles pale ale[6]!), besides tea and sugar, we (App. § 14) are all so over-joyed and confused that we cannot restrain[7] ourselves from falling to and[8] enjoying this sudden bounteous store. I beg you will charge[9] our apparent want of (an) thankfulness to our greediness. If we do not thank you sufficiently in words, rest assured we[10] feel what volumes could not describe.

For the next twenty-four hours we shall be too busy eating and drinking to think of anything else much; but I may say that the people[11] will cry out joyfully, while[12] their mouths are full of rice and fish: " Verily, our master has found the sea and his brothers, but we did not believe him until[13] he showed us the rice and the pambe (rum). We did not believe there[14] was any end to the great river; but God be praised for ever, for we shall see white people[15] to-morrow, and our wars[16] and troubles will be over !"

1, Anzeige von dem Empfange: 'supplies', here Warensendung, f.   2, Insert the adverb noch here.   3, It was exposed to my eyes, es war vor meinen Augen ausgebreitet; 'hungry', here gierig.   4, und — des für mich bestimmten Weißbrots; the article, in the Gen. case, must be repeated before each of the following nouns.   5, ye — it = o sehet, Ihr Götter.   6, Weißbier. 7, bezwingen; from falling to, zuzugreifen.   8, und diese uns so schnell und großmütig zugesandten Vorräte zu verzehren.   9, I beg you will charge this to his greediness, ich bitte Sie, dies seiner Gebgierde zur Last legen zu wollen. 10, we — describe = we feel more than could (App. § 33, and S. 2, N. 1) be described to you through (durch) volumes.   11, Leute.   12, Say 'while their mouth is still filled with rice and fish'.   13, ehe.   14, Say 'the great river had (See App. § 29) ever (je) an end.   15, Menschen.   16, Kämpfe und Beschwerden.   17, This letter, on the morning of the 7th of August, was despatched to Boma, the caravan following slowly, and reaching Boma on the 9th of August 1877, the 999th day from the date of their departure from Zanzibar. The expedition then embarked on board a steamer at Boma, and, on the 11th, descended the river Congo. After steaming northward from the mouth of the Congo for a few hours, the vessel entered the fine bay of Kabinda, on the southern shores of which the native town of that name in the county of Nyoyo is situate. The Expedition, after a stay of eight days at Kabinda, was kindly taken on board the Portuguese gunboat 'Tamega' to San Paulo de Loanda. Here they were treated with the utmost hospitality by the Portuguese and the officers of the English navy, who offered the Expedition a passage to Cape Town in H.M.S. 'Industry', Commander R. C. Dyer. The Cape of Good Hope was reached on the 21st of October. Here a telegram from the Lords of the British Admiralty was received, authorising the Commodore Francis William Sullivan to prepare H.M.S. 'Industry' for the reception of the Expedition and to convey them to Zanzibar, the end of their journey. On the 6th of November H.M.S. 'Industry' was equipped and ready for her voyage to Zanzibar, which was reached on the 20th of the same month. By this time the sick had, all but one, recovered, and had improved so much in appearance that few persons ignorant of what they had been, could have supposed that these were the living skeletons that had reeled from sheer weakness through Boma.

Section 150.

MR. STANLEY'S LETTER (continued).

II.

Dear Sirs,
        Though[1] strangers, I feel we shall be great friends, and[2] I shall always remember my feelings of gratefulness, when I first caught sight

of your supplies, and my poor, faithful, and brave people cried out :
"Master, we are saved!—food[3] is coming!"   *The* old and *the* young—
the men, *the* women, and *the* children—lifted their wearied and worn-
out[4] frames[5], and began to chant *lustily* an[6] extemporaneous song, in[7]
honour of the white people by (an) the great salt sea (the (S. 53, N. 9)
Atlantic) who had listened to their prayers. I had[8] to rush to my
tent to hide the tears that would issue[9], despite all my attempts to
composure[10].

. Gentlemen, that the blessing of God may attend your footsteps
whithersoever[11] you go, is the very earnest[12] prayer of

Yours faithfully,
H. M. STANLEY,

Commanding the Anglo-American Expedition.—

H. M. STANLEY, "THROUGH THE DARK CONTINENT."

1, obgleich wir uns noch fremd sind.   **2,** Say ' and I shall never forget the
feelings of gratefulness which I experienced (empfinden, insep. comp. str. v.),
when ', etc.   **3,** Say ' there come provisions '!   **4,** abgemagert.
5, Körper, m., which use in the Sing.   **6,** ein aus dem Stegreife entworfenes
Lied ; to chant = to sing.   **7,** in — people, den Weißen . . . zu Ehren; the words
zu Ehren must be placed at the end of the clause.   **8,** Use the Imperfect
of müssen.   **9,** to issue = to break forth, hervorbrechen.   **10,** to composure =
to compose myself.   **11,** The adverbial clause 'whithersoever you go ' may
be briefly rendered by the adverb ' stets '.   **12,** earnest = sincere ; faithfully,
ergeben (adject.).

Section 151.

RETURNED[1] KINDNESS.

When (S. 4, N. 2) the country near[2] Albany was newly settled, a
starving Indian came to the inn at Lichfield and asked for a night's
shelter and some supper, at[3] the same time confessing that, from[4]
failure in hunting, he had nothing[5] to pay. The hostess drove him
away with reproachful[6] epithets, and as the Indian was about (S. 6, N. 4)
scornfully to retire,—there being (S. 30, N. 4) no other inn for[7] many
a weary mile,—a[8] man, who was sitting by, directed the hostess to
supply[9] his wants, and promised to pay her. As[10] soon as the Indian's
supper was ended, he thanked his benefactor, and said he would some
day return his kindness. ¿ Several years thereafter[11] the settler was taken
a prisoner by a hostile tribe, and carried off to (S. 72, N. 4) Canada.   His
life was spared[12], but he was detained in[13] slavery.   One[14] day, however,
an Indian came to him, and bade the captive follow him.   The Indian
never told where they were going, nor[15] what was his object; *but* day
after[16] day the captive followed his mysterious guide, till one afternoon
they came suddenly on[17] a beautiful expanse of cultivated fields, with
many houses *rising amongst them.*   "Do you know that place?" asked
the Indian.   "Ah, yes—it is Lichfield !" and whilst the astonished exile[18]
had not yet recovered from his surprise and (S. 10, N. 9) amazement,
the Indian exclaimed: "And I am the starving Indian, on whom, at

this *very* place, you took [19] pity. And now that [20] I have repaid you,
I pray you go home!"—Dr. Dwight.

1, vergelten, insep. comp. str. v.   2, unweit; newly, eben; 'to settle', here
felenifieren.   3, at — confessing = on which occasion (wobei) he confessed.
4, wegen erfolgloſer Jagd.   5, nothing to pay = no money for (zu, contracted
with the dat. of the def. art.) paying.   6, reproachful epithets, Schelhwerte.
7, for — mile, meilenweit in der Runde.   8, 'a man', here = a guest. The
verb 'directed' (heißen, str. v.) must be placed before the subject, since the
subordinate clause precedes the principal one.   9, to supply a person's
wants, für die Bedürfniſſe eines Menſchen ſorgen.   10, Say 'As soon as the
Indian had eaten (verzehren) his supper'.   11, ſpäter.   12, verſchonen.
13, in slavery = as *a* slave; 'to detain', here gefangen halten.   14, Say
'One day, however, came an Indian to the prisoner with the intimation
(Weiſung, f.) to follow him'. This construction is necessary to avoid the
repetition of the pronoun 'ihm'.   15, nor — object = or else his intention.
16, für.   17, zu einer ſchönen Fläche urbar gemachter Felder.   18, exile =
settler.   19, to take pity on a person, ſich eines Menſchen erbarmen; supply
the adverb einmal (one day) before the verb.   20, that = since, da; to repay
a person, einem ſeine Schuld abtragen.

Section 152.

NEW-YEAR'S EVE[1].

I.

It was dreadfully cold; it snowed, and was beginning to grow dark;
it was the last evening of the year,—New-year's Eve. In this cold, a
poor little girl was wandering about the streets with [2] bare head and
bare feet. She had slippers on when she left home (Haus, with the
def. art.), but what was the good of them? They (Es) were the large,
old slippers of her mother's—so large that they fell off the little girl's
feet as she hurried across the street to [3] escape a carriage, which came [4]
galloping along at a great rate. The one slipper was not to be found,
and a boy ran off with the other.

So the little girl wandered about barefooted, with a quantity [5] of
matches in an old apron, whilst she held a box [6] of them in her
(S. 43, N. 9, *A*) hand. No one had bought *any* matches of her through [7]
the whole livelong day—no one had given her a single farthing [8].
Hungry, and pinched [9] with cold, the poor little girl crept [10] along, the
large flakes of snow covering (S. 55, N. 1; use während) her yellow
hair, which [11] curled round her face.

In [12] a corner between two houses, one projecting beyond the other,
she sought shelter. Huddling [13] herself up, she drew her poor little
feet, which were red and blue with cold, under her (ſich) as well *as* she
could, but she [14] was colder than ever, and [15] dared not go home
(S. 63, N. 8), for, as she had sold no matches, her cruel [16] father would
beat her. Besides [17], it was cold at home (S. 63, N. 8), for they lived
just [18] under the roof, and [19] the wind blew in, though straw and rags
had been stuffed in the large cracks. Her little hands were quite
benumbed with cold. Oh [20], how much good one match would do,

if she dared but (nur) take it out of the box and draw [21] it across the wall to warm her fingers in the flames!

1, Der Sylverſterabend.　　**2,** with — feet, barfuß und unbedeckten Hauptes, which place before 'about (durch) the streets'.　　**3,** to escape a carriage, einem Wagen aus dem Weg laufen. For the translation of the conjunction 'to' in this clause compare S. 19, N. 7.　　**4,** to come galloping along at a great rate, in vollem Galopp die Straße entlang kommen.　　**5,** a quantity = some. **6,** Schachtel, f.; of them = of the same.　　**7,** through — day, den ganzen Tag lang, which is best placed at the commencement of the period.　　**8,** Heller, m. **9,** to be pinched with cold, vor Kälte erſtarrt ſein.　　**10,** to creep along, ſich weiter ſchleppen.　　**11,** Say 'which in curls surrounded (umwallen, insep. comp. w. v.) her face.　　**12,** In — other, In einem durch ein hervorſpringendes Haus gebildeten Winkel.　　**13,** Say 'She huddled herself up (nie'berfauern, sep. comp. w. v.) and drew her', etc.　　**14,** I am cold, es friert mich.　　**15,** Say 'and yet she (App. § 24, *B*) dared (wagen, w. v.) not to go home'.　　**16,** 'cruel', here = severe.　　**17,** Say 'And also (App. § 14) at home it was cold'. **18,** 'just', here = immediately.　　**19,** Say 'through which the wind blew, although the large cracks (Spalte, f.) were stuffed (verſtopfen, insep. comp. w. v.) with straw and rags'.　　**20,** Say, 'Oh (Ach), how nice (ſchön) must (Imperf. Subj.) a match be'.　　**21,** Ein Zündhölzchen an der Mauer an'reiben, to draw a match across the wall.

Section 153.

NEW-YEAR'S EVE.

II.

She drew one out—"Ritsh!" how it sputtered[1] and burned! It burned with a warm, bright flame, like a candle, and she bent her hand round it (S. 4, N. 5, *B*), it was a wonderful light! It appeared to the little girl as if she were sitting[2] before a large iron stove, in which the fire burned brightly, and[3] gave out such comfort and such warmth. She stretched out her feet to warm them, too—but the flame went[4] out, the stove disappeared, and there she sat, still holding[5] a little bit of the burnt-out[4] match in her (S. 43, N. 9, *A*) hand.

Another was[6] lighted; it burned, and, where[7] the light fell upon the wall, that[8] became transparent, so that she could see into the room. There the table was covered with a cloth of dazzling white, and with fine china; and a roast goose was smoking most[9] temptingly upon it. But what was still more delightful, the goose sprang down from the table, and[10], with a knife and (S. 10, N. 9) fork *sticking* in its[11] back, waddled towards the little girl. Then[12] the match went out[4], and she saw nothing but the thick, cold wall.

She lighted a third one (S. 67, N. 3); and now she was sitting under the most splendid Christmas-tree. It was larger and more beautifully decorated[13] than the one (S. 16, N. 10) she had seen at Christmas[14] through the window at[15] the rich merchant's. Hundreds of[16] tapers were burning amongst the green branches, and painted[17] pictures, such[18] as she had seen in the shop-windows, looked down upon her. She stretched out[19] both *her* hands, when the match was burnt[4] out,—

1, fprühen, w. v.　　2, Use the Impf. Subj. according to App. § 33; as if, als.　　3, und ich weiß nicht wie viel Behaglichkeit und Wärme ausstrahlte.　　4, 'to go out', and 'to burn out', here erlöschen, insep. comp. str. v.　　5, The Present Participle may be used here in German, but where must it be placed?　　6, In which Voice is the verb here? Introduce the clause by the grammatical subject 'es', as explained in S. 104, N. 19.　　7, where = at (an) the place (Stelle, f.) where.　　8, diese.　　9, Use the superlative of hoch.　　10, Here follows the verb 'waddled'.　　11, in its = in the, contracted; towards, auf ... zu, which latter preposition place at the end of the whole period. 12, Then = Thereupon.　　13, aufputzen, sep. comp. w. v.　　14, at (an, contracted with the dat. of the def. art.) Christmas-day.　　15, The preposition 'at', in the signification of 'at the house of' is generally rendered by the preposition 'bei', which governs the dative; as—

At Easter we shall all dine *at my*　　Am Ostertage werden wir alle bei meiner
　　mother's.　　　　　　　　　　　　Mutter zu Mittag essen.

16, von.　　17, painted = coloured, bunt.　　18, such as, wie.　　19, Supply the pronominal adverb 'danach' before the particle aus, which stands at the end.

Section 154.

NEW-YEAR'S EVE.

III.

The countless lights rose higher and higher, and she now saw that they (es) were *the* stars, one of which fell[1], leaving a long line of light in the sky.

Some[2] one has (S. 29, N. 3) died just now, the girl said; for her old grandmother, who alone[3] had loved her, but who was now dead, had told her that[4] when a star fell, a soul took (App. §§ 28 and 30) its flight up to heaven.

She drew another match across the wall, and in the light it threw[5] around stood her old grandmother, so bright[6], so mild, and so loving.

"Grandmother," the little girl cried, "oh, take me with *you!* I know that you will disappear as soon as the match is burnt out, just like the warm stove, the delicious roast goose, and the Christmas-tree!" And hastily she lighted the[7] rest of the matches that remained in the box, for she wished to keep[8] her grandmother with her as long as possible; and the matches burnt so brightly, that it was lighter than day. Never before[9] had she seen her grandmother so beautiful and so tall, and behold, she[10] now took the little girl in her arms, and[11], in radiance and joy, flew high, high up with her into the heaven, where she felt neither (kein) cold, nor (kein) hunger, nor (und kein) fear any more[12],— for she was with God.

But, in the corner between the two houses, in the cold morning air, lay the little girl with pale cheeks and smiling lips. She was frozen[13] to death during the last night of the Old Year. The first light of the New Year shone upon the dead body of the little girl with the matches, one[14] box of which was nearly consumed. "She must have tried to warm herself," the people said; but no one knew of (von) the visions[15] she had had, or of the splendour that (S. 48, N. 6) surrounded her when she entered with her grandmother into the joys of a New Year.—After HANS ANDERSEN, "FAIRY TALES."

1, Say ' fell down and left (jurüd'laffen) a long line of light (Lidytftreifen, m.) in (an) the sky '. 2, This sentence is best introduced by the grammatical subject 'es', see S. 104, N. 19. 3, Say 'alone of all '. 4, that — fell; daß beim Herunterfallen eines Sternes; flight, Flug, m.; up to, ju, contracted with the dat. of the def. art. 5, to throw around, um fid) her verbreiten. 6, bright = friendly; mild, fanft; loving, liebreid). 7, the — box, die in der Schachtel fid) nod) befindlid)en Zündhölzer (Comp. S. 48, N. 6). 8, to keep with oneself, bei fid) behalten, insep. comp. str. v. tr. 9, juvor. 10, It will be best to begin this clause with the adv. 'now', and to turn the personal pronoun 'she' into the demonstrative pronoun 'the same', to agree with 'grandmother'. This will commend itself in order to avoid ambiguity. 11, Here follows the verb 'flew'; in radiance and joy, freudeftrahlend, adv.; high—heavens, mit ihr zum Himmel empor. 12, any more, mehr, before the verb; 'with', here bei. 13, erfrieren, insep. comp. str. v., to freeze to death. 14, Liter. 'of which nearly a whole box was burnt up'. 15, Traumbild, n.

Section 155.

PROVIDENCE[1] VINDICATING THE INNOCENT.

It is (S. 2, N. 1) recorded in history that a beautiful maiden named Blanche. the serf of[2] an ancient nobleman, was wooed[3] by her master's son. Not[4] admiring his character, she scorned[5] his suit. Upon this his *course of* love turned[6] to bitter hatred. Just[7] then a precious string of pearls confided (S. 7, N. 3, *B*) to the maiden's care was[8] lost. Her pseudo-lover[9] charged her with the theft, and, in[10] accordance with the customs of that rude age, she was doomed to die. On the day of the execution, as the innocent girl knelt to offer[11] her dying prayer, a[12] flash of lightning struck a statue of Justice, which adorned the market-place, to the dust. From[13] a destroyed bird's nest, built (S. 7, N. 3, *A*, and S. 48, N. 6) in a crevice of the image[14], dropped the lost[15] pearls, thus[16] declaring the maiden's innocence. In a moment the exultant crowd rushed to the scaffold, demanding her release. There she knelt beside the block, pale and beautiful, and with a smile of peace upon her lips. They (S. 134, N. 4) spoke[17]—she answered not. They touched her— she was dead! To preserve her memory they raised a statue there[18]; and to[19] this day, when[20] men gaze upon her image, they condemn her oppressor; they praise her for the purity of her character; they recognise the justice of Him whose[21] lightning testified her innocence.— W. SMITH.

1, Say, 'Providence (S. 3, N. 2) protects innocence.' 2, of—nobleman = of a nobleman of *an* old family (Gefd)led)t, n.). 3, umwer'ben, insep. comp. str. v. 4, = As his character displeased (mißfallen, insep. comp. str. v., governing the dat.) her. 5, verfd)mähen, insep. comp. w. v. tr. 6, fid) verwan'deln in. 7, Just then = Just at this time. 8, was lost = one missed; care, Dbhut, f. 9, = false lover. 10, in — customs = according to the law. 11, = to speak. 12, a — Justice . . . to the dust = fuhr ein

Blißſtrahl in die Statue der Gerechtigkeit ... und zerſchmetterte ſie.   13, Aus.
14, Bildſäule, f.   15, = missed.   16, Say 'and testified (bezeugen, w.
v. tr.) thus the maiden's innocence'.   17, Supply 'to her'.   18, daſelbſt.
19, bis auf den heutigen Tag.   20, Construe thus: 'those who look
at her image (Bildnis, n.) condemn her oppressor', and consider App.
§ 14.   21, In order to avoid a repetition of the same form of pronoun,
turn the last clause into: 'who with his lightning testified her innocence'.

Section 156.

NAPOLEON BONAPARTE[1].

I.

Napoleon understood his business[2]. He was a man who in each
moment and[3] emergency knew what[4] to do next. This[5] is an immense
comfort and refreshment to the spirits, not only of (S. 3, N. 2) kings,
but[6] of citizens. Few[7] men have any next; they live from hand to
mouth, without plan, are[8] ever at the end of their line, and, (S. 102,
N. 30) after each action, wait for[9] an impulse from abroad. Napoleon
would have been the first man of the world, if[10] his ends had been
purely public. As[11] he is, he inspires confidence and vigour by the
extraordinary unity of his action.

He is firm[12], sure, and self-denying; he sacrifices everything to his
aim[13]—money, troops, generals, his own safety even, and is not misled[14],
like common adventurers, by[15] the splendour of his own means. "Incidents ought not to govern policy," he said, "but[16] policy incidents."
"To[17] be hurried away by every event, is[18] to have no political system
at all." His victories were only so many doors[19], and[20] he never for a
moment lost sight of his way onward in the dazzle and uproar of the
present circumstances. He knew what to do, and he flew to his mark.

He[21] would shorten a straight line to come at his object. Horrible
anecdotes may no doubt be collected (S. 4, N. 4) from his history, of[22]
the price at which he bought his successes; but he must not, therefore,
be set[23] down as cruel, but only as one[24] who knew no impediment to
his will: not[25] bloodthirsty, not cruel; but woe to[26] what person stood
in his way! "Sire, General Clarke cannot combine with General Junot
for the dreadful fire of the Austrian battery." "Let[27] him carry the battery." "Sire, every regiment that approaches the heavy artillery is
sacrificed[28]. Sire[29], what orders?" "Forward! Forward!"

1, **Napoleon I.**, Kaiſer der Franzoſen, geboren den 15. Aug. 1769 zu Ajaccio
auf Korſika war der zweite Sohn des Patriziers Carlo Bonaparte und der Maria Latitia
Ramolini. Nachdem er ſeit 1779 die Kriegsſchulen zu Brienne und Paris beſucht hatte,
trat er am 1. Sept. 1785 als Lieutenant der Artillerie in die Armee ein. Im Jahre 1793
wurde er als Artilleriehauptmann ſeitens der Republik gegen die Aufſtändiſchen in Korſika
verwandt, welche ihn ächteten, da er als Landsmann gegen ſie kämpfte. Seit dem 12. Sept.
1793 Oberbefehlshaber des Belagerungsgeſchützes von Toulon, welches ſich in den Händen
der Engländer befand, zwang er den Platz am 19. Dez. zur Kapitulation, worauf er zum
Brigadegeneral der Artillerie befördert ward und in der Armee von Italien im Kriege
gegen Oſtreich diente. Nachdem er ſich vielfach ausgezeichnet hatte, wurde er im Februar
1796 zum Oberbefehlshaber der Armee von Italien ernannt, reorganiſierte dieſelbe, eroberte

in kurzem die Lombardei, schlug die Östreicher in mehreren großen Schlachten, zwang
Mantua zur Kapitulation, drang in Istrien, Kärnthen und Steiermark ein und schloß am
18. April 1797 zu Campo Formio den für Frankreich höchst günstigen Frieden mit
Östreich ab. Seit dem 9. März 1796 mit der verwitweten Generalin Josephine Beau-
harnais vermählt, ward er am 7. Febr. 1800 neben Cambacérès und Lebrun, welche ihm
beratend zur Seite standen, auf zehn Jahre zum ersten Konsul ernannt. Nach mehreren siegreichen Kriegen mit Östreich, Preußen, Rußland, England u. a., ward er im
Mai 1802 durch Senatsbeschluß auf weitere zehn Jahre und am 2. Aug. desselben
Jahres auf Lebenszeit zum Konsul ernannt. Am 8. Mai 1804 wurde er jedoch schon als
Napoleon I. zum erblichen Kaiser der Franzosen erklärt. Nun folgte eine fast ununter-
brochene Reihe von Kriegen mit fast allen europäischen Mächten, und als er im Jahre
1809 den Höhepunkt seiner Macht erreicht hatte, ließ er sich, seiner kinderlosen Ehe wegen,
von seiner ebenso klugen wie liebenswürdigen Gemahlin scheiden und vermählte sich am 2.
April 1810 mit Marie Luise, der Tochter Franz I. von Östreich. Als er jedoch 1812
Rußland den Krieg erklärte, mit der großen Armee in Rußland einzog, alles hinter sich
der verbrannte und zerstörte, dann aber durch die weltbekannte, stets denkwürdige Einä-
scherung der großen Hauptstadt Moskau seitens der beldenmütigen, verzweifelnden Einwohner gezwungen wurde, den Rückzug anzutreten, auf dem fast die ganze große Armee von
der fürchterlichen Kälte und die durch die Veröbung des Landes verursachte Hungersnot vernichtet wurde—schien das Glück ihn verlassen zu haben. Von dieser Zeit an folgte eine
Niederlage nach der andern, von denen die große Völkerschlacht bei Leipzig (18. Okt. 1813),
in welcher der unglückliche Kaiser den vereinigten Heeren der Preußen, Östreicher und
Russen gegenüber stand, die entscheidende war. Napoleon wurde in derselben gänzlich
geschlagen und die stiehende Armee von den Verbündeten unter Blüchers Führung ver-
folgt. Nach der Einnahme von Paris seitens der Alliirten am 31. März 1814 erfolgte
dann die durch den Senat erzwungene Abdankung des Kaisers und dessen Verbannung
nach der Insel Elba, von wo er jedoch schon anfangs März des Jahres 1815 zurückkehrte.
Sein bloßes Erscheinen war genügend, das französische Volk aufs neue für ihn zu begeistern.
Überall wurde er mit Jubel begrüßt, sein Vordringen war unwiderstehlich, die Armee ging
freudig zu ihm über, und schon am 14. März war der König Ludwig XVIII. gezwungen,
den jüngst bestiegenen Thron zu verlassen und sich durch die Flucht ins Ausland zu
retten.—Napoleons zweite Regierung war indessen nur von kurzer Dauer (100 Tage).
Der langersehnte Friede konnte nur durch seinen Untergang herbeigeführt werden, weshalb
die Großmächte Östreich, Rußland, Preußen und England am 25. März einen Alli-
anzvertrag abschlossen, durch den sie sich verbanden, Napoleon gemeinschaftlich zu be-
kämpfen und der Herrschaft desselben auf immer ein Ende zu machen. Dies gelang ihnen
auch bald, denn am 18. Juni 1815 wurden die noch übrigen, schnell von Napoleon
zusammengerafften Streitkräfte Frankreichs in der großen Schlacht bei Waterloo unter
Wellingtons und Blüchers Führung gänzlich vernichtet. Napoleon wollte am 21. Juni
zu Blois zu gunsten seines noch unmündigen Sohnes abdanken, seine Abdankung wurde
aber nicht angenommen, und als er sich am 3. Juli in Rochefort nach Amerika einschiffen
wollte, fand er den dortigen Hafen durch englische Kriegsschiffe gesperrt, worauf er sich unter
den Schutz Englands stellte und sich auf das Linienschiff Bellerophon begab. Auf
Beschluß der verbündeten Mächte wurde er nun als 'General Bonaparte' nach der
entlegenen Insel St. Helena transportiert, wo er am 16. Okt. 1815 anlangte und, in
Longwood wohnend, am 5. Mai 1821 in den Armen einiger ihm noch treu verbliebenen
Freunde eines natürlichen Todes starb. 2, = task. 3, and emergency, und in
jedem Notfalle. 4, what — next = what he must (Impf.) do next (zunächst).
5, This — spirits = This strengthens and refreshes the courage. 6, Read
S. 6, N. 10, and insert the adv. 'auch' here. 7, Say 'Only few men know
what they must do next'. 8, to be at the end of one's line (*or* to be at
one's wit's end), sich nie zu raten wissen. 9, auf eine göttliche Eingebung.
10, Say 'had his ends (= aims) been solely directed to (auf) the public welfare'.
Carefully study App. §§ 36 and 37. 11, This passage requires an altogether different setting; let us say: 'But notwithstanding (Trotzdem aber) he
inspires (erfüllen) us through the extraordinary unity (Einheit, f.) of (in) his

actions with confidence in (auf) his strength'.   **12,** firm = unshakable; sure, unfehlbar = never failing.   **13,** = purpose.   **14,** ir'releiten, sep. comp. w. v.   **15,** by — means, durch die Größe seiner ihm zu Gebote stehenden Hülfs= mittel.   **16,** 'but', here wohl aber.   **17,** to be hurried away, sich . . . hin und her treiben lassen.   **18,** is = signifies (heißen); 'to have', here = to follow, befolgen.   **19,** doors = gates (Pforten), through which he tried (suchen) to attain his aims (App. § 19).   This addition seems to be necessary to complete the underlying idea.   **20,** and — circumstances = and in (bei) the dazzle (Verblendung) and the confusion, which ruled (beherrschen) his time, he never lost sight of these aims.   To lose sight of a thing, etwas aus dem Auge verlieren. **21,** Say 'He would have liked (Impf. Subj. of gern haben in connection with the Past Participle of the verb) to shorten (abkürzen) a straight line, in order to attain his purpose'.   **22,** of — successes, welche alle Zeugnis davon ablegen, wie teuer er seine Erfolge erkaufte.   **23,** to set a person down as cruel, einen für grausam halten.   **24,** 'one', here = a man (S. 134, N. 9).   **25,** Say 'he was not', etc.   **26,** Say 'to the man who', etc.   **27,** Say 'He must carry (erobern) the battery'.   **28,** 'to be sacrificed', here dahin gerafft werden.   **29,** Was befehlen Ew. (abbreviation of Eure) Majestät?

Section 157.

NAPOLEON BONAPARTE.

II.

In the plenitude of his resources every obstacle seemed to vanish. "There[1] shall be no Alps," he said; and he built his perfect roads[2], climbing[3] by graded galleries their steepest precipices, until Italy was[4] as open to Paris as any town[5] in France. Having (S. 55, N. 1) decided what was to be done, he did that with[6] might and main. He[7] put out all his strength. He risked everything, and spared[8] nothing; neither ammunition, nor money, nor[9] troops, nor generals, nor[10] himself. If fighting[11] be the best mode of adjusting national differences (as[12] large majorities of men seem to agree), certainly Bonaparte was right in making it thorough[13].

He fought[14] sixty battles. He had never enough. Each victory was a new weapon. "My power would fall[15], were I not to support it by new achievements. Conquest has[16] made me what I am, and conquest must maintain me."

Before[17] he fought a battle, Bonaparte thought[18] little about what he should do in[18] case of success, but a great deal about what he should do in case of a reverse of fortune. The same prudence and good sense marked[19] all his behaviour[20]. His instructions[21] to his secretary at the palace are worth[22] remembering. He said: "During the night enter my chamber as seldom as possible. Do not awake me when you have any good news to communicate[23]; with[24] that there is no hurry; but when you have bad news, rouse me instantly, for then there is not a moment to be lost." His[25] achievement of business was immense, and[26] enlarges the known power of man. There have been (S. 82, N. 7) many working kings, from Ulysses to[27] William of Orange[28], but[29] none who accomplished a tithe of this man's performance.—EMERSON.

1, Es soll keine Alpen mehr geben.   **2,** perfect roads, Kunststraßen.   **3,** Say 'through which he by means of winding, (sich schlängeln) and gradually rising passes climbed the steepest precipices (Abhang, m.) of the Alps'.   **4,** was =

stood; to Paris = to the Parisians.   **The suffix er is used to form names
of male persons and of the inhabitants of countries and places; as —**
der Italiener, the Italian, from Italien; der Hamburger, the inhabitants of Ham-
burgh.   **5,** town in France = French (S. 101, N. 1) town.   **6,** with —
main, aus Leibeskräften.   **7,** Er setzte seine ganze Stärke daran.   **8,** schonen.
9, nor = neither.   **10,** und auch sich selbst nicht.   **11,** = war; be = is; mode,
Art und Weise.   **12,** Say 'as the majority of men seem (S. 107, N. 13) to
think (S. 64, N. 11)'.   **13,** to make (do) a thing thorough(ly), etwas gründ=
lich betreiben.   **14,** to fight battles, Schlachten liefern.   **15,** = sink.
16, = Conquests have; he has made me what I am, er hat mich zu dem gemacht,
was ich bin.   **17,** Ehre, adv.   **18,** to think about a thing, über etwas
nach'denken, read S. 87, N. 6; in — success, im Glücksfalle; in — fortune, im
Unglücksfalle.   **19,** aus'zeichnen.   **20,** Handlungsweise.   *All his* happiness,
sein ganzes Glück; *all our* family, unsere ganze Familie.   **21,** Verhaltungs=
befehl, m., directions for conduct; to, an.   **22,** This is not worth remembering, dies ist nicht der Beachtung wert.   **23,** melten.   **24,** Say literally
'these have no haste'.   **25,** His — business, Seine Arbeitskraft.   **26,** und
erweitert unsere bisherigen Vorstellungen von den im Menschen wohnenden Kräften.
27, bis auf.   **28,** Oranien. Commence this period with : 'From Ulysses',
29, doch keinen, der auch nur ein zehntel von den Thaten dieses Mannes vollbracht hätte
(App. § 33).

Section 158.

THE WARLIKE CHARACTER OF THE GERMANS.

The Germans fight as *a* nation.   Whatever[1] their birth[2] or (S. 10,
N. 9) profession, all are trained[3] soldiers.   The nation is the army; the
army is the nation.   Hence[4] they cannot be moved save at the bidding
of some grand principle, and the stirring[5] of some soul-penetrating[6] *and*
elevating sentiment; and yet they are as sensible[7] as any nation that
they abandon comfort[8], domestic ease, monetary independence, everything[9] which (S. 3, N. 7) men (= man) love and live for, in[10] order to
identify the nation and the army.   But they are willing to pay the price.
They count[11] hardihood of body and trained[12] courage of heart the
noblest riches of a nation. ¶They reckon[13] *that* national independence
and national greatness *are a* thousand times more precious than gold
and silver, and[15] that to die on the field of battle is better and happier
than to rot[14] and crumble away in sybaritic ease.   They[16] hold, too,
that[16] the cause of liberty, and the free noble spirit engendered by the
brotherhood of a nationality which affirms its oneness by noble acts[17], is
blessed by God, and that He will give[18] victory to the armies who go
forth to battle in (S. 3, N. 2) trust in[19] His name.   No wonder[20] they
fight and triumph[21].—ADMIRAL GARBETT.

1, Supply the verb 'be'.   **2,** = station, Stand, m.   **3,** = practised.
4, Say 'Hence they can be moved (erregen) only at (durch) the bidding (Gebet, n.)'.
5, Erweckung, f.   **6,** die Seele ergreifend.   **7,** 'to be sensible', here sich
bewußt sein.   **8,** here die Annehmlichkeiten des Lebens.   **9,** Say 'in short
give up everything', for the verb 'abandon' must be placed at the end of this
clause.   **10,** Say 'in order to prove the identity of the nation and the
army'.   **11,** halten (für).   **12,** here gestählt.   **13,** Say 'and feel
that it is better and nobler to die', etc.   **14,** vermodern; to crumble away,
verfallen; 'ease', here Gemächlichkeit.   **15,** Auch halten sie dafür.   **16,** Con-

strue thus: 'that God will bless the cause (Sache, f.) of liberty', and use the attributive constr. for the transl. of 'and the — nationality'. Any other constr. would be much too clumsy. **17,** = deeds. **18,** to give victory, den Sieg verleihen; to go forth to battle, in die Schlacht ziehen. **19,** auf. **20,** Supply 'then, that'. **21,** = conquer.

Section 159.

THE[1] WAY TO MASTER THE TEMPER.

A London (S. 157, N. 4) merchant, having[2] a dispute with a Quaker concerning a business account, determined[3] to institute a law-suit against him. Desirous of amicably settling[4] the matter, the Quaker called at the house of the merchant, when[5] the latter became so enraged that he vehemently[6] declared to his servant *that* he would (App. §§ 28 and 30) not see his opponent.[7] "Well, friend," said the Quaker quietly, "may[7] God put thee in a better mind." The merchant was[8] subdued by the kindness of the reply, and, after careful consideration, became convinced that[9] he was wrong. He sent[10] for the Quaker, and[11] after making a humble apology, he asked: "How were you able to bear my abuse[11] with so much patience?" "Friend," replied the Quaker, "I was naturally[12] as hot[13] and violent as thou *art*, but I knew that[14] to indulge my temper was sinful, and also very foolish. I observed that men in a passion always spoke very loud, and I thought that[15], if I could control my voice, I should keep down my passion. I therefore made[16] it a rule never to let it rise above a certain key; and by *a* careful observance of this rule I have, with the blessing of God[17], entirely mastered my[18] natural temper."—ALCOTT.

1, Wie man seinen Zorn beherrschen kann. **2,** Change 'having' into 'had'; the object is best placed after 'account'. **3,** Supply 'and' before 'determined'; to institute a law-suit against a person, einen gerichtlich belangen. **4,** to settle a matter amicably, eine Sache auf gütliche Weise erthun. Comp. S. 30, N. 4, and note that the Present Participle 'being' is understood at the commencement of this period. **5,** = whereupon. **6,** = emphatically, nachdrücklich. **7,** Say 'may God alter thy mind (Gesinnung, f.)'. **8,** to be subdued, sich besiegt fühlen; by, durch. **9,** 'that — wrong' may be briefly turned by 'of his wrong'. **10,** to send for a person, einen zu sich rufen lassen. **11,** 'and — asked'. This passage, literally translated, would be inelegant in German, say: 'humbly begged his pardon, and asked then'. Abuse, Beleidigung, f. **12,** von Natur. **13,** = passionate. **14,** = that it was sinful, etc.; to indulge one's temper, seinem Zorn freien Lauf lassen. **15,** = that I could (App. § 33) conquer my anger through mastering my voice (durch Beherrschung meiner Stimme). **16,** We make it a rule never to let our voices rise beyond a certain key, wir machen es uns zur Regel, unsere Stimmen nie über eine gewisse Tonhöhe hinaus zu erheben. **17,** = with God's help. **18,** = my natural inclination to (zu) anger (S. 3, N. 2).

Section 160.

OPINIONS[1] AS TO ENGLISH EDUCATION.

I.

This[2] energy of individual life and example acting throughout society constitute[3] the best practical education of Englishmen. Schools, academies, and colleges [4] give but the [5] merest beginning of culture in comparison with it (S. 4, N. 5). Far higher [6] and more practical is [7] the life-education daily given in our homes, in [8] the streets, behind (S. 3, N. 2) counters [9], in workshops, at the loom and behind the plough, in counting-houses and manufactories, and [10] in all the busy haunts of men. This is the education that [11] fits Englishmen for doing the work and acting the part of free men. This [12] is that final instruction as members of society, which Schiller designated "the education of the human race," consisting [13] in action, conduct [14], self-culture, self-control—all [15] that tends to discipline a man truly, and fit him for the proper performance of the duties of life—a *kind of* education not to be learnt (S. 7, N. 3 *B*) from (aus) books. Lord Bacon observes that [16] "Studies teach not their own use, but that there is (S. 82, N. 7) a wisdom without them and above them, won (S. 7, N. 3 *B*, and S. 2, N. 1) by (burch) observation, a remark that holds [17] true of [18] actual life, as well as of [19] the cultivation of the intellect itself. For *all* observation serves [20] to illustrate and enforce the lesson, that *a* man perfects himself by work much more than by reading [21],—*that* [22] it is life [23] rather than literature [21], action [24] rather than study, *and* character [25] rather than biography [26], which [27] tend perpetually to renovate mankind.

1, Ansichten über.   2, This — society. A good German rendering of the thought underlying this line is so difficult, that the author thinks it best to give at once his own translation, which he hopes will find acceptance : Diese im mehr selbständigen Leben sich entwickelnde Energie und das dadurch gegebene, auf die ganze Gesellschaft wirkende Beispiel.   3, aus' machen.   4, = universities ; 'to give', here gewähren.   5, = a mere.   6, = more important.   7, is — homes, ist die im täglichen Leben gewonnene Erziehung zu Hause.   8, auf.   9, Use this noun in the Sing.   10, und in den vielen andern Geschäftsstätten der Menschen.   11, Say 'that enables Englishmen as free men to do their work and their duty'.   12, This — designated = This education gives also to human society that instruction (Unterweisung, f.), which Schiller calls, etc. Johann Christoph Friedrich von Schiller, geboren am 10. Nov. 1759 zu Marbach, gestorben am 9. Mai 1805 zu Weimar, ist nächst Göthe (Siehe S. 110, N. 1) unstreitig die bedeutendste Erscheinung in der deutschen Litteratur. Als Dichter zeichnete er sich sowohl durch seine ideale, subjektive Richtung, wie auch durch hinreißenden Schwung echt poetischer Begeisterung aus, welche im Drama ihren Höhepunkt erreichte. Aber auch als Geschichtsschreiber und als philosophischer Schriftsteller hat er sich bei seiner Nation einen unsterblichen Namen erworben.   13, = and which consists in (S. 3, N. 2) action, etc.   14, in der sittlichen Auffassung.   15, = and in all that (here follows the verb 'consists', since this is the end of the relative clause introduced in Note 13), which (S. 3, N. 7) educates (bilten) man truly (wahrhaft) and fits (befähigen) him for (zu) the proper performance (= fulfilment) of his duties in life.   16, = that 'Studies do not teach us the application of the same, but', etc.   17, 'to hold true', here = to prove true.   18, = in practical life.   19, of — itself, in Bezug auf die Geistesbildung selbst.   20, = interprets (erklären) and proves the doctrine.   21, here Lektüre, f., with the art.   22, This conj. 'that' is best omitted, since a repetition of subordinate clauses must, as far as possible, be avoided.   23, = practical life ; 'rather than' seems here to be = 'and not'.   24, Thätigkeit, activity.   25, The English word 'character' is so varied in its application that it requires always the greatest discrimination to decide upon its translation, and in this case more than ever. After careful consideration it is thought to be equivalent here to : 'the personal dignity of a man'. **26,** bie Lebensbeſchreibung beſſelben. **27,** welche baju dienen, die Menſchheit ſtets von neuem ju beleben.

Section 161.

OPINIONS AS TO ENGLISH EDUCATION.

II.

Goethe (S. 5, N. 2), in *one of his* conversations with Eckermann at Weimar, once [1] observed: "It is very [2] strange, and I know not whether [3] it lies in race, in climate, in [4] soil, or in their healthy [5] education, but [6] certainly Englishmen seem to have a great advantage over most other men. We see here in Weimar only a [7] minimum of them, and [8] those, probably, by no means the best *specimens*, and yet what splendid fellows they are! And although they come here as seventeen-year-old [9] youths, yet they by no means feel strange in this strange land; on the contrary, their entrance [10] and bearing [11] in society is so confident [12] and quiet, that one would [13] think they were everywhere the masters, and the whole world belonged to them [14]."

"I should not like to affirm, for all that [15]," replied Eckermann [16], "that the English gentlemen in Weimar are cleverer, better educated, and better hearted than our young men."

"That is not the point [17]," said Goethe; "their superiority does not lie in such things; neither [18] does it lie in their birth and fortune [19]; it lies precisely [20] in their having [21] the courage to be what nature made them. There [22] is no halfness about [23] them. They are complete [24] men. Sometimes complete fools also, that I heartily [25] admit, but even that is something, and has its weight."

Thus (App. § 14), in [26] Goethe's eyes, the Englishmen fulfilled, to a great extent, the injunction [27] given by Lessing [28] to those who would be men:

"Think wrongly, if you please, but think for yourselves!"—S. SMILES, "SELF-HELP."

1, = one day.   **2,** 'Very' is often rendered by the superlative of the adv. ſehr.   **3,** 'whether it lies' may be elegantly translated by omitting the conjunction 'whether' and using the inversion.   **4,** im beimatlichen Boben.   **5,** heilſam.   **6,** Say 'but it seems to be certain that Englishmen possess a great superiority over most other men'.   **7,** a minimum = very few.   **8,** = and these (dies) are probably by no means the best, and yet (bennoch aber) they are (ſind es) splendid fellows!   **9,** a thirty-year-old man, ein breißigjähriger Mann.   **10,** Auftreten, n.   **11,** Benehmen, n. **12,** ſicher.   **13,** Render 'would' by the Impf. Subj. of mögen, since the sentence is equivalent to 'that one would be inclined to think'. The following verbs must be constructed according to App. §§ 29 and 30. **14.** Supply 'alone' after 'them'.   **15,** for all that, aber bech, to be placed before 'not'.   **16,** Johann Peter Eckermann, geboren 1792 ju Winſen in ter prenßiſchen Provinz Hannover, geſterben ten 3. Dez. 1854 ju Weimar, war viele Jahre als Göthes Privatſefretär thätig und iſt ter Welt am befannteſten burch die von ihm nach Göthes Tote veröffentlichten 'Geſpräche mit Göthe'. (Er war auch ter Herausgeber (editor) ven Göthes' Nachgelaſſenen Werfen'.   **17,** Sache, f.   **18,** auch

beſteht ſie nicht in.   19, = wealth; Comp. S. 10, N. 9.   20, = simply.
21, The English Gerund preceded by a possessive adjective and a preposition, must be translated by a regular subordinate clause with a conjunction and a finite verb; as—

His superiority lies *in his having* the courage to be what nature made him.	Seine Überlegenheit beſteht darin (S. 87, N. 6), daß er den Mut hat, das zu ſein, was er von Natur aus iſt.

22, Es.   23, an.   24, = whole.   25, = willingly; weight = value.
26, = according to the judgment of Göthe.   27, = advice; by, von; to, an; those = all such; who, die da.   28, (Goeth. Ephraim Leſſing, geboren den 22. Jan. 1729 zu Kamenz (Oberlauſitz), geſtorben den 15. Febr. 1781 in Braunſchweig, hat ſich durch ſeine äſthetiſch-kritiſchen Werke, wie auch durch ſeine Dramen, deren Form, Sprache, Methode und Inhalt faſt unerreichte Muſter ſind, einen unſterblichen Namen in der deutſchen Litteraturgeſchichte erworben.   Sein Wirken als genialer Kritiker, Forſcher und Dichter war von unermeßlichem Einfluß auf die nächſte Entwickelung unſerer Litteratur, die mit ihm und durch ihn ihrer Glanzperiode entgegenſchritt.

Section 162.

A ROYAL JUDGMENT.

A man and his wife named Lambrun had been many years in the service of the unfortunate Queen Mary Stuart, and were sincerely attached to her. The tragical death of that princess had such an effect on the husband that he did not long survive her, and the [1] widow, Margaret Lambrun, resolved to revenge, upon [2] Queen Elizabeth, the [3] death of two persons so dear to her. She (S. 5, N. 2) therefore disguised [4] herself in man's clothes, bought (S. 58, N. 8) a brace [5] *of* pistols, and went [6] to (S. 72, N. 4) London. Soon after, when the queen [7] appeared in [8] public, Margaret endeavoured to [9] make her way through the crowd in order to shoot her [10]; but one of the pistols fell [11], and she was immediately apprehended.

The [12] queen, being informed of the circumstance [13], ordered [14] the man to be brought before her, and said to him: "Well, Sir, who are you [15]? and why do you seek [16] to kill me?"—"Madam," replied Margaret, "I am a woman; I was a long time in the service of Queen Mary Stuart, whom you put [17] to death unjustly; her execution caused [18] the death of my dear husband, who was sincerely attached to her; and my affection for both *of them has* excited [19] me to revenge."—"And how do you think I ought to deal [20] with you?" asked Elizabeth.—"Do you speak as *a* queen or as *a* judge?" returned Margaret.—"As *a* queen."—"Then you ought to pardon [21] me," was the answer.—"And what security [22] can you give me that you will not attempt [16] my life again?"—"Madam, a [23] pardon granted upon conditions ceases to be a favour [24]."—"Well then," said the queen, "I pardon you, and trust to your gratitude for [25] my safety."—P. Sadler.

1, = his.   2, an, with the Dat. of the def. art. The words 'upon — Elizabeth' must be placed before the supine. Comp. App. § 1.   3, We lament the death of the two boys so dear to us, wir beweinen den Tod der beiden uns ſo teuren Knaben.   4, to disguise oneself in man's clothes, ſich als Mann verkleiden.   **5,** = a pair.   **6,** ſich begeben, insep. comp. str. v. refl.   **7,** Here place the adverbs ' soon after '.   **8,** öffentlich.   **9,** to make one's way, ſich einen Weg bahnen.   **10,** to shoot a person, auf einen ſchießen.   **11,** entfiel ihr.   **12,** Construe accord. to S. 55, N. 1, and S. 4, N. 4, (man).   **13.** Verſall, m.   **14,** ließ ſie den Mann vor ſich führen.   **15,** Use the 2nd pers. pl. (Ihr) here and in the following passages, since that was the pronoun generally used in addressing persons in olden times.   **16,** to seek to kill a person (*or* to attempt a person's life), einem nach dem Leben trachten.   **17,** to put a person to death unjustly, einen ungerechterweiſe hinrichten laſſen.   **18,** This caused the death of our child, dies koſtete unſerem Kinde das Leben.   The insertion of the adv. auch after the verb ' caused ' would considerably improve the German rendering.   **19,** to excite a person to revenge, einen zur Rache antreiben. Use the Impf.   **20,** verfahren.   **21.** begnadigen, v. tr.   **22,** Bürgſchaft, f.   **23,** a — conditions, eine bedingungsweiſe Begnadigung.   **24,** Gnade, f.   **25,** hinſichtlich, followed by the Gen.   The words ' to (auf) your gratitude ' are best placed at the end.

Section 163.

TACITUS.

I am glad to find[1], by your (= thy) letter just received, that you are reading Tacitus[2] with *some* relish.   His style is rather quaint[3] and enigmatical, which (S. 3, N. 7) makes[4] it difficult to the student ; but then[5] his pages[6] are filled with such admirable apothegms and maxims of political wisdom, as[7] infer the deepest knowledge of human nature ; and it is particularly necessary that any one intending to become a public speaker should[8] be master of his works, as[9] there is neither an ancient nor a modern author who affords such a selection of admirable quotations.   You should exercise yourself frequently in[10] trying to make translations of the[11] passages which most strike[12] you, trying[13] to invest[14] the sense of (S. 25, N. 5) Tacitus in as good English as you can.   This will answer[15] the double purpose of making yourself familiar with the Latin author, and giving you the command of[16] your own language, which no person will ever have[17] who[18] does not study composition in early life.—SIR WALTER SCOTT, " LETTERS TO HIS SON."

1, here erſehen ; by, aus.   **2,** Use the def. art. accord. to S. 25, N. 5.   **3,** — unusual and unclear (dunkel).   **4,** to make difficult, erſchweren ; student = pupil.   **5,** = on the other hand, andererſeits.   **6,** = writings, Schriften : filled with such, ſo voll von.   **7,** as infer = that they prove.   **8,** Say ' should thoroughly (gründlich) know his works '.   **9,** Say ' as there is (S. 82, N. 7) no classical nor (noch) modern author (Schriftſteller) '.   **10,** in trying = in the attempt, in dem Verſuche.   **11,** = such.   **12,** This passage struck me most, dieſe Stelle machte am meiſten Eindruck auf mich.   **13,** trying = and try.   **14,** wiedergeben, sep. comp. str. v. tr.   **15,** This does not answer my purpose, dies entſpricht meinem Zwecke nicht.   **16,** über.   **17,** = obtain.   **18,** welcher ſich nicht ſcheu in der Jugend in ſchriftlichen Aufſätzen übt.

Section 164.

HUMILITY.

I believe the first[1] test of a truly great man is his humility.   I do not mean by[2] humility, doubt of[3] his own power, or hesitation[4] in speaking[5] his opinions, but a right understanding of the relation between[6] what he can do and say, and[7] the rest of the world's sayings and doings. All great men not only know[8] their business[9], but usually know[10] that[11] they know it; they are not only right in their main opinions[12], but they usually know that they are right in them (S. 4, N. 5, *B*); only they do not think much of themselves on[13] that account. Arnolfo[14] knows he can build a good[15] dome at Florence; Albert[16] Dürer writes calmly[17] to one who had found fault with his work: "It cannot be better done;" Sir Isaac Newton knows that he has worked[18] out a problem or two that would have puzzled anybody[19] else:—only they do not expect their[20] fellow-men therefore to fall down and worship them; they[21] have a curious under-sense of powerlessness, feeling (S. 30, N. 4) that the greatness is[22] not in them, but through them; that they could (App. § 33) not do or be anything else than[23] what God made them. They see something divine and God-made[24] in every other man, and are endlessly, nay[25] incredibly merciful[26].—Anonymous.

1, = best; test, Prüfstein, m.   2, unter, which place at the head of the period; mean = understand.   3, an, with the Dat.   4, here Unentschlossen-heit.   5, aussprechen.   6, von.   7, = and of that which the remaining world can say and do.   8, = understand.   9, Sache, f.   10, wissen, after which insert the adv. auch.   11, that they understand the same (to agree with Sache).   12, Hauptansichten.   13, on that account, deswegen, which place after the Subj.; to think much of oneself, eine große Meinung von sich haben.   14, Arnolfo di Cambio, berühmter Baumeister und Bildhauer zu Florenz (1232–1300), baute den Dom St. Maria del fiore zu Florenz und das Taber-nakel zu St. Paolo in Rom.   15, = stately.   16, Albrecht Dürer, geboren den 20. Mai 1471 zu Nürnberg, gestorben den 6. April 1528 ebendaselbst, muß zu den hervorragendsten und vielseitigsten Künstlern gezählt werden, die je gelebt. Er war nicht allein ausgezeichneter Maler, sondern auch zugleich Kupferstecher (engraver on copper), Formschneider (moulder), Bildhauer (sculptor), Architekt und Schriftsteller (author) über die Kunst. Er war der Erfinder der Ätzkunst, erfand das Mittel, die Holzschnitte mit zwei Farben zu drucken, und vervollkommnete die Schriftgießerei (type-foundry), denn von ihm stammt die Form der deutschen Lettern.   17, gelassen; one, jemand.   18, to work out a problem or two, Probleme lösen.   19, anybody else, jeder andere, as Nom.   20, = that their fellow-men therefore (deshalb) must (sollen) fall down before them and worship (anbeten) them. The auxiliary sollen must be placed last, accord. to App. § 18.   21, they — powerlessness. This clause cannot be rendered in a literal way, but may be expressed thus: 'they recognise that they are, after all, only powerless'; after all, only, doch nur, which place after the Subj.   22, is not = manifests itself not (sich offenbaren).   23, als wozu Gott sie erschaffen.   24, Gotterschaffenes.   25, ja sogar.   26, = forbearing, nachsichtig.

Section 165.

RUSSIAN POLITICAL PRISONERS IN BANISHMENT.

I.

In the cheerless regions of[1] Arkangel, of which the aborigines say: "God made Russia, but the devil made Arkangel," there are (S. 82, N. 7) more than two hundred of those banished ones—men and women, all young, all (= and) poor, most[2] of them sent without trial, few[3] amongst them knowing even of what they are accused. Victor Ivanovitch[4] dines with his friend B., for instance, and[5] after a stroll along[6] the boulevards they separate. B. is arrested that[7] very evening, and when Victor, astonished and horror-stricken[8], hastens[9] to inquire the cause, he finds everybody[10], even B.'s *own* father, as[11] much in the dark as he *is himself;* all questions and petitions on[12] the subject receive[13] vague administrative answers; all friends and relatives are systematically discouraged and silenced; eagerly they wait for[14] the numerous political trials that[15] come on without intermission, hoping[16] to see the missing one's (S. 67, N. 3) name on[17] the list of criminals, or to see[18] his face once more, let[19] it be even in[20] the prisoner's dock ; but as[21] they wait and[22] watch, the prisoner[23] is, without any trial, en route for Arkangel.

Arrived[24] there, the routine (App. § 15) is the same for all ; whatever[25] the crime alleged, the age or sex, the[26] prisoner is taken to the police-ward,—a[27] dreary log-building, containing two sections, one for men, the other for women. The solitary table and chair in the room, the four walls, and even the ceiling, are covered[28] with the names of[29] youthful predecessors, whose pencilled[30] jests and clever caricatures bear[31] witness to the strength of confidence in themselves with which they began[32] their life in exile.

1, des Gouvernements Archangel.   2, most of them, meistens ; sent = sent there ; without trial = without any trial, ohne jegliches Verhör.   3, Say liter. 'of whom even but (nur) few know'.   4, Here follows 'for instance'; with = in company of.   5, Say 'und trennt sich von ihm nach', etc.   6, auf. 7, noch an demselben Abend.   8, aufs höchste erschrecken.   9, to hasten to inquire the cause, sich eiligst nach der Ursache erkundigen.   10, everybody = that all.   11, Supply 'are' (sich befinden) before 'as'.   12, über die Sache. 13, receive — answers = are vaguely (in unbestimmter Weise, which place after government) answered by (S. 106, N. 23) the government.   14, auf. 15, = that follow one another (auf einander folgen).   16, = in the hope. 17, in.   18, zu schauen (App. § 1); face, Angesicht, n.   19, let it be = be it even.   20, in — dock, vor den Schranken des Gerichts.   21, = whilst. 22, and watch = and attentively watch (bewachen) everything.   23, Insert the adv. schon after the subject ; en route for = on the way to.   24, Dort angekommen ; 'routine', here = treatment ; the words 'the same' are to be placed at the end of the clause.   25, whatever — sex, welches Verbrechens der Gefangene auch angeklagt und welches Alters und Geschlechts er auch sei.   26, the — ward = yet (so . . . doch) he is always taken (= conducted) to (in) the police-ward (Polizeiwache, f.).   27, a — women = that consists of (aus) a miserable block-house of (aus) two divisions, one of which is appointed for men and the other for women.   28, beschrieben, p. p.   29, of — predecessors = of the former (früher, adj.) youthful inhabitants of the same (to agree with room). 30, pencilled, mit Bleistift gezeichnet, which use attributively.   31, bear — themselves = prove the intensity (Größe, f.) of the confidence in themselves (Selbstvertrauen, n.).   32, 'to begin', here an'treten, sep. comp. str. v. tr.; ife in exile = banishment.

Section 166.

RUSSIAN POLITICAL PRISONERS IN BANISHMENT.

II.

In this dreary abode[1] a week or ten days is spent, when[2] the governor of Arkangel, after due reflection, marks out[3] for this dangerous personage some final place of exile (S. 76, N. 22, *B*), some [4] miserable little district town [5], such as Holmogor, Shenkoursk, Pinega, or Mexen. The [6] prisoner is then told his "documents" are ready, and a gendarme enters, saying [7] it is time to start [8]. The exile jumps into the jolting post-waggon, two gendarmes jump *in* after him, the bell above [9] the horse's neck begins to ring—and rings *on* for [10] days and weeks—through wood [11], *and* swamp, and plain, along [12] roads inconceivably drear and lonely, until the [13] weary convoy at length arrives at his destination. The little town is desolate and black [14], and consists of log-huts, two unpaved streets, and a wooden church painted green, and the [15] live-stock consists of ten or twelve raw-boned [16] horses, a small herd of sickly [17] cows, and thirty or forty reindeer. The population rarely (S. 102, N. 30) exceeds *one* (S. 132, N. 10) thousand [18], and consists of the Ispravnik [19], ten sub-altern [20] officers, the Arbiter [21] of the Peace, the [22] Crown Forester, a priest, a few shopkeepers, thirty or forty exiles, a [23] chain-gang of Russian felons, and a crowd [24] of Finnish beggars. On his arrival, the prisoner is driven straight to (S. 72, N. 4) the police-ward, where he is inspected [25] by (S. 106, N. 23) the Ispravnik, a (S. 53, N. 9) police officer, who is absolute lord and master of the district. This representative of the Government requires [26] of him to answer the following questions: His [27] name? How old? Married or single? Where from? The address of [28] parents, relations, or friends? Answers [29] to all of which are entered in the books.

1, Aufenthaltsort, m.; a — spent = spends (verbringen) the prisoner eight or ten days.   2, = whereupon.   3, to mark out, bezeichnen; for this = to this (Dat.); personage = character; some final = his definite (definitiv). The Dat. should be placed immediately after 'Arkangel'.   4, = a.   5, Kreis-stadt, f.; such as = as for example.   6, Construe this passage accord. to the following model: I am told the documents are destroyed, Es (S. 104, N. 19) wird mir mitgetheilt, daß die Papiere vernichtet sind.   7, mit dem Bemerken, daß, etc.   8, 'to start,' at a conveyance, a train, etc., is generally rendered by abfahren.   9, = at, an.   10, for years, jahrelang.   11, Use the pl. for this and the two following nouns.   12, auf. Read S. 128, N. 11.   13, the — convoy = the exhausted travellers.   14, black = gloomy. 15, Viehstand, m.   16, abgemagert.   17, siech.   18, Supply 'souls'. 19, This term may be used in its unaltered form, but is perhaps better rendered by 'Polizeipräsident', m.   20, Unterbeamte, m.   21, Friedensrichter. 22, Nom. der kaiserliche Forstbeamte.   23, einem Haufen russischer Verbrecher in Ketten.   24, = number.   25, = examined; who — district = with absolute (unumschränkt) power (Vollmacht, f.) over the whole district.   26, begehren; to answer = the answer, die Beantwortung, followed by the Gen., but without art.   27, = your.   28, Say 'of your parents'.   29, Say 'and the answers to (auf, with Acc.) these questions are all entered (ein'tragen) in the books.

Section 167.

RUSSIAN POLITICAL PRISONERS IN BANISHMENT.

III.

A [1] solemn promise is then exacted of him that he will not give lessons of [2] any kind, or [3] try to teach [4] anyone; that every letter (S. 48, N. 6)

he writes will go through the Ispravnik's hands, and[5] that he will follow
no occupation except shoemaking, carpentering, or field labour.   He is
then[6] told he (App. § 28) is free, but[7] at the same time is solemnly
warned that[8] should he attempt to pass the limits of the town, he would
be shot down like a dog rather than be allowed to escape; and[9], should
he be taken alive, would be sent off to Eastern Siberia without further
formality than that of the Ispravnik's personal order.

The poor fellow takes up his little bundle, and[10], fully realising that
he has now bidden[11] farewell to the culture and material[12] comfort of
his past[13] life, he walks[14] out into the cheerless street.   A group of
exiles, all pale and emaciated, are (S. 107, N. 13) there[15] to (S. 19, N. 7)
greet him, take[16] him to *some of* their miserable lodgings, and feverishly
demand[17] news from home.   The new comer gazes on them as *one* in
a dream ; some are melancholy, and almost mad, others nervously
irritable, and the remainder have evidently tried to find solace in[18] drink.
They live (S. 116, N. 17) in[19] communities of twos and threes, have food,
a scanty provision of clothes, money[20], and books in common, and consider[21] it their sacred duty to help each other in every emergency,
without[22] distinction of (S. 3, N. 2, and S. 10, N. 9) sex, rank, or age.
The noble by[23] birth get sixteen shillings[24] a month from Government
for their maintenance, and[25] commoners only ten, although many of
them are married, and[26] sent into exile with young families[27].

1, Say ‘Hereupon one demands (verlangen) of him the solemn promise’.
2, not of any kind, feinerlei, adj. (indeclinable).   3, or try = and not try.
The auxiliary verb of mood ‘*will*’ need be expressed but once, and stands, of
course?   4, unterrichten, insep. comp. w. v. tr.   5, Say ‘and that he
besides (außer) shoemaking (Schumacherei, f., with def. art.), carpentering and
field-labour, will carry on (treiben) no (feinerlei) occupation.   6, ‘then’,
here (Endlich), with which begin the clause, and construe accord. to S. 4, N. 4
(man).   7, but —warned, aber zugleich fündigt man ihm an.   8, that —
escape.   This passage requires an altogether different construction in German ;
say ‘they (man) would upon (bei) an attempt, to go beyond (überschreiten, insep.
comp. str. v. tr.) the limits of the town, not allow him to escape, but rather
(vielmehr) shoot him down like a dog (liter. —but him rather like a dog shoot
down, niederschießen).   9. Say ‘should he however be caught (einfangen) alive,
(je) they (man) would send him without further formality (Formalität, f.), upon
the simple order of the Ispravnik to the East of Siberia.   10, and —
realising = and well knowing (pres. p.).   11, to bid farewell, Lebewohl
sagen.   12, materielle Bequemlichkeiten (Nom. pl.), which use with the def.
art. in the Dat. pl.   13, = former.   14, to walk out into the street,
in die Straße hinaus'schreiten.   15, = outside.   16, Supply the pron.
‘these’ before the verb take (führen, i. e. lead); to = into.   17. to demand
news from home, einen nach Nachrichten aus der Heimat fragen.   18, in drink,
im Trunke.   19, in — threes, je zwei oder drei zusammen.   20, Supply
‘as also’ before ‘money’; in common, gemeinschaftlich.   21, My parents
consider it their duty to help their neighbours in every emergency, meine
Eltern halten es für ihre Pflicht, ihren Nachbarn in jeder Not und Gefahr beizustehen.
22, Insert ‘und zwar’ before ‘without’, which will improve the rendering
very much.   23, von.   24, 1 sh. = 1 Mark; a month, monatlich, jeden
Monat, or alle Monate.   25, doch die Bürgerlichen ; repeat ‘Mark’ after ‘ten’.
26, and sent = and are being sent (see S. 2, N. 1).   27, = children.

Section 168.

RUSSIAN POLITICAL PRISONERS IN BANISHMENT.

IV.

Daily a gendarme visits[1] their lodgings, inspects[2] the premises when
and how he pleases[3], and now[4] and then makes some mysterious entry
in his note book.   Should[5] any of their number carry a warm dinner, a
pair of newly-mended boots, or a change of linen to some passing exile
lodged for the moment in the police-ward, it is just as likely as not
marked against him as a crime.   It is a crime to[6] come and see a friend
off, or accompany[7] him a little on the way.   In[8] fact, should the Ispravnik feel[9] out of sorts—the effect of cards[10] and drink—he[11] vents
his bad temper on the exiles; and as[12] cards and drink are the only
amusements in these dreary regions, crimes[13] are often marked down
against the exiles in astonishing numbers, and[14] a report of them sent
to the Governor of the province.

Winter lasts eight months, a[15] period during which the surrounding[16]
country presents the appearance of a noiseless[17], lifeless, frozen marsh.
No roads, no communication with the outer world, no means of[18] escape.
In course of time almost every exile is attacked[19] by nervous convulsions, soon[20] followed by prolonged apathy and complete prostration.
Some of them contrive[21] to forge passports, and by a miracle, as[22] it
were, make their escape ; but the great majority of these victims of the
Third Section[23] either go mad, commit suicide, or die of[24] delirium
tremens.—JAMES ALLEN.

1, visits = comes into.   2, = who inspects (unterſuchen) the house.
3, Do as you please, thun Sie, wie es Ihnen beliebt.   4, now and then, dann und
wann, or von Zeit zu Zeit, after which insert the adverbs auch wohl; some = a ;
to make an entry in a book, eine Bemerkung in ein Buch eintragen.   5, Arrange
this period in the following manner: ' Should one of them to a for the moment
in the police-ward lodged (untergebracht) and passing (durchreiſent) exile ever (je)
a warm dinner, a pair of newly-soled boots, or some clean linen (Wäſche, f.)
bring, then (je) is (Passive) to him this very (S. 161, N. 2) likely as a crime
ascribed (zur Laſt geſchrieben).   6, He came and saw his friend off, er ſagte
ſeinem abreiſenden Freunde Lebewohl.   7, Will you accompany me a little on
my way?   Wollen Sie mich auf meinem Wege eine kleine Strecke begleiten?   8, = In
short, Kurz.   9, to feel out of sorts, übler Laune ſein.   Insert the adv. einmal
after the subject.   10, = card-playing ; see S. 3, N. 2, and S. 10, N. 9.
11, he — exiles, ſo müſſen ihm die Verbannten dafür büßen.   12, The adverbial
circumstance of place ' in — regions ' is best placed immediately after the conj.
13, crimes — numbers = an astonishing number of crimes is often ascribed to
the exiles.   Read App. § 5.   14, and — sent to = and reported (melden)
to.   15, a — which = during which time.   16, = whole.   17, See
S. 71, N. 2, which rule applies likewise to adjectives; 'frozen', here zu Eis
erſtarrt.   18, zu, contracted with the art.   19, 'to be attacked', here
heimgeſucht werden.   20, = upon which soon follows a state (Zuſtand, m.) of
prolonged (dauernd) apathy (Stumpfſinn, m.) and complete (gänzlich) prostration
(Hinfälligkeit der Lebenskräfte).   21, He contrived to forge a passport, es gelang
ihm, einen falſchen Paß herzuſtellen.   22, as it were, gleichſam, which place

after 'and'; by = through, burd); to make one's escape, entfommen, insep. comp.
str. v. intr.   23, 'Die dritte Abteilung' nennt man in Rußland das gefürchtete
Departement des Polizeiministeriums, welches mit der geheimen Polizei betraut ist.
24, an, contracted with the Dat. of the def. art.

Section 169.

TAHITI [1].

I.

At[2] daylight Tahiti, an island which must for ever remain[3] classical
to the voyager in the South Sea, was in view.   At a distance the appearance[4] was not attractive.   The[5] luxuriant vegetation of the lower[6] part
could not yet be seen; and as the clouds rolled[7] past, only the wildest[9]
and most precipitous peaks showed themselves[8] towards[10] the centre of
the island.   As soon as we anchored in[11] Matavai Bay we[12] were surrounded by canoes.   After dinner we landed and enjoyed the delights[13]
always[14] produced by the first impressions of a fine country.   A crowd
of men, women, and children was collected on the shore, *ready* to (S. 19,
N. 7) receive us with laughing, merry faces.   They[15] marshalled us towards
the house of (S. 10, N. 2) Mr. Wilson, the[16] missionary of the district,
who met[17] us on the road, and gave[18] us a very fine reception.   After
sitting[19] a short time in his house, we separated from our host to[20] walk
about, and[21] returned in the evening.

The[22] land capable of cultivation is[23] scarcely in any part more than
a fringe of low alluvial soil, accumulated round[24] the base of the mountains, and[25] protected from the waves of the sea by a coral reef, which
encircles the entire line of coast.   Within the reef there[26] is an expanse
of smooth water, like that of a lake, where[27] the canoes of the natives
can ply with safety, and where[28] ships anchor.   The low land, which[29]
comes down to the beach of coral sand, is covered[30] by the most beautiful productions of[31] the intertropical regions.   In the midst of bananas[32],
orange, cocoa-nut, and bread-fruit trees, spots[33] are cleared where yams[34],
potatoes, the sugar-cane, and pine-apples are cultivated[35].

1, Tahiti ist die größte der Gesellschaftsinseln (Society Islands) im stillen Meere
oder der Südsee (Pacific Ocean) und besitzt ungefähr 9200 Einwohner, welche seit 1815
durch englische Missionäre zum Christentum bekehrt sind.   Die Bibel ist in die Sprache
der Eingebornen übersetzt, und auch in den Kirchen und Schulen wird in der Landessprache
gepredigt und gelehrt.   2, = At the break of day (Beim Tagesanbruch) we saw
Tahiti.   3, = appear, erscheinen.   The words 'to — Sea' must be placed
after the rel. pron., and are followed by 'for ever' (stets).   4, = view.
5, Use the active Voice of the verb with 'man', which should commence the
clause.   6, 'lower', here niedriger belegen.   7, rolled past, an uns
vorüberzogen.   8, Supply 'to us' after 'themselves'.   9, wüst.   10, = in
the middle.   11, in der Bucht von Matavai.   12, = we found ourselves
surrounded by (von) canoes (Baumkahn, m.).   13, Freuen.   14, Say
'which the first sight of a fine country always produces (hervor rufen) within
us'.   15, = These conducted us.   16, des Bezirksmissionärs.   17, He
will meet me on the road, er wird mir halbwegs entge genfommen.   18, to give
a person a very fine reception, einen höchst freundlich bewillfommnen.   19, ver.

weilen; construe this clause accord. to S. 55, N. 1.   20, Inf. einen Spaziergang machen.   21, = from which we returned in the evening (abends).
22, Der kulturfähige Teil der Insel.   23, is — soil = consists nearly every-.
where only of (aus) a narrow strip of low (niedrig belegen) alluvial land (use the
Gen. without the art.).   24, round the base, rings herum am Fuße.   25, Say
'and is protected'; from, ver.   26, there is = finds itself (sich befinden);
an expanse of water, eine ausgedehnte Wasserfläche; 'smooth', here fast spiegelglatt.
27, The literal rendering of this passage would not read well, say 'which (to
agree with Wasserfläche) affords (App. § 5) perfect (völlig) safety to the canoes of
the natives'.   28, = in which.   29, = which reaches down (hinun'ter-
reichen) to (bis zu) the beach consisting of coral-sand.—Use the attributive
const., S. 48, N. 6.   30, 'covered', here bewachsen; by, mit.   31, der
zwischen den Tropen belegenen Gegenden.   32, See S. 71, N. 2.   33, to
clear a spot (of trees, etc.), eine Stelle urbar machen.   34, Damswurzeln.
35, kauen.

Section 170.

TAHITI.

II.

Even the brush-wood is[1] an imported fruit-tree, *namely*, the guava[2],
which grows in abundance here. In Brazil I have often admired the
varied[3] beauty of the bananas (S. 71, N. 2), palms, and orange-trees
contrasted[4] together; and here we also have the bread-fruit[5], conspicuous[6] from its large, glossy, *and* deeply digitated leaves. It is
admirable[7] to behold groves of a tree, sending[8] forth its branches with
the vigour of an English oak, loaded[9] with large *and* most nutritious
fruit[10].

However[11] seldom the usefulness of an object can account for the
pleasure of beholding it, in the case of these beautiful woods, the knowledge of their high productiveness, no doubt, enters largely into the feeling of admiration. The[12] little winding paths, cool from the surrounding
shade, led to the scattered[13] houses, the owners of which everywhere
gave[14] us a cheerful[15] *and* most hospitable reception.

I[16] was pleased with nothing so much as with the inhabitants. There[17]
is a mildness in the expression of their countenances which at once
banishes the idea of[18] a savage, and an intelligence[19] which shows that
they are[20] advancing in civilisation. The common people, when working,
keep[21] the upper part of their bodies quite naked; and[22] it is then that
the Tahitians are seen to advantage. They are very tall, broad-shouldered,
athletic, and well proportioned. It (S. 4, N. 4, man) has been remarked
that[23] it requires little habit to make a dark skin more pleasing and
natural to the eye of a European than his own colour.

1, = consists of.   2, der Guavabaum, dessen pomeranzenartige (orange-like)
Früchte in Zucker eingemacht oder auch in Gelee verwandelt verjanet werden.   3, mannigfaltig.   4, Say 'which form such a great contrast'.   5, Brotbaum, m.
6, conspicuous, welcher ... sogleich auffällt, i. e. strikes the eye; from, durch; its
deeply digitated leaves, seine tief eingeschnittenen, fingerförmigen Blätter.
7, = splendid; groves of a tree = a forest of trees.   8, = spreading out
their, etc.   9, = and are at the same time (dabei) loaded.   10, Use

this noun in the pl.   **11,** Arrange this period thus: 'Although the usefulness of an object perhaps only seldom explains to us the pleasure, which we experience at the sight of the same, yet (ſo ... ted) our admiration at the sight of these splendid groves (Wälder) is no doubt considerably influenced by (= through) our knowledge of (von) their great fertility.   **12,** The—shade = The narrow, winding (ſich ſchlängelnd), shady *and* cool foot-paths.   **13,** zerſtreut liegend.   **14,** gewähren.   **15,** freundlich, but here wohlwollend, in order to avoid a repetition of the same term, since 'hospitable' must be turned by gaſtfreundlich; reception, Aufnahme, f.   **16,** Say ' Nothing gave (machen) me greater joy than just (gerade) the inhabitants'.   **17,** Say 'The expression of their faces (Ihr Geſichtsausdruck) bears a mildness (Sanftmut, f.), which', etc. **18,** = of savages.   **19,** Intelligenz, f.   **20,** are advancing = make progress. **21,** = they have. It is a matter of course that the conj. 'when' must commence the period.   **22,** = and just then one sees the Tahitians (die Tahitianer) to advantage (= in the best light).   **23,** = that after *a* short time a dark skin appears to the eye of a European more pleasing and more natural than his own.

Section 171.

TAHITI.

III.

A white man bathing (S. 16, N. 4) by the side of a Tahitian was [1] like a plant bleached (S. 7, N. 3, attrib.) by the gardener's art compared [2] with a fine dark-green *one* growing vigorously [3] in the field. Most of the men are tatooed, and the ornaments follow the curvature [4] of the body so [5] gracefully, that they [6] have a very elegant effect. The most common pattern, varying [7] in its details, is *somewhat* like [16] the crown of a palm-tree. It springs [8] from the central line of the back, and gracefully curls [9] round both sides. The simile may [10] be a fanciful one, but I [11] thought the body of a man thus ornamented [12] was (App. §§ 29 and 30) like [13] the trunk of a noble tree embraced [14] by a delicate creeper.

Many of the elder people [15] had their feet covered with small figures, so [16] placed as to resemble a sock. This fashion, however, is partly gone [17] by, and has been succeeded [18] by others. Here [19], although fashion is far from immutable, every one must abide [20] by that prevailing at his youth. An old man has thus [21] his age for ever stamped on his body, and *he* cannot assume [22] the airs of a young dandy. The women are tatooed in the same manner as the men, and [23] very commonly on their fingers.

In [24] returning to the boat, we witnessed [25] a very pretty scene. Numbers [26] of children were playing on the beach, and had lighted bonfires, which illuminated the placid sea and [27] surrounding trees; others, in [28] circles, were singing Tahitian verses. We seated ourselves on the sand, and [29] joined their party. The songs were impromptu [30], and [31] I believe related to our arrival. One little girl sang a line [32], which [33] the rest took up in parts, forming [34] a very pretty chorus. The whole scene made [35] us unequivocally aware that [36] we were seated on the shore of an island in the far-famed South Sea.—CHARLES DARWIN.

1, = appeared.   2, = in (contracted with the Dat. of the def. art.)
comparison.   3, = in full vigour (Kraft, f.).   4, Kurvatur, f.   5, auf
eine so anmutige Weise.   6, they have a = they are of.   7, varying —
details = the single parts of which often differ (abweichen) from each other.
8, springs from, geht ... aus; from — back, vom Rückgrat (spine).   9, to curl
round, sich um ... herumwinden.   10, may — one = is perhaps fanciful (phan-
tastisch).   11, ich dachte bei mir selbst.   12, Use the attribut. const.
13, wie.   14, = which is embraced (umschlingen, insep. comp. str. v.) by
(S. 106, N. 23) a delicate (zart) creeper (Schlingpflanze, f.).   15, = men.
16, = which were so arranged that they resembled (gleichen, to be like, str. v.
governing the Dat.) a sock.   17, = antiquated, veraltet.   18, verdrängt,
i. e. displaced.   19, Say 'Although fashion here is far from (weit davon
entfernt) being (S. 1, N. 3) immutable.   20, to abide by a thing, bei etwas
verbleiben. Use the attributive constr. in this clause.   21, Auf diese Weise,
which place at the head of the period. 'Old', here bejahrt; 'to stamp', here
aufprägen.   22, to assume the airs of a dandy, den Stutzer spielen.
Render 'not' by 'not possibly', unmöglich.   23, = but generally also.
24, = When we returned to the vessel.   25, Yesterday I witnessed a very
pretty scene, gestern bot sich mir ein sehr hübsches Schauspiel dar.   26, = Numerous
children.   27, und die in der Nähe stehenden Bäume.   28, = who formed
a circle (Kreis, m.), sang verses in their mother-tongue (i. e. native language).
29, = and joined them (sich anschließen, sep. comp. str. v. refl., governing the
Dat.).   30, aus dem Stegreif.   31, = and related (sich beziehen, insep. comp.
irreg. v. refl.), I believe (inverted), to (auf) our arrival.   32, the 'line' of
a verse is generally rendered by 'Strophe', f.   33, which — parts, welche
von den übrigen mehrstimmig aufgenommen wurde.   34, = and formed.
35, made — aware, legte unzweifelhaftes Zeugnis davon ab.   36, = that we
found ourselves.   37, here vielbesungen, adj.

Section 172.

AUDUBON[1], THE AMERICAN ORNITHOLOGIST, RELATES HOW NEARLY[2] A THOUSAND OF HIS ORIGINAL DRAWINGS WERE DESTROYED.

I left the village *of* Henderson, in Kentucky, situated[3] on the banks
of the Ohio, where I[4] resided for several years, to proceed[5] to Phila-
delphia on business. I (S. 115, N. 1) looked[6] to my drawings before
my departure, placed them carefully in a wooden box, and gave[7] them
in charge of a relative, with[8] injunctions to see that no injury should
happen to them. My absence was of (= lasted) several months ; and
when I returned, after[9] having enjoyed the pleasures of home *for* a few
days, I inquired[10] after my box, and[11] what I was pleased to call my
treasure. The box was produced[12] and opened; but[13], reader, feel for
me—a pair *of* Norway rats had taken possession of the whole, and
reared a young family among the gnawed[14] bits of paper, which, but[15]
a month previous, had represented nearly a thousand inhabitants of[16]
the air! The burning heat which[17] instantly rushed through my brain
was too great without[18] affecting my whole nervous system. I slept
for (S. 166, N. 10) several nights, and the days passed like[19] days of
oblivion—until[20] the animal powers being recalled into action, through
the strength of my constitution, I[21] took up my gun, my note-book and

my pencils, and went forth to the woods as gaily as if nothing had happened. I [22] felt pleased that I might now make better drawings than before ; and, ere a period not exceeding three years had elapsed, my portfolio was again filled.—JOHN AUDUBON.

1, Jehn James Nububen, der berühmte amerikanische Ornithologe (oder Vogel= kundige), geboren den 4. Mai 1780 in Louisiana, gestorben den 27. Januar 1851 zu New=York, befuhr die Ströme und Flüsse des Westens, um die Vögel zu beobachten und zu zeichnen.   2, nearly a thousand, nahe an tausend.   3, Use the attributive constr., and see S. 7. N. 3, and S. 48, N. 6.   4, = I had resided for (seit). 5, reisen ; on business, in Geschäften.   6, to look to a thing, nach etwas sehen. 7, to give a thing in charge to a person, einem etwas über ge`ben.   8, = with the express command to protect (bewahren) them from (ver) any (jeder) injury. 9, = and had enjoyed. The pleasures of home, die Freuden der Häuslichkeit. 10, to inquire after a thing, nach etwas fragen.   11, = and after (nach) my treasure, as I was pleased to call its contents (wie ich dessen Inhalt gerne zu bezeichnen pflegte).   12, = brought.   13, = but have pity on (mit) me, O reader !   14, zernagt ; bits of paper, Papierfetzen.   15, noch ver einem Menat.   16, der Lüfte, which is the poetic form.   17, = which instantly took possession of my brain (Gehirn, n.). To take possession of a thing, sich einer Sache bemächtigen.   18, um nicht auch mein ganzes Nervensystem zu erschüttern. 19, like — oblivion, im gänzlichen Vergessen alles Geschehenen.   20, = till my vital powers (Lebenskräfte) were reanimated (wieder angeregt waren, App. § 17) through the strength of my constitution (Natur, f.).   21, Say 'and I was able (imstande sein) to take up (ergreifen) my gun (Büchse, f.), my sketch-book and my pencils to (S. 19, N. 7) go therewith again as (so) cheerfully into the woods as if nothing had happened (als ob nichts vergefallen wäre)'.   22, Say 'It gave me pleasure to think that I would now perhaps produce better drawings than ever (je) before ; and even before (noch ehe) three years had passed away, my portfolio was again filled with drawings.

Section 173.

THE BATTLE OF[1] KASSASSIN.

I.

Mahsamah, Monday, August 28, 1882.

At[2] seven this morning, guns were heard in the direction of Kassassin, which is[3] four miles to our front. The troops were called[4] under arms, the Cavalry, consisting of the Household Cavalry[5] and 7th Dragoon Guards, saddled *up*, and the Infantry fell[6] in in readiness to[7] march to the assistance of the force there under General Graham. That officer, however, sent a[8] message saying that the firing was in the enemy's camp, and[9] was inexplicable, except upon the supposition that the Egyptians were fighting[10] among themselves.

At[11] eleven o'clock, however, the flags of the signallers at Kassassin were in motion, and (S. 104, N. 19) the news came that the enemy were approaching[12]. The Cavalry again turned out[13] and rode *off* to Kassassin. As the enemy approached, General Graham opened fire with his two guns, and[14] the Egyptian artillery replied. The 19th Hussars[15] came on[16] to the place from Mahuta, where General Willis has his headquarters.

The enemy made no attack, but halted at[17] a considerable distance from the camp, and kept [18] up a continued shell-fire, but at a distance altogether [18] out of range. Their conduct [19] was, indeed, altogether inexplicable. The Cavalry remained out all day, and the Infantry *here* were kept in readiness to march at [20] a moment's notice, but as the enemy made [21] no movement in advance, they were not called *forward* to the front.

The heat was terrific [22] all day, the [23] sun beating down with almost insupportable force upon the wide sand waste. It [24] had been hard work for horses and men. No shade was obtainable [25], and the hot wind raised [26] great dust storms, which penetrated everywhere and made breathing difficult. The brigade of Guards (S. 36, N. 7, *A*) fell in under arms [2ª] ready [29] to march, but the Cavalry returned and reported that the enemy had fallen back [30], after [31] keeping the troops the whole day out in the full force of the sun.

1, bei. The very graphic account of the Battle of Kassassin given in Sections 173-177 was written by the correspondent of the London ' Standard ', who was with the cavalry at Mahsamah. Kassassin (also called Kassassin Lock) is four miles west from Mahsamah Station, which, only a few days previous to this action, was captured from the Egyptians by General Drury Lowe. The Egyptians had established a camp at that place, and, 'after the capture, the Household Cavalry and the Dragoon Guards were stationed there, under the command of General Drury Lowe, as a reserve to the small force that held Kassassin Lock, an important fortified position occupied by General Graham. The enemy, under the rebel-leader Arabi, held the strongly fortified camp of Tel-el-Kebir, about twelve miles west from Kassassin. Arabi's stronghold (Tel-el-Kebir) was stormed and captured by the English under their skilful Commander-in-chief Sir Garnet Wolseley (now Lord Wolesley of Cairo), on Wednesday, September 13, when the rebel-army was totally beaten, and the Egyptian war brought to a successful issue. **2,** Say ' This (Heute) morning *at* 7 o'clock we (man) heard *the* thunder of cannons (comp. n.)', etc. **3,** = is situated; to our front = before us. **4,** to call under arms, zu ben Waffen rufen. **5,** Nom. Pl. Garbefüraffiere; the 1st Dragoon Guards, bas erste Dragoner Garberegi-ment. **6,** fell – readiness, stellte sich in Reih und Glied. **7,** um ben bert unter General Graham stehenten Truppen zu Hülfe zu eilen. **8,** a — saying – a messenger with the information (Nachricht, f.). **9,** and — supposition, und baß man sich basselbe nur burch bie Vermutung erflären fönne. **10,** The rebels fight among themselves, bie Empörer befämpfen sich unter einander. **11,** = At 11 o'clock, however, we (man) saw the flag-signals (S. 76, N. 22, *A*) at Kassassin. **12,** heran'rücten. Comp. 107, N. 13. **13,** = got ready (sich fertig machen). **14,** which was answered (erwietern) by the Egyptian artillery. **15,** Hufaren-regiment, n. **16,** on — place = here (hieher). **17,** at a = in. **18,** to keep up a continued shell-fire, ein ununterbrochenes Bombarbement (pronounced as in French) unterhal'ten. **18,** welche außer dem Bereiche ber Schußweite lag. **19,** Hautlungsweise, f.; indeed = really; altogether, ganz. **20,** at — notice = any moment. **21,** to make a movement in advance, ver'rücten. **22,** = ex-traordinary great. **23,** = and the sun shone down, etc.; ' force ', here Glut, f. **24,** = Horses and men had had hard work (here einen schweren Stand haben). **25,** = to be found. **26,** Staubwelfen auf treiben. **27,** here hin'bringen. **28,** to fall in under arms, unter Waffen treten. **29,** = and held itself ready to march (sich zum Abmarsch bereit halten). **30,** to fall back, sich zurück'ziehen. See App. §§ 28 and 22. The auxiliary in this clause is best omitted to avoid its repetition, the next sentence containing the same. **31,** = after he (i. e. the enemy) had kept (zurückhalten, App. § 30) the troops the whole day at (bei) the great heat of the sun (comp. n. S. 76, N. 22; use u as a connecting link, since fem. nouns ending in e in olden times used to take u as an inflection for the Gen., Dat., and Acc. Sing., as well as for the Pl.) in the field.

Section 174.

THE BATTLE OF KASSASSIN.

II.

Ismailia[1], Tuesday, August 29,
3 o'clock in the morning.

Scarcely had the Cavalry unsaddled, and[2] horses and men begun to eat, when the[3] sound of artillery was heard (S. 4, N. 4, man) again at Kassassin, and by[4] the heavy *and* continuous roar[5] it was evident[6] that this time the attack was[7] in earnest. Again the wearied men saddled their no less weary horses and[8] prepared to advance. The[9] sun was still beating down fiercely even at that late hour, and the hot withering[10] wind was raising[11] the sand clouds so high that it was impossible to see what was going[12] on, but through the dust and haze numerous[13] jets of smoke from the guns were visible.

The cannonade increased[14] in violence, and the Cavalry moved[15] away to the right, the[16] Artillery following them, and pressed[17] round towards the flank of the enemy's Infantry. With[18] the movement of such masses of men and horses the dust rose over the whole scene thicker than ever, and it was impossible to obtain[19] more than a general idea of what was going on; while the sun set in[20] a red glare over the sandy plain.

The Cavalry pushed[21] still further to the right until[22] hidden from the enemy by some low sand hills, and[23] then goaded their weary horses into as fast a trot as the heavy sand and their weary condition would permit.

It was evident that it was the General's intention to repeat the tactics of the previous fight, and that he meant[24] to get round the enemy's rear. It was a striking proof of his confidence in[25] his troops that (S. 66, N. 15), with[26] tired horses and night approaching, he should attempt this manœuvre against an enemy of unknown strength and with[27] fresh horses. Against any other enemy it would have been rash[28], but the result proved that General Drury Lowe did not over-estimate the fighting powers[29] of his men.

1, Ismailia, then the head quarters of Sir Garnet Wolseley, is 21 miles east of Kassassin, on the Suez Canal. In the morning, morgens. 2, and = and scarcely had; 'men', here Reiter; to begin to eat, mit dem Essen anfangen. 3, the — artillery, Artilleriesalven. 4, = through, durch; heavy — loud. 5, Kanonendonner, m. 6, — clear. 7, = was meant in earnest (ernstlich, adv.). See App § 17. 8, und rüsteten sich zum Vorrücken. 9, Say 'Even at (zu) this late hour the sun sent down burning rays', and insert the adv. noch before 'burning'. 10, versengent. 11, treiben. 12, to go on, vergehen. 13, numerous — guns, zahlreiche aus den Kanonen aufsteigende Rauchsäulen. 14, = became more and more violent (immer with the comparative form of the adj.). 15, to move away, abziehen : to the right, nach rechts. 16, = whilst the A. followed them (ihr, to agree with Kavallerie in the fem. Sing.) 17, 'to press round', here seitwärts vordringen; towards,

auf; 'of — infantry' may be briefly expressed by 'of the hostile Infantry'.
18, With — horses, Durch die maſſenhafte Truppenbewegung.   19, 'to obtain',
here ſich . . . machen; of what was going on, von dem Verlaufe des Gefechts, which
place after the pron. ſich.   20, in — glare, mit blendend rotem Glanze, which
place before the verb, which stands?   21, vor'dringen.   22, until — enemy,
bis dieſelbe den Blicken des Feindes . . . entzogen war.   23, Render 'and —
permit' freely, and say 'und ſprengten dann ihre ermüdeten Pferde zum möglichſt
ſchnellen Trabe an'.   24, gedenken; to — rear, dem Feinde in den Rücken zu fallen.
The Impf. of the verb gedenken stands, of course, after fallen, accord. to App.
§ 19.   25, welches er zu ſeinen Truppen hegte.   26, = in spite of
the tired horses and the approaching (heran'nahen) night.   27, = in the
possession of fresh horses.   28, unbeſonnen, i. e. imprudent.   29, fighting
powers, Stärke, f.; 'men', here = troops.

Section 175.

THE BATTLE OF KASSASSIN.

III.

Soon[1] darkness came down rapidly upon us. The rattle and roar of[2]
combat on[3] our left never ceased, and it was evident that the two thousand Infantry[4] at Kassassin were hard pressed. Presently[5] the moonlight
streamed palely over the grey sand, but the clouds of dust obscured[6] the
advancing horsemen, who sometimes trotted, sometimes[7] walked.

By about seven o'clock we had got in the rear of the firing[8], and[9]
wheeled in that direction, advancing[10] very slowly to[11] allow the Artillery
to[12] come up. We could see the flashes of[13] the enemy's artillery *gleam*
on the horizon like the flicker of incessant summer lightning[14].

We slowly drew[15] nearer to the scene of conflict. It was almost dark[16],
but, unfortunately, we showed up[17] a black mass against the bright
moonlit sky and ground[18], and[19] the sudden rush of shell through the
air, followed[20] by an explosion far in our rear, showed that the enemy
had at last discovered us. They[21] were about fifteen hundred yards[22]
away, and[23] we saw nine flashes, one after another, at short intervals,
spurt out, no[24] longer like sheet lightning, but in angry jets of flame.
Almost simultaneously the sky above us seemed to[24] be torn in pieces as
by (=through) a mighty hurricane. Shells screamed[25] and burst[26], and
shrapnel bullets[27] tore up the sand on either side of us.

The brigade now moved[28] to the right to[29] disconcert their aim, and
the next salvo of shell missed us. We moved quickly forward, and the
gunners again saw us, and the shells burst over and around. Yet,
strangely[30], but few were hit, though it seemed as if the storm[31] would
mow men and horses down by squadrons[32].

1, = Soon after (darauf) the darkness (Dunkel, n.) of the night descended
(hernie'derſteigen) rapidly upon us.   2, = of the.   3, zu.   4, Infan-
teriſten.   5, = Now streamed the pale moonlight, etc.   6, = concealed;
horsemen, Reiterei, f. Sing.   7, zuweilen auch im Schritt dahinritt.   8, = enemy;
got = arrived.   9, und ſchwenkten der Richtung zu, aus der das Schieſſen kam.
10, = advanced (vor'wärtsreiten) however only very slowly.   11, to allow =
to (S. 19, N. 7) give time to.   12, Inf. heraus'kommen.   13, = of the
hostile artillery.   14, = sheet lightning, Wetterleuchten, n.   15, to

draw near, ſich nähern. **16,** The fact of its being dark soon after seven at the end of August is explained when we remember that there is no twilight in Egypt. **17,** = we formed. **18,** Erboten, m. **19,** und das Saufen einer plöglich die Luſt durchfliegenden Bombe. **20,** = which exploded far behind us. **21,** = He (the enemy). **22,** = steps, Schritte; away, von uns entfernt. **23,** Arrange this sentence literally thus: and now saw we nine at (in) short intervals one another (einander) following cannon-shots (Kanonenſchüſſe) spurt out (hervor'bligen). **24,** welche nicht mehr dem Wetterleuchten, ſondern verzehrenden Feuerſtrömen glichen; to — pieces, zu zerreißen. **25,** ſauſen. **26,** plagen . . . in der Luſt. **27,** Granaten. **28,** ab'ſchwenken. **29,** um dem Ziele des Feindes aus dem Wege zu gehen. **30,** ſonderbarerweiſe. **31,** der Kugelregen. **32,** men and horses by squadrons = whole squadrons of (von) men (Menſchen) and horses.—To mow down, hernie'dermähen.

Section 176.

THE BATTLE OF KASSASSIN.

IV.

Now [1] tiny flashes, with the sharp ping of bullets, told that the enemy's Infantry were also at work, whilst [2] a horse here and a man there dropped [3] in the ranks.

The battery having (S. 30, N. 4) by this time come up, the Cavalry moved [4] to the right, in order to [5] allow them to come into action, and *in a few seconds*, after taking up their ground, our guns spoke [6] out their answer to the enemy's fire.

The Cavalry now advanced [7] from the left, the [8] 7th Dragoons leading. Under [9] cover of these the Life Guards formed for a charge, and [10] by word of command the Dragoons opened [11] right and left to allow them to pass. Already Herbert Stewart, General Drury Lowe's brigade-major, had passed [12] down the line the word: "The Cavalry are to charge the guns!" Sir Baker Russell was in front (= at the head), and shouted: "Now we have them. Charge!"

Away [13] went the long line, disappearing [14] almost instantly in the darkness and dust, and *away* behind them went [15] the 7th Dragoons, keeping [16] (S. 16, N. 4) on either flank of the Guards.

We [17], remaining in the rear, had the full benefit of the storm and shot which was to greet the advancing horsemen (Reiterei, f.) and of whom from (S. 102, N. 4) this moment we saw no more till the battle was over; *and* only (S. 109, N. 5) then we learned [18] what they had done.

Led by Baker Russell, they charged [19] straight at the guns, sabring [20] the gunners as they passed, and [21] dashing into and cutting down the flying Infantry beyond them. Russell's horse was shot under him, but he seized another and kept with [22] his men.

The battle was ended [23] at a stroke, and a scene of wild confusion ensued [24]; some guns were [25] still firing, bodies [26] of Infantry still kept up a fusillade, and numerous bodies [27] of horses and men dotted the moon-lit plain.

Being now separated altogether from the Cavalry, with [28] the enemy intervening between us, myself and two companions endeavoured to find our [23] way round to Kassassin. It was an adventurous ride, for several shells burst near us, but before we reached the camp, the conflict was at an end.

1, = At (Jn) this moment (App. § 14) flashes of lightning (kleine Blitze) and the sharp ping (Knallen, n.) of bullets betrayed that also the hostile Infantry were (= was) engaged in the attack (beim Angriff betheiligt sein).   2, Place 'here' after 'whilst', and 'there' after 'and'.   3, zu Boden fallen.   4, 'to move', here ab'ziehen, sep. comp. irreg. v.   5, = in order to allow (gestatten) the same (to agree with 'battery') to begin the combat.   6, spoke out their answer to = answered (erwiedern), v. tr.   7, vor'rücken.   8, = and (und zwar) the 7th Regiment of Dr. at (an) the head (Spitze, f.).   9, = Under their (dessen) cover (Schutz, m.) formed the Life Guards (die Garbekürassiere) a line of attack (eine Angriffslinie).   10, = and upon a given command.   11, = opened . . . the ranks (Reihen).   12, to pass the word, den Befehl ergehen lassen; down = all along, längs.   13, Die lange Linie sprengte davon.   14, = and disappeared.   15, away . . . went = followed.   16, to keep, sich halten; on, zu, either flank = both flanks.   17, = Since we remained (zurückbleiben) behind all, (so) we had the full effect of the shower of shot (Kugelregen, m.)   18, = heard.   19, to charge straight at the guns, die feindliche Artillerie sogleich an'greifen.   20, = sabred down; as they passed, auf ihrem Zuge.   21, = and dashed (sprengen) into the ranks of the flying Infantry behind the same, which they (sie, f. Sing. to agree with die Reiterei) cut down (nie'dermetzeln).   22, bei: men = regiment.   23, = with one stroke (Schlag, m.) at an end (zu Ende).   24, = followed.   25, = thundered still.   26, einzelne Teile.   27, bodies — plain = and numerous bodies (Haufen) of Cavalry were still here and there upon the moonlit plain visible.   28, = and the enemy stood between us. (The verb must stand last, since also this clause is a depending one, co-ordinated to the preceding clause by the conjunction 'and'.)   29, our way round, einen Weg seitwärts.

Section 177.

THE BATTLE OF KASSASSIN.

V.

The Infantry there[1] had indeed had a hot time of it[2]. Hundreds of shells had (S. 29, N. 3) burst in the confined[3] space, and the shelter trenches[4] afforded but an insufficient protection. On the left of the position[5], next to the Canal, were[6] the Marine Artillery, then came the 46th, and next[7] to them the 84th[8], the[9] slight earthworks sweeping round again in a semi-circle almost to the Canal. The Mounted[10] Infantry were in front under Captain Pigott, who[11] has received a wound, having been shot through the thigh.

The Egyptians came on with great bravery, and in spite of the[12] heavy fire of our men[13], were rapidly gaining ground, and would soon have rushed[14] into the entrenchments, when the roar of our guns on[15] their left rear, followed[16] by the rush of our Cavalry, proved[17] too much for them, and from (S. 102, N. 4) that moment they thought only of flight.

Our casualties are surprisingly[18] small considering[19] the fire to which our men were exposed. Lieutenant Edwards, of the Mounted Infantry, was[20] shot in the arm, Surgeon-Major[21] Shaw, of the 46th, was[22] killed, and *some* ten or a dozen men, but, fortunately, the Remington bullet wounds rather than kills; the hospital was crowded [23] with wounded men.

About 10 o'clock the Cavalry came in [24] in high spirits over their brilliant achievement. Many, of course, are missing in the darkness, but will, no doubt, turn up [25] in the morning. Upon their [26] return from the pursuit they [27] were unable to find the guns over which they had charged, but these [28] will doubtless be discovered at sunrise. After learning from them [29] the events [30] of the charge, I [31] started to ride here to get off [32] my despatches,—a [33] distance of twenty-four miles. This solitary ride over the dismal desert by moonlight was not [34] the least exciting part of an exciting day.

Late [35] as it was, I found at (auf) the different posts the men [36] busy at work entrenching, and met troops also on [37] their march to reinforce those at the front.

The enemy's force [38] *engaged* was estimated at 13,000. The Egyptians fought well until our Cavalry and guns took [39] them in the rear, and, had [40] it not been for the gallantry of the defenders of Kassassin, would [41] have carried the positon before our reinforcements came upon the scene.

At [42] the time I left, the losses were unknown, but were [43] supposed to be about twenty killed and a hundred wounded.

As [44] I am writing, Sir Garnet Wolseley and [45] the entire army are marching to the front.—The Correspondent of the London "Standard."

1, there, fertig, which is an attributive adj., to be placed before the noun 'Infantry'.　　2, to have a hot time of it, einen schweren Stand haben.　3, = narrow.　　4, die Schanzgräben.　　5, = camp.　　6, = stood.　7, next to them = finally.　　8, Supply 'regiment'.　　9, = whilst the insignificant entrenchments (Verschanzungen) swept round in a semicircle almost to (bis zu) the canal. 'To sweep round,' here sich hinschlängeln, of which the pron. sich must be placed immediately after the subject, and the verb?　10, feritten, adj.　　11, = who was wounded (S. 2, N. 1) and had received a shot through the thigh.　　12, Nom. das lebhafte Schießen.　　13, = troops; were rapidly gaining ground = advanced rapidly (schnell vorwärtsrücken, sep. comp. w. v. intr. Where must you place the verb? and where the separable particle?　　14, to rush into the entrenchments, in die Schanzwerke dringen (str. v.).　15, on — rear, an ihrer linken Flanke.　　16, mit der daranf folgende unerwartete Angriff unserer Kavallerie.　　17, = had not terrified them (einen in Schrecken jagen).　　18, = extraordinarily.　　19, = if one considers (bedenfen), that our troops were exposed to a really murderous fire.　　20, = is wounded; in, an, contracted with the Dat. of the def. art.　　21, Stabsarzt.　　22, was—kills; and ten or a dozen (zehn bis zwölf) men (= privates, Gemeine) are killed, but fortunately the Remington bullet (Kugel, f.) is but (nur) rarely fatal (ist . . . von tödlicher Wirkung).　　23, = quite full of. The wounded man, der Verwundete.　　24, = returned; in high spirits, höchst erfreut.　　25, to turn up, sich wieder ein stellen; 'in the morning', here morgen früh.　　26, = the; from their pursuit, von ihrer Verfolgung.　　27, Literally = could the Cavalry the cannons, which they had conquered, not find again (wiederfinden).　　28, = the same.　　29, = the horsemen (Kavalleristen).　　30, = details, Einzelheiten.　31, ritt ich nach hier ab.　　32, = send off.　　33, Commence a new period here, and say: 'The distance from Kassassin to here [Ismailia] is (beträgt) 24 miles'.　　34, = by no means, keineswegs, adv.　　35, = Notwithstanding the late hour.　　36, Mannschaften.　　37, on their march, welche auf dem Marsch begriffen waren.　　38, Streitkräfte, pl.; was = were; at

13,000, an 13,000 Mann.   **39,** = attacked.   **40,** hätten bie Verteibiger
von Kaffaffin nicht eine folche Tapferfeit bewiesen, so, etc.   **41,** = the enemy
would.   **42,** = When I rode away.   **43,** = were estimated at (auf)
about, etc.   **44,** = Whilst.   **45,** = with.

Section 178.

HOW THE DUKE OF WELLINGTON WAS DECEIVED.

"I (S. 115, N. 1) got famously taken in [1] on that occasion," said the
Duke of Wellington once. "The troops had [2] taken to plundering a
good deal. It was necessary to [3] stop it, and I issued an order announcing [4] that the [5] first man taken in the act should be hanged upon the spot.
One day, just as we were sitting [6] down to dinner, three men [7] were
brought to the door of the tent by the provost. They had been taken
in [8] the act of plundering, and I had nothing for it [9] but to command that
they (S. 4, N. 4, man) should be taken away and hanged in some place
where they might be seen by the whole column in its march next day.
I had *a good* many guests with [10] me on that day, and among the rest, I
think, Lord Nugent. They [11] seemed dreadfully shocked, and could not
eat *their dinner*. I did not eat myself, but, as I told them, I could not
indulge my feelings [12]; I must do my duty. Well [13], the dinner went off
rather gravely; and next morning, sure enough [14], three men in uniform
were seen hanging (S. 78, N. 14, *B*) from the branches of a tree close to
the high road. It was a terrible example, which produced [15] the desired
effect, for there was no more plundering. Some months afterwards I
learned that one of my staff [16] had taken counsel with Dr. Hume, and as
three men had (S. 29, N. 3) just died in the hospital, they had hung
them [17] up and let the three culprits return to their regiments."
  "Were you not very angry, Duke [18]?"
  "Well [19], I suppose I was at first; but [20] as I had no wish to take the
poor fellows' lives and only wanted the example, and as the example had
the desired effect (S. 27, N. 8), my anger soon died out [21], and I confess
to you that [22] I am very glad now that the three lives were spared."—
HISTORICAL ANECDOTES.

1, to be famously taken in, gehörig angeführt werden ; once, eines Tages.
2, = had begun to plunder ; a good deal, tüchtig.   **3,** to — it = to make an
end of this nuisance, biefem Unwesen ein Ende zu machen.   **4,** announcing
that = according to which, wonach.   **5,** the — act = the first man (ber erste)
whom one would take in the act.   To take a person in the act, einen auf
frischer That ertappen.   **6,** to sit down to dinner, sich zu Tische setzen.   **7,** Leute.
8, in — plundering, beim Plündern.   **9,** He has nothing for it, es bleibt ihm
nichts anderes übrig; but, als; in, an; might=could, Impf. Subj.; column =
army; in its march, verbeimarschierend, adj. qualifying 'army'.   **10,** bei ; place
'I think' after 'and'; among the rest = among others.   **11,** = These
seemed to be very much shocked (ergriffen) at (von) the occurrence.   **12,** to
indulge one's feelings, seinen Gefühlen freien Lauf lassen.   **13,** Gut ; went —
gravely, ging ein wenig ernsthaft vonstatten.   **14,** auch wirklich, which place after
the subject, and construe the sentence in the Active Voice with the pron.
man ; men = soldiers.   **15,** = had. There was no more talking, es wurde
nicht mehr gesprochen.   **16,** = one of my staff-officers (Stabsoffiziere) ; to take

counsel in a matter with a friend, eine Sache mit einem Freunde besprechen.
17, = these; culprits = condemned men (der Verurteilte, Nom. Sing.).　18, Waren
(Eure (Ew.) Hoheit nicht sehr erstaunt darüber?　19, Nun ja, anfangs vielleicht
war ich's.　20, = however (aber), since I did not wish (wollen) the death of
the poor fellows, but (sondern) only the example (Here follows the verb).　21, 'to
die out', here ersterben, insep. comp. str. v.　22, To avoid a repetition of
subordinate clauses, say: 'that I am very glad (froh) now at (über) the preservation (Rettung) of the 3 men (Leute).

Section 179.

A LETTER FROM DR. HENRY DANSON TO[1] MR. JOHN FORSTER, ON[2] CHARLES DICKENS'S[3] SCHOOL-LIFE.

I.

My impression is[4] that I was a schoolfellow of Dickens for nearly two
years. He left[5] before me, I think about fifteen years of age. The school,
called (S. 7, N. 3, *B*) *the* Wellington Academy, was in *the* Hampstead
Road at the north-east corner of Granby Street. The school-house was
afterwards taken down[6] on account of the London and North-Western
Railway. It was considered at the time[7] a very superior sort of school,
one of the best indeed[8] in that part of London; but it was most shamefully mismanaged[9], and the boys[10] made but very little progress. The
proprietor, Mr. Jones, was a Welshman[11]; a most[12] ignorant fellow, and
a mere tyrant, whose chief employment was[13] to scourge the boys. Dickens
has[14] given a very lively account of this place in his paper *entitled* " Our
School," but it is very mythical in many respects, and[16] more especially in the compliment he pays in it to himself. I do not remember
that Dickens distinguished himself in any way[16], or carried off *any* prizes.
My belief is[17] that he did not learn Greek or Latin there, and you will
remember[18] there is no allusion to the classics in *any of* his writings. He
was a handsome, curly-headed lad[19], full of animation and animal spirits,
and[20] probably was connected with every mischievous prank in the school.

1, an.　2, über.　3, Charles Dickens, geboren den 7. Febr. 1812 zu
Portsmouth, gestorben den 9. Juni 1870 auf seinem Landsitze bei Leuden, begann seine
schriftstellerische Thätigkeit unter dem angenommenen Namen Boz, welcher ihn schnell
berühmt machte. Er begründete seinen Ruf als englischer Humorist durch die 'Sketches
of London' (1836), und namentlich durch die 'Pickwick Papers' (1837), welches
unstreitig das beliebteste, aber auch vielleicht das beste seiner zahlreichen Werke ist. Er
gründete 1845 die Zeitung 'Daily News', sowie 1850 die Zeitschrift 'Household
Words', welche seit 1860 den Titel 'All the year round' führt. Er besuchte zweimal,
im Jahre 1842 und 1868, die Vereinigten Staaten von Nord Amerika, von wo er das
zweite Mal durch seine vielbesuchten Vorlesungen aus seinen eigenen Werken eine reiche
Ernte heimführte. Von seinen späteren Werken sind 'Oliver Twist', 'Nicholas
Nickelby', 'David Copperfield', 'Dombey and Son', 'Martin Chuzzlewit',
und 'A Christmas Carol' die bekanntesten und besten. Es mag interessant sein, hier
zu bemerken, daß seit dem Tode des berühmten und höchst beliebten Verfassers (d. h. in 16
Jahren) von seinen Werken 4,539,000 Bände verkauft werden sind.　4, = I remember still, that, etc. Place the advl. circumstance of time 'for — years'
before 'a — Dickens'.　5, Supply 'the school' here; before me = earlier
than I; I think = and as I think.　6, to take down (of buildings), nieder-
reißen.　7, damals; I consider this a very superior sort of school, ich halte dies

für eine ganz vorzügliche Schule.   8, one — indeed = and was indeed (auch
wirklich) one of the best.   9, This institution is most shamefully mismanaged, diese Anstalt wird ganz außerordentlich schlecht verwaltet.   10, boys =
school-boys or pupils, Schüler; to make little progress, geringe Fortschritte machen.
11, Wallifer.   12, most = highly, höchst: 'fellow', here = man; 'mere',
here = real, wahr.   13, darin bestand (comp. S. 87, N. 6); to scourge = to
chastise, züchtigen.   14, Insert 'to us' after the auxiliary; of, über; place =
institution; 'paper', here Schrift, f.   Place 'in — School' after 'to us'.
15, und zwar besonders in Bezug auf die Schmeicheleien, die er sich selbst darin zollt.
16, in any way = ever, je; to carry off prizes, Schulpreise erhalten. Use the verbs
in the Pluperfect Subjunctive, accord. to App. § 33; the auxiliary, however,
must be used but once, and this at the very end.   17, = I believe; not
. . . or = neither . . . nor.   18, = and you know. Is there no allusion to
the classics? bezieht er sich nie auf die klassische Litteratur?   19, = He was a
handsome boy with curly hair. Full — spirits = voller Leben und Lebenskraft.
20, = who; to be connected with an action, bei einer Handlung beteiligt sein;
a mischievous prank, ein muthwilliger Possenstreich.

Section 180.

A LETTER FROM DR. HENRY DANSON TO MR. JOHN FORSTER, ON CHARLES DICKENS'S SCHOOL-LIFE.

II.

I do not think (S. 64, N. 11) he[1] came in for any of Mr. Jones's
scourging propensity; in fact, together with myself, he was only a day-
pupil, and[2] with these there was a wholesome fear of tales being carried
home to the parents. His personal appearance at that time[3] is vividly
brought home to me in the portrait of him taken a few years later by
Mr. Lawrence. He resided (S. 116, N. 17) with[4] his friends, in a very
small house in a street leading out of Seymour Street, north of Mr.
Judkin's chapel.

Depend on it, he was *quite* a self-made man, and his wonderful knowledge and command (Beherrschung, f.) of the English language must[5]
have been acquired by long and patient study after leaving his last
school.

I have no recollection of the boy you name[6]. Dickens's chief[7] associates were, I think[8], Tobin, Mr. Thomas, Bray, and myself. The first
named[9] was his chief ally, and his acquaintance with him appears to
have continued many[10] years *afterwards*. About that time[11] the Penny
and Saturday magazines (S. 71, N. 2) were published weekly, and *were*
greedily read by (S. 106, N. 23) us. We kept bees, white mice, and
other living things, clandestinely[12], in our desks, and the mechanical
arts were a good deal cultivated, in[13] the shape of coach-building, and
making pumps and boats, the motive power of which was the white
mice.

I think at that time Dickens took to writing[14] small tales, and we had
a sort *of* club for[15] lending and circulating them. Dickens was also very
strong[16] in using a sort of lingo, which made us[17] quite unintelligible to
bystanders.

1, = that he had to suffer from the scourging propensity (Prügelmanie, f.) of his teacher, for, like myself, etc. 2, und diesen gegenüber war stets zu befürchten, daß sie bei den Eltern zu Hause aus der Schule plaudern würden. 3, Sein damaliges Aussehen; is vividly brought home to me = is again vividly brought (führen) before my (S. 43, N. 9, A and B) eyes; in—Lawrence (Liter.) = 'through the some years later by (von) Mr. L. painted picture of him', which place immediately after the copula (wird) and the dative of the personal pronoun indicating the possessor. 4, bei; in — Street = in a side-street (comp. n. S. 76, N. 22, B [n]), not far from Seymour Street. 5, must — acquired = he must have acquired. To acquire, sich erwerben, insep. comp. str. v. refl.; by, durch; 'long', here langjährig; after — school = after his school-time. 6, = I cannot remember (sich einer Sache erinnern) the boy whose name you mention (anführen). 7, hauptsächlich, adj. 8, Inverted constr. 9, Ersterer; render 'chief ally' by a comp. n., and turn 'chief' by Haupt. 10, Insert the adv. noch before 'many'; to continue, fortdauern. 11, Um diese Zeit. 12, to keep clandestinely, versteckt halten; things = creatures; a — cultivated, eifrig geübt. 13, in — mice = for we made coaches, pumps and boats, which then were set in motion by the white mice. 14, took to writing = began to write. 15, for—them, Liter. = among (unter) the members of which the same (to agree with 'tales') circulated (zirkulieren). 16, = great; in — lingo, im Gebrauch einer gewissen lauterwälschen Geheimsprache. 17, made us = was; to bystanders = to the uninitiated, den Uneingeweihten.

Section 181.

A LETTER FROM DR. HENRY DANSON TO MR. JOHN FORSTER, ON CHARLES DICKENS'S SCHOOL-LIFE.

III.

We were very strong, too, in theatricals[1]. We mounted[2] small theatres, and got up very gorgeous scenery to[3] illustrate "The Miller and his Men," and other pieces. I remember the[4] present *Mr.* Beverley, the scene painter, assisted us in this (S. 4, N. 5). Dickens was always the leader[5] at these plays, which were occasionally presented with much solemnity before an audience[6] of boys, and in *the* presence of the ushers. My brother, assisted by Dickens, got up[7] "The Miller and his Men" in a very gorgeous form. Master[8] Beverley constructed the mill for us, in such a way[9] that it could tumble to pieces with the assistance of crackers. At one representation, the fireworks in the last scene, ending with the destruction of the mill, were so *very* real[10] that the police interfered, and knocked violently at the door. Dickens's after-taste for theatricals might have had[11] its origin in these small affairs.

I quite[12] remember Dickens[13] one day heading us in Drummond Street in pretending to be poor boys, and asking the passers-by for charity, especially old ladies, one of whom told[14] us she had no money for beggar-boys.

On these adventures, and especially when the old ladies were quite staggered[15] by the impudence of the demand, Dickens would explode with laughter and then take to his heels.

I met him one Sunday morning shortly after he had left the school, and[16] we very piously attended the morning service at Seymour Street

chapel. I am sorry to say [17] Master [18] Dickens did not attend in the slightest
degree to the service, but (S. 6, N. 10) incited me to laughter by declaring
(S. 111, N. 6) his dinner was ready, and the potatoes would be spoiled [19].
In fact, he behaved in such a manner [20] that it was lucky for us we were not
ejected from the chapel.—From J. Forster's " Life of Charles Dickens."

1, in theatralifchen Aufführungen.   2, = made ; to get up, verfertigen.
3, Say 'to illustrate (in Scene fetsen) the piece', etc.   Men, Leute.   4, = that
the ; scene painter, Decorationsmaler, which is best placed before the name.
5, ber Tonangeber ; at, bei.   6, = assembly ; boys = pupils ; ushers = assistant
masters, Unterlehrer.   7, to get up, in Scene fetsen, of which the part ' in
Scene ' is to be treated like the separable particle of a comp. sep. verb.   Place
the verb immediately after ' brother ', and supply 'the piece ' before ' The —
Men'; In — form = very (ganz) gorgeously.   8, = The young.   9, auf
folche Weife ; with the assistance, mit Hülfe.   10, realiftifch ; to interfere, fich
hineinmifchen.   11, might have had = perhaps had.   Commence the sentence
with ' Perhaps'. ' After-taste ', Berliebe, f. ; affairs = performances, Borftellungen.
12, noch ganz beutlich.   13, = that Dickens led (au'leiten) us one day in
Drummond Street to pretend to be (fich gebärden . . . als) poor boys and to ask
the passers-by for (um) alms (milde Gaben).   14, = observed (bemerfen).
15, ' to be quite staggered ', here ganz verblüfft ba'ftehen ; by — demand = through
the impudent demand ; to explode with laughter, vor Lachen faft berften ; to take
to one's heels, fchnell bavon laufen ; and — heels = and ran then quickly away.
16, = and we went very (ganz) piously to church in Seymour St., to attend the
morning service (um bem Morgengottesbienfte beizuwohnen).   17, Ich muß leiber
befennen.   18, = that the young D. not paid the least attention to the
service. To pay attention to a thing, einer Sache Aufmerffamfeit widmen.
19, = would get cold.   20, = He behaved really so.   That — us = that
we must (Impf.) esteem (fchätsen) ourselves lucky, not to be ejected from
church.—He was ejected from church, er wurde aus ber Kirche geworfen.

Section 182.

SIR JOSEPH PAXTON [1].

Sir Joseph Paxton was acting as gardener to [2] the Duke of Devonshire
when the Committee of the Exhibition of 1851 advertised for plans of a
building. The architects and engineers seem to have been very much at
fault [3] when Paxton submitted his design, and its novelty and remarkable
suitability for the purposes intended, at once secured its adoption [4].   The
first sketch was made upon a piece of blotting-paper in the rooms of the
Midland Railway Company [5] at Derby ; and the first rough [6] sketch indicated [7] the principal features of the building as accurately as the most
finished drawings which were afterwards prepared.   The great [8] idea of
the Crystal Palace was as palpable [9] on the blotting-paper as if it had
been set forth in all the glory of water-colour and gold-framing [10].
Was it a sudden idea,—an inspiration of genius [11],—flashing upon the
mind of one [12] who, though no architect, must at least [13] have been something like a poet?—Not at all [14].   The architect of the Crystal Palace was
simply a man who cultivated opportunities [15],—a laborious, painstaking [16]
man, whose life had been a life of labour, of diligent self-improvement, of
assiduous cultivation of knowledge [17].   As [18] Sir Joseph Paxton himself
has shown, in a lecture before the Society of Arts, the idea was slowly and

patiently elaborated by experiments extending over many years [19]. The
Exhibition of 1851 merely afforded him *the* opportunity of putting
forward his idea [20]—the right thing at the right time—and the result was
what we have seen.—S. SMILES, "SELF-HELP."

1, Joseph Parton, geb. den 3. Aug. 1803, gest. den 8. Juni 1865, wurde zunächst
Kunstgärtner beim Herzog von Devonshire, zeichnete sich jedoch bald durch seine genialen
Schöpfungen so sehr aus, daß der Herzog ihn zum Gartendirektor und Verwalter seiner
großartigen Besitzung in Chatsworth ernannte. Die wundervollen Gartenanlagen und
Gewächshäuser daselbst legen noch heute Zeugnis ab von seiner Genialität. Das große
Gewächshaus, welches aus Eisen und Glas erbaut und 300 Fuß lang und 140 Fuß breit ist,
diente ihm später als Grundlage des von ihm eingereichten Entwurfes für das Ausstellungsgebäude von 1851 im Hyde Park zu London und des später von ihm in Sydenham errichteten
Krystalpalastes. Seine Verdienste um die große Weltindustrieausstellung von 1851 wurden
von der Königin dadurch anerkannt, daß sie ihm die Ritterwürde verlieh. Sir Joseph
Parton wurde im Jahre 1854 zum Parlamentsmitgliede für Coventry gewählt und hat
sich um die Baukunst und das Eisenbahnwesen manche Verdienste erworben. Er ist auch
der Verfasser vieler Zeitschriften und Werke über die Gartenkunst.   **2,** to act as
gardener to a person, bei einem als Kunstgärtner angestellt sein ; advertised —
building, öffentlich zur Einsendung von Plänen für ein Ausstellungsgebäude aufforderte.
I propose to commence the period with the subordinate clause ' when —
building '.   **3,** to be very much at fault, in großer Verlegenheit sein ; to submit
a design (of a building), einen Entwurf ein'reichen.   **4,** and — adoption = and
as the same (agreeing with Entwurf) was quite new and remarkably suitable
to its purpose (zweckentsprechend), it was at once accepted.   **5,** in — company = in the waiting-rooms of the railway station.   **6,** = hasty, flüchtig.
7, an'deuten.   **8,** = grand, großartig.   **9,** klar dargestellt, p. p.   **10,** as —
framing = as if one had embellished (aus'schmücken) it with beautiful water-
colours and gold framing.   **11,** an — genius = the inspiration of a genius
(Genie, n., pronounced as in French).   **12,** flashing — one = which suddenly
(auf einmal) filled the mind of a man.   **13,** Insert the adv. doch before ' at
least ' (mindestens) ; something like = more or less.   **14,** Ganz und gar nicht !
15, to cultivate opportunities, Gelegenheiten zu benutzen wissen.   **16,** strebsam ;
of — full of, voller.   **17,** of — knowledge, und unverdrossenen Strebens nach Kennt-
nissen.   **18,** = Like, wie ; has shown = declared ; in — Arts, in einem vor dem
Kunstvereine gehaltenen Vortrage, which place immediately after the subject.
19, ' by — years ' may be briefly rendered by durch langjährige Versuche or
Experimente, which place after ' idea'; slowly = gradually ; patiently, beharrlich ;
to elaborate, aus'arbeiten.   **20,** of — idea = to bring his idea before (ver)
the public (Öffentlichkeit, f.) ; the right thing, das Rechte ; at, zu, contracted with
the def. art.

Section 183.

REBECCA DESCRIBES THE SIEGE OF TORQUILSTONE
(App. § 5) TO THE WOUNDED IVANHOE [1].

I.

"And I must lie here like a bed-ridden [2] monk," exclaimed Ivanhoe,
" while the game [3] that gives me [4] freedom or death is played out by *the
hand of* others! Look from the window [5] once again, kind maiden, but
beware that you are not marked by the archers [6]. Look out once more,
and tell me if [7] they yet advance [8] to the storm."

With patient [9] courage, strengthened by the interval which she had
employed in mental devotion [10], Rebecca again took post [11] at the lattice,

sheltering herself[12], however, by means of a large *and* ancient shield so as not to be visible from beneath [13].

"What dost thou see, Rebecca?" again demanded the wounded knight.

"Nothing but the [14] cloud of arrows flying so thick as to dazzle mine eyes [15], and to hide the bowmen who shoot them."

"That cannot endure [16]," said Ivanhoe; "if they press not right on [17] to carry the castle by pure force of arms (S. 27, N. 8), the archery may [18] avail but little against stone walls and bulwarks. Look for [19] the Black Knight, fair Rebecca, and see how he bears himself [20]; for as the leader *is*, so will his followers be [21]."

"I see him not," said Rebecca.

"Foul craven [22]!" exclaimed Ivanhoe; "does he blench [23] from the helm when the wind blows highest [24]?"

1, Ivanhoe, a novel by Sir Walter Scott, is the most brilliant and splendid of romances in the English language. Rebecca, the Jewess, was Scott's favourite character. The Scene is laid in England in the reign of Richard I., who assumes the name of the 'Black Knight' in this story, and we are introduced to Robin Hood in Sherwood Forest, banquets in Saxon halls, tournaments, and all the pomp of ancient chivalry. Sir Wilfred Ivanhoe is the favourite of Richard I. and disinherited son of the Saxon Cedric of Rotherwood. Having distinguished himself as a crusader, he returns to England and, disguised as a palmer, goes to Rotherwood, where he meets Rowéna, his father's ward, with whom he is in love; but, through his separation from his true love, we see him more as the friend of Rebecca and her father, Isaac of York, to both of whom he shows repeated acts of kindness, and completely wins the affections of the beautiful Jewess, who, by her gentle, meek, yet noble and high-toned disposition, quite throws into the shade her more successful rival Rowéna. In the grand tournament at Ashby Ivanhoe appears as the 'Disinherited Knight', and overthrows all comers. He is, however, wounded, and carried from the crowded lists by Rebecca's servants. After having attended to his wounds, Rebecca and her father are about to transport their friend in a litter to Doncaster, when they are surprised by a number of armed men, headed by the Templar Brian de Bois-Guilbert, who take them prisoners and bring them, along with Cedric and Rowéna, who likewise have been made captives, to Torquilstone, the Castle of Front-de-Bœuf, Ivanhoe's enemy. During their imprisonment the castle is besieged by the Black Knight, who, in his adventurous spirit, having joined a band of yeomen and outlaws, demands the deliverance of the prisoners. The castle falls into the hands of the besiegers, Front-de-Bœuf perishing in the flames of the burning castle; King Richard pleads for Ivanhoe to Cedric, reconciles the father to his son, and the young knight marries Rowéna.　　2, bettlägerig. 3, = combat.　　4, Insert 'either' here; gives = brings; played out = is fought out; by, ven.　　5, to look from the window, zum Fenster hinaus'sehen. Use the 2nd pers. sing. when Ivanhoe addresses Rebecca.　　6, that — archers = that (= in order that, damit) the archers *may* not notice thee. 7, ob.　　8, heran'rücken.　　9, unverdrossen.　　10, und durch die von ihr zur stillen Andacht benutzte Pause gestärkt.　　11, took post = placed herself; at, an.　　12, sich verbergen, insep. comp. str. v. refl.; say 'sheltered herself how-ever;' by means of = behind.　　13, as — beneath = that she could not be seen from beneath (unten).　　14, = a; flying so thick = which fly in such masses (use the Sing.) through the air; 'to fly through', here durchflie'gen, insep. comp. str. v.　　15, as — eyes = that they dazzle my eyes: and to hide = and conceal from my eyes (Blick, m.); 'to shoot', here ab'schießen.

16, lange fe fortbauern.　　**17,** to press right on, fchnell ver'bringen; to =and; to carry a fortress by pure force of arms, eine Feftung burch Waffengewalt ein'neh= men.　　**18,** = will; avail, nützen; but = only; bulwarks, Befeftigungen. **19,** fuchen.　　**20,** 'to bear oneself', here fich halten, str. v. refl.　　**21,** fo bie Geführten.　　**22,** Verruchter Feigling!　　**23,** =to give way, zurück= weichen, sep. comp. str. v.; helm=rudder, Steuerruber, n.　　**24,** highest = strongest. **The relative superlative of adverbs** is formed by placing am before the superlative of the adjective, and giving it the dative termination en, like the predicative form of adjectives. Comp. S. 120, N. 14.

Section 184.

REBECCA DESCRIBES THE SIEGE OF TORQUILSTONE TO THE WOUNDED IVANHOE.

II.

" He blenches not! he blenches not!" said Rebecca, "I see him now; he leads a body of men [1] close under the outer barrier [2] of the barbican. They pull down the piles and palisades; they hew down the barriers with axes.—His high black plume floats abroad over the throng [3], like a raven over the field of the slain [4].—They have made a breach in the barriers—they rush in—they are thrust back! Front-de-Bœuf heads the defenders; I see his gigantic form above the press [5]. They throng [6] again to (S. 72, N. 4) the breach, and the pass is disputed hand to hand and man to man [7]. God of Jacob! it is the meeting of two fierce tides— the conflict of two oceans moved by adverse winds [8]!"

She turned her head from the lattice, as if (S. 27, N. 7) unable longer to endure a sight so terrible (S. 128, N. 11).

"Look forth again, Rebecca," said Ivanhoe, mistaking [9] the cause of her retiring; "the archery must in some degree [10] have ceased, since they are now fighting hand to hand.—Look again, there is [11] now less danger."

Rebecca again looked forth, and almost immediately exclaimed: "Help, O prophets of the law! Front-de-Bœuf and the Black Knight fight hand to hand on [12] the breach, amid [13] the roar of their followers [14], who watch [15] the progress of the strife.—Heaven strike [16] (App. § 34) *with* the cause (Sache, f.) of the oppressed and the captive!"

She then [17] uttered a loud shriek, and exclaimed: "He is down [18]!— He is down!"

1, eine Schar Kämpfer.　　**2,** 'barrier' may here be rendered by Befe= ftigungen, Schanzfäble, or Verfchanzungen. Every Gothic castle and city had, beyond the outer walls, a fortification composed of palisades, called the barriers, which were often the scene of severe skirmishes, as these had neces- sarily to be carried before the walls themselves could be approached. The 'barbacan' or '*barbican*' was the outer wall of an ancient castle or town, and may be rendered by ' Zwingmauer, f.'　　**3,** flattert boch über ter Menge in ter Luft umher.　　**4,** =battle-field.　　**5,** Getränge, n.　　**6,** to throng = to press forward, fich vorwärts brängen, sep. comp. w. v. refl.　　**7,** and — man = they fight for (um) the pass (Durchgang, m.) and struggle (kämpfen) man against man.　　**8,** it — winds = it is like the meeting (Aneinanterftoßen) of two fierce tides (Sturmflut, f.), like the conflict (Zufammenftoßen, n.) of two oceans (Weltmeer, n.) which are moved (fort'treiben, sep. comp. str. v.) by adverse (entgegengefeßt) winds.　　**9,** unrichtig teuten. Construe accord. to S. 16, N. 4:

of her retiring = of this movement.   10, in some degree = almost.
11, there is, es ist . . . vorhanden.   Comp. S. 104, N. 19.   12, ver.
13, während, with Gen.   14, Anhänger.   15, mit Aufmerksamkeit
verfolgen.   16, = defend, v. tr.   17, = hereupon, which place first.
To utter a shriek, einen Schrei ausstoßen.   18, = fallen.

Section 185.

REBECCA DESCRIBES THE SIEGE OF TORQUILSTONE TO THE WOUNDED IVANHOE.

III.

"Who is down?" cried Ivanhoe; "for[1] our dear Lady's sake, tell me who has fallen?"

"The Black Knight," answered Rebecca faintly[2]; then instantly again shouted with joyful eagerness[3]: "But[4] no—but no!—the name of the Lord of hosts be blessed[5]!—he is on foot[6] again, and fights as if there were twenty men's strength in his single arm[7].—His sword is broken—he snatches[8] an axe from a yeoman—he presses[9] Front-de-Bœuf with blow on blow.—The giant stoops and totters like an oak under the steel of the woodman[10]—he falls—he falls!"

"Front-de-Bœuf?" exclaimed Ivanhoe.

"Front-de-Bœuf!" answered the Jewess; "his men[11] rush to the rescue[12], headed (S. 102, N. 3) by (von) the haughty Templar[13]—their united force compels the champion[14] to pause.—They drag Front-de-Bœuf within the walls[15]."

"The assailants have won[16] the barriers, have they not?" said Ivanhoe.

"They have—they have[17]!" exclaimed Rebecca—"and they press[18] the besieged hard upon the outer wall; some plant ladders[19], some swarm like bees (S. 3, N. 2) and endeavour to ascend upon the shoulders of each other[20]—down go[21] stones, beams, and trunks of trees upon their heads, and as fast as they bear the wounded to the rear[22], fresh men[23] supply their places in the assault.—Great God, hast thou given men thine own image[24], that (S. 183, N. 6) it should be thus cruelly defaced[25] by[26] the hands of their brethren?"

1, = for the sake of (um . . . willen) the holy Virgin.   2, mit schwacher Stimme.   3, then — eagerness = but cried immediately (gleich darauf) with joyful surprise.   4, Doch.   5, gepriesen.   6, to be on foot, auf den Beinen sein.   7, as — arm = as if (als ob) his arm possessed (Impf. Subj. App. 33) the strength of 20 men.   8, to snatch a thing from a person, einem etwas entreißen, insep. comp. str. v. tr.; a yeoman, ein Freisasse, m. Comp. App. § 5; 'axe', here = battle-axe, Streitart, f.   9, 'to press', here weiter zurückträngen, sep. comp. w. v. tr.; with blow on blow, mit jedem Schlage. 10, = wood-cutter.   11, Leute.   12, He rushed to my rescue, er eilte mir zu Hülfe. 13, Der Tempelherr war Brian de Bois-Guilbert. Comp. S. 183, N. 1.   14, = hero; to pause = to stop fighting, mit dem Fechten inne zuhalten. 15, 'within the walls' may be briefly rendered by hinein.   16, = taken, ein nehmen, sep. comp. irreg. v. tr.; turn 'barriers' by Verschanzungen; have they not? nicht wahr?   17, Ja — ja!   18, here bedrängen; hard, heftig; upon, auf, with Dat.   19, to plant ladders, Leitern an die Mauer stellen.

20, = of the others. **21,** down go, es werden ... herniedergeworfen. Comp. S. 104, N. 19. **22,** and — rear = and as soon as (so wie) the wounded are carried away (hinwegtragen). Comp. S. 2, N. 1. **23,** = other combatants (Streiter). He supplied my place in the assault of the castle, er nahm meine Stelle bei der Erstürmung des Schlosses wieder ein. **24,** Say 'hast thou created men (S. 134, N. 9) after thy own image (Bild, n.)'. **25,** entstellen, insep. comp. w. v.; Use the Pres. Subj. of the Passive voice, and comp. App. §§ 29 and 35. **26, by** = through, durch; the hands = the hand.

Section 186.

REBECCA DESCRIBES THE SIEGE OF TORQUILSTONE TO THE WOUNDED IVANHOE.

IV.

"Think not of that (S. 4, N. 5, *B*)," said Ivanhoe; "this is[1] no time for such thoughts. Who yield? Who push their way[2]?"

"The ladders are thrown down," replied Rebecca shuddering; "the soldiers lie grovelling[3] under them like crushed reptiles. The besieged have the better[4]."

"Saint George, strike[5] for us!" exclaimed the Knight; "do the false yeomen give way[6]?"

"No!" exclaimed Rebecca, "they bear[7] themselves right yeomanly— the Black Knight approaches the postern with his huge axe—the thundering blows which he deals[8] you may[9] hear *them* above all the din[10] and shouts of the battle.—Stones and beams are hailed down[11] on the bold champion—he regards them no more than if they were[12] thistle-down[13] or feathers!"

"By Saint George," said Ivanhoe, raising (S. 111, N. 6) himself joyfully on his couch, "methought[14] there was (S. 82, N. 7, and App. § 33) but one man in England that[15] might do such a deed!"

"The postern gate shakes[16]," continued Rebecca; "it crashes—it is splintered by[17] his blows—they rush in—the outwork is won[18].—O God, they hurl the defenders from the battlements—they throw them into the moat.—O men, if ye[19] be indeed men, spare them that can resist no longer!"

"The bridge—the bridge which communicates with the castle—have they won[20] that pass?" exclaimed Ivanhoe.

"No," replied Rebecca, "the Templar has destroyed the plank on which they crossed[21]—few[22] of the defenders escaped with him into the castle—the shrieks and cries[23] which you hear tell the fate of the others.—Alas! I see it is still more difficult to look upon[24] victory (S. 3, N. 2) than upon battle."—Sir Walter Scott, "Ivanhoe."

1, = we have; for, zu. **2,** to push one's way, vorwärts dringen. **3,** auf dem Bauche. **4,** to have the better, die Oberhand haben. **5,** = fight. **6,** zurückweichen. **7,** 'to bear oneself', here sich halten; right yeomanly = like true (echt) yeomen. **8,** to deal blows, Streiche führen. **9,** = can; See S. 92, N. 5, and App. § 14; above, über ... hinaus. **10,** Getöse, n. **11,** = thrown down. **12,** than — were = than he would regard (beachten). **13,** Distelwolle. **14,** = I thought; see S. 64, N. 11; but = only. **15,** der

einer folchen That fähig wäre! 16, wacfeln. 17, von, 18, = taken,
ein'nehmen, sep. comp. irreg. v. tr. 19, ihr; to spare a man, eines Menschen schonen:
render 'them' by the Gen. of the demonstr. pron.; that — longer = who can
defend themselves no longer. 20, erfämpft; that pass, tiefen Durchgang.
21, to cross on a plank, über eine Planfe schreiten. 22, = only few; escaped =
have escaped (entfom'men, insep. comp. irreg. v., S. 29, N. 3). 23, das laute
Schreien und Klagen; you = thou; tell, verrät. 24, 'to look upon a
thing', here etwas mit an'sehen, v. tr.

Section 187.

THE FAVOURITE HARES[1].

I.

In the year 1774, being (S. 55, N. 1) much indisposed both in mind
and body[2], incapable of diverting myself either[3] with company or books,
and yet in a condition[4] that made some diversion necessary[5], I was glad
of anything that would engage my attention[6], without fatiguing it.

The children of a neighbour of mine had a leveret given them for a
play-thing[7]; it was at that time about three months old. Understanding
better how to tease the poor creature than to feed it, and soon becoming
weary of their charge[8], they readily consented[9] that their father, who
saw it pining[10] and growing leaner every day, should offer[11] it to my
acceptance. I was willing enough to take the prisoner under my protection, perceiving that (S. 66, N. 15), in the management[12] of such an
animal, and in the attempt to tame it, I should find just that sort of
employment which my case required[13]. It was soon known among the
neighbours that I was pleased[14] with the present, and the consequence
of it was, that[15] in a short time I had as many leverets offered to
me as would have stocked a paddock[16]. I undertook the care[17] of
three, which it is necessary that I should here distinguish by the names I
gave them[18]: Puss, Tiny, and Bess. Notwithstanding the two feminine
appellatives, I must inform[19] you they were all males.

1, Die in dieser und den drei darauf folgenden Abschnitten gegebene interessante Erzäh-
lung ist den Schriften des wohlbekannten englischen Dichters und Schriftstellers William
Cowper entnommen, welcher am 26. November 1731 im Pfarrhause von Great Berkhamp-
stead in Hertfordshire geboren wurde und am 25. April 1780 starb. Seine beste Schöpfung
ist unstreitig die von ihm mit dem Titel: 'The Task' benannte Dichtung, durch welche
er seinen Ruf als Dichter begründete, und welche von keinem seiner späteren Werke über-
troffen wurde. 2, to be much indisposed both in mind and body, sowohl
geistig als auch körperlich zerrüttet sein. 3, incapable — either = and could
neither divert myself (sich zerstreuen); with, durch, which repeat before books;
or = nor. 4, mich aber dabei so befand. 5, that — necessary = that
some diversion was necessary. 6, I shall be glad of anything that will
engage my attention, ich werde gern alles ergreifen, was meine Aufmerksamkeit fesseln
kann. 7, zum Spielen, which place after the auxiliary 'had'; given them,
geschenkt erhalten. 8, to become weary of one's charge, seines Schützlings
überdrüssig werden. 9, I readily consented, ich hatte nichts dagegen. 10, sich
ab'zehren. 11, should offer = offered it. We offered it to his acceptance,
wir boten es ihm zum Geschenk an. 12, = treatment. 13, I hope he will

find just that sort of employment which his case requires, ich hoffe, er wird gerade die für seinen Zustand passende Beschäftigung finden.   14, My father will be greatly pleased with the picture, das Bild wird meinem Vater große Freude machen. 15, Read App. § 21. In order to avoid a repetition of the conjunction daß, it is advisable to construe the clause ' that — me ' = there were (es wurden, S. 104, N. 19) offered to me in *a* short time so many leverets. ' To offer ', here zum Geschenk anbieten.   16, as — paddock, daß ich einen Wildpark damit hätte ausrüsten können.   17, Pflege.   18, which — them = the names of which I must mention (an´führen) here, in order to distinguish them from one another ; I called them.   19, bemerken ; you = to the reader ; they = the little animals (for which use the diminutive).

Section 188.

THE FAVOURITE HARES.

II.

Immediately commencing carpenter, I built[1] them houses to sleep in. Each leveret had a separate apartment, so contrived[2] that it could be kept perfectly sweet and clean[3]. In the daytime[4] the animals had the range[5] of the hall, and at night[6] retired each to his own bed, never intruding into that of another[7].

Puss grew presently familiar, would leap[8] into my lap, raise himself[9] upon his hinder feet, and bite the hair from my temples. He would suffer[10] me to take him up, and to carry him about in my arms, and has more than once fallen fast asleep upon my knees. He was ill three days, during which time I nursed him, kept him apart from his fellows, that[11] they might not molest him (for, like many other wild animals, they per- secute[12] one of their own species that is sick), and by constant care[13], and with a variety of herbs, restored him to perfect health[14]. No crea- ture could be more grateful than (S. 104, N. 19) my patient after his recovery, a sentiment which he most significantly expressed by licking[15] my hand, first the back of it[16], then the palm, then every finger separately[17], then[18] between all *the* fingers, as if (S. 27, N. 7) anxious to leave no part of it unsaluted ; a ceremony[19] which he *never* performed but once again[20] upon a similar occasion.

1, I became at once *a* carpenter and made, etc.   2, ein´richten; see S. 7, N. 3, *B*.   3, rein und sauber.   4, Des Tags.   5, We had the range of the whole house, wir konnten im ganzen Hause umher´laufen.   6, des Nachts. 7, never — other = and none ever (je) went (sich begeben) into the bed of another. 8, would leap = leapt. Comp. S. 101, N. 22.   9, = placed himself. 10, = He allowed (gestatten) me ; has fallen = fell ; to fall asleep, ein´schlafen. 11, = in order that, damit ; might = could.   12, = torment, quälen ; one = sick = the sick *ones* of their own species (Gattung, f.).   13, = nursing, Pflege, f. ; with a variety = various.   14, He restored me to perfect health, er stellte meine Gesundheit ganz wieder her.   15, durch das Belecken.   16, und zwar beleckte er zuerst den Rücken derselben.   17, = singly, adj., to be placed before ' finger '.   18, = and finally he licked even, beleckte er mich auch.   19, here Förmlichkeit, f.   20, but once again, nur noch einmal ; upon, bei.

Section 189.

THE FAVOURITE HARES.

III.

Finding him extremely tractable, I made it my[1] custom to carry him always after breakfast into the garden, where he hid himself generally under the leaves of a vine, sleeping[2] or chewing the cud till evening; in the leaves also of that vine he found a favourite repast[3]. I had not long habituated him to *this taste of* liberty, before[4] he began to be impatient for the return of the time[5] when he might enjoy it[6]. He would invite me to the garden[7] by drumming (S. 111, N. 6) upon my knee, and by (S. 185, N. 26) a look of such expression[8] as it was not possible to misinterpret. If the[9] rhetoric did not immediately succeed, he would take the skirt of my coat (S. 36, N. 7, *A*) between his teeth, and pull it with all *his* force[10]. Thus Puss might be said to be perfectly tamed[11]; the shyness of his nature was done away[12], and, on the whole[13], it was visible by many symptoms, which I have not room to enumerate[14], that he was happier in human society than when (S. 27, N. 7) shut up with[15] his natural companions.

Not so Tiny; upon him the kindest[16] treatment had not the least effect. He too was sick, and in his sickness had an equal share of my attention[17]; but when, after his recovery, I took the liberty to stroke him, he would grunt, strike with his fore feet, spring forward, and bite[18]. He was, however[19], entertaining in his way; even his surliness was matter of mirth[20], and in his play he preserved such an air of gravity[21], and performed his feats with such solemnity of manner[22], that in (an) him too I had an agreeable companion.

1, jur.   **2,** Use this and the following verb in the Imperfect, preceded by 'and'; to chew the cud, sein Futter wiederkäuen.   **3,** in — repast, auch aß er die Blätter des Weinstocks besonders gern.   **4,** = when; insert the adv. schon after 'he'.   **5,** to — time = to long impatiently for the time. **6,** when — it = when (S. 131, N. 4) he could again enjoy this liberty.   **7,** - to come into the garden with him.   **8,** Render 'of such expression' by the adj. 'expressive'; as = that, followed by man and the active form of the verb.   **9,** = his; and construe according to the following example: He will never succeed, er wird nie seinen Zweck erreichen.   **10.** Supply the adv. 'forward' after this noun.   **11,** Say 'And so (somit) I may (dürfen) perhaps (wohl) say of "Puss" that he was quite tamed'.   **12,** = his natural shyness was conquered.   **13,** überhaupt; visible = clear.   **14,** = which (S. 66, N. 15) on account of want of (an) room I cannot enumerate here. **15,** 'to be shut up', here sich ausschließlich befinden; with, bei.   **16,** liebreich. **17,** in — attention = and during his sickness I nursed him with equal (gleich) attention.   **18,** Supply 'at (nach) me' here.   **19,** Supply 'also' here; in, auf.   **20,** = amusing.   **21,** = such a grave air (Miene, f.).   **22,** = solemn dignity.

Section 190.

THE FAVOURITE HARES.

IV.

Bess, who died soon after he was full grown[1], and whose death was occasioned by his being turned (S. 161, N. 21, and S. 87, N. 6) into his box, which had been washed, while it was yet damp[2], was a hare of great humour and drollery[3]. Puss was tamed by gentle usage; Tiny was not to be tamed at all; and Bess had a[4] courage and confidence that made him tame from the beginning[5]. I always admitted them into the parlour after supper, when (S. 131, N. 4), the[6] carpet affording their feet a firm hold, they would frisk, *and* bound, and play *a* thousand gambols, in[7] which Bess, being remarkably strong and fearless, was always superior to the rest. One evening, the cat being in the room, it had the hardiness to pat Bess upon the cheek, an indignity which[8] he resented by drumming upon her (S. 43, N. 9, *B*) back with such violence that the cat was happy to escape from *under* his paws, and[9] hide herself.

I describe the animals as having had each a character of his own[10]. Such they were in fact[11], and their countenances were so expressive of that character, that, when I looked only on the face of either, I immediately knew which it was[12].—WILLIAM COWPER, "THE GENTLEMAN'S MAGAZINE, 1784."

1, völlig ausgewachsen fein. 2, which — damp = which after having been washed (nach der Reinigung) was yet damp. 3, = was a very facetious *and* droll hare. 4, = so much. 5, = that he became tame from the very (gleich im) beginning. 6, Place the clause 'the — hold' after 'they — gambols': To play gambols resscrlide Luftsprünge machen. 7, in which = in (bei) which games. 8, an indignity which = which offence. 9, Say 'and to be able to hide herself'. 10, as — own = as if each of the same had had (Pluperf. Subj.) his own character. 11, = That was however (aber auch) really the case. 12, that — was = that from (aus) the face of each I could at once distinguish (erkennen) who it (= he) was.

Section 191.

PRINCE BISMARCK'S HOME[1].

After crossing the threshold I found myself in a small, plain apartment—the reception-room—in the centre of which stands a simple little polished table with four legs. This is a relic of historical significance. A brass plate let into the square top[2] bears *the* following inscription : "At this table the preliminaries of peace between Germany and France were signed, February 26th, 1871, at Versailles, No. 14 Rue de Provence." In the centre of the table is[3] a round piece *of* green cloth, and on it are visible a number of spots[4] caused by (S. 185, N. 26) the drippings[5] from the candles used on the momentous occasion of the negotiations between the Chancellor and Jules Favre[6]. The table was the property of the lady in whose house the Chancellor was quartered[7], and of whom he bought it. In the same room stands a gigantic wardrobe richly sculptured[8], and a second wardrobe (S. 5, N. 2), according to Castellan (S. 10, N. 2) Hackmack's explanation, was made from[9] the wood of a linden tree, in the shade of which Prince Bismarck, when a[10] merry student at Göttingen, had frequently reposed. The adjoining room is the Prince's study. A bookcase contains a small library[11] for immediate use and for reference, among its books being a French account of[12] the peace negotiations of 1871. The writing-desk occupies the centre of the room. A polished fire-screen, highly[13] ornamented and of Asiatic origin, is a present from the Chinese Embassy in Berlin. On the mantel-piece stands a bronze statuette, about three feet high, representing the Grand Elector—a present from the Emperor. A slip of paper attached to the Marshal's baton in the Elector's outstretched hand, bears the Imperial autograph[14]: "To[15] Prince Bismarck—Christmas, 1880,—W." On the wall, behind the statuette, hangs, in a richly gilt frame, a painting by[16] Hünten, representing the attack of dragoons of the guard on French infantry at Mars-la-Tour; the Chancellor's two sons, Herbert and William, being[17] in the midst of the fight.—The Correspondent of the London "Daily News."

1, here Hauseinrichtung. 2, here Tisch; the plate was let into the table, die Platte war in den Tisch hineingelegt. 3, = lies. 4, and — spots = and upon the same one sees still some spots. 5, das Lesen; render 'from the' by the Gen. of the def. art., and turn 'used — negotiations' by 'during the momentous negotiations'. 6, Jules Favre, geboren den 21. März 1809 zu Lyon, machte sich zuerst als Redner und gewandter Advokat einen Namen, beschäftigte sich jedoch später auch mit der Politik, wo er stets zur demokratischen Partei gehörte. Nach der Februarrevolution von 1848 wurde er Generalsekretär im Ministerium des Innern, kann Mitglied der Nationalversammlung, in der er als Gegner des zum Präsidenten gewählten Prinzen Ludwig Napoleon auftrat. Im Jahre 1858 in den gesetzgebenden Körper gewählt, wurde er nach dem Sturze des Kaiserreichs und der Erklärung der Republik Mitglied der Regierung der Nationalverteidigung und Minister des Äußern, als welcher er im Jahre 1871 zu Versailles und Frankfurt a/M mit dem Fürsten Bismarck über den Frieden unterhandelte. Am 2. August 1871 zog er sich jedoch vom politischen Leben zurück und starb am 19. Januar 1880. 7, = lived (S. 116, N. 17). 8, richly sculptured, mit reicher Bildhauerarbeit verziert, which use attributively, as explained in S. 7, N. 3, A); 'wardrobe', here Wandschrank. 9, aus. 10, when a — as. 11, Supply 'intended' (bestimmt) here, and place the words 'intended for (zu, contracted with the def. art.) — reference' before 'library'. 12, über. 13, höchst künstlerisch; and — origin = and made (verfertigen) in Asia, all to be placed before 'screen'. 14, trägt die vom Kaiser eigenhändig geschriebenen Worte. 15, Dem. 16, von. 17, = are, sich befinden.

Section 192.

ROYAL BENEVOLENCE.

Frederick the Great, King of Prussia[1], once rang the bell[2] of his cabinet; but as nobody answered[3], he opened the door of the ante-chamber, and there found his page fast asleep[4] upon a chair[5]. He went up to awake him, but, coming nearer, he observed a paper in his pocket, upon which something was written[6]. This excited his curiosity. He pulled it out, and found that it was a letter from the page's mother, the contents of which were nearly as follows[7]: "She returned her son many thanks[8] for the money he had saved out of his salary and sent to her, which had proved a very timely assistance[9]. God would certainly reward him for it, and if he continued to serve God and his king faithfully and conscientiously, he could not fail of success[10] and prosperity in this world[11]." Upon reading (S. 55, N. 1) this, the king stepped softly into his closet, fetched a rouleau[12] *of* ducats, and put it with the letter into the page's pocket (S. 43, N. 9, *B*). He then rang again till the page awoke and came into his closet. " You have[13] been asleep, I suppose?" said the king. The page could not deny it, stammered out an excuse[14], put, in his embarrassment, his hand into his pocket, and felt the rouleau *of* ducats. He immediately pulled it out, turned[15] pale, and looked at the king with tears in his eyes. "What is the matter with you?" said the king. "Oh!" replied the page, "somebody has contrived[16] my ruin: I know nothing of this money." "What God bestows[17]," resumed the king, "He bestows in sleep. Send the money to your mother (App. § 5), give my respects to her[18], and inform her that I will take care[19] of both her and you."—W. BUCK.

1, Friedrich der Große, König von Preußen, wurde am 24. Januar 1712 in Berlin geboren und war der Sohn des Königs Friedrich Wilhelm I, der den den Künsten und Wissenschaften ergebenen Jüngling oft tyrannisch und hart behandelte und ihn selbst gegen seine Neigung im Jahre 1733 mit der Prinzessin Elisabeth Christine von Braunschweig-Bevern vermählte. Nach dem Tode seines Vaters bestieg er am 31. Mai 1740 den preußischen Thron, auf dem er bald Gelegenheit fand, seine bedeutenden Talente als Staatsmann und Feldherr zu bethätigen. Die Geschichte nennt ihn wohl mit Recht den größten Fürsten, Feldherrn und Staatsmann seiner Zeit, und als er am 17. August 1786 auf seinem Lustschlosse zu Sanssouci starb, hinterließ er seinem Nachfolger ein um 1325 Quadratmeilen vergrößertes Reich, einen Schatz von über 70 Millionen Thalern, eine Armee von 200,000 Mann und einen kräftig emporblühenden Staat. **2,** to ring the bell, die Glocke ziehen; of = in. **3,** = appeared. **4,** in tiefem Schlafe. **5,** Supply here sitzen. **6,** The clause 'upon — written' may be briefly rendered by 'beschrieben', to be placed before paper, inflected as an adj. **7,** were . . . as follows, folgendermaßen lautete. **8,** to return a person many thanks, einem vielmals danken. Construe this and the following passages according to App. §§ 28, 30 and 31. **9,** Place the words 'sent to her' before 'money', attributively, and render 'which — assistance' by und ihr sehr gelegen gekommen sei. **10,** You cannot fail of success, das Glück kann dir nicht fehlen. **11,** = life. **12,** Reise, f. **13,** = Thou hast, after which place the adv. wohl = I suppose. **14,** = stammered some words of (der) excuse. **15,** = became. **16,** ersonnen. **17,** = gives. **18,** give — her, grüße sie von mir. **19,** to take care of a person, für einen sorgen; of — you = of both of you. He saw both of us, Er sah uns beide.

Section 193.

TELEGRAPHY (S. 3, N. 2) AMONG BIRDS.

I watch[1] a flock[2] *of* crows who, by some own correspondent of theirs, have learned that Farmer Blyth will hold a ploughing match on his grounds[3], and have in consequence summoned their brethren[4] to a diet *of* worms. How unconcerned they look, as if worms were nothing to them[5]! How grave, as if it were an Ecclesiastical Convocation[6], and they had no thought of earthly things[7]! Yet point[8] a gun, or anything like it towards them, and in a moment (App. § 14) the young birds even whose backs seemed turned to you[9] will give a flutter[10] of their wings, which appears an involuntary struggle[11], but in reality is as significant a danger-signal as a red flag on a railway[12], and is sufficient to clear the field. Nor [=And yet . . . . not] are those crows exceptionally wise. All their feathered brethren [13] have made a sacred compact [14] that never with their consent shall salt be put upon their tails. The sparrows are not so idle that [15] they do not pass the word to each other when crumbs are falling thick [16] from some rich man's table. The doves, though they look so innocent (S. 27, N. 8) do not spend [17] all their time in cooing love-songs and cradle-lullabies [18], or in pruning their rainbow-feathers. They have a Telegraphy of their own [19], and [20] by a mere peck, or a [baß] ruffle of their feathers, can direct each other to the fields where the autumn wheat [21] is germinating best, or [22] the garden where the green peas are fullest and brightest [23].—Professor C. Wilson.

1, beobachten.   2, Schar, f.   3, to hold a ploughing match on one's grounds, auf seinem Felde pflügen lassen.   4, =friends; 'diet', here Gericht, n. 5, This is nothing to me, dies geht mich nichts an. See App. § 33.   6, Kir= chenversammlung, f.   7, to have no thought of earthly things, an nichts Irdisches denken.   8, The huntsman pointed a gun towards me, der Jäger richtete eine Flinte auf mich.   9, whose — you = that apparently seemed to turn their (S. 43, N. 9, B) back to thee.   10, to give a flutter, eine leichte flatternde Bewegung machen; of=with.   11, an involuntary struggle = quite involuntary (unwillkürlich).   12, =in the railway-service (S. 36, N. 7, A).   13, =All birds.   14, Supply 'among (unter) one another' here.   15, als daß; to pass the word = to give a hint.   16, to fall thick, im Überflusse auf die Erde fallen.   17, verbringen.   18, in — lullabies, mit dem Girren von Liebes= und Wiegenliedern.   19, We have a library of our own, wir haben unsere eigene Bibliothek.   20, Here follows the verb 'can'; supply 'with the beak' after 'peck'.   21, = where the wheat in autumn.   22, The prep. 'to' must be repeated here.   23, = stand thickest and best (schön). See S. 183, N. 24.

Section 194.

THE HANSE [1].

I.

About the end of the twelfth century commerce began to extend to-wards the north of Europe. Along the German shores of the Baltic (S. 36, N. 7, A) sprang up [2] thriving towns, which sent out ships to (S. 72, N. 4) Russia, Norway, England, and other parts, and exchanged the raw materials which they thus acquired (S. 48, N. 6) for the merchandise of Southern Europe and the Levant, which reached them both by land and sea [3]. Before [4] *the* middle of the thirteenth century, this trade had become so valuable as to excite [5] the rapacity, not only of numerous pirates who infested [6] the seas, but [7] of princes (S. 3, N. 2) and nobles, who exacted arbitrary and excessive tolls.

To defend their interests against these assailants, the chief [8] ports entered into a league, binding themselves [9] to [zu] *afford* mutual aid and protection. Lübeck and Hamburg stood at the head of this association; Bremen ranked next [10]; and one after another the principal towns gave in their adhesion, the movement spreading from east to west [11]. The numbers of the league [12] fluctuated, but at one time it is known (S. 4, N. 4, man) to have comprised more than ninety different towns. In the fourteenth century its authority [13] extended greatly, for [14] it rallied around it the chief commercial towns of the interior, such as Cologne, Dortmund, Münster, Brunswick, Magdeburg, etc. The Hanse had for its object the protection and development of commerce, the maintenance of existing and the acquisition of new privileges [15] The association was governed by a Diet [16], to which each town sent representatives, and which met once in three years [17] in Lübeck. As the confederation expanded, it became necessary to divide it into several provinces [18], of which the capitals were Lübeck, Cologne, Brunswick, and Dantzic.

1, Die Hansa.   2, entstehen, insep. comp. irreg. v.   3, welche sie sowohl auf dem Lande als auch auf dem Seewege bezogen.   4, - Already before.   5, = that it excited; place 'not only' before 'rapacity'.   6, unsicher machen. 7, = but also that (to agree with 'rapacity').   8, = most important; to enter into a league, ein Bündnis mit einander schließen.   9, = whereby they bound themselves (sich verpflichten). Aid and protection, Schutz und Trutz. 10, = hereupon came Bremen.   11, and — west = and afterwards one great town after the other joined the league, which expanded (sich ausbreiten) from east to west.   12, Liter. = The number of the towns in the league. 13, = power.   14, for — it, denn es traten ihm . . . bei.   15, The — privileges = The protection and the development of commerce, the maintenance of existing and the acquisition of new privileges were the object (Zweck, m.) of the Hanse.   16, = The business (Angelegenheiten, pl.) of the league was conducted by (durch) a Diet (here den Hansetag).   17, alle drei Jahre einmal.   18, here Bezirke (or Quartiere).

Section 195.

THE HANSE.

II.

In Russia the Hanse found a valuable and most virgin field [1] for its commercial enterprises. Thence it drew [2] large supplies of timber, flax, hemp, ropes, skins, furs, wax, and tallow ; bestowing in return [3] (for the trade was only one of barter), salt, herrings, and coarse cloth, for the mass of the peasants ; and [4] brocades, jewels, wines, and other articles of luxury, for the wealthy boyards and princes. A factory at Novgorod conducted these transactions. Another factory at Bergen placed the Hanse in direct contact [5] with Norway and Sweden. This was an establishment of considerable magnitude, comprising twenty-two courts, and serving not only as a lodging for the staff of agents and clerks [6], but as a warehouse [7] *for the goods.* The chief exports from this quarter were timber, resin, sperm oil, *and,* above all [9], salted fish—a (S. 53, N. 9) commodity [10] in great demand at a time when Europe was still Catholic and fasted faithfully on the appointed days. The Hanse had [11] two other large factories, one in Bruges, employing three hundred agents. and another in London.

Year by year [12] the Hanse grew more rich and powerful. New branches of business were opened up, new factories *were* founded. Kings and princes were glad [13] to be on good terms with so influential a body. Ambassadors from the Kings of England, France, Sweden, and Denmark, and even from the Emperor himself, waited on [14] the Diet, to ask [15] favours, and to offer trading privileges in return. The original object of the league—mutual protection—was reasonable and legitimate, but was gradually expanded into [16] a policy of forcible aggression and imperious monopoly. Not only were foreigners, in [17] their voyages to (S. 72, N. 4) the Hanse towns, compelled to employ Hanseatic ships, but [18] the commerce of the north-east and west of Europe was almost exclusively in the hands of the league.

1, and most virgin field = and hitherto quite unused field.   **2,** beziehen, insep. comp. irr. v. tr.   **3,** bestowing in return = Liter. which it (fie, to agree with bie Hanſa) for (gegen) . . . exchanged. The verb stands, of course, after 'princes', and the clause 'for — barter' is best placed after it.   **4,** Repeat the preposition gegen here.   **5,** Place 'in — contact' after 'Sweden'. **6,** for — clerks, ben Beamten unb Unterbeamten, which place after 'only'. Render 'as a' by zu, contracted with the dat. of the def. art.   **7,** = but was also used as a (als) warehouse.   **8,** beſtanben aus.   **9,** = but especially. The prep. ans must be repeated here.   **10,** Artifel, m.; in — demand, welcher . . . in greſer Nachfrage ſtanb.   **11,** Supply the adv. noch here. **12,** Bon Jahr zu Jahr.   **13,** freß; to be on good terms, auf freunbſchaftlichem Fuß ſtehen; with — body, mit bem mächtigen Stäbtebunbe, which place after 'glad'. **14,** = appeared before (ver).   **15,** erbitten; favours, Gunſtbezengungen ; in return, bafür.   **16,** zu; of — monopoly, ber Gewaltherrſchaft unb bes Menepels; 'to expand', here umgeſtalten.   **17,** auf.   **18,** but . . . was, ſonbern es beſanb ſich auch; of = in.

Section 196.

THE HANSE.

III.

There were no bounds to its greed and selfishness [1]. It did its utmost to crush all growing trade [2], navigation, and even manufactures, which in the least interfered with its gains [3]. It warned away [4] all strangers [5] from the Baltic ; and when it found them there, it seized and destroyed their vessels [6]. In order to maintain this monopoly, it [7] was ready to make [8] the greatest sacrifices, to equip fleets, and sustain long and costly campaigns. With Denmark it waged a desperate war ; and it also came into collision [9] with Sweden and Norway. From [10] these contests it came off victorious, and the whole of Scandinavia was compelled to acknowledge its commercial supremacy [11]. It [12] had a rupture also with the Netherlands, whose flag it banished from the Baltic [13].

These unbounded pretensions naturally excited a great deal of ill feeling [14] against the Hanse, and, in the end, proved fatal [15] to it. One after another [16], the markets which it had been accustomed to regard as its own private estates, threw off their allegiance, and admitted [17] the traders of other nations. Then [18] *it was that* the league began to suffer in another way from its narrow-minded selfishness. As long as it had exclusive command of [19] foreign sources of supply, it did not trouble itself to develop the resources of Germany—indeed it rather endeavoured [20] to repress them, when it thought that others were likely to profit by them ; but when one by one its monopolies exploded [21], it found reason to repent that it had neglected to cultivate [22] the productive powers of its own country.

These causes, combined [23] with the change [24] of route to India, led to the gradual decline of this famous confederation [25]; and at the last general assembly, held at Lübeck in 1630, the deputies from the several cities appeared merely to declare their secession [26]. In a modified form [27], however, the Hanse lingered on [28] till the beginning of the present century—the [29] shadow of a great name. The Free Cities of Lübeck, Hamburg, Bremen, and Frankfort-on-the-Maine, are now only nominally the representatives of the Hanse.—J. H. FYFE.

1, = Its greed and selfishness had no bounds.   2, to crush all growing trade, allen Handel ... im Keime zu ersticken; the adj. 'all' must be repeated before the two following nouns.   3, which — gains, sobald die Interessen des Bundes im geringsten dadurch beeinträchtigt wurden.   4, = drove away.   5, = foreign ships. 6, their vessels = them.   The passage 'and — vessels' is best rendered by the Passive Voice.   'To seize', here mit Beschlag belegen.   7, = the league. 8, to make a sacrifice, ein Opfer bringen.   9, to come into collision with a person, sich mit einem entzweien.   10, Aus; to come off, hervorgehen; it = the same.   11, dessen kommerzielle Überlegenheit.   12, It is better, for the sake of distinctness, to change the pronoun 'it' into 'the league'.   13, Use the Passive Voice to render 'whose — Baltic'.   14, a — feeling - great hatred. 15, to prove fatal = to become dangerous.   16, Place 'one —another' after 'threw', and commence the sentence with 'The markets'; it – the same; as — estates, als ihre eigenen Gebiete; threw off their allegiance, warfen . . . das ihnen aufgedrungene Joch von sich.   17, 'to admit a person', here einem den Zutritt gestatten.   18, = Upon that.   19, Herrschaft über; sources of supply, Zufuhrquellen.   20, er bemühte sich vielmehr.   21, but — exploded = but when its monopolies (Handelsprivilegien) were one after another taken away (entreißen) from it (ihm, to be placed after 'monopolies').   22, to culti-vate = the cultivation (Pflege, f.); 'the — country' may be briefly rendered by der inländischen Produktionskraft.   23, = in combination.   24, Verlegung, f.; route, Landweg, m.   25, Städtebund, m.   26, der Austritt aus dem Bunde.   27, beschränkt.   28, however, the Hansa lingered on, fristete die Hansa jedoch noch . . . ein kümmerliches Dasein.   29, = the mere.

Section 197.

COMING TO TERMS [1].

One of the most distinguished artists in Paris [2] painted for a lady occupying a brilliant position in society her portrait [3], with [4] the intention of placing it in an exhibition afterwards. The lady, although a long time celebrated for her beauty [5], had arrived at that age [6] which is seldom admitted (fifty years), but [7] endeavoured to conceal it through cosmetics, and showed herself as beautiful and captivating as in her younger days [=years]. Paris is full of resources, and ointments are to be obtained there [8] to heal the wounds of time.

Our heroine had her portrait taken [9] in the most graceful attitude; splendidly dressed, and leaning on an arm-chair, she looked smiling into the glass, which should return [10] her the most amiable compliments.

The painter made [11] a most striking likeness, but this was a great mistake—a flattering one was expected [12], *and the lady* subsequently [13] declared that she did not recognise herself (App. § 28) in this painting, and the portrait was left on the painter's hands [14]. The artist, feeling himself hurt in his pride, was too good a philosopher to keep a portrait worth three thousand francs quietly on his hands [15], and an idea of vengeance presented itself to his mind [16], which he put into execution at once.

A short time before the day fixed for [17] the opening of the art-exhibition at the Louvre [18], the lady was secretly informed that her portrait was ornamented with certain accessories rather compromising her [19]. She went immediately to the artist. There was the portrait! It was the same striking likeness certainly; but the painter had thinned the hair, and the lady so faithfully painted [20] held in her hand two large tresses of false hair. On the toilet table were several small bottles, labelled thus [21]: "White-Wash," "Vegetable Red," "Cosmetic [22], to efface wrinkles," "Lotion, to dye the hair in a minute [23]."

"It is abominable," said the lady, greatly excited.

"Of what do you complain?" coolly replied the artist. "Did you not declare (S. 48, N. 2, and App. § 28) that it was not your portrait? You are right, it is a mere fancy sketch [24], and as such I shall send it to the exhibition."

"What, Sir, do you intend to exhibit this painting?"

"Certainly [25], Madam; but as *a* cabinet picture [26], since the catalogue will indicate it under the title *of* 'The Coquette of Fifty Years.'"

At this the lady fainted, but soon recovered, and then paid at once for the portrait [27]. The accessories were effaced [28] in her presence, the portrait was restored to its original state, and the three thousand francs were transferred [29] to the purse of the painter.—THE YOUNG LADIES' JOURNAL.

---

1. = The Compromise.   2, An artist in Berlin, ein Berliner Künstler. 3, 'painted — portrait' may be briefly rendered = painted the portrait of a high-placed (hochgestellt) lady.   4, in.   5, = Although the lady was for a long time (seit lange) celebrated for (wegen) her beauty (see S. 27, N. 8). 6, = she had now reached that age; admitted = confessed (eingestanden). 7, = however, to be placed after 'endeavoured'.   8, and — time = and offers (darbieten) ointments, which heal all *the* wounds of time.   9, to have one's portrait taken, sich malen lassen.   10, = tell.   11, schaffen, str. v. tr.; a most striking likeness, ein höchst ähnliches Bild.   12, = the lady expected one that flattered her (S. 48, N. 6).   13, mithin, to be placed after 'declared'.   14, and — hands = and refused the acceptance of the same (to agree with 'painting').   15, to keep a portrait quietly on one's hands, ein Portrait ganz ruhig bei sich liegen lassen.   16, and — mind = and devised a plan of vengeance (S. 36, N. 7, *A*).   17, zu.   18, im Louvre.   19, daß ihr Portrait mit gewissen sie kompromittierenden Zusätzen verziert sei.   20, und die treu nach der Natur gemalte Dame; a tress of false hair, eine falsche Haarflechte. 21, = with *the* following labels (Etikette, f.).   22, Schönheitswasser.   23, Haartinktur zum augenblicklichen Färben der Haare.   24, = it is only the production of my fancy.   25, Allerdings.   26, als Genrebild, the first component of which being pronounced as in French.   27, for — portrait = the price of the picture.   28, beseitigen.   29, ein'verleiben, p. p. einverleibt.

Section 198.

FALSE PRIDE.

Have pity on[1] the youth who is ashamed to be seen carrying[2] a parcel. Such a youth will never climb the hill[3]; he will never be honoured and respected by sensible, respectable[4] men. And yet how many there are (S. 82, N. 7) who have the failing[5]. Do you know the story of the young man who came *down* from a country town of New Hampshire, and entered the great wholesale establishment of the Lawrences—Abbot and Amos—in Boston[6]? He was a young merchant who had just commenced business[7]. He had money enough *with which* to purchase a certain quantity *of* goods, and wished to get as many more on credit[8], if they (S. 134, N. 4) would trust[9] him.

Mr. Lawrence shook his head. The young man could offer no security, and the old[10] merchants did not consider it good *policy* to give credit to an unknown and untried young man. The youthful customer did not blame them. He said he should probably do the same himself by one whom he did not know[11]. "However," he added, "I hope I may grow into your confidence one of these days[12]."

Then he paid *for* the goods he had purchased; and when they had been done up[13], he was asked where he would have them sent[14]. "I will take[15] them myself," was the answer. "But the parcel is heavy," said the clerk. "And I am young and strong," answered the customer. "No, I will take the parcel on my shoulder. I cannot earn half a dollar more easily or more honestly." And he had taken the parcel on his shoulder, and had approached the door, when Mr. Lawrence came out of his office, where[16] he had been a spectator of the scene, and called the youth back. "You can have all *the* goods you want, young man[17]," he said. "Make your own selection, and set your own time for payment[18]. He who is willing to help himself, will not betray[19] those who are willing to help him."

And the old merchant was not mistaken. That young man became one of his most valuable customers, and one of his valued[20] friends.

When Jerome Napoleon Bonaparte, son of (S. 25, N. 5) King Jerome of Westphalia and nephew of the Emperor Napoleon I., was a student of[21] Harvard College, in Cambridgeshire, he was one day carrying a bundle of clothing[22] from his washer-woman's to his dormitory[23], when he was met by a companion[24], who asked him, with much surprise, why he had not had the bundle sent to his room.

"Why should I do that?" asked the prince. "Why[25]," said his companion with a little touch of embarrassment, "you know it doesn't look well to carry one's own bundle like a common labourer."

"Bah[26]," cried Jerome, laughing, "I trust I shall never be ashamed to be seen bearing[27] anything (S. 3, N. 7) that belongs to a Bonaparte!"— THE NEW YORK HERALD.

1, mit.   2, = with.   3, = Such a one will never get on (vorwärts kommen). 4, jelitr.   5, = this fault.   6, from — Boston = from (aus) a small town in N. H. to Boston, and there entered the great (großartig) wholesale establishment (Waarenlager) of Messrs. Lawrence—Abbot and Amos? **7,** I have just commenced business, ich habe mich soeben etabliert. **8,** to get a thing on credit, etwas auf Kredit entnehmen ; as many more, noch einmal so viele. **9,** to trust a person, einem Vertrauen schenken. **10,** = experienced. **11,** by — know, einem Unbekannten gegenüber, to be placed after 'should' and the grammatical object 'es'. To do the same oneself, es auch so machen. **12,** I may — days = that I shall gain (sich erwerben) one of these days (vermaleinst) your confidence. **13,** = were packed. **14,** = where they should be sent. **15,** = carry. **16,** von wo ; to be a spectator of a scene, eine Scene mit ansehen. **17,** Herr. **18,** to set one's own time for payment, den Zahlungstermin selbst bestimmen. **19,** betrügen. **20,** = best. **21,** was — of = studied in. **22,** mit Wäsche. **23,** = 'lodging' here. **24,** I was met by a companion, ein Freund begegnete mir. **25,** Sie; his = the ; with — embarrassment, etwas verlegen ; you know, doch, to be placed after the verb ; to carry = if one carries. **26,** = Nonsense ! **27,** to be seen bearing = to bear.

Section 199.

ANECDOTES OF[1] GREAT STATESMEN.

I.

ABRAHAM LINCOLN[2].

The night previous to the meeting of the Convocation[3] of Chicago, Mr. Lincoln did not get home until[4] eleven o'clock *at night*. In the morning[5] Mrs. Lincoln, who possessed a most amiable disposition, remonstrated with her good husband at breakfast. She kindly, but firmly, informed him[6] that politics[7] were leading him into bad habits, especially (S. 87, N. 6) to keeping late hours[8] and drinking at the rum shops. She did not like it; she had to sit up[9], and also the children were kept awake[10]. "And now, Abraham," she continued, "let me tell you[11] that to-night I will go to bed at ten o'clock. If you come before that hour, well and good[12]; if not[13], I will not get up and let you in[14]." Ten o'clock came that night, and true to her word, Mrs. Lincoln went to bed with her children[15]. About an hour later Mr. Lincoln knocked at[16] the door. He knocked once, twice, and even three times before[17] an upper window was raised and the nightcap of a female looked out. "Who is there?" "I." "You know what I told you, Abraham?" "Yes, but, wife, I have *got* something very particular to tell you. Let me in!" "I don't want to hear. It is political stuff[18]." "Wife, it is very important. There is[19] a telegraphic despatch, and I have been nominated for the Presidency[20]." "Oh, Abraham, this is awful! Now I know you have been drinking. I only suspected it before, and you may just go and sleep where you got your liquor[21]!" And down went the window with a slam[22]. The next day confirmed the truth of the news that the humble husband had been nominated to rule[23] over millions.—THE NEW YORK HERALD.

II.

PRINCE BISMARCK (S. 138, N. 12) AND LORD BEACONSFIELD[24].

Amongst a number of amusing anecdotes of Lord Beaconsfield is one of[25] the State banquet given at Berlin at the time of the Congress, when [26] he sat next to Prince Bismarck and opposite to the Crown Princess of Germany. Near to him was a trophy of "bonbons," on the papers of which were [27] miniature photographs of the German Emperor and other members of the Prussian royal family. After the feast was over [28], the lord was busily engaged (S. 87, N. 6) in securing [29] some of these sweets to take home as a [зum] remembrance of the occasion [c], when Prince Bismarck suddenly caught him by the arm and so startled him that he dropped his spoil and exclaimed: "I see, not only does Prince Bismarck give nothing away, but (S. 6, N. 10) he does not allow anybody to help himself." The German Chancellor, on discovering (S. 55, N. 1) that he had interrupted Lord Beaconsfield in a feat of annexation [31], burst into a hearty laugh, and retorted: "It is true that [32] I give nothing away; but, as you see, I am always ready for an honest alliance." So saying, he turned to the table and executed an energetic raid upon [33] the "bonbons," part of which he handed over to his British colleague.—THE CORRESPONDENT OF "THE LONDON DAILY TELEGRAPH."

1, über, with Acc. 2, **Abraham Lincoln**, Präsident der Vereinigten Staaten von Nord Amerika, war der Sohn eines einfachen Landmannes und wurde am 12. Februar 1809 im Staate Kentucki geboren. Seine Jugenderziehung war nur eine höchst mangelhafte, denn man sagt, er habe nur ein Jahr die Schule besucht; trotz der ungünstigsten Verhältnisse gelang es ihm aber dennoch, sich durch beharrliches Selbststudium zum gewandten Advokaten, tüchtigen Redner und einflußreichen Politiker heranzubilden. Er wurde Abgeordneter für die Legislatur des Staates Illinois, Mitglied des Kongresses und des Senats, und ward endlich im Jahre 1860, gerade in dem kritischen Augenblicke, wo die Südstaaten, welche die Ausdehnung der Sklaverei forderten, sich weg u Verweigerung dieser Forderung von der Union lossagten, von den Republikanern zum Präsidenten der Vereinigten Staaten gewählt. Gleich nach seiner Wahl zur Führung des Staatsruders erfolgte der Ausbruch jenes stets denkwürdigen Bürgerkrieges seitens der Union und der sich empörenten Südstaaten, welcher fünf Jahre lang mit mörderischer Wut das Land zerrüttete und endlich mit der gänzlichen Abschaffung der Sklaverei und der Besiegung der Südstaaten endete. Kaum war er jedoch im März 1865 zum zweiten Male durch ungeheure Stimmenmehrheit von der Union zum Präsidenten erwählt worden, und kaum waren die Streitkräfte der Südstaaten auf immer gebrochen und vernichtet, a s der gefeierte Staatsmann am 14. April 1865 bei Gelegenheit einer Theatervorstellung im Ford'schen Theater zu Washington der ruchlosen Hand eines von der demokratischen Partei angereizten Mörders, des Schauspielers John Willes Booth, zum Opfer fiel. So endete das Leben eines Mannes, welcher als guter, rechtschaffener Bürger, als einflußreicher Staatsmann und als edelmütiger Befreier von fünf Millionen Sklaven von seinem Vaterlande stets in dankbarem Andenken gehalten werden wird. 3, Neuvent, m.; of, зu. 4, not until, erst. 5, Say 'The next morning at (beim) breakfast', and comp. App. § 14. She remonstrated with her good husband, sie machte ihrem guten Manne einige Vorstellungen über sein langes Ausbleiben. The words 'einige — Ausbleiben' must stand at the end of the period. 6, = She told him in a kind, but (doch) determined tone. 7, die Politik, always used in the Sing.; into, зu. 8, to keep late hours, spät nach Hause kommen. App. § 28 and 30. To drink at the rum shops, die Wirtshäuser besuchen. 9, aufbleiben. 10, = could not sleep. 11, = I will tell you. 12, = well, then, I will be glad. 13, Liter. = comest thou however not. 14, ins Haus lassen. 15, Say 'Now, when it (Als es nun) struck ten that night, Mrs. Lincoln with her children went to bed, as she had promised. 16, an, with Acc. 17, else; an — raised = a window was opened up-stairs (eben). 18, Unsinn. 19, bei ist . . . gekommen. 20, for the Presidency = President. Comp. S. 27, N. 4.

21, = go again and sleep there where you have been drinking!   **22,** = and the window was closed with a slam (wieber zugeworfen).   **23,** to rule = ruler. **24, Benjamin Disraeli, Lord Beaconsfield,** geboren in London am 21. December 1804, gestorben am 19. April 1881 auf seinem Landsitze Hughenden, ausgezeichneter Litterat, berühmter Staatsmann, glänzender Redner und langjähriger Führer der konservativen Partei, steht bei seinen bewundernden Landsleuten jetzt noch in so frischem Andenken, daß es dem Verfasser der Kürze wegen erlaubt sein möge, auf seine glänzenden Erfolge weiter nicht einzugehen.   **25,** in Bezug auf; use the attributive construction, as explained in S. 7, N. 3, *A*, and S. 48, N. 6.   **26,** bei bem.   **27,** on — were = which were ornamented with.   **28,** nach aufgehobener Tafel.   **29,** here sich an'eignen.   **30,** an das Fest.   **31,** Amerieueverjuch, m.   **32,** It — that, Freilich.   **33,** = and made an energetic (tüchtig) attack upon (auf).

Section 200.

THE POWER OF MUSIC.

On one occasion when young Chopin[1] had been travelling for several days in the slow *fashion of* German diligences, he was delighted and surprised, on stopping at a small post-house, to discover a grand pianoforte in one of the rooms[2], and still more surprised to find it in tune[3]— thanks, probably, to the musical taste of the postmaster's family. He sat down instantly and began to improvise in[4] his peculiarly happy manner. One by one the travellers were attracted by the unwonted sweet sounds. One of them even allowed[5] his beloved pipe to go out in his ecstasy, and the postmaster, his wife, and his two daughters joined the group of listeners. Unmindful of his audience, of the journey, the lapse of time[6], and everything but the music, Chopin continued to play, and his companions[7] to listen in rapt attention, when they were suddenly roused by a stentorian[8] voice, which made the windows rattle, calling out[9]: " The horses are ready, gentlemen !" The postmaster roared out an anathema[10] against the disturber—the postillion—and the passengers cast angry glances at him. Chopin started from his seat, but was instantly surrounded by his audience, who entreated him to continue. " But we have been here for some time," said Chopin, consulting his watch, "and are due in Posen already[11]." " Stay and play, noble young artist," cried the postmaster, " I will find you courier's horses if you will only remain a little longer." "Do be persuaded[12]," added the postmaster's wife, almost threatening the artist with an embrace[13]. What could he do but resume his place at the instrument? When at last he paused, the servant appeared with wine ; the host's daughter served the artist first, and then the travellers, upon which the postmaster proposed a cheer for[14] the musician, in which all joined[15]. The ladies in their gratitude filled the carriage pockets with the best eatables and wine the house contained ; and when at last the artist rose to go[16], his gigantic host seized him in his arms and triumphantly bore him to[17] the carriage ! Long[18] years afterwards Chopin would recall (S. 101, N. 22) this little incident with pleasure, and declare that the plaudits of the press had never given him more delight than the homage[19] of these simple music-loving Germans.— MANCHESTER TIT-BITS.

1, Frédéric François Chopin, der berühmte Klaviervirtuose und Komponist, dessen melodieenreiche Masurkas, Walzer, Notturnos, Balladen, Polenaisen und Etüden seinen Namen überall bekannt gemacht haben, wurde im Jahre 1810 zu Zelazowawola bei War= schau geboren, und starb am 17. October 1849 in Paris, wo er sich seit dem Jahre 1831 niedergelassen hatte. On one occasion, einst.   2, he — rooms = and was stopping at (ver) a small post-house, he was delighted and surprised to discover a grand pianoforte (Flügel, m.) in one of the rooms.   3, to — tune = when he found it in good tune.   4, auf; peculiarly = peculiar; happy = charming. 5, lassen.   6, Zeitverlauf, m.   7, Say 'whilst his travelling-companions listened to him', etc.   8, = mighty.   9, = through which even the windows rattled (erklirren), and which cried.   10, einen Fluch ausstoßen. 11, I am due in London already, ich sollte bereits in London sein. The words ' said — watch' are best placed after the quotation.   12, sich überreden lassen.   13, die in ihrem Entzücken den Künstler fast umarmt hätte.   14, to propose a cheer for a person, ein Hoch auf einen ausbringen.   15, here ein= stimmen.   16, here zur Abreise.   17, in . . . hinein.   18, Noch viele. 19, die Ehrenbezeugungen.

Section 201.

THE TWO SCHOOLBOYS, OR EYES AND NO EYES[1].

I.

" Well, Robert, where have you been walking[2] this afternoon?" said a tutor to one of his pupils, at the close[3] of a holiday.

Robert.—I have been to Millthorp-Heath, and so round by[4] the wind-mill upon Camp-Mount, and home through the meadows by the river side.

Tutor.—Well, that is a pleasant round[5].

Robert.—I thought[6] it very dull, sir; I scarcely met with a single person. I would much rather have gone[7] along the turnpike-road.

Tutor.—To be sure, if seeing men and horses is your object[8], you are, indeed, better entertained on the high-road. But did you not see William (S. 48, N. 2)?

Robert.—We set out together[9]; but he lagged behind in the lane, and so[10] I walked on and left him.

Tutor.—That was a pity. He would have been company for you.

Robert.—Oh, he is so tedious, always stopping to look at this thing or that! I would rather walk alone[11]. I dare say he is not come yet.

Tutor.—Here he comes. Well, William, where have you been?

William.—Oh, the pleasantest walk[12]! I went all over Millthorp-Heath, and so up to the mill at the top of the hill, and then down among the green meadows by the side of the river home again.

Tutor.—Why, that is just the round Robert has been taking, and he complains of *its* dulness and prefers the high-road.

William.—I wonder at that. I am sure I hardly took a step that did not delight me; and I have brought home my handkerchief full of curiosities[13].

Tutor.—Suppose [14], then, you give us an account of what amused you so much. I fancy it will [15] be as new to Robert as to me.

William.—I will do it readily. The lane leading to the heath, you know, is close [16] and sandy, so I did not mind it much, but made the best of my way [17]. However, I spied a curious thing enough [18] in the hedge. It was an old crab-tree, out of which grew a bunch of something green [19], quite different from the tree itself. Here is a branch of it.

Tutor.—Ah! this is mistletoe, a plant of great fame [20] for the use made of it by the Druids of old [21], in their religious rites and incantations. It bears [22] a very slimy, white berry, of which bird-lime may be made, whence [23] its Latin name "viscum." It is one of those plants which do not grow in the ground by a root of their own [24], but fix themselves upon other plants; whence [25] they have been humourously [26] styled "parasitical," as being hangers on, or dependents. It was the mistletoe of the oak that the Druids particularly honoured.

1, ober Sehen und nicht Sehen.   2, walking, auf deinem Spaziergange. Use the 2nd pers. sing. when the tutor addresses the boy, but the 3rd pers. pl. when the boy addresses the tutor.   3, am Abend.   4, and — by = dann bei . . . vorüber. Camp-Mount, der Lagerberg; Millthorp-Heath, die Millthorper Heide. 5, = tour or walk.   6, = I have found.   7, Use the Pluperfect Subj. accord. to App. § 32; along — road, die Chaussee.   8, = if you want to see men and horses. — I am better entertained there, ich werde mich dort besser amü- sieren.   9, = We went away from home together.   10, = therefore; and left him = and troubled no more about him (sich um einen kümmern).   11, Ich gehe viel lieber allein. I dare say, wohl, adv., to be placed after the auxiliary. 12, = Oh, it was a splendid walk! All over = through the whole of; and so = then; and then = and from there; among = through.   13, = curious things. 14, Nun.   15, = It will certainly.   16, eingepfercht.   17, so — way = and therefore I left almost everything unnoticed there and went on as fast as pos- sible.   18, = something most curious.   19, a — green = a green plant. 20, = a well (allgemein) known plant.   21, = the old Druids; in, bei. 22, = has.   23, und daher.   24, which — own, welche nicht in der Erd- wurzeln.   25, weshalb.   26, scherzhafterweise; parasitical, Parasiten: as — dependents, das heißt Schmarotzer oder Abhänglinge.

Section 202.

THE TWO SCHOOLBOYS, OR EYES AND NO EYES.

II.

William.—A little further on I saw a green woodpecker [1] fly to a tree, and run up the trunk like a cat.

Tutor.—That was [2] to seek *for* insects which live in the bark of trees. For that purpose the woodpeckers bore holes into the bark with their strong bills, whereby they do [3] a great deal of damage to the trees.

William.—What beautiful birds they are [4]!

Tutor.—Yes; the woodpecker has, from its colour and size, been called the English parrot (S. 4, N. 4, man).

William.—When I got upon the heath, how charming it was[5]! The air was so fresh, and the prospect on every side[6] so free and unbounded! The heath was all covered with gay flowers, many of which I had never observed before. There were[7] at least three different kinds (S. 36, N. 7 A) of heath (I have them in my handkerchief here) and gorse, and broom, and bell-flowers; and many others of all colours, of which I will beg you presently to tell me the names[8].

Tutor.—That I will do readily.

William.—I saw, too, several birds that were new to me. There was a pretty grayish one, of the size of a lark, that was hopping about some great stones; and when he flew he showed a great deal of white above his tail[9].

Tutor.—That was a wheat-ear[10]. They are reckoned very delicious birds to eat[11], and frequent the *open* downs in[12] Sussex, and some other counties, in great number.

William.—There was a flock of lapwings upon a marshy part of the heath[13] that amused me much. As I came near them, some of them kept flying round and round[14], just over my head, and crying, "Pewit," "Pewit," so distinctly, one might almost fancy they spoke[15]. I thought I should have caught[16] one of them, for he flew as if one of his wings was broken (App. § 33), and often tumbled close to the ground; but as I came near, he always contrived[17] to get away.

Tutor.—Ha, ha! you were finely taken in, then[18]! This was all an artifice of the bird's, to entice you away from its nest, for the lapwings build upon the bare ground, and their nests would easily be observed, did they not draw off[19] the attention of intruders, by their loud cries and counterfeit lameness.

William.—I wish I had known that[20], for the bird led me a long chase[21], often over shoes in water. However, this was the cause [ravou, S. 161, N. 21] of my falling in with[22] an old man and a boy, who were cutting[23] and piling up turf for fuel. I had a great deal of talk with them about the manner of preparing the turf, and the price it sells at[24]. They gave me, too, a creature I never saw before—a young viper, which they had just killed. I have seen several common snakes, but this is thicker in proportion, and of a darker colour than they *are*.

1, Grünſpecht, m.; to, auf. 2, = That he did. 3, zu'fügen. 4, = They (Es) are really charming birds! 5, = But upon the heath it was charming! 6, nach allen Seiten hin; all = quite. 7, Es waren derr. 8, deren Namen ich mir noch von Ihnen erbitten will. 9, and — tail, und beim Fliegen über dem Schwanze weiß befiedert war. 10, Steinpacker, m.; or Weißkehlchen, n. 11, They — eat = These birds are very much valued (ſchäßen) on account of their flesh. 12, = and live in the downs of. 13, = In the marshy part of the heath I saw a flock (Schar) of lapwings. 14, round and round, immer im Kreiſe herum. 15, one — spoke, daß ich faſt wähnte, ſie ſprechen zu hören. 16, = I should be able to catch. 17, gelang es ihm immer. 18, dann ſind du ſchön angeführt werden! 19, did — off, ſuchten ſie nicht . . . daven abzulenken, intruders = unbidden guests. 20, Das hätte ich vorher wiſſen ſollen. 21, = for the bird caused (veranlaßen) me to run a long time after it (hinter einem herjagen). 22, of — with = that I met. 23, ſtechen, str. v. 24, about — at, über die Zubereitungsweiſe und die Verkaufspreiſe des Torfes.

Section 203.

THE TWO SCHOOLBOYS, OR EYES AND NO EYES.

III.

TUTOR.—True.   Vipers frequent[1] those turfy, boggy grounds[2] pretty much, and I have known several turf-cutters bitten by them.

WILLIAM.—They are very venomous, are they not?

TUTOR.—Enough so[3] to make their wounds painful and dangerous, though they seldom prove fatal.

WILLIAM.—Well, I then took my course[4] up to the windmill on the mount.   I climbed up the steps of the mill, in order to get a better view of the country round[5].   What an extensive prospect!   I counted fifteen church steeples; I saw several gentlemen's houses[6] peeping out from the midst of green woods and plantations[7]; and I could trace the windings[8] of the river all along the low grounds, till it was lost behind a ridge of hills[9].   But I will tell you what I mean to do[10], if you will give me leave.

TUTOR.—What is that[11]?

WILLIAM.—I will go again and take with me Carey's county map[12], by which I shall probably be able to make out most of the places.

TUTOR.—You shall have it; and I will go with you, and take my pocket spying-glass.

WILLIAM.—I shall be very glad of that.   Well, a thought struck me, that, as the hill is called Camp-Mount, there might probably be some remains of ditches and mounds[13] with which I have read that camps were surrounded.   And I really believe I discovered something of that sort[14] running one side of the mount.

TUTOR.—Very likely you might[15].   I know antiquaries have described such remains as existing there, which some suppose to be Roman, others Danish[16].   We will examine them when we go.

WILLIAM.—From the hill I went straight down to the meadows below, and walked on the side of a brook that runs[17] into the river.   It[18] was all bordered with reeds and tall flowering-plants (S. 16, N. 10), quite different from those I had seen on the heath.   As I was getting down[19] the bank to reach one of them, I heard something plunge into the water near me.   It was a large water-rat, and I saw it swim over to the other side, and go[20] into its hole.   There were[21] a great many large dragon-flies all about the stream.   I caught one of the finest, and have him here in a leaf.   But how I longed to catch a bird that I saw hovering[22] over the water, and every now and then darting into it!   It was all over a mixture of the most beautiful green and blue, with some orange colour[23]. It was somewhat less than a thrush, and had a large head and bill, and a short tail.

1, = live in.   2, Gegenten.   3, = venomous enough.   4, = thereupon I went.   5, I had a fine view of the country round, ich kennte die Umgegend gut überblicken.   6, herrschaftliche Häuser.   7, Parkanlagen.   8, der sich schlängelnde Lauf, as Nom.; low grounds = meadows.   9, Hügelrücken, m.   10, = will do.   Supply 'dazu' after 'leave'.   11, Was denn?   12, Bezuſſarte; by which = by (mit) the help of which; 'to make out', here beſtimmen, w. v. tr.; places, Ortſchaften.   13, Well — mounds. This passage may be construed thus: 'Now, since (Da nun) the hill is called Camp-Mount, a thought struck me that there are (ſich befinden) probably some remains of ditches and mounds (Erdwall, m)'. I have read = as I have read.   14, etwas derartiges; running one side = on the one side.   15, = That is quite (gerne) possible. 16, to be — Danish, daß ſie römiſchen, andere aber, daß ſie däniſchen Urſprungs ſind. 17, ſich ergießen.   18, = The brook: bordered = overgrown, bewachſen. 19, hinunterſteigen: to reach ~ to pluck.   20, = creep. Read S. 78, N. 14, B. 21, Es waren dort, after which place the words 'all — stream', am Bache. 22, umherfliegen: every — then, dann und wann; 'to dart', here hinunterſchießen; into it = into the same.   23, It — colour = His plumage (Gefieder) consisted of (aus) a mixture of the finest green and blue with a small addition (Zuſatz, m.) of orange colour (Orangengelb).

Section 204.

THE TWO SCHOOLBOYS, OR EYES AND NO EYES.
IV.

TUTOR.—I can tell you what that bird was—a kingfisher, the celebrated halcyon of the ancients, about which so many tales are told. It lives on[1] fish, which it catches in the manner you saw. It builds in holes on the banks, and is a shy, retired[2] bird, never to be seen far from the stream it inhabits.

WILLIAM.—I must try to get another sight of him, for I never saw (S. 48, N. 2) a bird that pleased me so much. Well, I followed this little brook till it entered[3] the river, and then took[4] the path that runs along the bank. On the opposite side, I observed several little birds running along the bank, and making a piping noise[5]. They were[6] brown and white, and about as big as a snipe.

TUTOR.—I suppose they [es] were sand-pipers[7]; one of the numerous family of birds (S. 36, N. 7, A) that get their living[8] by wading among the shallows and picking up worms and insects.

WILLIAM.—There were a great many swallows, too, sporting[9] above the surface of the water, that entertained me with their motions. Sometimes[10] they dashed down into the stream[11]; sometimes they pursued one another so quickly, that the eye could scarcely follow them. In one place, where a steep sand-bank rose high above the river, I observed many of them go in and out of holes with which the bank was bored full[12].

TUTOR.—Those [Das] were sand-martins[13], the smallest of our species of swallows. They are of a mouse-colour above, and white beneath. They[14] make their nests, and bring up their young, in these holes, which run a great depth, and by their situation are secure from all plunderers.

WILLIAM.—A little further I saw a man in a boat, who was catching eels in an odd way[15]. He had a long pole with broad iron prongs[16] at the end; just like Neptune's trident[17], only there were five prongs instead of three. This he pushed straight down into the mud, in the deepest parts of the river, and fetched up the eels sticking between the prongs.

TUTOR.—I know the method. It is called the spearing of eels[18].

WILLIAM.—While I was looking at him, a heron came flying over my head, with his large flagging wings. He alighted[19] at the next turn of the river, and I crept softly behind the bank to watch his motions. He had waded into the water as far as his long legs would allow him[20] and was standing there motionless with his neck drawn in, looking[21] intently on the stream. Presently he darted his long bill as quick as lightning into the water, and drew out a fish, which he swallowed. I saw him catch another in the same manner. He then took alarm[22] at some noise I made, and flew away slowly to a wood at some distance, where he settled.

1, von; in — saw, auf die von dir beobachtete Weise.   **2,** die Einsamkeit liebend; never — inhabits = which goes never far away (sich entfernen) from the stream (Gewässer, n.) where it has its nest.   **3,** sich ergießen, str. v. refl.   **4,** betreten, str. v. tr.   **5,** running — noise, am Ufer entlang hüpfen und pfeifen.   **6,** = looked; and = and were.   **7,** Strandläufer.   **8,** 'to get one's living', here sich seine Nahrung verschaffen. Read S. 87, N. 6; among the shallows, an den seichten Stellen; to wade, umherwaten; and picking up = in order to pick up.   **9,** 'to sport', here sein Spiel treiben; that = and.   **10,** bald.   **11,** = water.   **12,** I — full = I observed that many of them crept into the holes that were in great number (Menge, f.) bored (hinein'bohren) into the bank, but then (dann aber) came out again.   **13,** Uferschwalben.   **14,** Commence this period with 'In these holes — plunderers'; to make a nest, ein Nest bauen; to bring up the young, die Jungen groß ziehen.   **15,** auf wunderliche Weise.   **16,** Zinke, f.   **17,** Dreizack, m.   **18,** das Aalstechen.   **19,** sich auf die Erde niederlassen.   **20,** Insert the grammatical object es before 'him'.   **21,** = and looked intently (mit gespannter Aufmerksamkeit) down upon the water (auf . . . hernieder).   **22,** to take alarm at something, durch etwas in Furcht gesetzt werden.

Section 205.

THE TWO SCHOOLBOYS, OR EYES AND NO EYES.

V.

TUTOR.—Probably his nest was there, for herons build upon the loftiest tree they can find, and sometimes in society together, like rooks. Formerly, when these birds were valued for the amusement of hawking[1], many gentlemen had their heronries[2], and a few are still remaining.

WILLIAM.—I think (S. 64, N. 11) they are the largest wild birds we have.

TUTOR.—They are of great length and spread of wing[3], but their bodies are comparatively small.

WILLIAM.—I then turned homeward, across the meadows, where I stopped awhile, to look at[4] a large flock of starlings, which kept flying about at no great distance. I could not tell at first what to make of them[5], for they rose altogether from the ground as thick as a swarm of bees, and formed *themselves into* a kind[5] of black cloud, hovering over the field. After taking a short round[7], they settled again, but presently rose in the same manner. I dare say[8] there were hundreds of them.

TUTOR.—Perhaps so[9]; for in the fenny counties their flocks are so numerous[10] as to break down whole acres of reeds, by settling on them[11].

This disposition [12] of starlings to fly in close swarms was remarked even by Homer, who compares the foe (S. 48, N. 6) flying from one of his heroes to a cloud of starlings retiring dismayed at the approach of the hawk.

WILLIAM.—After I had left the meadows, I crossed [13] the corn-fields in the way to our house, and passed close by a deep marl-pit. Looking into it, I saw, on one of the sides, a cluster of what [14] I took to be shells; and upon going down, I picked up a clod of marl [15], which was quite full of them; but how sea-shells can get there, I cannot imagine.

TUTOR.—I do not wonder at your surprise, since many philosophers have been much perplexed to account for the same appearance [16]. It is not uncommon to find [17] great quantities of shells and relics of marine animals, even in the bowels of high mountains, very remote from the sea.

WILLIAM.—I got [18] to the high field next to our house just as the sun was setting, and I stood looking at it till it was quite lost [19]. What a glorious sight! The clouds were tinged with purple, crimson, and yellow of all shades and hues, and the clear sky varied from blue to a fine green at the horizon. But how large the sun appears just as it sets! I think it seems twice as big as when it is over-head.

1, for — hawking = on account of the amusement which they afforded through hawking (die Falkenjagd). 2, Meierstand, m. 3, They — wing — They have very large, long wings. 4, = to observe; to keep flying about, umberstiegen; at — distance, in nur geringer Entfernung von mir. 5, = I could not recognise them at first. 'To rise', here sich in die Luft emporschwingen; thick, dicht. 6, a kind, gleichsam; hovering — field, als sie über dem Felde hin und her schwebten. 7, = After they had been flying about *for* a short time. 8, 'I dare say' may be briefly rendered by the adv. gewiß. Read S. 104, N. 19. 9, Das ist leicht möglich. 10, = they exist (verbanten sein) in such masses; as to = that they. 11, = when they settle upon the same (to agree with 'reeds'). 12, = peculiarity. 13, = I went through the corn-fields home again. 14, a — what, eine zusammengeballte Masse, welche. 15, Nom. ein Klumpen (m.) Mergel; of them = of shells. 16, since — appearance, da schon viele Naturforscher sich über die Erklärung dieser Erscheinung den Kopf zerbrochen haben. 17, = that one finds. 18, gelangen; to, auf; high field, Anhöhe, f. 19, = till it had entirely disappeared at the (am) horizon.

Section 206.

THE TWO SCHOOLBOYS, OR EYES AND NO EYES.
VI.

TUTOR.—It does so [1]; and you *may* probably have observed the same apparent enlargement of the moon at its rising [2].

WILLIAM.—I have [3]; but pray what is the reason of this?

TUTOR.—It is an optical deception, depending upon principles which I cannot well explain to you, till you know more of that *branch of* science. But what a number of new ideas this afternoon's walk has afforded you. I do not wonder that you found it amusing [4], and it has been very instructive too. Did you see (S. 48, N. 2) nothing of all these sights, Robert?

Robert.—I saw some of them, but I did not take particular notice of them.

Tutor.—Why not?

Robert.—I do not know. I did not care about them; and I made the best of my way home [5].

Tutor.—That would have been (App. § 33) right, if you had been sent on a message [6]; but as you only walked for amusement [7], it would have been wiser to have sought out as many sources of it as possible [8]. But as it is [9]: one man walks through the world with the eyes open, and another with them shut, and [10] upon this difference depends all the [11] superiority the one acquires above the other. I have known sailors [12] who have been in all the quarters of the world, and could tell you nothing but [13] the signs of the tippling houses they frequented [14] in different ports, and the price and quality of the liquor. On the other hand [15], a Franklin could not even cross the Channel without making some observation useful to mankind [16]. While many a vacant, thoughtless youth is whirled throughout Europe [17], without gaining [18] a single idea worth crossing a street for [19], the observing eye and inquiring mind find matter of improvement and delight [20] in every ramble *in town or country* Do you then, William, continue to make use of your eyes; and you, Robert, learn that eyes were given you to use.—Dr. Aikin.

1, = Quite right.　　2, of — rising, beim Aufgange des Mondes.　　3, = Yes. 4, = interesting.　　5, and — home = and went home as quickly as possible. 6, if — message, hätte man dich ausgeschickt, um eine Besorgung zu verrichten.　　7, to walk for amusement, einen Spaziergang machen.　　8, to — possible, hättest du denselben so viel wie möglich auszubreiten gesucht.　　9, Es ist aber nun einmal so; one man, der eine; another, der andere.　　10, and just (gerade).　　11, = the great. 12, Schiffer.　　13, and — but, dennoch aber von nichts anderem zu erzählen wußten, als von.　　14, = visited.　　15, Andererseits hingegen.　　16, Use the attributive construction.　　17, ganz Europa durchfliegt.　　18, sich aneignen. 19, worth — for = for (wegen) which it would have been worth while to go over the street.　　20, zur Belehrung und zum Genusse. The words 'in every ramble' must be placed after 'mind'.

Section 207.

THE KING AND THE MILLER.

I.

In the reign [1] of Frederick the Great (see S. 192, N. 1), king of Prussia, there was [2] a mill near Potsdam which obstructed the view from the windows of the palace of Sans Souci. Annoyed by this drawback to his favourite residence [3], the king sent [4] to the owner of the mill inquiring the price for which he would sell it. "For no price," was the reply of the sturdy Prussian; and in a moment of anger the monarch gave orders [5] that the mill should be pulled down. " The king may do this," said the miller, quietly folding his arms; "but there are (S. 82, N. 7) laws in Prussia, and he will find them out [6]". Forthwith he commenced a lawsuit against the monarch, the issue of which was [7], that the court gave a decision against His Majesty, compelling him [8] to rebuild the mill, and in addition [9] to pay a large sum of money as a compensation for the injury he had done [10]. The king felt mortified (S. 87, N. 6) at having been worsted by one of his subjects, but had the magnanimity to say, addressing [11] his courtiers : " I am glad to find that there are just laws and upright judges in my kingdom who are bold enough to decide against me when they think I am in the wrong." Many years afterwards (App. § 14), a descendant of the honest miller, who had in *due* course of time succeeded to the hereditary possession of the property [12], found himself involved in pecuniary difficulties that had become insurmountable.

1, = At (ʒu) the time of the reign. See S. 53, N. 9.   2, there — Potsdam = stood near (bei) Potsdam a mill.   3, Der seinem Lieblingsschlosse hierdurch erwachsende Nachteil vertroß ten König sehr.   4, = and he sent.   5, = the order.   6, = and he will soon convince himself of it.   7, the — was, welcher damit entete.   8, = and compelled him.   9, and in addition, mit noch ebendrein ; sum — compensation, Entschädigungssumme, f.   10, Supply 'to the miller'.   11, = to.   12, Liter. = who in course of time *and* through inheritance had come into the possession of the mill.

Section 208.

THE KING AND THE MILLER.

II.

In his distress he wrote to Frederick William IV, who was at that time king of Prussia, reminding him of the refusal experienced by Frederick the Great at the hands [1] of his ancestor the miller, and stating [2] that [3] if His Majesty now wished to obtain possession of the property, he would, in his present embarrassed circumstances, most willingly dispose of the mill. The king immediately wrote, with his own hand [4], *the* following reply :

" My Dear Neighbour,

I cannot allow you to sell the mill. It must remain in the possession of your family as long as one of your descendants survives [5], for the building belongs [6] to the history of Prussia, and is a standing [7] memorial of the integrity of our judges and the impartiality of our laws. I am sorry, however, to hear that you are in straitened circumstances, and therefore send you six thousand dollars [8] to pay off your debts, and hope the sum will be sufficient for the purpose. Consider me [9] always

Your affectionate [10] neighbour,

FREDERICK WILLIAM."

The mill still stands, and is occupied by the [11] descendants of the resolute miller who had the fortitude to thwart the despotic monarch in his desire [12] to improve the prospect from the windows of his palace.— CHAMBERS'S " SHORT STORIES."

1, reminding — hands = reminded him of the refusal (abschlägige Antwort) which Fred. the Gr. had received at the hands (seitens).   2, stated.   3, that he would in his present embarrassed circumstances most willingly sell the mill, if, etc. 'To obtain possession of the property', here das Besitzthum käuflich erwerben.   4, with — hand, eigenhändig, adj., which use after 'following'.   **5,** noch am Leben sein.   **6,** an'gehören.   **7,** bleibend, adj.; to, an.   **8,** Thaler (m.), formerly the standard coin in Germany, and equal to 3 sh. English.   **9,** = I remain always.   **10,** here wohlwollend, adj. **11,** = and is still in the possession of the.   **12,** to thwart — desire = to oppose (sich einer Sache widersetzen) the desire of the despotic king.

Section 209.

A FRIEND IN NEED (S. 3, N. 2).

I.

One wet wintry night, when a gentleman was hurrying along[1] one of the crowded thoroughfares of London, his attention was arrested by a lean, hungry-looking dog which rushed past him. He observed that it had a collar[2] round its neck, to which a basket was attached. If it was (App. § 36) a dog that ran on errands[3], he thought that surely its owner would feed it better, and its ribs would not look so spare. Thinking that there was some mystery connected with the animal[4], he resolved to follow it[5]. After a[6] time it turned up a narrow lane into a stable-yard, where some coachmen and hostlers were loitering about. It then got up on its hind-legs, and began walking about in circles[7]. The bystanders, surprised at this strange proceeding, formed round in a ring and looked on. It walked five times round, standing[8] erect, and looking fixedly before it like a soldier on duty[9], evidently doing its utmost[10] to make the company laugh. After taking a short rest, it began its performance[11] again, but this time on its fore-feet, pretending to stand[12] on its (S. 43, N. 9) head. Tiring of this[13], it lay down in the middle of the ring, feigning to be dead[14], and going through all the convulsions of a dying dog, breathing heavily, panting, suffering the lower jaw to fall[15], and then turning over motionless. It did this so well, that a woman in the crowd exclaimed :· "Poor beast!" and drew her hand across her eyes[16]. Having lain still a minute, with its eyes closed, it got up and shook itself, to show that the performance[17] was over. It then went round begging on its hind-legs, standing[18] a little while before each of the spectators, and earnestly watching[19] to see whether they put their hands into their pockets or not. The basket round its neck had a slit in the lid, into which the coppers might be dropped.

1, to hurry along, hindeilen, insep. comp. w. v. Place 'one — night' after 'gentleman'; wet = rainy; thoroughfares = streets.   **2,** here Halsband, n.; round its neck, um.   **3,** to run on errands, Besorgungen aus'richten; and — spare = and it would not look so dreadfully lean.   **4,** = Since the matter appeared very mysterious (räthselhaft) to him.   **5,** = the animal.   **6,** furz; turned up = ran into; into = which led to.   **7,** im Kreise.   **8,** = held himself. **9,** auf dem Posten.   **10,** = and did evidently his best.   **11,** here = tricks, Kunststücke.   **12,** = and did (sich anstellen) as if he stood (App. § 33). **13,** = Hereupon.   **14,** to feign to be dead, sich todt stellen. The Present Participles in this passage must be rendered by the Imperfect in German. **15,** = dropped (fallen lassen) the lower jaw.   **16,** mit der Hand über die Augen fahren.   **17,** Verstellung, f.   **18,** stille stehen.   **19,** = and watched (beobachten) them quite earnestly (ernsthaft).

Section 210.

A FRIEND IN NEED.

II.

The gentleman put in a shilling, and stooped down to read a crumpled piece of paper which hung loosely from the collar. It bore these words, written in a[1] shaky hand : "This is the dog of a poor man who is bedridden. It earns bread for its master. Good people, do not prevent it from returning to its home." On receiving (S. 55, N. 1) *any* money, the poor creature returned thanks by a wag of its tail. Almost every one of the spectators gave the dog something, and when it had finished collecting the money, it barked once or twice, as if to say good-bye, and then scampered off. On entering the principal street, it quickened its pace[2], and the gentleman finding it impossible to keep up with it[3], hailed[4] a cab, and, much to the driver's amazement[5], cried : "Follow that dog." After a time the dog bolted up a narrow alley[6], through which the cab could not pass[7]. The gentleman alighted, and followed the dog through a dark close up[8] to the garret of a rickety dwelling. Pulling the string attached to the latch, the dog opened the door, and the stranger followed. Its master lay dying[9] on a wretched bed, supported[10] by the earnings of the faithful creature, who practised[11] the same tricks alone as it used to do under its master's superintendence. Death soon ended[12] the poor man's sufferings, and the dog followed the coffin to the grave. The gentleman took home the dog, but next morning the poor beast howled impatiently for[13] the basket to go its rounds as usual. It went with the pennies to the cemetery and laid them on a grave, whining[14] mournfully, and trying to scratch up the earth. Twice more it went out all day, and brought back the money for its master; but, on finding the money untouched, it lay down at full length upon the grave. The next morning it did not go its rounds, for it was dead.—CHAMBERS's "SHORT STORIES."

1, in a = with.   2, here Lauf, m.   3, to keep up with a person, gleichen Schritt mit einem halten.   4, au'rufen, sep. comp. str. w. tr.   5, = to the great amazement of the driver.   6, plötzlich in einen Durchgang hinein'laufen. 7, passieren.   8, Passage, f.; to = into ; rickety, baufällig.   9, im Sterben. 10, = and was supported (unterhalten or verforgen).   11, here aus'üben. 12, einer Sache (Dat.) ein Ende machen.   13, nach; 'to go one's rounds ', here seine Runde wieder an'treten.   14, = whereby he whined.

Section 211.

MY FIRST GUINEA.

I well remember[1], when I was very young, possessing for the first time a guinea. I remember too that this circumstance cost me no little perplexity and anxiety. As I passed along the streets, the fear of losing my guinea induced me oftentimes to take it out of my pocket to look at it. First I put[2] it in one pocket, then I took it out and put it in another;

after a while I took it out of the second pocket and placed[2] it in another, really perplexed[3] what to do with it (S. 27, N. 7).

At last my attention was arrested by a book-auction. I stepped in and looked about me. First one lot[4] was put up, and then another, and sold to the highest bidder[5]. At last I ventured to the table, just as the auctioneer was putting up "The History of the World," in two large folio volumes. I instantly thrust[2] my hand into my (S. 43, N. 9) pocket, and began turning over[6] my guinea, considering whether I should have money enough to buy this lot. The bidding proceeded[7], and at last I ventured to bid too. "Halloo! my little man!" said the auctioneer, "what! (S. 27, N. 7) not content with less than the world?" This remark greatly confused me, and drew the attention of the whole company[8] toward me, who[9], seeing (S. 30, N. 4) me anxious[10] to possess the books, refrained from bidding against me; and so, "The World" was knocked down[11] to me at a very moderate price.

How to get[12] these huge books home was the next consideration[13]. The auctioneer offered to send them, but I, not knowing what sort of creatures auctioneers were[14], determined to take them myself; so, after[15] the assistant had tied them up, I marched out of the room with these huge books upon my shoulder, like Samson with the gates of Gaza, amid the smiles of all present.

When I reached my home, after the servant had opened the door, the first person I met was my sainted mother.

"My dear boy," she said, "what have you *got* there? I thought you would not keep your guinea long."

"Do not be angry, mother," said I, throwing the books down upon the table. "I have bought 'The World' for nine shillings."

This was on a Saturday, and I well remember sitting up[16] till it was well-nigh midnight, turning over[17] this "History of the World." The books became my delight, and were carefully read through and through.

When I grew older, I became at length a Christian, and my love of books[18], among other things, led me to desire to be a Christian minister[19]. To the possession of these books I attribute, in a great measure, any honours that have been added to my name in connection with literature. I have not mentioned this anecdote to gratify any foolish feeling[20], but to encourage in all whom I see before me that[21] love of literature which has afforded me such unspeakable pleasure—pleasure[22] which I would not have been without for all the riches of the Indies[23].—THE REV. DR. VAUGHAN.

1, Supply 'the time' here; to remember, fich erinnern, governs the Gen.; possessing = and possessed.   2, ſtecken.   3, fich in großer Verlegenheit befinden.   4, Partie, f.; to put up to auction, to public sale, zur Verſteigerung bringen, unter den Hammer bringen, or zum öffentlichen Verkauf ſtellen.   5, der Meiſtbietende; to, an.   6, herum'treten; considering = and considered (über-le'gen, insep. comp. w. v.).   7, verſtatten gehen.   8, = of all the persons present (die Anweſenden); toward, auf.   9, Finish first the clause 'who refrained from bidding against me', and then commence the other, and use this construction in all cases where it can possibly be employed.   10, We are anxious to buy the property, wir möchten das Beſitztum gerne kaufen.

11, to knock down an article to the last bidder, einen Artifel dem zuletzt Bietenden zu schlagen. 12, to get home, nach Hause schaffen. 13, Erwägung, f. 14, = but since I had not yet any experience in such matters, I determined, etc. 15, so, after = and when. 16, = that I sat up. 17, = and turned over (durchblät'tern, insep. comp. w. v.). 18, Liebhaberei (f.) für Bücher. 19, = to become *a* Christian Minister (Geistlicher). 20, Supply 'of vanity' here. 21, = the; of, zu, contracted with the Dat. of the def. art. 22, = a pleasure (Genuß, m.) 23, = of India.

Section 212.

THE GREEN VAULTS IN DRESDEN.

Dresden, May 11, 1845.

We were fortunate in seeing the Green Vaults or " Das grüne Gewölbe," a collection of jewels and costly articles [1], unsurpassed in Europe (S. 7, N. 3, *A*). Admittance is only granted to six persons at a time, who pay a fee [2] of two thalers. The customary way is to employ a "valet de place [3]," who goes round from one hotel to another, until he has collected the required number, when [4] he brings them together and conducts them to the keeper who has charge of the treasures. The first hall into which we were ushered contained works in bronze [5]. They were all small, and chosen with regard to their artistical value. The next room contained statues, and vases ornamented with reliefs, in ivory. The most remarkable work was the fall of Lucifer and his angels, containing ninety-two figures in all [6], carved out of a single piece *of* ivory sixteen inches high! It was the work of an Italian monk, and cost him many years of hard labour [7].

However costly the contents of these halls (S. 27, N. 7), they were only an introduction to those which followed. Each one exceeded the other in splendour and costliness. The walls were covered to the ceiling with rows of goblets, vases, etc., of polished jasper, agate, and lapis lazuli. We saw two goblets, each prized at six thousand thalers, made of gold and precious stones; also the great pearl called the Spanish Dwarf, nearly as large as a pullet's egg; globes and vases cut entirely out of *the* mountain crystal; magnificent Nuremberg watches and clocks, and a great number of figures made ingeniously of rough [8] pearls and diamonds. The seventh hall contains the coronation robes of Augustus II, king of Poland, and many costly specimens of carving in wood [9]. A cherry-stone is shown in a glass case, which has one hundred and twenty-five faces, all perfectly finished, carved upon it [10]. The next room we entered sent back a glare of splendour [11] that perfectly dazzled us. It was all gold, diamond, ruby, and sapphire. Every case sent out a glow and a glitter that it seemed like a cage of imprisoned lightnings [12]. Wherever the eye turned it was met by a blaze of broken rainbows. They were there by hundreds [13], and every gem was a fortune. We here saw the largest known onyx, nearly seven inches long, and four inches broad! One of the most remarkable works is the throne and court of Aurungzebe, the Indian king, by Dinglinger, a celebrated goldsmith of the last century. It contains one hundred and thirty-two figures, all of enamelled gold, and each one most perfectly and elaborately finished. It was purchased by Prince Augustus for fifty-eight thousand thalers, which was not an exorbitant sum, considering that the making of it occupied Dinglinger and thirteen workmen for seven years!

It is almost impossible to estimate the value of the treasures these halls contain. That of gold and jewels alone must be many millions of dollars, and the amount of labour expended on these toys of royalty is incredible.—Bayard Taylor, " Views Afoot."

1, Köſtlichkeiten. **2,** Eintrittsgeld, n. **3,** Generally one engages a ' valet de place ' (ein Lohnbedienter, Nom.). **4,** = and then. **5,** Bronzeſachen. **6,** im Ganzen. **7,** hard labour, angeſtreugte Arbeit. **8,** here ungeſchliffen. **9,** Holzſchnitzereien. **10,** which — it = upon which are carved 125 faces, which are all perfectly finished (ausgebildet). **11,** wiederſtrahlte von einem herrlichen Glanze; ' perfectly ', here förmlich. **12,** Aus jedem Kaſten erſtrahlte ſo viel Glanz und Licht, daß es ſchien, es entſtrömten ihm tauſend Blitze. **13,** = There were (Es waren dert) hundreds of gems.

Section 213.

THE DEATH OF LITTLE NELL.

She was dead. No sleep (S. 27, N. 7) so beautiful and calm, so free from trace[1] of pain, so fair to look upon. She seemed[2] a creature fresh from the hand of God, and waiting for the breath of life; not one who had lived and suffered death. Her couch was dressed with here and there some winterberries and green leaves, gathered in a spot she had been used to favour. " When I die, put near me something[3] that has loved the light, and had the sky above it always." These were her words.

She was dead. Dear (S. 10, N. 2), gentle, patient, noble Nell was dead. Her little bird—a poor, slight thing[4], the pressure of the finger would have crushed—was stirring nimbly in its cage; and the strong heart of its child-mistress[5] was mute and motionless for ever! Where were the traces of her early cares, her sufferings and fatigues? All gone[6]. Sorrow was dead, *indeed* in her[7]; but peace and perfect happiness were born[8]—imaged in her tranquil beauty and (S. 10, N. 9) profound repose.

And still her former self lay there, unaltered in this change[8]. Yes, the old fireside[9] had smiled upon that same sweet face; it had passed like a dream through haunts of misery and care—at the door of the poor schoolmaster on the summer evening, before the furnace-fire upon the cold wet night, at the still bedside of the dying boy[10], there had been the same mild and loving look. So shall we know the angels in their majesty after death.—Charles Dickens, " The Old Curiosity Shop."

1, = from the traces. **2,** = seemed to be a creature (Kreatur, f.). Fresh — God, erſt ſeeben aus der Hand Gottes hervorgegangen, which use attributively before ' creature '; breath, Otem, m. **3,** kann gebet mir etwas mit. **4,** ein armſeliges kleines Ding. **5,** ſindliche Herrin, Nom. **6,** Alles war verſchwunden. **7,** war in ihr erſterben; were born, waren dafür wieder in ihr erſtanten; imaged in, wie es . . . bezeugte : her tranquil beauty = her tranquil beautiful face (Antlitz, n.).   **8,** Liter. = And still (dennoch) lay her former self in this change (Berwandt: lung) unaltered there.   **9,** der häusliche Herd ; 'to smile upon', here auf etwas hernie'derlächeln.   **10,** = brother.

Section 214.

THE CHILDHOOD OF ROBERT CLIVE[1].

Some lineaments of the character of the man were early discerned in the child.   There remain[2] letters written by his relations when he was in his seventh year ; and from[3] these letters it appears that, even at that early age, his strong will and his fiery passions, sustained by a constitutional intrepidity[4], had begun to cause great uneasiness to his family. " Fighting," says one of his uncles, " to which he is out of measure addicted, gives his temper such a fierceness and imperiousness, that he flies out on every occasion[5]."   The old people of the neighbourhood still remember to have heard from their parents how Bob Clive climbed to the top of the lofty steeple of Market Drayton, and with what terror the inhabitants saw (S. 78, N. 14, B) him seated on a stone spout near the summit.   They also relate how he formed all the idle lads of the town into a kind of predatory army[6], and compelled the shop-keepers to submit to a tribute of apples and halfpence, in consideration of which[7] he guaranteed the security of their windows.   He was sent from school to school, making very little progress in his learning[8], and gaining for himself everywhere the character of an exceedingly naughty boy.   One of his masters, it is said, was sagacious enough to prophesy that the idle lad would make a great figure in the world[9].—LORD MACAULAY, " LORD CLIVE."

1, Robert Lord Clive, geboren den 29. September 1725, gestorben den 22. November 1774, war der Begründer des brittischen Reiches in Indien.   **2,** Es existieren noch. **3,** aus ; it appears, ergiebt sich.   **4,** welche durch die ihm angeborene Unerschrocken: heit noch unterstützt wurden.   **5,** daß er bei jeder Gelegenheit in heftigen Zorn gerät. **6,** He formed of them a kind of predatory army, er bildete aus ihnen eine Art Räuberbande.   **7,** in — which, wofür.   **8,** = studies.   **9,** to make a great figure in the world, eine große Rolle in der Welt spielen.

Section 215.

AN ADVENTURE WITH A LION.

I.

It is well[1] known that if one of a troop of lions is killed, the others take the hint[2], and leave that part of the country.   So[3] the next time the herds were attacked, I went with the people, in order to encourage them to rid themselves of the annoyance by destroying[4] one of the marauders. We found the lions on a small hill about a quarter of a mile in length[5], which was covered with trees.   A circle of men was formed round it, and they gradually closed up[6], ascending pretty near to each other.   Being down below on the plain with a native schoolmaster, named Mebalwe, a most excellent man (S. 53, N. 9), I saw one of the lions sitting (S. 78,

N. 14, B) on a *piece of* rock within the now-closed circle *of men*. Mebalwe fired at him before I could[7], and the ball struck the rock on which the animal was sitting. He bit at the spot struck, as a dog does at a stick or stone thrown at him ; then leaping away[8], broke through the opening circle, and escaped unhurt. The men were afraid to attack him on account of their belief in [an] witchcraft. When the circle was re-formed, we saw two other lions in it; but were afraid[9] to fire lest we should strike the men, and they allowed the beasts to burst through also. If (App. § 36) the Bakatta had acted according to the custom of the country, they would have speared the lions in their attempt to get out. Seeing we could not get[10] them to kill one of the lions, we bent our footsteps[11] towards the village ; in going round the end of the hill, however, I saw one of the beasts sitting on a *piece of* rock as before, but this time he had a little bush in front. Being about thirty yards[12] off, I took a good aim at his body through the bush, and fired both barrels into it. The men then called out: "He is shot! he is shot!" Others cried: "He has been shot by another man, too; let us go to him!" I did not see any one else shoot at him, but I saw the lion's tail[13] erected in anger behind the bush, and turning to the people, said: "Stop a little till I load[14] again."

1, = generally. 2, es sich zur Warnung dienen lassen. 3, So, Als nun; the next time, wiederum, which place after the subject. 4, durch Vertilgung, which place, with 'one — marauders', immediately after the reflective pronoun 'sich'. 5, Use the attributive construction. 6, and — up, welche sich allmählich enger an einander anschließen ; ascending = and ascended (den Berg hinauf= steigen). 7, ehe ich es thun tonnte. 8, = and when, hereupon, he sprang away, he, etc. 9, = but ventured not; lest, aus Furcht, daß; render 'should' by the Imperf. Subj. of mögen. 10, dahin bringen. 11, we went (schreiten). 12, = steps; distances are generally measured by *steps* in Ger- many. 13, a lion's *tail*, Schweif, m. ; in, aus. 14, = have loaded.

Section 216.

AN ADVENTURE WITH A LION.

II.

When (S. 27, N. 7) in the act[1] of ramming down the bullets, I heard a shout. Starting, and looking half round, I saw the lion just in the act of springing[2] upon me. I was upon a little height; he caught my shoulder as he sprang[3], and we both came to the ground below together. Growl- ing (S. 55, N. 1, während) horribly close to my ear, he shook me as a terrier dog does a rat. The shock produced a stupor similar to that which seems to be felt by a mouse after the first shake of the cat. It caused a sort of dreaminess, in which there was[4] no sense of pain nor feeling of terror, though I was quite conscious of all that was happening. It was like what[5] patients, particularly under the influence of chloroform, describe, who see all the operation, but do not feel the knife. This sin- gular condition was not the result of any mental process. The shake annihilated fear, and allowed no sense of horror[6] in looking round at the beast. This peculiar state is probably produced in all animals killed by the carnivora [7]; and, if so [8], is a merciful provision by our benevolent creator for lessening the pain of death (S. 76, N. 22, *B*, 1). Turning round to relieve myself of the weight, as he had one paw on the back of my head [9], I saw his eyes directed to Mebalwe, who was trying to shoot him at a distance of ten or fifteen yards. His gun, a flint one [10], missed fire in both barrels; the lion immediately left me, and attacking Mebalwe, bit [11] his thigh. Another man, whose life I had saved before, after he had been tossed [12] by a buffalo, attempted to spear the lion while he was biting Mebalwe. He left Mebalwe, and caught this man by the shoulder; but, at that moment, the bullets he had received took effect [13], and he fell down dead. The whole was the work of a few moments, and must have been his paroxysm of dying rage. In order to take out the charm from him, the Bakatla on the following day made a huge bonfire over his carcass, which was declared to be that of the largest lion they had ever seen. Besides crunching the bone into splinters, he left [14] eleven teeth wounds on the upper part of my arm.—DR. LIVINGSTONE.

1, 'to be in the act of doing anything', here bei etwas beschäftigt sein. Read S. 87, N. 6, which rule applies in this case likewise. 2, 'in the act of springing', here = about (im Begriff) to spring. 3, as he sprang, im Sprunge, with which commence the clause. 4, in — was = which possessed. 5, — I found myself in that state (Zustand, m.), which. 6, und flöße mir keinen Schrecken ein. 7. here reißende Tiere. 8, = and if this is the case, it is, etc. 9, on — head, auf meinem Hinterkopfe. 10, His — one, Seine Flinte; to miss fire, versagen. 11, and — bit = attacked M., and bit. etc. 12, in die Luft schleudern. 13, to take effect, zu wirken anfangen. 14. zurücklassen.

Section 217.

THE BURNING OF MOSCOW. (Comp. S. 156, N. 1.)

I.

On the 14th *of* September, 1812, while the rear-guard of the Russians were in the act (S. 216, N. 1) of evacuating Moscow, Napoleon reached the hill called the Mount of Salvation [1], because *it is* there *where* the natives kneel and cross themselves at first sight of the Holy City.

Moscow seemed as lordly and striking [2] as ever, with the steeples of its thirty churches, and its copper domes glittering in the sun; its palaces of Eastern architecture mingled with trees, and surrounded with gardens [3]; and its Kremlin [4], a huge triangular mass of towers, [5] something between a palace and a castle, which rose like a citadel out of the general [6] mass of groves and buildings. But not a chimney sent up smoke [7], not a man appeared on the battlements, or at the gates. Napoleon gazed [8] every moment expecting to see a train of bearded boyards arriving to (S. 19, N. 7) fling themselves at his feet, and place their wealth at his disposal. His first exclamation was: "Behold at last that celebrated city!" His next: "It was full [9] time!" His army, less regardful of the past or the future [10], fixed their eyes on the goal of their wishes, and a shout of "Moscow! Moscow!" passed from rank to rank.

Bonaparte, as if unwilling to encounter the sight of the empty streets, stopped immediately on entering the first suburb. His troops were quartered in the desolate city. During the first few hours after their arrival [11], an obscure rumour, which could not be traced [12], but one of those which are sometimes found to get abroad before the approach of some awful certainty [13], announced that the city would be endangered by fire in the course of the night [14].

1, Nom. ber feligmachende Berg.. **2**, = majestic. **3**, feinen im orienta: lifchen Stile erbauten, mit Bäumen und Gärten umgebenen Palästen. **4**, Kreml, m. **5**, einem ungeheuren, dreiedigen, mit vielen Türmen verzierten Gebäude; something — castle, welches zwischen einem Palaste und einem Schloße die Mitte hielt; which = and. **6**, = great; groves, Baumgruppen. **7**, = smoked; not a man = nobody. **8**, blickte . . . darauf hin. **9**, = high. **10**, less — future, Liter. = which troubled itself (sich bekümmern) only about (um) the present (Gegenwart, f.). **11**, Here follows the predicate 'announced'. **12**, = the origin of which could not be traced (ausfündig machen). See S. 4, N. 4 (man). **13**, = event. **14**, = that the town during the night would be exposed to a great conflagration.

Section 218.

THE BURNING OF MOSCOW.

II.

The report seemed to arise from [1] those evident circumstances which rendered the event probable, but no one took any notice of it, until [2] at midnight, *when* the soldiers were startled from their quarters by the report that the town was in flames (App. § 28). The memorable conflagration began amongst [3] the coachmakers' warehouses and work-shops in the Bazaar, *which was* the richest district of the city. It was imputed to accident, and the progress of the flames was subdued by the exertions of the French soldiers. Napoleon, who had been roused by the tumult, hurried to the spot [4]; and when the alarm seemed at an end [5], he retired, not to his former quarters in the suburbs, but to the Kremlin, the hereditary palace of the only sovereign whom he had ever treated as an equal [6], and over whom his successful arms had now attained such an apparently [7] immense superiority. Yet he did not suffer himself to be dazzled by the advantages he had attained, but availed himself of the light of the blazing Bazaar, to write to the Emperor proposals of peace with his own hand [8]. They were despatched by a Russian officer of rank, who had been disabled by indisposition from following the army. But no answer was ever returned [9].

Next day the flames had disappeared, and the French officers luxuriously [10] employed themselves (S. 87, N. 6) in selecting out of the deserted palaces of Moscow, that which best pleased the fancy of each for his residence. At night the flames again arose in the north and west quarters of the city. As the greater part of the houses were built of wood, the conflagration spread with the most dreadful rapidity.

1, = to have arisen from (entstehen (aus), conjugated with sein). **2**, Supply 'at last' here and omit the comma and the conj. 'when'. To be startled from one's quarters, von seinem Nachtlager aufgeschreckt werden. **3**, = in; warehouse, Magazin, n. **4**, herbeieilen. **5**, = and when the danger seemed to be over. **6,** wie feinc#gleichen. **7,** apparently, wie es schien, which place after the adv. ' now '. **8,** Say ' to write to the Emperor with his own hands (eigenhändig, adj. used attributively) a letter, in which he offered him proposals of peace (S. 76, N. 22, *B*). **9,** = The same (to agree with 'proposals of peace') remained however unanswered. **10,** prachtliebend, which use as adj. before ' French officers '.

Section 219.

THE BURNING OF MOSCOW.

III.

This was at first imputed to the blazing brands [= pieces of wood] and sparkles which were carried by the wind; but at length it was observed, that, as often as the wind changed[1],—and it changed three times in that terrible night,—new flames broke always forth in that direction, where[2] the existing gale was calculated to direct them on[3] the Kremlin. These horrors were[4] increased by the chance[5] of explosion. There was, though as yet unknown to the French, a magazine of powder in the Kremlin; besides that, a park of artillery, with its ammunition, was drawn up[6] under the Emperor's window. Morning (S. 3, N. 2) came, and with it a dreadful scene. During the whole night, the metropolis had glared[7] with a thick and suffocating atmosphere, of almost palpable smoke. The flames defied the efforts of the French soldiery, and it is said that the fountains of the city had been rendered inaccessible, the water-pipes cut, and the fire-engines destroyed or carried off.

Then came the reports of fire-balls having been found burning in deserted houses ; of men and women, that, like demons, had been seen openly spreading the flames, and who were said to be[8] furnished with combustibles for rendering their dreadful work more secure. Several wretches against[9] whom such acts had been charged, were seized (S. 2, N. 1) upon, and, probably without much inquiry, *were* shot on the spot. While it was almost impossible to keep the roof of the Kremlin free of the burning brands which the wind showered down[10], Napoleon watched from the windows the course of the fire which devoured his fair conquest, and the exclamation burst from him[11] : " These are indeed Scythians !"

1, as — changed, bei jedem Winterwechsel ; it = the wind. **2,** where = which through (durch) ; to calculate, berechnen (auf) ; read S. 87, N. 6. **3,** = to. **4,** Insert here the adv. noch. **5,** = possibility ; of, von, followed by the plural. **6,** = put up, aufstellen. **7,** = had been filled. **8,** The Emperor is said to be dead, der Kaiser soll tot sein. **9,** against — charged = who were (welche) accused (beschuldigen) of such a deed. **10,** = which were carried away by (S. 106, N. 23) the wind in great number (Menge, f.). **11,** = and he exclaimed involuntarily (unwillkürlich).

Section 220.

THE BURNING OF MOSCOW.

IV.

The equinoctial gales rose higher and higher[1] upon the third night, and extended the flames, with which there was no longer any human power of contending[2]. At the dead[3] hour of midnight, the Kremlin itself was found to be on fire. A soldier of the Russian police, charged with being incendiary[4], was turned over[5] to the summary[6] vengeance of the Imperial Guard. Bonaparte was then, at length, persuaded, by the entreaties of all around him, to relinquish his quarters in the Kremlin, to which, as the visible mark of his conquest, he had seemed to cling with the tenacity of a lion holding a fragment of his prey. He encountered both difficulty and danger in retiring from the palace, and, before he could gain the city gate, he had to traverse with his suite streets arched with fire[7], and in which the very air they breathed was suffocating. At length he gained the open country, and took up his abode in a palace of the Czar's called Petrowsky, about a French league from the city. As he looked back on the fire, which, under the influence of the autumnal wind, swelled and surged round the Kremlin, like an infernal ocean around a sable Pandemonium[8], he could not suppress the ominous expression: "This bodes us great misfortune!"

The fire continued to triumph unopposed, and consumed in a few days what it had cost centuries to raise. "Palaces and temples," says a Russian author, "monuments of art, and miracles of luxury, the remains of ages which had passed away, and those which had been the creation of yesterday; the tombs of ancestors, and the nursery-cradles[9] of the present generation, were indiscriminately destroyed. Nothing was left of Moscow save the remembrance of the city, and the deep resolution to avenge its fall."

The fire raged till the 19th of September with unabated violence, and then began to slacken for want of fuel. It is said four-fifths of this great city were laid in ruins.—Sir Walter Scott.

1, immer ſtärker werden; upon = during, with which commence the period. 2, there was no longer ... of contending = could no longer contend. 3, = quiet.   4, This man is charged with being incendiary, man beſchuldigt dieſen Mann der Brandſtiftung.   5, übergeben, with Dat.   6, here = immediate, ſofertig, adj.   7, über denen von beiden Seiten ein Feuermeer emporſchlug. 8, um ein ſchwarzes Pandämonium (ein Dämonentempel, das Reich des Satans). 9, die Geburtsſtätten, N. Pl.

Section 221.

CHRISTMAS IN GERMANY.

I.

Frankfort-on-the-Maine, Jan. 2, 1845.

We have lately[1] witnessed the most beautiful and interesting of all German festivals — Christmas — which is celebrated in a style truly characteristic of the[2] people. About the commencement of December, the Christmarkt, or fair, was opened in the Römerberg[3], and has continued to the present time. The booths, decorated with green boughs, were filled with toys of various kinds, among which, during the first days, the figure of St. Nicholas was conspicuous. There were[4] bunches of wax candles to illuminate[5] the Christmas tree, gingerbread with printed mottoes in poetry[6], beautiful little earthenware, basket-work, and a wilderness[7] *of* playthings. The sixth of December, being Nicholas day[14], the booths were lighted up, and the square was filled with boys, running from one stand to another, all shouting and talking together in the most joyous confusion[8]. Nurses were going around, carrying the smaller children in their arms, and parents bought presents decorated with sprigs of pine and carried them away.

Many of the tables had *bundles of* rods with gilded bands, which were to be used that evening by the persons who represented St. Nicholas. In the family with whom we reside, one of our German friends dressed himself[9] very grotesquely with a mask, fur robe, and long tapering cap. He came in with a *bunch of* rods, a sack, and a broom for[10] sceptre. After we all had received our share of the beating, he threw the contents of his bag on the table, and while we were scrambling for the nuts and apples, gave us many smart raps over the fingers. In many families the children are made to say[11]: "I thank you[12], Herr Nicholas," and the rods are hung up in the room until Christmas, to keep them in good behaviour[13]. This[14] was only a forerunner of the "Christkindchen's" coming. The Nicholas is the punishing spirit, and the "Christkindchen" the rewarding one.

1, fürzlich. 2, Render 'of the' by the Dat. of the def. art., and use the attributive construction for 'truly — people'. 3, auf dem Römerberge, a large square (Plaß, m.) in the City. 4, Es waren dort. 5, zur Er: leuchtung. 6, = verses. 7, = great number, Menge, f. 8, = excitement. 9, sich verkleiden. 10, als. 11, läßt man die Kinder sagen. 12, Euch. 13, um die Kleinen daran zu erinnern, sich gut zu betragen. 14, Der St. (S. 103, N. 33) Nicolaustag; forerunner, Vorfeier, f.

Section 222.

CHRISTMAS IN GERMANY.

II.

When this time was over, we all began preparing secretly our presents for Christmas. Every day there was[1] a consultation about the things which should be obtained[2]. It was so arranged that we should interchange presents, but nobody must[3] know beforehand what he would receive. What pleasure there was in all these secret purchases and preparations! Scarcely anything was thought or spoken of but Christmas, and every day the consultations became more numerous and secret. The trees were bought some time before-hand, but as we Americans were to witness the festival for the first time, we were not allowed to see them prepared, in order that the effect might be as great as possible. The market in the Römerberg *Square* grew constantly larger and more brilliant. Every night it was illuminated with lamps and thronged with people. Quite a forest sprang up in the street before our door. The old stone house opposite, with the traces of so many centuries on its dark face, seemed to stand in the midst of a garden. It was a pleasure to go out every evening and see the children rushing to and fro, shouting and selecting toys from the booths and talking all the time of the Christmas that was so near (S. 48, N. 6).   The poor people went with[4] their little presents hid under their cloaks, lest their children might see them; every heart was glad, and every countenance wore a smile of secret pleasure.

Finally, the day before Christmas arrived.   The streets were so full, I[5] could scarcely make my way through[6], and the sale of trees went on[7] more rapidly than ever.   These were[8] usually branches of pine or fir, set upright[9] in a little miniature garden of moss.   When the lamps were lighted at night, our street had the appearance of an illuminated garden. We were prohibited from entering the rooms upstairs in which the grand ceremony was to take place, being obliged[10] to take our seats in those arranged for the guests, and to await with impatience the hour when the " Christkindchen " should call us.

1, ſtatt'finten.   2, = procured, auſſchaffen.   3, = but that nobody should.   4, went with = had.   5, = that I.   6, to make one's way through, ſich einen Weg durch die Menge bahnen.   7, vonſtatten gehen. 8, beſtehen (aus).   9, welche . . . hineingeſtellt waren.   10, = and were obliged.

Section 223.

CHRISTMAS IN GERMANY.

III.

Several relatives of the family came (S. 104, N. 19), and, what was more agreeable, they brought with them five or six children.   I was anxious to see how they would view the ceremony[1].   Finally, in the midst of an interesting conversation, we heard the bell ringing at the head of[2] the stairs.   We all started up, and made for[3] the door.   I ran up the steps with the children at my heels, and at the top met[4] a blaze of dazzling light, coming from the open door.   In each room stood a great table, on which presents were arranged, amid flowers and wreaths.   From[5] the centre rose the beautiful Christmas tree, covered with wax tapers to the very top, which made the room nearly as light as day[6], while every bough was hung with sweetmeats and gilded nuts.   The children ran shouting around the table, hunting[7] their presents, while the older persons had theirs pointed out to them.   I had a little library of German authors *as my share;* and many of the others received quite valuable gifts.

But how beautiful was the heartfelt joy that shone on every countenance! As each one discovered his presents, he embraced the givers, and it was a scene of unmingled joy[8].   It is a glorious feast, this Christmas time!   What a chorus from happy hearts went up on that evening to Heaven!   Full of poetry and feeling, and glad associations, it is here anticipated with delight, and leaves a pleasant memory behind it.   We may laugh at such simple festivals at home, and prefer to shake our- selves loose from every shackle[9] that bears the rust of the past, but we should certainly be happier if some of these beautiful old customs were better honoured.   They renew the bond of feeling[10] between families and friends, and strengthen their kindly sympathy; even life-long associates require occasions of this kind to freshen the tie that binds them together[11]. —BAYARD TAYLOR, " VIEWS AFOOT."

1, wie sie sich bei dem Feste benehmen würden.   **2,** at the head of, eben auf.
3, = ran towards.   **4,** = found.   **5,** = In; rose = stood.   **6,** as —
day, tageshell; 'to make', here erleuchten.   **7,** = and searched for (nach).
8, = empfangen.   **9,** Use this noun in the pl., Fesseln; bears = bear.
10, = love; to — together, um das sie verbindende Band fester zu schürzen.

Section 224.

NEW-YEAR'S EVE (S. 152, N. 1) IN GERMANY.

New-Year's Eve is also favoured with a peculiar celebration[1] in Germany. Everybody remains up and makes himself merry until midnight. The Christmas trees are again lighted, and while the tapers are burning out, the family play for[2] articles which they have purchased and hung on the boughs. It is so arranged that each one shall win as much as he gives, and the change[3] of articles creates much amusement. One of the ladies rejoiced in the possession of a red silk handkerchief and a cake of soap, while a cup and saucer and a pair of scissors fell to my lot. As midnight drew near, the noise became louder in the streets, and companies of people, some of them[4] singing in chorus, passed by on their way to the Zeil[5]. Finally, it struck a quarter to twelve, the windows were opened, and every one waited anxiously for the clock to strike twelve. At the first sound, such a cry arose as one may imagine when thirty or forty thousand persons all set their lungs going[6] at once. Everybody in the house, in the street, over the whole city, shouted: " Prost Neujahr[7]! "

In families, all the members embrace each other, with wishes of happiness for the new year. Then the windows are thrown open, and they cry to their neighbours or those passing by.

After we had exchanged congratulations, three of us set out for the Zeil. The streets were full of people, shouting to one another and to those standing at the open windows. We failed not to cry: " Prost Neujahr!" wherever we saw a damsel at the window, and the words came back to us more musically than we sent them. Along the Zeil the spectacle was most singular. The great wide street was filled with companies of men, marching up and down, while from the mass rang up one deafening, unending shout, that seemed to pierce the black sky above. The whole scene looked stranger and wilder in the flickering light of the swinging lamps[8], and I could not help thinking it must resemble a night in Paris, during the French Revolution.—BAYARD TAYLOR, " VIEWS AFOOT."

1, is — celebration = is celebrated in (auf) *a* peculiar way.   **2,** um.
3, Tausch or Austausch, m.   **4,** = of whom some were.   **5,** die Zeil is one of the principal streets in Frankfort a/M.   **6,** to set going, in Bewegung setzen.   **7,** Properly: Prosit Neujahr! A happy New-Year to you!   **8,** Before the introduction of gas, the lamps hung in the middle of the street on ropes which were attached to the houses on both sides of the street.

Section 225.

THE TWO ROBBERS.

I.

WE OFTEN CONDEMN IN OTHERS WHAT WE PRACTISE OURSELVES.

(Alexander the Great in his tent. A man with a fierce countenance, chained and fettered, brought before him.)

ALEXANDER.—What, art thou the Thracian robber, of whose exploits I have heard so much?

ROBBER.—I am a Thracian, and a soldier.

ALEXANDER.—A soldier?—a thief, a plunderer, an assassin! the pest of the country! I could honour thy courage, but I must detest and punish thy crimes.

ROBBER.—What have I done of which you can complain[1]?

ALEXANDER.—Hast thou not set at defiance my authority, violated the public peace, and passed thy life[2] in injuring the persons[3] and properties of thy fellow-subjects[4]?

ROBBER.—Alexander! I am your captive. I must hear what you please to say, and endure what you please to inflict. But my soul is unconquered; and if I reply at all[5] to your reproaches, I will reply like a free man.

ALEXANDER.—Speak freely. Far be it from me to take[6] the advantage of my power, to silence those with whom I deign to converse!

ROBBER.—I must then answer your question by another. How have you passed your life?

ALEXANDER.—Like a hero. Ask Fame[7], and she will tell you. Among the brave, I have been the bravest; among sovereigns, the noblest; among conquerors, the mightiest.

1, ſich über etwas beflagen. Use the 2nd person Plural when the robber addresses Alexander.   2, und dein Leben damit zugebracht.   3, = the personal safety.   4, deiner Nebenmenſchen.   5, überhaupt.   6, = to use.
7, 'Fame,' here Fama, die Göttin des Ruhmes.   FAME, or FAMA, was a poetical deity, represented as having wings and blowing a trumpet. A temple was dedicated to her by the Romans.

Section 226.

THE TWO ROBBERS.

II.

ROBBER.—And does not Fame speak of me too? Was there (S. 82, N. 7) ever a bolder captain of a more valiant band? Was there ever— but I scorn to boast. You yourself know that I have not been easily subdued.

ALEXANDER.—Still, what are you but a robber, a base, dishonest robber?

ROBBER.—And what is a conqueror? Have not you, too, gone about the earth[1] like an evil genius, blasting[2] the fair fruits of peace and industry, plundering, ravaging, killing [3] without law, without justice, merely to gratify an insatiable lust for dominion? All that I have done to a single district with *a* hundred followers, you have done to whole nations with a hundred thousand. If I have stripped individuals [4], you (S. 27, N. 8) have ruined kings and princes. If I have burned a few hamlets, you have desolated the most flourishing kingdoms and cities of the earth. What is then the difference [5], but that, as you were born a king, and I a private man [6], you have been able to become a mightier robber than I?

ALEXANDER.—But if I have taken like a king, I have given like a king. If I have subverted empires, I have founded greater. I have cherished [7] arts, commerce, and philosophy.

ROBBER.—I, too, have freely given to the poor, what I took from the rich. I have established order and discipline among the most ferocious of mankind [8], and have stretched out my protecting arm over the oppressed. I know, indeed, little of the philosophy you talk of; but I believe neither you nor I will ever atone to the world for the mischiefs we have done.

ALEXANDER.—Leave me!—Take off his chains, and use him well. Are we, then, so much like?—Alexander and a Robber?—Let me reflect [9].—DR. AIKIN.

1, 'to go about the earth' here über die Erde her'ziehen, conjugated with sein. **2,** = to (um ... zu) blast, vernichten. **3,** = Have you not plundered, ravaged and killed. **4,** = robbed common citizens. **5,** Besteht denn zwischen uns beiden ein anderer Unterschied als der, daß; followed by 'you have — than I', according to S. 211, N. 9. **6,** = common citizen. **7,** here = protected. **8,** = of all men. **9,** Ich will darüber nachdenken.

Section 227.

A TOUCHING SCENE AT SEA.

I.

Two weeks ago [1] on board an English steamer, a little ragged boy, aged nine years, was discovered on the fourth day of the voyage *out* from Liverpool to New York, and carried before the first mate, whose duty it was to deal with such cases. When questioned as to his object in being stowed away [2], and who brought him on board, the boy, who had a beautiful sunny face, and eyes that looked like the very mirrors of truth, replied that his stepfather did it, because he could not afford [3] to keep him, nor to pay his passage *out* to Halifax, where he had an aunt who [4] was well off, and to whose house he was going. The mate did not believe the story, in spite of the winning face and truthful [5] accents of the boy. He had seen too much of stow-aways [6] to be easily deceived by them, he said; and it was his firm conviction that the boy had been brought on board and provided with food by the sailors. The little fellow was very roughly handled in consequence. Day by day he was questioned and re-questioned, but always with the same result. He did not know a sailor on board, and his father alone had secreted him, and given him the food which he ate. At [7] last the mate, wearied by the boy's persistence in the same story, and perhaps a little anxious to inculpate the sailors, seized him one day by the collar, and dragging him to the fore[8], told him that (S. 211, N. 9) unless he would tell the truth in ten minutes from that time, he would hang him from the yard-arm.

1, Bor vierzehn Tagen, after which place predicate and subject [one discovered], since, as a rule, only *one* part of the adjuncts to the predicate should be placed before it.   **2**, as — away ~ warum er aufs Schiff geschmuggelt sei (App. §§ 28 and 30).   **3**, I cannot afford to keep you, meine Mittel gestatten mir nicht, dich zu ernähren.   **4**, The relative clause 'who — off' may be avoided by using the adjective 'wohlhabend' before 'aunt'.   **5**, here glaubwürdig; accents, Sprache.   **6**, 'the stow-away' may perhaps be rendered by der Eingeschmuggelte.   **7**, It will easily be seen that, on account of the length of this period and of the many dependent clauses contained therein, it requires an altogether different form of construction in German. The author will, however, refrain from indicating the form to be used, the student being by this time expected to have attained sufficient skill and practice for dealing with such cases.   **8**, aufs Vorderteil des Schiffes.

Section 228.

A TOUCHING SCENE AT SEA.
II.

He then made him sit down under it on the deck. All around him were the passengers and sailors of the watch, and in front of him stood the inexorable mate, with his chronometer in his hand, and the other officers of the ship by his side. It was the finest sight, said our informant[1], that he ever beheld—to see the pale, proud, sorrowful face of that noble boy, his head erect, his beautiful eyes bright through the tears that suffused them. When eight minutes had fled[2], the mate told him he had but two minutes to live, and advised him to speak the truth and save his life; but he replied with the utmost simplicity and sincerity by asking (S. 111, N. 6) the mate if he might pray. The mate said nothing, but nodded his head, turned as pale as a ghost[3], and shook *with trembling* like a reed with[4] the wind. And there, all eyes turned on him, the brave and noble little fellow, this poor waif, whom society owned not, and whose own stepfather could not care for him — there he knelt, with clasped hands, and eyes turned up to heaven, while he repeated[5] audibly the Lord's Prayer, and prayed the Lord Jesus to take him to heaven. There then occurred (S. 104, N. 19) a scene as at Pentecost. Sobs broke[6] from the strong hard hearts, as the mate sprang forward to the boy, and kissed and blessed him, and told him how sincerely he believed his story, and how glad he was that he had been willing enough to face death[7] and to sacrifice his life for the truth of his word.—REV. E. DAVIES.

1, Place 'said — informant (here Gewährsmann, m.)' after 'that — beheld'. **2**, = were over.   **3**, as — ghost, geisterbleich.   **4**, = in.   **5**, = said; audibly = aloud.   **6**, (Ein Schluchzen entrang sich, followed by the Dat.   **7**, to face death, dem Tode ins Antlitz schauen, or dem Tode trotzbieten.

Section 229.

AN ORATION ON THE POWER OF HABIT.

I.

I will now speak of a habit which I believe[1] is, more than any other, debasing, degrading, and embruting to man[2], both[3] physically, intellectually, and morally. I am not going to give you an address[4] *full* of my favourite theme [temperance], but I must speak of it[5]. I must speak of it before this assembly, for I shall never see you again till we meet on that day when we shall see things as they are[6]. Let me then speak of one habit which, in its power, and[7] influence, and[8] fascination, seems to rear its head like a Goliath or Saul above all its kindred agencies of demoralization; I allude to[9] the habit of using intoxicating liquors as a beverage, until that habit becomes a fascination[10]. You will allow me to give[11] my opinions upon these points freely. I consider drunkenness not merely to be a moral evil, but also a physical evil, and[12] it depends a great deal more upon the temperament, *and* the constitution, and disposition of the young man, whether if he falls into the drinking usages of society, it becomes a habit or not, than it does upon his strength of mind or firmness of purpose[13].

Take a young man, and he shall be full of fire[14] and poetry. He shall be[15] of a nervous temperament and generous heart; fond of society, and open and manly in everything he does. Every one loves him. That is the man most liable to become intemperate.

1, = as I believe.   2, is . . . to man, auf den Menſchen wirſt.   3, 'both', hier und zwar.   4, to give an address to a person, einem eine Rede halten; of, über.   5, ich muß daſſelbe aber wenigſtens berühren (allude to).   6, Render 'for — are' Liter. = for we shall see one another only (S. 109, N. 5) on that day, when (we) we shall see (ſchauen) the things in their true form (Geſtalt, f.).   7, = in its.   8, = and its.   9, = I mean; of using — beverage = of drinking intoxicating liquors.   10, until — fascination, bis dieſe Gewohnheit einen zauberhaften Reiz auf den Menſchen ausübt.   11, = express.   12, Say 'and when a young man once follows the general habit of taking intoxicating liquors, it depends, etc.'   13, his — purpose, ſeine Geiſtes= oder Willenskraft.   14, = who is full of (voller) fire.   15, The student will do well to omit the words 'He shall be' and join this period to the preceding one.

Section 230.

AN ORATION ON THE POWER OF HABIT.

II.

He enters[1] into the outer circle of the whirlpool, and throws care to the winds[2]. There he thinks to stay, but he gets nearer and nearer to the fatal gulf, until he is swept into the vortex before he dreamed of danger. This thing, habit[3], comes gradually. Many a man who has acquired[4] a habit of drinking, but does not exactly proceed to excess[5], is rescued simply by possessing certain physical qualities which his poor unfortunate friend had not. You say: "I am not so foolish as to become a drunkard!" So He thought once. You say: "I can leave it off[6] when

I like," as if He at first had not had (App. § 33) the power to leave it off when he liked. You say: "I have too sound an intellect to become a drunkard," as if He were born without an intellect. You say: "I have too much pride in myself, too much self-respect," as if He were not once as proud as you." *The way* men acquire this habit, *is* by looking on those[7] who proceed to excess as naturally inferior to themselves. The difference between you and the drunkard is just this, that you could leave off[8] the habit, but won't; he would[9] with all his heart and soul, but cannot. I tell you, young men[10], that while the power of a bad habit is stripping you of nerve [pl.], *and* (S. 10, N. 9) energy, and freshness of feeling[11], it does not destroy your responsibility. You are accountable to God for every power, *and* talent, and influence with which you have been endowed.

1, = approaches.   2, to throw care to the winds, ſich feine Sorgen machen. 3, = What one calls habit.   4, to acquire a habit, in eine Gewohnheit verfallen. 5, der dieſelbe jedoch eigentlich nicht übertreibt.   6, to leave off, aufhören.   7, = by considering (halten) those ; to proceed to excess, ſich dem Übermaß ergeben ; as — themselves = as (für) *being* worse than themselves.   8, here aufgeben. 9, = and that he would give it up.   10, Commence the period with ' Young men '.   11, Gefühlsfriſche, f.

Section 231.

AN ORATION ON THE POWER OF HABIT.

III.

If you say: "Should I find the practice by experience to be injurious, I will give it up," surely that is not common sense[1]. You might as well say: "I will put my hand into the nest of the rattlesnake, and when I find out that he has stuck his fangs into me[2], I will draw it out and get cured."

I remember riding from[3] Buffalo to the Niagara Falls, and said to a gentleman: "What river is that, Sir?" "That," he said, "is Niagara River[4]." "Well, it is a beautiful stream," said I, "bright, and fair, and glossy; how far off are the rapids[5]?" "Only a mile or two," was the reply. "Is it possible that (S. 66, N. 15) only a mile or two from us we shall find the water in the turbulence which it must show *when* near the falls?" "You will find it so, Sir." And so I did find it ; and that first sight of the Niagara I shall never forget. Now, launch your boat on that Niagara river ; it is bright, smooth, beautiful, and glossy. There is a ripple at the bow[6], and the silvery wake[7] you leave behind adds to your enjoyment. Down the stream you glide ; oars, sails, and helm are in proper trim, and you set out[8] on your pleasure excursion[9]. Suddenly some one cries out from the bank : "Young men, ahoy[10]!" "What is it[11]!"—"The rapids are below you[12]!"—"Ha, ha! we have heard of the rapids, but we are not so foolish as to get there[13]. If we go [=If it goes] too fast, then up with the helm[14], then set the mast in the socket[15], hoist the sail, and speed to land[16]. Then on[17], boys ; don't be alarmed—there's no danger !"

1, = reasonable.   2, stuck — me = bitten me.   3, riding from that
I during a journey from ; change 'and said to ' into 'asked'.   4, Use the
def. art.   5, die Stromſchnellen.   6, Das Waſſer träuſelt ſich am Bug des Bootes.
7, Kielwaſſer, n.   8, 'to set out on', here an'treten, v. tr.   9, Vergnügungsteur.
10, Ohei! of which pronounce every vowel separately and slowly in the
German way.   11, Was giebts.   12, are below you, ſind dort unten nicht
weit von euch!   13, as — there, ſo weit zu fahren.   14, dann ſchnell das
Steuerruder hinein.   15, dann richten wir den Maſt auf.   16, und eilen ans
Land!   17, Daher nur immer vorwärts.

Section 232.

AN ORATION ON THE POWER OF HABIT.

IV.

" Young men, ahoy, *there!*"—" What is it?"—" The rapids are below
you!"—" Ha, ha! we will laugh and quaff; all things delight us. What
care we for the future? No man ever saw it. 'Sufficient for the day is
the evil thereof[1].' We will enjoy life while we may[2]; we will catch
pleasure as it flies. This is enjoyment; time enough[3] to steer out of
danger when we are driving swiftly with the current."—" Young men,
ahoy!"—" What is it?"—" Beware! Beware! The rapids are below
you!"—Now you see water foaming[4] all around you.—See how fast you
pass that point!—Up with the helm!—Now turn[5]!—Pull hard[6]—
quick!—quick!—pull for your lives!—pull till[7] the blood starts from the
nostrils, and the veins stand like whipcord upon the brow! Set the mast
in the socket! hoist the sail! Ah, ah!—it is too late! Shrieking,
cursing, howling, blaspheming, over you go[8]!—Thousands go over the
rapids of Intemperance[9] every year, through the power of evil habit,
crying out all the while[10]: " When I find out that it is injuring me, I
will give it up!" The power of evil habit, I repeat, is fascinating[11], is
deceptive; and man may go on arguing and coming to conclusions
while on the way down to destruction[12].—J. B. GOUGH.

1, (So iſt genug, daß ein jeglicher Tag ſeine eigene Plage habe!   2, ſo lange
wir es noch können.   3, es bleibt uns noch Zeit genug.   4, ſchäumendes
Waſſer.   5, 'to turn', here um'kehren.   6, Pull, Rudert; 'hard', here
aus Leibeskräften.   7, Supply the pron. euch here; starts streams; from
the nostrils, and der Naſe.   8, ſtürzt ihr in den Abgrund hinunter!   9, Trunk-
ſucht, f., seems to be the right expression here, although the dictionaries
translate the word by Unmäßigkeit, f., and Völlerei, f.   10, und rufen immer.
11, here beſtrickend; is = and.   12, and — destruction = and often we are
still occupied with arguing a matter (eine Sache gründlich zu erörtern) in order
to come (gelangen) to a definite conclusion, when we are (ſich befinden) already
on the way to destruction (Verderben, n.).

Section 233.

A CURIOUS STORY[1].

I.

We heard a curious story[1] at Tristan[2] about two Germans who had
settled nearly two years before on Inaccessible Island[3]. Once a year

about the month *of* December, the Tristan men go [4] to the two outlying islands to pick up the few seals which are still to be found there.   On two of these occasions they had seen the Germans, and within a few months smoke had risen from the island, which they attributed [5] to their having fired (S. 161, N. 21) some of the brushwood; but as they had seen or heard nothing of them since, they thought the probability was that they had perished.   Captain Nares [6] wished to visit the other islands, and to ascertain the fate of the two men was an additional object in doing so [7].

Next morning we were close under Inaccessible Island, the second in size of the little group of three.   The ship was surrounded by multitudes of penguins [8], and as few of us had any previous personal acquaintance with this eccentric form of life [9], we followed their movements with great interest.   The penguin as a rule swims under water, rising now and then and resting on the surface, like one of the ordinary water-birds, but more frequently with its body entirely covered, and only lifting its head from time to time to breathe.

The structure of Inaccessible Island is very much the same as Tristan, only the pre-eminent feature [10] of the latter, the snowy cone, is wanting. A wall of volcanic rocks, about the same height as the cliff at Tristan, and which one is inclined to believe to have been at one time continuous with it, entirely surrounds Inaccessible Island, falling for the most part sheer [11] into the sea, and it seems that it slopes sufficiently to allow a tolerably easy ascent to the plateau on the top at one point only.

1, This story is taken from Mr. W. J. J. Spry's most interesting account of 'The Cruise of the Challenger'.   The Tristan d'Acunha group of islands (bie Erfrischungsinseln), so named from the Portuguese navigator who discovered it early in the 16th century, lies in mid-ocean, about 1300 miles south of St. Helena and 1500 miles west of the Cape of Good Hope, nearly on a line between the Cape of Good Hope and Cape Horn; it is thus probably the most isolated and remote of all the abodes of men.   The group consists of the larger Island of Tristan and two smaller islands—Inaccessible Island, about 18 miles south-west from Tristan, and Nightingale Island, twenty miles south of the main island.   Tristan only is permanently inhabited, the other two are visited from time to time by sealers.   In the year 1829 Tristan was inhabited by 27 families; in 1836 it possessed a population of 42; in 1852 the population had risen to 85, and in 1867 this number was only exceeded by one.   2, Auf ter Insel Tristan, which place at the head of the period; about, über, with Acc. 3, The author finds that the best German maps use the English name of 'Inaccessible Island' unaltered.   This is also the case with 'Nightingale Island'. 4, fahren; 'to go', when used in the sense of 'travelling, riding (in a carriage), driving, sailing, etc.', is mostly rendered by reisen (generally used for greater distances) or by fahren.   When used in the sense of 'riding on horseback,' it is rendered by reiten.   5, = which they attributed to the circumstance.   6, Captain Nares was the commander of 'The Challenger' at that time.   7, and — so = and as he was anxious (begierig) to ascertain (erforschen) the fate of the two men, the voyage [there, dahin] was at once determined upon.   8, ter Pinguin, pl. e.   9, with — life, mit dieser eigentümlichen Vogelart.   10, - the characteristic peculiarity. 11, = straight.

Section 234.

A CURIOUS STORY.

II.

There is a shallow bay in which the ship anchored in fifteen fathoms on the east side of the island; and there, as in Tristan, a narrow belt of low ground, extending for about a mile along the shore, is interposed between the cliff and the sea. A pretty waterfall tossed itself down, about the middle of the bay, over the cliff from the plateau above. A little way down it was nearly lost in spray, like the Staubbach of Schaffhausen, and collected itself again into a rivulet [1], where it regained the rock at the lower level. A hut built of stones and clay, and roofed with spars and thatch, lay in a little hollow [2] near the waterfall, and the two Germans, in excellent health and spirits, but enraptured at the sight of the ship and longing for a passage anywhere out of the island, were [3] down on the beach, waiting for the first boat. Their story is a curious one [4], and as Captain Nares agreed [5] to take them to the Cape, we had ample time to get an account of their adventures, and to supplement from their experience such crude notions of the nature of the place as we could gather during our short stay [6].

Frederick and Gustav Stoltenhoff are sons of a dyer in Aix-la-Chapelle (Aachen). Frederick, the elder, was employed in a merchant's office in Aix-la-Chapelle at the time of the Franco-German war (1870). He was called on to serve in the German army, where he attained the rank of a lieutenant, and took part in the siege of Metz and Thionville. At the end of the campaign he was discharged, and returned home to find his old situation filled up.

1, gestaltete sich jedoch wieder zu einem kleinen Bache.   2, Vertiefung, f. 3, = stood. Consult S. 5, N. 2.   4, = very (höchst) curious.   5, = granted them their request.   6, Let the student endeavour to construe this passage by means of the attributive construction, which will prove excellent practice.

Section 235.

A CURIOUS STORY.

III.

In the meantime, his younger brother, Gustav, who was a sailor and had already made several trips, had joined [1] on the 1st of August, 1870, at Greenock, as an ordinary seaman, the English ship "Beacon Light," bound for Rangoon. On the way out [2], the cargo, which consisted of coal, caught fire [3] when they were from [4] six to seven hundred miles north-west of Tristan d'Acunha, and for (S. 166, N. 10) three days all hands [5] were doing their utmost to extinguish the fire. On the third day, the hatches, which had been battened down, to exclude the air, blew up [6], the main hatch carrying overboard [7] the second mate who had been

standing on it at the time of the explosion. The boats had been pro-
visioned beforehand, ready to leave the ship. Two of the crew were
drowned through one of the boats being swamped[8], and the survivors, to
the number of sixteen, were stowed in the long-boat. Up to this time
the ship had been nearing Tristan with a fair wind at the rate of[9] six
knots an hour[10], so that they had now only about three hundred miles
to go. They abandoned the ship on Friday; on Saturday afternoon they
sighted Tristan, and on the following day a boat came off to their assistance
and towed them ashore.

The shipwrecked crew remained for eighteen days at Tristan d' Acunha,
during which time they were treated with all kindness and hospitality.
They were relieved by the ill-fated " Northfleet," bound for Aden with
coal, and Gustav Stoltenhoff found his way back to Aix-la-Chapelle.

1, to join a ship, fid) einem Schiffe verheuern.   **2**, = On the voyage thither
(tenthin).   **3**, to catch fire, in Brand geraten.   **4**, = about, ungefähr.
5, 'all hands', here = all sailors, die ganze Mannschaft, alle Matrosen, alle Schiffsleute.
6, in die Luft sprengen; the hatches, die Luken; the main hatch, die große Luke.
7, = and the main hatch carried overboard (über Bord schleudern).   **8**, = through
the sinking of one of the boats.   **9**, 'at the rate of', referring to the
rapidity of motion, is rendered by '**mit einer Schnelligkeit von**', but when
referring to price, is generally rendered by '**zum Preise von**'.   **10**, an
hour, **in der Stunde, per Stunde**, or **die Stunde**. He receives 20 marks
a week, er erhält 20 Mark die Woche (or wöchentlich).

Section 236.

A CURIOUS STORY.

IV.

During his stay at Tristan he heard that a large number of seals were
to be had among the islands[1], and he seems to have been greatly pleased
with the Tristaners and to have formed a project of returning there.
When he got home, his brother had just got back from the war and
was unemployed; he infected him with his notion[2], and the two agreed[3]
to join in a venture to Tristan to see what they could (App. § 33) make[4]
by seal-hunting and barter.

They accordingly sailed for[5] St. Helena in August 1871, and on the
6th of November left St. Helena for Tristan in an American whaler
bound on a cruise[6] in the South Atlantic. The captain of the whaler,
who had been often at Tristan d' Acunha, had some doubt of the reception which the young men would get[7] if they went as permanent
settlers[8] there, and he spoke so strongly of the advantages of Inaccessible
Island, on account of the greater productiveness of the soil, and of its
being the centre[9] of the seal-fishing, that they changed their plans and
were landed on the west side of Inaccessible Island on the 27th of
November 1871,—early in summer. A quarter of an hour after, the
whaler departed, leaving them the only inhabitants of one of the most
remote spots on the face of the earth. They do not seem, however, to
have been in the least depressed by their isolation.

The same day the younger brother clambered up to the plateau with the help of the tussock grass [10], in search of goats or pigs, and remained there all night, and on the following day the two set to work to build themselves a hut for shelter. They had reached the end of their voyage by no means unprovided, and the inventory of their belongings [11] is curious.

1, in der Gegend der Inseln. 2, = he persuaded (gewinnen, str. v. tr.) his brother for his plan. 3, überein'kommen; to join — to Tristan = to undertake the adventurous voyage to Tristan. 4, = earn. 5, = to. 6, The vessel is bound on a cruise in the Atlantic, das Schiff ist dazu bestimmt, im atlantischen Ozean umherzukreuzen. 7, had — get = doubted (zweifelte daran) that the young men would be kindly (freundlich) received (aufnehmen). Use the active voice with 'man'. 8, He went there as a permanent settler, er ließ sich dort dauernd nieder. 9, = and of its central (zentral) position for seal-fishing. 10, das Tussockgras. 11, here Habseligkeiten, Nom. Pl.

Section 237.

A CURIOUS STORY.

V.

They had an old whale-boat [1] which they had bought at St. Helena, with mast, sails, and oars, three spars for a roof, a door, and a glazed window; a wheel-barrow, two spades and a shovel, two pickaxes, a saw, a hammer, two chisels, two or three gimlets, and some nails; a kettle, a frying-pan, two sauce-pans, knives and forks, and some crockery; two blankets each, and empty covers [2] which they afterwards filled with sea-birds' down. They had a lamp, a bottle of oil, and six dozen boxes of Bryant and May's matches.

For internal use [3] they had two hundred pounds *of* flour, two hundred pounds *of* rice, one hundred pounds *of* biscuits, twenty pounds *of* coffee, ten pounds *of* tea, thirty pounds *of* sugar, three pounds *of* table-salt, a little pepper, eight pounds *of* tobacco, five bottles *of* gin, six bottles *of* Cape wine [4], six bottles *of* vinegar, and some Epsom salts. A barrel *of* coarse salt was provided for curing seal-skins, and forty empty casks were intended for oil. Their arms and ammunition consisted of a short English rifle, an old German fowling-piece, two and a half pounds *of* powder, two hundred bullets, and four sheath-knives [5]. The captain of the whaler gave them some seed potatoes, and they had a collection of the ordinary garden seeds.

When they had been four days on the island, they had a visit from a party of men from Tristan, who had come on their annual sealing excursion. They were ten days on Inaccessible, and were very friendly in their intercourse with the new comers.

1, the whale-boat, das beim Walfischfang gebräuchliche Boot. We have not a compound noun to render the English term. Say 'They had an old boat, which had been used (braugt) for whale-fishing and which they had bought in (S. 46, N. 6) the Island *of* St. Helena. 2, here Überzug, m., pl. Überzüge. 3, für ihre körperlichen Bedürfnisse. 4, Kapwein, m. 5, Jagdmesser, m.

Section 238.

A CURIOUS STORY.

VI.

They told them that the north side of the island was better suited for a settlement, and transported all their goods (S. 236, N. 11) thither in one of their boats. Being familiar with the place, they showed them generally their way about and the different passes by which the plateau might be reached, and they taught them how to build [1] to withstand the violent winds, and how to thatch with tussock-grass. Immediately after they left, the brothers set about building a house and clearing some ground [2] for potatoes and other vegetables. They killed nineteen seals, and prepared the skins, but they were unable to make any [3] quantity of oil. Towards the end of the sealing season their boat got damaged in the surf, and they were obliged to cut it in two [4], patch up the best half of it, and use it as best they could [5] in smooth weather, close to shore.

They went from time to time to the upper plateau and shot goats and pigs. When they first arrived, they counted a flock of twenty-three goats; three of these were killed during the summer of 1871–1872 by the Tristan people (S. 157, N. 4), and six by themselves; the remaining fourteen remained over the winter of 1872. The flesh of the goats they found extremely delicate. Pigs were much more numerous, but their flesh was not so palatable, from their feeding [6] principally on sea-birds; that of the boars was especially rank. They found the pigs very valuable, however, in yielding an abundant supply of lard [7], which they used for frying their potatoes.

1, = how they must (Imp. Subj.) build.   **2,** to clear the ground (= land), eine Strecke Landes urbar machen.   **3,** here erzielen; any = a large.   **4,** to cut in two, entzwei schneiden, sep. comp. irr. v.   **5,** = as well as possible.   **6,** from their feeding = as they lived; on, von.   **7,** in — lard = on account of their lard (Schmalz, n.).

Section 239.

A CURIOUS STORY.

VII.

In the month of April 1872, a singular misfortune befell them. While burning some of the brushwood below to make a clearing, the tussock-grass in the gully [1], by which they had been in the habit [2] of ascending the cliff, caught fire, and as it had been only by its assistance that they had been able to scramble up to the plateau, their only hunting-ground was now inaccessible from the strip of beach on which their hut and garden stood, which was closed in on either side by a headland jutting into the sea. While their half-boat remained seaworthy, they were able to paddle round in fine weather to the west side of the island, where there was an access to the top; but the "sea-cart," as they called it, was washed off the beach and broken up in June, and after that the only way they had of reaching the plateau was by swimming round the headland—a risky feat, even in the finest weather, in these wild regions.

In winter it was found to be impossible to reach the terrace, and as their supply of food was low, they experienced considerable privations during their first winter. Their daily allowance of food was reduced to a quantity just sufficient to maintain life, and in August they were little better than skeletons[3].

Help was, however, near. Early in August a multitude of penguins landed[4] hard by their hut,—stupid[5] animals, which will scarcely get out of one's way, and are easily knocked down with a stick[6], and with fleshy breasts, wholesome enough, though with a rather fishy taste; and in the end of August the females began to lay large blue eggs, sufficiently delicate in flavour.

1, Vertiefung, f.   2, I was in the habit of ascending the mountain every day, id pflegte täglich ben Berg zu ersteigen.   3, = und im August waren sie fast zu Steletten geworden.   4, = settled, sich niederlassen.   5, Begin a new period here and say: 'These are stupid animals', etc.   6, and -stick, sich leicht mit einem Stoct niederschlagen lassen; and with — taste = and have a fleshy breast, which (supply zwar here) yields (bieten) a wholesome food, but (jedoch) possesses a rather (etwas) fishy taste.—The whole period is difficult to translate into good German; the author considers it therefore necessary to assist the student.

Section 240.

A CURIOUS STORY.

VIII.

A French barque hove-to off the beach[1] in the middle of September, and in her they shipped their seal-skins, and bartered penguins' eggs with her for biscuits and tobacco. Had the bark arrived a week earlier, the brothers would have left the island; but the eggs had set them up again[2], and they determined to remain a little longer. In October, a schooner, which proved[3] to be "The Themis," a whaler from the Cape of Good Hope, was seen standing towards the island. A gale *of wind* blew[4] her off for a couple of days, but she returned and landed some men from Tristan, who had crossed[5] to see what the hermits were about[6]. Their guests remained a day and a half, and then returned to Tristan.

Early in November, that is, early in the second summer, the brothers thus swam round the eastern headland:—Frederick with their blankets, the rifle, and a spare suit of clothes[7]—Gustav with powder, matches, and the kettle in an oil-cask. They mounted by the help of the tussock-grass to the top of the cliff, went over to the west side of the plateau, and there built a small hut, where they remained a month, living on goats' flesh and fresh pork.

On the 10th of December they returned home, mended their thatch, dug[8] the early potatoes, and put the garden in order.

On the 19th of December the Tristan men made their second sealing expedition. They remained nine days on the island, and killed forty seals, one sea-elephant, and eight of the remaining[9] twelve goats. They left some flour in exchange for an oil-cask, and this was the last communication between the brothers and the outer world until the "Challenger" called eight months later.

1, legte fidh . . . unweit ber Jufel vor Anter.   **2,** = had strengthened them again.   **3,** fidh erweifen als.   **4,** = drove.   **5,** = who had come over.   **6,** = doing.   **7,** a spare suit of clothes, ein Referveanzug, m. **8,** here aufnehmen; early potatoes, frühzeitige Kartoffeln.   **9,** noch übrig.

Section 241.

A CURIOUS STORY.

IX.

In January Frederick swam round the point[1] again, and mounted the cliff. He shot four pigs, ran[2] the fat into buckets, and threw the hams down to his brother on the beach below. He saw the four last goats, but spared[3] them to increase their number. In February a boat came to the west side from Tristan, and its crew killed the four goats, and departed without communicating with the Stoltenhoffs[4].

The relations between the Tristan people and the brothers does not appear to have been so cordial latterly as it was at first, and the Stoltenhoffs believe that[5] the intention of their neighbours in killing the goats, and in delaying from time to time to bring them some live stock, which they had promised them, was to force them to leave the island. It may have been so, for the Tristan men had been in the habit of making a yearly sealing expedition to Inaccessible Island, and no doubt the presence of the energetic strangers lessened their chance of success.

In March the brothers once more swam round the point, and ascended the cliff. After staying on the plateau together for a few days, it was settled that Frederick should remain above to procure (S. 58, N. 8) a stock of lard for the winter, Gustav returning to the hut and storing it[6]. When a pig was killed, the hide, with the fat in it, was rolled up, secured with thongs of skin, and thrown over the cliff, where Gustav then ran the lard into a cask.

1, Santfivise, f.   **2,** laufen laffen.   **3,** verfdhenen.   **4,** = without having seen the Stoltenhoffs.   **5,** = that their neighbours killed the goats and delayed, etc., . . . in order to force them, etc.   **6,** um es zuzubereiten.

Section 242.

A CURIOUS STORY.

X.

During the second winter, the privations of the brothers do not seem to have been great. They were getting accustomed to their mode of life, and had always sufficient food, such as it was[1]. They were remarkably well educated. Both could speak and read English fluently, and the elder had a good knowledge of French. Their library consisted of eight volumes: Schoedler's Natural History, a German Atlas, Charles O'Malley, Captain Morrell's Voyages, two old volumes of a monthly magazine[2], Hamlet and Coriolanus with French notes, and Schiller's poems. These books they came to know almost by heart[3], but they had considerable resources in themselves, in the intelligent interest they took in the ever-changing appearances of nature.

When the "Challenger" arrived, they were preparing for another summer; but the peculiar food, and the want of variety in it, were beginning to tell upon them, for all their original stores were exhausted, with the exception of the Epsom salts, which were untouched, neither of them having had an hour's illness during their sojourn; and they were heartily glad of a passage to the Cape.

Frederick came to the ship before we left for the South in December. He was then comfortably settled in a situation in a merchant's office in Cape Town, and Gustav was on his way home to see his people [4] before resuming the thread of his roving sailor's life.—W. J. J. SPRY, "THE CRUISE OF THE CHALLENGER."

1, and — was = and the food at their disposal (und die ihnen zu Gebote stehende Nahrung) was at least always sufficient (ausreichend).   2, a monthly magazine, eine Monatsschrift.   3, = they knew at last almost by heart.   4, = friends or relations.

Section 243.

HOW THE BANK OF ENGLAND WAS HUMBLED.

I.

Once, many years ago, a bill of exchange for a large amount was drawn [1] by Anselm Rothschild, of Frankfort, on Nathan Rothschild, of London.   When the gentleman who held it arrived in London, Nathan was away, and he took the bit of paper to the Bank of England and asked them to discount it.

The managers were very stiff.   With haughty assurance they informed the holder that they discounted only their own bills; they said they had nothing to do with the bills of private persons.   They did not stop to reflect with whom they had to deal.   Those shrewd old gentlemen in charge of the bank of the realm should have known and remembered that that bit of paper bore the signature of a man more powerful than they—more powerful, because independent of a thousand-and-one hampers that rested upon them.   " Umph," exclaimed Nathan Rothschild, when the answer of the Bank was repeated to him.   "Private persons! I will let these important gentlemen know with what sort of private persons they have to deal."

And then Nathan Rothschild went to work.   He had an object in view [2]—to humble the Bank of England—and he meant to do it [3].   He sent agents to the Continent and through the United Kingdom, and three weeks were spent in gathering up notes of the smaller denominations of the Bank's own issue [4].

One morning, bright and early, Nathan Rothschild presented himself at the Bank, and drew forth from his pocket-book a five-pound note, which he desired to have cashed.   Five sovereigns were counted out to him, the officers looking with astonishment upon seeing Baron Rothschild troubling himself personally about so trivial a matter.   The baron examined the coins one by one, and, having satisfied himself of their good quality, slipped them into a canvas bag, and then drew out and presented another five-pound note.   The same operation was repeated, save that the baron took the trouble to take a small pair of scales from his pocket to weigh one of the pieces, for the law gave him that right.

1, to draw a bill of exchange, einen 𝔚ech𝔣el ziehen.   2, Er hatte 𝔣ich das Ziel ge𝔣teckt.   3, und er wollte alles daran 𝔣etzen, dies Ziel zu erreichen.   4, in gathering — issue, die auf kleinere Summen lautenden, von der engli𝔣chen 𝔅ank in Umlauf ge𝔣etzten 𝔅anknoten aufzukaufen.

Section 244.

HOW THE BANK OF ENGLAND WAS HUMBLED.

II.

Two—three—ten—twenty—a hundred—five hundred five-pound notes were presented and cashed. When one pocket-book was emptied, another was brought forth; and when a canvas bag had been filled with gold, it was passed to a servant who was in waiting. And so he went on until the hour arrived for closing the Bank; at the same time he had nine of the employés of his house engaged in the same work. So it resulted that ten men of the house of Rothschild had kept every teller[1] of the Bank busy for seven hours, and exchanged *somewhere* about £22,000. Not another customer had been able to get his wants attended to. The English like oddity. Let a man do anything original, and they will generally applaud. So the people of the Bank contrived to smile[2] at the eccentricity of Baron Rothschild, and when the time came for closing the Bank, they were not a tenth part so much annoyed as were[3] the customers from abroad[4] whose business had not been attended to. The bank officials smiled that evening, but—

On the following morning, when the bank opened[5], Nathan Rothschild appeared again, accompanied by his nine faithful helpers, this time bringing with him, as far as the street entrance, four heavy two-horse drays, for the purpose of carting away the gold, for to-day the baron had bills of a larger amount. Ah! the officers of the Bank smiled no more, and a trembling seized them when the banker monarch said, with stern simplicity and directness:

"Ah! these gentlemen refuse to take my bills! Be it so. I am resolved that I will not keep one of theirs. It is the House of Rothschild against the Bank of England[6]." The Bank of England opened its eyes very wide. Within a week, the House of Rothschild could be demanding gold which it did not possess. The gentlemen at the head of affairs saw very plainly that in a determined tilt[7] the Bank must go to the wall[8]. There was but one way out of the dilemma, and they took it. Notice was at once publicly given[9] that thenceforth the Bank of England would cash the bills of Rothschild *the same* as its own.—Tɪᴛ-Bɪᴛs.

1, =cashier, 𝔎a𝔣𝔣ierer.   2, contrived to smile=smiled.   3, they — were, ärgerten 𝔣ie 𝔣ich nicht halb 𝔣o 𝔣ehr, wie.   4, 'the customers from abroad' seems to be used here in the sense of 'the numerous customers'.   5, = was opened.   6, Es handelt 𝔣ich darum, ob das 𝔥aus 𝔑oth𝔣child oder die engli𝔣che 𝔅ank den Sieg davon tragen wird!   7, =struggle, 𝔎ampf, m.   8, to go to the wall, den kürzeren ziehen.   9, Es wurde öffentlich angezeigt.

Section 245.

MORGAN PRUSSIA[1].

I.

MORGAN, the gay and handsome son of a low Irish farmer, tired of home, went to take the chances of the world, and seek his fortune. By what means he traversed England, or made his way to France, is not told. But he at length crossed France, and, probably without much knowledge or much care whether he was moving to the north or the south pole, found himself in the Prussian territory. This was in the day of Frederick William I. (1713–1740), famous for his tall regiment of guards. He had but one ambition, that of inspecting twice a day a regiment of a thousand grenadiers, not one of whom was less than six feet and a half high. Morgan was an Irish giant, and was instantly seized by the Prussian recruiting sergeants, who forced him to "volunteer" into the tall battalion. This turn of fate was totally out of the Irishman's calculation; and the prospect of carrying a musket till his dying day on the Potsdam parade[2], after having made up his mind to live by his wits and rove the world, more than once tempted him to think of leaving his musket and honour behind him, and fairly trying his chance for escape. But the attempt was always found impracticable; the frontier was too closely watched, and Morgan still marched up and down the Potsdam parade with a disconsolate heart, when one evening a Turkish recruit was brought in; for the king looked to nothing but the thews and sinews of a man, and the Turk was full seven feet high.

"How much did his majesty give for catching that heathen?" said Morgan to his corporal. "Four hundred dollars[3]," was the answer. Morgan burst out into an exclamation of astonishment at this waste of royal treasure upon a Turk. "Why, they cannot be got for less," replied the corporal. "What a pity my five brothers cannot hear of it!" said Morgan, "I am a dwarf to any one of them, and the sound of half the money would bring them all over immediately." As the discovery of a tall recruit was the well-known road to favoritism, five were worth at least a pair of colours to the corporal[4]. The conversation was immediately carried to the sergeant, and from him, through the gradation of officers, to the colonel, who took the first opportunity of mentioning it to the king. The colonel was instantly ordered to question Morgan; but he at once lost all recollection of the subject. "He had no brothers; he had made the regiment his father, and mother, and relations, and there he hoped to live and die." But he was urged still more strongly, and at length confessed that he had brothers, even above the regimental standard, but that nothing on earth could stir them from their spades.

1, Morgan der Preuße.   2, auf dem Paradeplatz zu Potsdam.   3. Thaler.
4, five — corporal, so würden fünf derselben dem Korporal wenigstens eine Fähnrichsstelle eintragen.

Section 246.

MORGAN PRUSSIA.

II.

After some time the king inquired for the five recruits, and was indignant when he was told of the impossibility of enlisting them. "Send the fellow himself," he exclaimed, "and let him bring them back." The order was given; but Morgan was broken-hearted "at the idea of so long an absence from the regiment." He applied to the colonel to have the order revoked, or at least given to some one else. But this was out of the question, for the king's word was always irrevocable; and Morgan, with a disconsolate face, prepared to set out upon his mission. But a new difficulty struck him. "How was he to make his brothers come, unless he showed them the recruiting money?" This objection was at last obviated by the advance of a sum equal to about three hundred pounds sterling, as a first instalment for the purchase of his family. Like a loyal grenadier the Irishman was now ready to attempt anything for his colonel or his king, and Morgan began his journey. But, as he was stepping out of the gates of Potsdam, another difficulty occurred; and he returned to tell the colonel that of all people existing the Irish were the most apt to doubt a traveller's story, they being in the habit of a good deal of exercise in that style themselves [1]; and that when he should go back to his own country, and tell them of the capital treatment and sure promotion that a soldier met with in the guards, the probability was, that they would laugh in his face. As to the money, "there were some who would not scruple to say that he stole it, or tricked some one out of it. But, undoubtedly, when they saw him walking back only as a common soldier, he was sure they would not believe a syllable, let him say what he would about rising in the service."

The objection was intelligible enough, and the colonel represented it to the king, who, doubly outrageous at the delay, swore a grenadier's oath, ordered Morgan to be made a sub-lieutenant, and, with sword and epaulets, sent him instantly across the Rhine to convince his five brothers of the rapidity of Prussian promotion. Morgan flew to his home in the county of Carlow, delighted the firesides for many a mile round with his having outwitted a king and a whole battalion of grenadiers, laid out his recruiting money on land, and became a man of estate at the expense of the Prussian treasury.

One ceremony remains to be recorded. Once a year, on the anniversary of the day on which he left Potsdam and its giants behind, he climbed a hill within a short distance of his house, turned himself in the direction of Prussia, and, with the most contemptuous gesture which he could contrive, bade good-bye to his majesty. The ruse was long a great source of amusement, and its hero, like other heroes, bore through life the name earned by his exploit—Morgan Prussia.—KING GEORGE THE FOURTH.

1, they being — themselves, ba auch fie im Erzählen von dergleichen Geschichten eine große Fertigkeit besäßen.

Section 247.

THE TERRIBLE WINTER OF 1784.

About the middle of the month of April, in the year 1784, three hundred thousand miserable beings, dying from cold and hunger, groaned in Paris alone—in that Paris where, in spite of the boast that scarcely another city contained so many rich people, nothing had been prepared to prevent the poor from perishing of cold and wretchedness.

For the last four months, the same leaden sky had driven the poor from the villages into the town, as it sent the wolves from the woods into the villages.

No more bread.   No more wood.

No more bread for those who felt this cold—and no more wood to bake it.   All the provisions which had been collected, Paris had devoured in a month.   The Provost, short-sighted and incapable, did not know how to procure for Paris, which was under his care, the wood which might have been collected in the neighbourhood.   When it froze, he said the frost prevented the horses from bringing it; when it thawed, he pleaded want of horses and conveyances.   Louis XVI., ever good and humane, always ready to attend to the physical wants of his people, although he overlooked their social ones, began by contributing a sum of 200,000 francs for horses and carts, and insisting on their immediate use.   Still the demand continued greater than the supply.

At first no one was allowed to carry away from the public timber-yard more than a cart-load of wood; then that was limited to half the quantity.   Soon long strings of people might be seen waiting outside the timber-yards, as they were afterwards seen at the bakers' shops.   The king gave away the whole of his private income in charity.   He procured 3,000,000 francs by a grant and applied it to the relief of the sufferers, declaring that every other need must give way before that of cold and famine.   The queen, on her part, gave 500 louis from her purse.   The convents, the hospitals, and the public buildings were thrown open as places of asylum for the poor, who came in crowds for the sake of the fires that were kept there.

They kept hoping for a thaw, but heaven seemed inflexible.   Every evening the same copper-coloured sky disappointed their hopes; and the stars shone bright and clear as funeral torches through the long, cold nights, which hardened again and again the snow that fell during the day.   All day long, thousands of workmen, with spades and shovels, cleared away the snow from before the houses, so that on each side of the streets, already too narrow for the traffic, rose a high, thick wall, blocking up the way.   Soon these masses of snow and ice became so large that the shops were obscured by them, and they were obliged to allow it to remain where it fell.

Paris could do no more.   She gave in, and allowed the winter to do its worst.   December, January, February, and March passed thus,

although now and then a few days' thaw changed the streets, whose
sewers were blocked up, into running streams.   Horses were drowned,
and carriages destroyed, in the streets, some of which could only be
traversed in boats.   People went to the markets to see the fisherwomen
serving their customers with immense leathern boots on, inside which
their trousers were pushed, and with their petticoats tucked round their
waists, all laughing, gesticulating, and splashing each other as they stood
in the water.

These thaws, however, were but transitory ; the frost returned, harder
and more obstinate than ever, and recourse was had to sledges, pushed
along by skaters, or drawn by roughshod horses along the causeways,
which were like polished mirrors.   The Seine, frozen many feet deep, had
become the place of rendezvous for all idlers, who assembled there to skate
or slide, until, warmed by exercise, they ran to the nearest fire, lest the
perspiration should freeze upon them.   All trembled for the time when,
the water communications being stopped, and the roads impassable,
provisions could no longer be sent in, and began to fear that Paris would
perish from want.

The king, in this extremity, called a council.   They decided to implore
all bishops, abbés, and monks to leave Paris and retire to their dioceses
or convents ; and all those magistrates and officials who, preferring the
opera to their duties, had crowded to Paris, to return to their homes ;
for all these people used large quantities of wood in their hotels, and
consumed no small amount of food.   There were still the country
gentlemen, who were also to be entreated to leave.   But M. Lenoir,
lieutenant of police, observed to the king that, as none of these people
were criminals, and could not therefore be compelled to leave Paris in
a day, they would probably be so long thinking about it, that the thaw
would come before their departure, which would then be more hurtful
than useful.

All this care and pity of the king and queen, however, excited the
ingenious gratitude of the people, who raised monuments to them, as
ephemeral as the feelings which prompted them.   Obelisks and pillars
of snow and ice, engraved with their names, were to be seen all over
Paris.

At the end of March the thaw began, but by fits and starts, constant
returns of frost prolonging the miseries of the people.   Indeed, in the
beginning of April it appeared to set in harder than ever, and the half-
thawed streets, frozen again, became so slippery and dangerous, that
nothing was seen but broken limbs and accidents of all kinds.   The
snow prevented the carriages from being heard, and the police had
enough to do, through the reckless driving of the aristocracy, to preserve
from the wheels those who were spared by cold and hunger.—AFTER
ALEXANDER DUMAS, "THE QUEEN'S NECKLACE."

Section 248.

A STORY WORTH READING.

I.

Soon after the promulgation of Methodism[1] in England it spread with great rapidity over the counties of Devon and Cornwall, and especially among the miners and lower orders. For a long period after its introduction the clergy and higher classes of society in the west of England manifested a dislike to the new doctrines which can scarcely be imagined in these days of modern toleration. It was thought by many young gentlemen good sport to break the windows and nail up the doors of a Methodist chapel[2]. The robbery of a Wesleyan preacher[3], as a spree, by two young gentlemen, became the subject of an investigation, and the frolicsome young men had to pay very dearly for their practical joke.

Among the uninstructed local preachers was one known by the name of "The Old Gardener." This old man was no common character—indeed he was quite original, and by far the most popular preacher among the disciples of John Wesley in the vicinity.

He kept a small nursery garden about two miles from the town of St. A——, working hard at his occupation of gardener by day, and praying and preaching to his fellow-sinners, as he called them, in the evening. He lived in the poorest manner, giving away all the surplus of his earnings in charity, distributing Bibles, and promoting to the utmost of his ability the extension of Methodism. His complexion was a sort of dirty, dark, iron grey, and his whole appearance lean and grotesque. Although extremely ignorant, he possessed no small degree of cunning; of this the following incident affords ample evidence :—

"The Old Gardener" was once subjected to a burglary and attempt at robbery. He lived with his wife in a small and somewhat dilapidated cottage, not far from the high road. Three young "squires," who all despised and hated Methodism, having heard that the old man had been recently making a collection to build a Methodist chapel, thought it would be a good frolic to rob him temporarily of the proceeds of this collection. The result of the frolic is best related in the words of one of the actors :—

"We set out," said he, "upon our expedition with blackened faces, upon a dark night, a little before twelve o'clock. We had dined late, and all of us had Dutch as well as Cornish courage; yet I confess, when it came to the point[4], I felt myself a coward. I began to reflect that it was but a dastardly frolic to frighten the poor old man and his wife in the dead of night."

"The clock struck twelve. 'Now comes the watching time of the night,' exclaimed Tom."

"' Don't let us frighten the poor couple out of their wits,' said I."

"' No,' said Ryder, 'we will be gentle robbers—gentle as Robin Hood and Little John.'"

"I said that I would rather return than proceed. 'Recollect,' said I,

' the old fellow is an old soldier, as well as a saint, and fears nothing human.' "

" ' Nonsense,' exclaimed Ryder, ' here goes⁵.'   He pressed the feeble door of the cottage in which the old man resided; it immediately gave way and flew open.   We entered and found ourselves in a sort of kitchen.   To our great surprise there was a light shining from an inner room.   This made us all hesitate."

1, Nom. die Lehre der Methodisten.   2, of a — chapel, einer den Methodisten gehörenden Kapelle.   3, eines wesleyischen Predigers.   4, als es wirklich ernst wurde.   5, komm nur!

Section 249.

A STORY WORTH READING.

II.

" ' Who is out there at this time of the night ?' exclaimed a hoarse voice from within.   I knew it to be the unmistakable voice of ' The Old Gardener.' "

" ' Give us your money, and no harm shall befal you,' said Tom, ' but we must have your money.' "

" ' The Lord will be my defence,' rejoined ' The Old Gardener.' ' You shall have no money from me; all in the house is the Lord's— take it if you dare.' "

" ' We must and will have it,' said we, as we entered the inner room. after taking the precaution of fastening the chamber-door as we entered."

" We soon wished we had suffered it to remain open, as you will see."

" Now, consider us face to face with ' The Old Gardener,' and a pretty sight was presented.   Three ruffians (ourselves) with white waggoners' frocks and blackened faces; before us ' The Old Gardener,' sitting on the side of his bed.   He wore a red worsted nightcap, a checked shirt. and a flannel jacket; his iron grey face, fringed with a grizzly beard, looking as cool and undismayed as if he had been in the pulpit preaching."

" A table was by the side of the bed, and immediately in front of him, on a large deal table, was an open Bible, close to which we observed, to our horror, a heap of gunpowder, large enough to blow up a castle.   A candle was burning on the table, and the old fellow had a steel in one hand and a large flint in the other.   We were all three paralysed.   The wild, iron-faced, determined look of ' The Old Gardener,' the candle, flint and steel, and the great heap of powder, absolutely froze our blood, and made cowards of us all.   The gardener saw the impression he had made."

" ' What! do you want to rob and murder?' exclaimed he ; ' I think you had better join with me in prayer, miserable sinners that you all are! Repent, and you may be saved.   You will soon be in another world.' "

" Ryder first recovered his speech."

"'Please to hear me, Mr. Gardener. I feel that we have been wrong, and if we may depart we will make reparation, and give you all the money we have in our pockets.'"

"We laid our purses on the table before him."

"'The Lord has delivered you into my hands. It was so revealed to me in a dream. We shall all soon be in another world. Pray, let us pray.'"

"And down he fell upon his knees, close to the table, with the candle burning, and the ugly flint and steel in his hand. He prayed and prayed. At last he appeared exhausted. He stopped and eyed the purses, and then emptied one of them out on the table. He appeared surprised, and, I thought, gratified at the largeness of its contents."

"We now thought we should have leave to retire; but, to our dismay, 'The Old Gardener' said:

"'Now, we will praise God by singing the 100th Psalm.'"

"This was agony to us all. After the Psalm, the old man took up the second purse, and while he was examining its contents, Ryder, who was close behind Tom and myself, whispered softly:

"'I have unfastened the door, and when you hear me move, make a rush.'"

"'The Old Gardener,' then, pouring out the contents of the second purse, exclaimed:

"'Why, there is almost enough to build our new house of God. Let me see what the third contains.'"

"He took up the third purse."

"'Now,' whispered Ryder, 'make a rush.'"

"We did so; and at the same moment heard the old fellow hammering away at his flint and steel. We expected to be instantly blown into fragments. The front door, however, flew open before us: and the next moment we found ourselves in the garden. The night was pitchy dark. We rushed blindly through brambles and prickly shrubs, ran our heads against trees, and then forced our way through a thick hedge. At last, with scratched faces, torn hands, and tattered clothes, we tumbled over a bank into the high road.

Section 250.

A STORY WORTH READING.

III.

"Our horses we soon found, and we galloped to Ryder's residence. Lights were produced, and we sat down. We were black, ragged, and dirty. We looked at each other, and, in spite of our miserable adventure, roared with laughter."

"'We may laugh,' exclaimed Tom, 'but if this adventure becomes known, and we are found out, Cornwall will be too hot for us the next seven years. We have made a pretty night of it. We have lost our money, been obliged to pretend to pray for two long hours, before a great heap of gunpowder, while that grim-faced, ugly, red-capped brute threatened us with an immediate passage into eternity. And our money

forsooth must go to build a meeting-house!   Bah!   It is truly horrible.
The old fellow has played the old soldier on us with a vengeance, and we
shall be the laughing-stock of the whole country.'"

"The affair was not yet ended.   Reports were spread that three men
disguised as black demons, with horns and tails, had entered the cottage
of 'The Old Gardener,' who had not only terrified them, but had
frightened them out of a good sum of money, which he intended to devote to the building of a new Methodist meeting-house.   It was given
out that on the following Sunday 'The Old Gardener' intended to
preach a sermon, and afterwards solicit subscriptions for the meeting-
house, when he would relate the remarkable manner in which he had
been providentially assisted with funds for the building.   Our mortifica-
tion was complete.   Tom, whose hatred of Methodism was intense, declared he would blow up the meeting-house as soon as it was built.
Our curiosity, however, was excited, and we all three determined to hear
our adventure of the night related by 'The Old Gardener,' if we could
contrive to be present without being suspected."

"Sunday evening arrived.   The meeting-house was crammed to suffo-
cation; and with the dull lights then burning in the chapel, we had no
difficulty in concealing ourselves.   The sermon was short, but the statement of our adventure was related most minutely and circumstantially in
the old man's quaint, homely, and humorous phraseology.   This evening
he seemed to excel himself, and was exultingly humorous."

"'I never,' said he, 'saw black faces pray with greater devotion.
I have some doubt, however,' he slily observed, 'if their prayers were
quite heavenward.   They sometimes turned their faces towards the door,
but a lifting of the flint and steel kept them quiet.'"

"He then added, with a shake of the head and an exulting laugh:
'But they had not smelt powder like the old soldier they came to rob.
No, no; it was a large heap—ay, large enough to frighten old General
Clive himself.   The candle was lighted, the flint and steel were ready.
You may ask, my friends, if I myself was not afraid.   No, no, my dear
friends,' shouted he, 'this large stock of apparent gunpowder was—it
was my whole year's stock of leek (onion) seed!'"

"The whole congregation somewhat irreverently laughed; even the
saints almost shouted; many clapped their hands.   I was for a moment
stupefied by the announcement, but at last could hardly suppress my
own laughter."

"We subscribed to the fund to avoid suspicion, and left the meeting.
After the sermon we joined each other, but could not speak.   We could
hardly chuckle 'leek-seed,' and then roared with laughter."

"It was a good joke, though not exactly to our taste.   It has, however, more than once served for subsequent amusement."

"The chapel was built with the money collected by the gardener.
Time and circumstances now induce me to think that there has been no
detriment to morality or religion by the erection of the meeting-house,
which was afterwards known as 'The Leek-seed Chapel.'"—St. James's
Magazine.

APPENDIX.

A. ESSENTIALS OF CONSTRUCTION.

I. PRINCIPAL AND CO-ORDINATE CLAUSES.

(See § 24.)

§ 1. **Infinitives, Participles, and that form of the Infinitive preceded by zu which is called Supine, stand at the end of the clause;** as—

Er war ärmlich, aber doch sauber gekleidet.	He was poorly, but yet neatly dressed.
Sein zürnender Oheim hatte ihn zu sich gerufen.	His angry uncle had bid him come to him.
Seine Tante wird morgen zu uns kommen.	His aunt will come to us to-morrow.
Sie hat uns versprochen, morgen zu kommen.	She has promised us to come to-morrow.

§ 2. In a clause containing *both* an infinitive and a participle, **the infinitive stands last;** as—

Der Diener würde es nicht gethan haben, wenn er ihn nicht freundlich darum gebeten hätte.	The servant would not have done it, if he had not kindly asked him to do it.
Der Brief muß gut geschrieben werden, denn er enthält wichtige Mitteilungen.	The letter must be well written, for it contains important communications.

§ 3. In a clause containing **two infinitives, the one governing the other stands last;** as—

Er mag mit einem solchen Menschen nichts zu thun haben.	He does not like to have anything to do with such a man.

§ 4. **Separable prefixes of compound verbs are placed at the end of the clause when the verb is used in a *simple tense*;** as—

Der König ging jeden Morgen um elf Uhr aus und kam gegen zwölf Uhr zurück.	The king went out every morning at eleven o'clock and returned towards twelve o'clock.

§ 5. In a clause containing **two objects, both expressed by nouns, that of the person stands before that of the thing;** as—

Am nächsten Abend gab er dem Manne das Geld zurück.	The next evening he returned the money to the man.

§ 6. When *both* objects represent *persons,* the accusative generally stands first; as—

Man hat den Verbrecher dem Richter überliefert.	They have delivered the criminal to the judge.

§ 7. In clauses containing *two* objects, one being *a personal pronoun* and the other *a noun,* the pronoun stands first; as—

Der fremde Herr gab mir einige Äpfel und Birnen.	The stranger gave me some apples and pears.

§ 8. When both objects are personal pronouns, the accusative *generally stands* first; as—

Sie hat es mir gesagt.	She has said it to me.
Man hat sie ihm genommen.	They have taken her away from him.

§ 9. *A.* Adverbial expressions of time generally stand before the object (except it is a pronoun) and always before adverbial expressions of manner and place; as—

Wir haben gestern drei Briefe erhalten.	Yesterday we received three letters.
Er ist heute plötzlich nach London abgereist.	He has suddenly left for London to-day.

But we must say—

Wir haben Sie heute mit Ungeduld erwartet. (Sie pers. pron.)	We have been expecting you to-day with impatience.

B. Adverbial expressions of manner and place generally stand before the Infinitive or Participle when the verb is in a compound tense, but take the last place in the clause when the verb is in a simple tense; as—

Die Schüler haben ihre Aufgaben sehr gut gemacht.	The pupils have done their lessons *very well.*
Sie machen ihre Aufgaben immer sehr gut.	They do their lessons always very well.
Sind Sie gestern im Theater gewesen?	Were you *at the theatre yesterday?*
Ich* gehe nie ins Theater.	I* *never* go *to the theatre.*

§ 10. The negation nicht stands after the accusative; as—

Er schreibt den Brief nicht, sondern sein Bruder.	He is not writing the letter, but his brother is.
Er hat den Brief nicht geschrieben.	He has not written the letter.

§ 11. In questions nicht sometimes stands before the accusative; as—

Haben Sie nicht meinen Brief erhalten?	Have you not received my letter?

§ 12. In general the negation nicht stands before that part of the sentence which it affects; as—

Ich bin nicht krank gewesen.	I have not been ill.
Wir sprechen nicht von ihm, sondern von seinem Vetter.	We do not speak of him, but of his cousin.
Die Natur hatte sie nicht mit Schönheit ausgestattet.	Nature had not endowed her with beauty.

---

* When the subject, which may be preceded by its attributes, occupies the first place in a principal clause, either the copula or the verb must follow immediately.

II. INVERTED CONSTRUCTION.

§ 13. The *ordinary* way of arranging the words is to place the subject and its adjuncts first, and the predicate with its adjuncts after; as—

Der gute Vater (subj.) ist heute Morgen mit seinen drei Töchtern nach London abgereist (predicate with adjuncts).	The good father has left this morning for London with his three daughters.

But this construction is sometimes inverted, so as to place the predicate, or a part of the predicate, before the subject. This is the case:

(*a*) In interrogative clauses; as—

Kommt der Mann heute?	Does the man come to-day?
Ist der Vater nach London abgereist?	Has the father left for London?
Hat er kein Geld bei sich?	Has he no money about him?

(*b*) In imperative clauses; as—

Senden Sie diesen Brief zur Post!	Send this letter to the post-office!

(*c*) In exclamatory clauses; as—

Hätte er auf mich gehört!	Would he had listened to me!

(*d*) In subordinate clauses beginning with an adverbial conjunction. (See § 124 of Lange's German Grammar.)

§ 14. The *ordinary* way of arranging the words is often departed from for the sake of emphasizing a part of the predicate. In this case the part to be emphasized is placed at the *beginning* of the sentence, and the construction must be inverted, that is to say the subject must be placed after the verb; as—

Die letzten Worte hatte der junge Mensch mit gehobener Stimme gesprochen.	The last words the young man had spoken with an elevated tone of voice.
Heute kann er nicht abreisen, sondern morgen.	He cannot depart to-day, but to-morrow.
Mit dem zwölf Uhr Zuge kann er nicht mehr fahren, denn es ist zu spät.	He cannot go by the twelve o'clock train, for it is too late.

These sentences would read in the *ordinary* construction: Der junge Mensch hatte die letzten Worte mit gehobener Stimme gesprochen. Er kann nicht heute abreisen, sondern morgen. Er kann nicht mehr mit dem zwölf Uhr Zuge fahren, denn es ist zu spät. The words „Die letzten Worte," „heute," „mit dem zwölf Uhr Zuge," have been made *emphatic* by being placed at the *beginning* of the sentence, which required the *verb* and the *subject* to interchange places.

§ 15. Sometimes a subordinate clause (that is to say a clause dependent on another clause, without which it would not be understood) is made emphatic by being placed before the principal clause. Then also the subject of the *principal clause* must be placed after the verb; as—

Als er in die Stube kam, fand er mich am Schreibtische.	When he came into the room, he found me at the desk.

In this example the *principal* clause is „er fand mich am Schreibtische," and the *subordinate* clause is contained in the words „Als er in die Stube kam;" this latter clause has been emphasized by being placed before the principal clause, but it required the *principal* clause to be *inverted*, so as to place the *subject* (er) after the *verb* (fand).

Here are some more examples of the same class:

Weil er ein guter Junge ist, will ich ihm
seine Bitte gewähren.

Because he is a good fellow, I will
grant his request.

Nachdem er gegessen und getrunken hatte,
ging er nach Hause.

After having eaten and drunk, he
went home.

III. SUBORDINATE CLAUSES.

(See § 24.)

§ 16. In subordinate clauses beginning with a relative pronoun, a relative conjunction, or a subordinative conjunction, **the verb** stands at the end; as—

Man zeigte mir ein Buch, das viele schöne
Bilder enthielt.

They showed me a book which contained many beautiful pictures.

Wir waren im Zimmer, als er eintrat.

We were in the room when he entered.

§ 17. When the verb is in a compound tense, the **auxiliary** verb stands last; as—

Nachdem sie ihn begrüßt hatte, kam
sie schnell auf mich zu.

After she had welcomed him, she
approached me quickly.

§ 18. When there are *two* verbs, one of which is a verb of mood, **the verb of mood stands last**; as—

Er sagte, daß er nicht kommen könne.

He said that he could not come.

§ 19. When there are *two* verbs, the one being an infinitive, and the other an inflected verb, **the inflected verb stands last**; as—

Der Sohn starb gerade zu der Stunde,
in welcher sein Vater ihn wieder-
zusehen hoffte.

The son died the very hour his father
hoped to see him again.

§ 20. When there are *two infinitives* and *an auxiliary verb*, the **auxiliary** verb has the first place, whilst the governing infinitive stands last; as—

Er überlegte, wie er es werde vermeiden
können. (können is the governing
verb.)

He considered how he might be able
to avoid it.

Er sagte, daß er es nicht habe thun
mögen. (mögen is the governing
verb.)

He said that he did not like to
do it.

§ 21. Sometimes the conjunction, which generally connects the sub-ordinate clause with the principal clause, *is omitted and understood.* In this case the construction is like that of a *principal clause;* as—

Er fürchtete, ich könne mich erkälten.
(Er fürchtete, daß ich mich erkälten
könne.)

He was afraid I might catch
cold.

§ 22. Sometimes the **auxiliary** verb is omitted *and understood;* as—

Daß er mir genommen (wurde), ist
mein größtes Leid.

That he was taken from me is my
greatest sorrow.

§ 23. In subordinate clauses the prefixes of separable compound verbs are not separated from the verb; as—

Er war so beschäftigt, daß er in vierzehn
Tagen nicht ausging.

He was so busy that he did not go
out for a fortnight.

§ 24. *A.* The co-ordinative conjunctions—aber, allein, denn, nämlich, oder, sondern, sowohl — als, and und — serve to connect two or more independent statements with each other, which have either one common subject or predicate, or have each a subject and predicate of their own (co-ordinate clauses). **Co-ordinative conjunctions do not affect the regular order of construction** explained in §§ 1–12, and generally stand at the beginning of the co-ordinate clauses which they introduce; but aber and nämlich are often placed after the verb, and sometimes even stand in the middle of the clause; as—

> Die Frau war dem Manne früh gestorben; dieser ließ dem hinterlassenen Kinde aber jede mögliche Sorgfalt angedeihen.

A subordinate clause, i.e. a clause dependent on another clause, without which it would not be understood, is joined to a principal clause by means of a relative pronoun, or a conjunction, which latter may be either a relative, a subordinative, or an adverbial conjunction. (See § 124 of Lange's German Grammar.) The effect produced upon the construction by relative pronouns, relative conjunctions, and subordinative conjunctions has been explained in §§ 16–23.

B. **Adverbial conjunctions, like all other adverbial expressions commencing a clause, require the verb to stand before the subject,** as has been pointed out in § 124 of Lange's German Grammar.

B. THE INDICATIVE MOOD.

§ 25. The Indicative Mood is the Mood of Actuality, whilst the Subjunctive Mood is the Mood of Possibility. The nature of the Indicative may be said to be *objective*, because it is used to express positive facts. The nature of the Subjunctive may be said to be *subjective*, because it represents the statement made as a mere subjective supposition, or as resting on the mere hearsay evidence of other persons.

The Indicative Mood denotes Positiveness and Certainty.

Conjunctions never determine the mood in which a verb is to be used. The mood is always determined by the nature of the statement we wish to make. So one and the same verb may be followed, in the dependent clause, either by the Indicative or the Subjunctive Mood.

EXAMPLES.

Der Gefangene ist tot; er ist heute Morgen gestorben. (Positive statement.) — The prisoner is dead; he died this morning.

Ich bin überzeugt, daß er es gesagt hat. (Certainty.) — I am convinced that he has said it.

Der Mensch ist sterblich. (A fact.) — Man is mortal.

Ich habe gehört, daß er zum Minister ernannt ist. — I have heard that he has been appointed a minister, (and I do not doubt it).

(Here the Indicative Mood is used, because I wish to imply that I have *no doubt* about the accuracy of the statement.)

Ich habe gehört, daß er zum Minister ernannt sei (see § 30). — I have heard that he has been appointed a minister, (but I rather doubt it).

(Here the Subjunctive Mood is used because I wish to express a *doubt* about the accuracy of the statement, which is expressed in English by the words 'but I rather doubt it.')

C. THE SUBJUNCTIVE (OR CONJUNCTIVE) MOOD.
(See § 25.)

§ 26. Since, in the best modern works of English Literature, we frequently find the Indicative employed instead of the Subjunctive in clauses of uncertainty and supposition, and since, with the exception of the verb *to be*, it is evidently the tendency of the English language to reject the distinction of the Subjunctive Mood, the student will encounter no small difficulty in learning the right use of the German Subjunctive, which is most extensively used, and gives often great power, conciseness, and elegance to the mode of speaking.

The Subjunctive Mood is used both in principal and subordinate clauses, and **denotes Uncertainty and Supposition.**

EXAMPLES.

Man sagt er sei gestorben (see § 29). (Uncertainty.)	People say (i. e. it is rumoured) he is dead.
Plato glaubte, daß nur ein Gott sei. (Supposition.)	Plato thought that there was only *one* God, (but that it was a matter of doubt).

§ 27. **The Subjunctive expresses Command, Wish, and Concession.**

EXAMPLES.

Er nehme seine Weile, wie's Brauch ist! (Schiller.) (Command.)	Let him take his distance as it is customary!
Gott sei mit dir! (Wish.)	God be with you!
Er gehe, wohin er Lust hat. (Concession.)	He may go wherever he pleases.

§ 28. **The Subjunctive is used in Indirect Speech** (oratio obliqua), i. e. when words which have been actually spoken are *quoted* not as they were spoken, but *in substance only*; it stands especially after the verbs sagen, to say; erzählen, to relate; melden, to report; berichten, to relate, to report; hören, to hear; as—

Er sagte ihm, er sei ein Verschwender.	He told him he was a spendthrift.
Sie behauptete, sie habe den Brief nicht erhalten.	She asserted that she had not got the letter.
Sein Freund meldete, daß er nicht kommen könne, mich zu besuchen.	His friend reported that he could not come to see me.

§ 29. **The Subjunctive is used when the statement made in the subordinate clause is intended to be represented not as a fact, but as a mere idea, as a mere conception of the person speaking.** We find it, therefore, especially after verbs denoting *a request, a wish, a hope, an apprehension, a permission, an advice,* and *a command;* as—

meinen, to mean.	wollen, to be willing.
glauben, to believe.	bitten, to ask.
vermuten, to presume.	befehlen, to command.
zweifeln, to doubt.	verlangen, to demand.
scheinen, to seem.	ermahnen, to admonish.
hoffen, to hope.	raten, to advise.
fürchten, to fear.	bestehen, to insist upon,

And others of a like meaning.

EXAMPLES.

Laſſen Sie uns hoffen, daß unſer Streben von Erfolg ſein werde.	Let us hope that our endeavours may be successful.
Ich bat ihn, daß er mir helfen möge.	I asked him to help me.
Ich fürchtete, daß er ein Bein gebrochen habe.	I was afraid that he had broken a leg.
Wir bitten, daß der Gefangene frei gelaſſen werde.	We request that the prisoner be released.
Er zweifelt daran, daß man ihn für unſchuldig erklären werde.	He doubts if he will be declared innocent.
Wir werden ſtets verlangen, daß man uns unſere Rechte gewähre.	We shall always demand that our rights be given to us.
Ich rate dir, daß du fleißiger werdeſt.	I advise you to become more industrious.
Ich beſtehe darauf, daß ſich der Lord entferne. (Schiller.)	I insist upon the Lord's retiring.

§ 30. With regard to the *Tense* in which the Subjunctive ought to stand in subordinate clauses of the character mentioned above, the general rule is, that—

> We use the same tense of the Subjunctive Mood which, in direct speech, or in a principal clause, would be used in the Indicative Mood,

except that

> the Perfect of the Subjunctive is used instead of the Imperfect of the Indicative, and that the Pluperfect of the Indicative is changed into the Perfect of the Subjunctive, with the help of one of the conjunctions ehe, bevor, and nachdem.

The following table will make this clear:—

Direct Speech.	Indirect Speech.
Er ſagte: „Ich leſe." (Present.)	Er ſagte, er leſe. (Present Subj.)
Er ſagte: „Ich habe geleſen." (Perfect.)	Er ſagte, er habe geleſen. (Perfect Subj.)
Er ſagte: „Ich werde leſen." (First Future.)	Er ſagte, er werde leſen. (First Future Subjunctive.)
Er ſagte: „Ich werde geleſen haben (Second Future), wenn mein Freund mich abholen wird." (First Future.)	Er ſagte, er werde geleſen haben (Second Future Subj.), wenn ſein Freund ihn abholen werde (First Future Subjunctive).
But—	
Er ſagte: „Ich las, als ſein Freund ſchrieb." (Imperfect.)	Er ſagte, er habe geleſen, als ſein Freund geſchrieben habe. (Perfect Subjunctive.)
Er ſagte: „Ich hatte geleſen (Pluperfect), als mein Freund ſchrieb." (Imperfect.)	Er ſagte, er habe geleſen (Perfect Subjunctive), ehe ſein Freund geſchrieben habe. (Perfect Subjunctive.)

It will be seen, therefore, that the verb in the subordinate clause stands either in the Present, in the Perfect, or in the Future.

EXAMPLES.

Der Diener antwortete, er sei nicht im stande die Arbeit zu thun, denn er sei zu schwach. (Present Subj.)	The servant answered that he was unable to do the work, for he was too weak.
Er erzählte mir, er habe ein Unglück gehabt. (Perfect Subj.)	He told me he had met with a misfortune.
Sie behauptete, daß sie nie in ihrem Leben krank gewesen sei. (Perfect Subj.)	She affirmed that she had never been ill in all her life.
Er sagte, daß er sich um eine Stelle bewerben werde. (First Future.)	He said that he was going to apply for a situation.

§ 31. **The Imperfect and Pluperfect Subjunctive, however, must be used instead of the Present and Perfect Subjunctive, and the Conditional instead of the Future Subjunctive,** when any ambiguity might arise as to the mood employed, that is to say in cases where the form of the Present, of the Perfect, or of the Future is *identical* both in the Indicative and the Subjunctive Mood. For example, in the sentence—

„Sie sagte mir, ihre Töchter gingen niemals auf Bälle;" 'She said to me that her daughters never went to balls;'

the verb gingen stands in the *Imperfect Subjunctive* and *not* in the *Present*, because the third person plural of the Present Indicative and the corresponding person of the Present Subjunctive *are identical* in the conjugation of this verb. Both are „sie geben," the verb, therefore, must be put in the *Imperfect Subjunctive* to show clearly the mood employed.

§ 32. **The Subjunctive is employed in adverbial clauses of purpose and of manner,** when the subordinate clause generally begins with the conjunctions daß, auf daß, damit, and als ob; as—

Du sollst deinen Vater und deine Mutter ehren, auf daß dir's wohlgehe und du lange lebest auf Erden.	Thou shalt honour thy father and thy mother, that thou mayest prosper and thy days be long on earth.
Ist es nicht, als ob dies Volk mich zum Gott mache? (Schiller.)	Does it not seem as if the people meant to make a God of me?

§ 33. **The Imperfect Subjunctive and the Pluperfect Subjunctive** are used to express something possible, or something capable of being done, also to denote a mere supposition on the part of the speaker, or for the purpose of stating an opinion with *caution* or *modesty*; as—

Es könnte sein, daß er nicht zu Hause wäre.	Literally: It might be possible that he were not at home, i.e. He may possibly not be at home.
Ich hätte wohl Lust, ihm einen Besuch zu machen.	I should like indeed to pay him a visit.
Ich wüßte wohl, was zu thun wäre.	I fancy I know what ought to be done.
Es wäre vielleicht besser, das Unternehmen aufzugeben.	Perhaps it would be better to give up the undertaking.

§ 34. **To express a wish** we use the *Present Subjunctive*, when we believe in the fulfilment of the wish, but the *Imperfect Subjunctive*, when we want to indicate that the fulfilment of the wish is unlikely, and even impossible; as—

Gott sei mit dir!	God be with you!
Möge er bald gesund werden!	May he soon recover his health!
Lang lebe der König!	Long live the king!
Gott helfe mir! (Luther.)	May God help me!

But with the Imperfect Subjunctive:

Möchte er balb gefund werden!	Would he might soon recover his health!
Wenn er boch noch lebte!	I would he were still alive!
Möchte er balb kommen!	Would he might soon come!

§ 35. It must always be remembered that both moods (the Indicative and the Subjunctive) may stand in Principal Clauses as well as in Subordinate Clauses, since *their use depends alone on the nature of the statement we wish to make* (see § 25). Nor has the notion connected with the verb standing in the principal clause an absolute influence on the mood to be used in the subordinate clause. The Indicative stands in subordinate clauses not merely after verbs expressing Certainty, but also after such as denote Belief, Supposition, and Doubt, when the statement contained in the subordinate clause is represented *objectively*, i.e. as being based upon a fact, or as being, in the speaker's opinion, not open to any doubt. So we say—

Ich glaube, baß er in ber Schlacht geblieben ist (not fei).	I believe that he was killed in battle.
Ich weiß nicht, ob er lebt, ober ob er tot ist.	I do not know whether he is alive, or whether he is dead.
Ich zweifle, baß ber Kranke genefen wirb.	I doubt if the patient will recover.
Ich hoffe, baß er sich wohl befindet.	I hope that he is well.

But when the statement contained in the subordinate clause is represented *subjectively*, i.e. as being based upon a mere idea or belief, the correctness of which is still open to doubt, the Subjunctive must be used; as—

Man glaubt, man sagt, etc., er fei in ber Schlacht geblieben.	People believe, people say, etc., that he was killed in battle, (but it is still doubtful).
Er fürchtet, baß man ihn verraten habe.	He is afraid that they have betrayed him, (yet he does not know).

D. THE CONDITIONAL MOOD.

§ 36. The Conditional is the mood for representing a state or an event as dependent on another, which other, however, is not based upon a real fact, but is a mere hypothesis or supposition. As such we use not only the First and Second Conditional (ich würde, etc.), as given in the tables of verbs, but also the Imperfect and Pluperfect Subjunctive. The latter two, in fact, may be called the simple forms of the Conditional Mood, and the former (ich würde, etc.) the compound forms. Every true conditional statement consists of two clauses: (a) the hypothetical clause, which contains the supposition, (b) the conditioning clause, which contains the inference drawn from that supposition; as—

> If I had money (hypothetical clause),
> I should like to travel (conditioning clause).

The Imperfect and Pluperfect Subjunctive may be used in both clauses, but the First and Second Conditional (ich würde, etc.—see the tables of verbs) can only be used in conditioning clauses.

The conditioning clause is often introduced by „so."

EXAMPLES.

Wenn ich Gelb hätte, ginge ich gern auf Reisen (or würde ich gern auf Reisen gehen).	If I had money, I should like to travel.

Wenn es heute schönes Wetter gewesen wäre, so würden wir ausgegangen sein.	If the weather had been fine to-day, we should have gone out.
Dieser Mann könnte glücklicher sein, wenn er das Spiel nicht zu sehr liebte.	This man might be happier, if he were not too fond of gambling.
Er würde gesund sein (or er wäre gesund), wenn er mäßiger lebte.	He would be healthy, if he were more temperate.

§ 37.   The Conditional is sometimes used *elliptically*; as—

Ja, ich würde gekommen sein!	Yes, I should have come! (i.e. if I had been able to do so, *understood*).
Unter den Umständen hätte ich es gewiß gethan.	I am sure, under the circumstances I should have done it (i.e. if I had been placed in the same situation).
Wäre ich reich, würde ich Sie sofort bezahlen.	Were I rich, I should pay you directly.

SYNOPSIS OF THE CHANGES

WHICH

THE GERMAN SPELLING HAS UNDERGONE THROUGH THE

GOVERNMENT REGULATIONS OF 1880*.

A. Vokale. (Vowels.)

Write

Ä, Ö, Ü (instead of Ae, Oe, Ue) in: die Äpfel (*apples*); die Öfen (*ovens, stoves*); der Überrock (*overcoat*), etc. In foreign words ä, ü (for Greek and French ai and French u) in: der Pädagog (*pedagogue*); der Kapitän (*captain*); die Lektüre (*reading*), etc.

ay (instead of ai) in: Bayern (*Bavaria*); der Bayer (*the Bavarian*); bayerisch, adj. (*Bavarian*), and derivatives.

ei (instead of ai) in: der Heide (*heathen*); die Heide (*heath*); das Getreide (*grain*); der Weizen (*wheat*), etc.—**But:** die Bai (*bay*); der Hai (*shark*); der Hain (*grove*); der Kaiser (*emperor*); der Laib (*loaf*); der Laich (*spawn* [of fish]); das Laichen (*spawning*); die Laichzeit (*spawning-time*): der Laie (*layman*); der Mai (*May*); die Maid (*maid, maiden*); der Mais (*maize*); maischen (*to mash* [in brewing]); die Saite (*string*); der Waid (*dyer's woad*); der or die Waise (*orphan* (boy or girl)), and derivatives.

> **Nouns terminating in -ee and -ie—**
> take in the plural **en**, which inflection forms a separate syllable, as: die Armee' (*army*), *pl.* die Armee'en (*armies*); der or die See' (*lake or sea*), *pl.* die See'en (*lakes or seas*); die Melodie' (*melody*), *pl.* die Melodie'en (*melodies*); die Theorie' (*theory*), *pl.* die Theorie'en (*theories*), etc. **But:** das Komitee' (*committee*), *pl.* die Komitee's (*committees*); das Knie' (*knee*), *pl.* die Knie'e.

eu 1. (instead of äu) in: deuchten (*to appear, to seem*); mir deucht (*it seems to me, methinks*); ihm deuchte (*he thought*); (durch)-bleuen (*to give* [one] *a hearty drubbing, to beat* [one] *black and blue*); [but: (durch)-bläuen (*to make or dye blue*)]; der Greuel (*horror*); leugnen (*to deny*); verleumden (*to slander*), etc.

2. in the termination **eur** (sounded as in French), in: der Commandeur (*commander*); der Redacteur (*editor*), etc.

i (instead of y) in: der Gips (*plaster of Paris*); die Silbe (*syllable*); der Sirup (*syrup*); der Vampir (*vampire*), etc. [Comp. ay.]

---

*1. Regeln und Wörterverzeichnis für die deutsche Rechtschreibung zum Gebrauch in den preußischen Schulen. Berlin, Weidmannsche Buchhandlung 2. Regeln und Wörterverzeichnis für die deutsche Rechtschreibung zum Gebrauch in den bayerischen Schulen. München, Expedition des Kgl. Zentral-Schulbücher-Verlags.

Write:

ie (instead of i) in the verbal termination **ie'ren,** as in: ſtudie'ren (*to study*); ſpa=
zie'ren (*to go for a walk*); marſchie'ren (*to march*); probie'ren (*to try, to test*);
hantie'ren (*to handle, to manage*), etc.—and in their derivatives, as in: die
Hantie'rung (*management, business, profession*), etc.; also in: gieb (*give*), and
derivatives.

ou (*pronounced as in French*, instead of u) in words coming from the French, as
die Fenrage (*forage*); der Fenrier (*quarter master*); der Fournier (*veneer*), etc.

Only one Vowel (instead of two)—

in: bar (*bare, destitute of;* [of money]: *in cash*); die Barſchaft (*ready money,
cash in hand*); das Maß (*measure*); das Schaf (*sheep*); die Schar (*troop, herd*);
der Star (*starling;* [in medicine]: *cataract*); die Wage (*scales*); die Ware (*goods*);
der Herd (*hearth*); die Herde (*herd, flock*); das Kamel (*camel*); das Los (*lot, fate*);
loſen (*to cast lots*); die Loſung (*the casting or drawing of lots*); der Schoß (*lap,
middle;* [of dress]: *skirt, or tail*); etc.

B. Konſonanten. (Consonants.)

d (instead of dt) in: der Tod (*death*); todkrank (*sick unto death*); todmüde (*tired to
death*); die Todſünde (*deadly* or *mortal sin*); tödlich (*deadly, mortal, fatal*), etc.—
Comp. letter **t** (instead of dt).

f (instead of ph) in: Adolf (*Adolphus*); der Elefant (*elephant*); der Faſan (*pheasant*);
Rudolf (*Ralph*); Weſtfalen (*Westphalia*), etc.—But: der Epheu (*ivy*) from the
old German word Ebheu.

h 1. **h remains as a sign of lengthening a syllable :—**

　(a) **In syllables beginning with a t-sound and containing a long
vowel, but not a diphthong or a double vowel,** as in: die That
(*deed*); die Thräne (*tear*); der Thron (*throne*); der Thor (*fool*); das
Thor (*gate*); thun (*to do*); that (*did*); gethan (*done*), etc. [Comp.
h, 2 (a).]

　(b) **before l, m, n, and r,** as in: allmählich (*gradually*); befehlen (*to
command*); nehmen (*to take*); wohnen (*to live, to reside*); lehren (*to
teach*), etc. **Exceptions:** die Feme (*an old secret criminal court in
Westphalia*) and derivatives, as: der Femrichter (*a judge of that court*),
and derivatives.

　(c) **in:** die Fehde (*feud, quarrel*); die Mahd (*mowing*), from mähen (*to mow*);
der Draht (*wire*) from drehen (*to turn*); die Naht (*seam*), from nähen (*to
sew*), and other words derived from verbs containing an aspirated **h.**

　(d) **in a few proper names,** as in: Bertha, Günther, Martha, Mathilde,
Theobald, Theodor, etc.

　(e) **in many nouns originally Greek,** as: die Kathedra'le (*cathedral*);
das Thema (*theme*); die Theologie'; die Theorie'; das Thermome'ter; der
Pa'nther, etc.

2. **h is not retained after t :—**

　(a) **in syllables beginning with a t-sound and containing a diphthong or a double vowel,** as in: der Tau (*dew*); das Tau (*rope*); der

Write:

Teer (*tar*); teeren (*to tar*); der or das Teil (*part,* or *share*); teuer (*dear*); das Tier (*animal*); verteidigen (*to defend*), etc., and derivatives.—Exception: der Thee (*tea*), and derivatives.

(b) in the suffixes **tum** and **tüm** (formerly thum and thüm), as in: das Eigentum (*property*); das Königtum (*kingdom*); das Ungetüm (*monster*), etc.

(c) **at the end of syllables, and at the beginning of syllables before a short vowel,** as in:—die Armut (*poverty*); der Atem (*breath*); atmen (*to breathe*); die Blüte (*blossom*); die Flut (*flood*); das Gerät (*tools*); die Glut (*glow*); der Kot (*dirt*); das Lot (*a weight of half an ounce, now obsolete*); der Met (*mead*); die Miete (*rent; a corn or hay-stack; mite*); der Mut (*courage*); die Not (*need*); nötigen (*to urge; to invite; to compel*); der or die Pate (*god-father or god-mother*); der Rat (*advice*); raten (*to advise; to guess*); das Rätsel (*riddle*); rot (*red*); die Röte (*redness*); die Rute (*rod*); der Turm (*tower*); der Wert (*value*); wert (*worth, dear*); der Wirt (*host, landlord*); die Wut (*rage*), and derivatives, as: ratlos (*without advice or means: helpless*); wertvoll (*valuable, precious*); das Wirtshaus (*inn*), etc.

Mark well: hurra! (*hurra!*).

k 1. (instead of *c*) **in many words originally Greek,** as in: die Akademie' (*academy*); praktisch (*practical*); die Arithmetik (*arithmetic*); die Physik (*natural philosophy*), etc.—But: der Charakter; die Melancholie'.

2. (instead of *c* and *qu*) **in many words originally Latin or French,** but which have become quite germanised, and are now looked upon as altogether German words, as: der Advokat (*lawyer*); das Boskett (*thicket*) from the French: le bosquet; das Lokal (*locality*); das Publikum (*public*); vakant (*vacant*); der Vulkan (*volcano*), etc.—More especially in words terminating in . . . **kel,** as in: der Artikel; die Partikel; die Floskel (*flourish*), pl. die Floskeln (*fine words, frequently made use of with a deceptive purpose*).

3. (instead of *c*) **in words with the prefixes Ko=, Kol=, Kom=, Kon=, Kor=,** and also in syllables containing a **k**-sound followed by **t** (. . . **kt**), as in: die Kopie' (*copy*); die Kolonie' (*colony*); der Kommandant (*commander*); der Konstabler (*constable*); das Konzert (*concert*); die Korrespondenz (*correspondence*), etc.; die Didaktik (*didactics*); das Edikt (*edict*), etc.—But: das Diktum, because not germanised, etc.—

Mark well: der Kaffee' (*coffee*), but: das Café (*a fine restaurant where mostly coffee is served*).

NOTE. In foreign words which have preserved a foreign pronunciation, or certain foreign forms of spelling or inflection, do not use **k,** but **c,** as in: die Campagne (*campaign*); der Commis (*clerk*); das Flacon (*smelling-bottle*); der Redacteur (*editor*); die Adjectiva (*adjectives*), etc.

Doubtful Orthography. We find: Konzert *and* Concert, n.; Karzer (*prison in schools and universities*) *and* Carcer, m.; Komitee' *and* Comité', n.; Kompanie' *and* Compagnie', f.; konzentrisch (*concentric*) *and* concentrisch; Konzession

Write:

and Conceſſio'n, f.; Konzi'l (*council*) and Conci'l, n.; klaſſifizie'ren (*to classify*) and claſſificie'ren; Ku'rſus (*course of study*) and Cu'rſus, m.; korre'kt and corre'ct; Konjunktio'n and Conjunctio'n, etc., etc.

From these examples it will be seen that the mode of spelling is fluctuating between k and c, and c and z, in many words which originally contained the letter c. The first way is to be preferred, and strongly recommended, in all the words given above, and many others in common use that contain a k or a z-sound and are quite germanised in spelling and inflection. (Comp. C. 3.)

Use also k instead of c in words of Greek origin which have preserved the k-sound, as:—Anekdo'te, katho'liſch, Komö'die, Diale'kt, etc.— [Comp. B, letter k, 1.]—And write c and cq, as before, in: Acce'nt, Accuſati'v, Acquiſitio'n, etc.—

:nis (instead of niß) as a suffix of nouns, as in: das Ereignis (*event*); das Begräbnis (*burial*); das Verhältnis (*relation*); das Vermächtnis (*bequest*), etc.—

The prefix miß..., however, remains unchanged, as in: das Mi'ßverſtändnis (*misunderstanding*), pl. die Mi'ßverſtändniſſe.

s (instead of ß) in deshalb (*therefore*); deswegen (*therefore, for this reason*); indes (*meanwhile, whilst; however*); unterdes (*meanwhile, whilst*); weshalb (*why*); weswegen (*why*), etc.—

sf (instead of ſſ) in: dasſelbe (*the same*); desſelben (*of the same*); diesſeits (*on this side*), etc.

st (instead of ſt) in: Dienstag (*Tuesday*); Geburtstag (*birthday*); Frühlingstag (*spring-day*), and other compound nouns in which s occurs as a sign of the Genitive and is followed by a t.

ſſ between two vowels, the first one of which is short, as in laſſen (*to let, to leave*); die Taſſe (*cup*); trotz deſſen (*in spite of that*); weſſen (*whose*), etc.—

ß 1. between two vowels, the first one of which is long, as in: bü'ßen (*to atone for*); ſchießen (*to shoot*), etc.

2. before t, and at the end of words, as in: er läßt (*he leaves*); ihr laßt (*you leave*); gebü'ßt (*atoned for*); laß (*let*); der Kuß (*kiss*), etc.—

t (instead of dt) in: der Tote (*a dead man* or *person*); tot (*dead*); töten (*to kill*); der Totſchlag (*manslaughter*); der Totengräber (*gravedigger*), etc.—Comp. letter d (instead of dt.)

t (instead of d) in: das Brot (*bread*).

t (and never z) in the accented and original Latin combinations:—tia', tie', tio', as in: martia'liſch, Patie'nt, m., Natio'n, f., Traditio'n, f., Motio'n, etc.

But write: Gra'zie, Ingredie'nzien, etc., e being unaccented.

z 1. (instead of tz) after a long vowel, as in: die Bre'zel (*biscuit in the shape of a twisted ring, cracknel*); du'zen (*to call a person thou*), etc.

2. (instead of Cz and Sc) in: der Zar (*czar*); das Zepter (*sceptre*), etc.

3. (instead of ce) regularly at the end of foreign words with German pronunciation and terminating in French in ce, and in Latin in tia, tius, tium, cius, cium, as in: das Benefi'z, die Juſti'z, das Hoſpi'z, die Mili'z, die Noti'z; die Differe'nz, die Sente'nz, die Bala'nz; die Fina'nzen, die Novi'ze, die Allia'nz.

bie Diſta′nʒ, etc.—(But with foreign pronunciation: Alliance, Diſtance, etc.)

4. also in words quite germanised, as: ber Beʒi′rk (*district, circuit*); bie La′nʒe (*lance*); bie Poliʒei′ (*police*); ber Poliʒi′ſt (*policeman*); bas Terʒero′l (*pocket-pistol*); bas Terʒe′tt (*trio*), etc.—But write: Cä′ſar, bie Cäſu′r (*cesure, cesura*); bie Ce′ber, bie Celebritä′t, bie Cenſu′r (*censorship*), cenſie′ren (*to censure, to review*), ber Ce′ntis me′ter, bie Cerea′lien (*cereals*), bas Cöliba′t, ber Ci′rfumſte′r, bas Lyce′um, etc.

5. (instead of c) in verbs terminating in ... ie′ren, as: fabriʒie′ren (*to manufacture*); muſiʒie′ren (*to make music*); publiʒie′ren (*to publish*), etc.

Note. In many words which originally contained the letter c, the mode of spelling is unsettled and fluctuating between c and ʒ, as in: Mebiʒi′n and Mebici′n, f.; bas Reʒept and Recept, n. (*prescription, recipe*); Prinʒi′p and Princi′p, n. (*principle*); Proʒe′nt and Proce′nt, n. (*per cent.*); Proʒe′ß and Proce′ß, m., etc.—[Read carefully B, Note to letter k, also letter t of B, and General Observations on the Spelling of Foreign Words, where additional examples are given.]

C. Allgemeine Bemerkungen über die Schreibung der Frembwörter.

(General Observations on the Spelling of Foreign Words.)

1. With foreign words containing sounds and combinations of sounds not originally German, THE GENERAL PRINCIPLE regarding their orthography is that, their foreign pronunciation being preserved, also the foreign garb of their orthography is retained.

So, for example, we use:—

oi (sounded as in French) in: bie Memoi′ren (*memoirs*); bie Toile′tte (*toilet*).

g and j (sounded as in French) in: bie Baga′ge (*luggage*); bas Legi′s (*lodgings*); ber Genba′rm (*a police-officer on horseback*); bas Genie′ (*genius; a man of great talent*); ber Ingenieu′r (*engineer*); bas Journa′l (*journal, magazine*); rangie′ren (*to arrange*), etc.—But with German pronunciation: ber Genera′l (*general*); genia′l (*highly gifted*); bie Genialitä′t (*geniality, originality*), etc.—

gu (sounded as in French) in: ber Champa′gner (*champaign*); bie Lorgne′tte (*lorgnette, eye-glass*), etc.

ll (sounded like English l followed by y) in: bas Bataillo′n (*battalion*); bas Bi′llard (*billiards*); bas Bille′t (*ticket; note*); ber Poſtillo′n (*postillion*), etc.

n (sounded as in French, but not quite so nasal) in: bie Nua′nce (*gradation of colours*); bas Baſſi′n (*reservoir*); ber Refrai′n (*refrain*); ber Raye′n (*ray of light*; [of a fortification]: *radius*); bas Violonce′ll (*violoncello*), etc.

2. Many foreign words, on the other hand, composed of German

sounds, which might be indicated by German letters, have as yet preserved their original orthography. So we find:—

ai (for the sound of ä) in: die Chaiſe (*chaise*), from the French;

au *and* eau (for the sound of o) in: die Sauce (*sauce*); das Bureau (*office*), from the French;

ch (for the sound of ſch) in: die Chauffee' (*turnpike-road*), from the French;

ch (for the Greek ſ-sound) in: der *or* das Chor (*choir or chorus*), from the Greek;

ph (for the sound of f) in: der Philoſo'ph (*philosopher*), from the Greek;

th (for the sound of t) in: der Thron (*throne*), from the Greek; and

v (for the German w-sound) in: viole'tt (*violet-blue*, adj.), from the French.

3. **Again we find foreign words which, being in common use and composed of German sounds, have become entirely germanised, and wear a German garb**; as: die Tru'ppe (*troop, company*), French: la troupe; die Gru'ppe (*group*), French: la groupe; der Disku'rs (*discourse*), French: le discours; der Sekretä'r (*secretary*), French: le secrétaire.

It follows from the three preceding paragraphs:—that it is impossible to reduce the spelling of foreign words to any fixed principles, and that there exists at present much uncertainty and inconsistency respecting the spelling of such words.   [Comp. B, Consonants, Note to letter ſ, also B, letter x, where additional examples are given.]

D.   Kleinſchreibung und Zuſammenziehung.

(Small Initials [*instead of Capitals*] and Contractions.)

USE SMALL INITIALS:—

1. **With Nouns used as Prepositions, Conjunctions, Indefinite Numerals, and Adverbs,** as in: angeſichts (*in the face of*); infolge (*in conse-quence of*); behufs (*on behalf of*);—falls (*in case of*);—ein bißchen (*a bit, a little*); ein paar (*a few, some, some few*);—anfangs (*in the beginning*); teils (*partly*); einesteils (*on the one part or hand*); andernteils (*on the other part or hand*); meinerseits (*on my part*); morgens (*in the morning*); abends (*in the evening*); vormittags (*in the fore-noon*) [but: des Morgens, des Abends, heute Nachmittag, etc., Sonntags, Montags, etc.]; überhaupt (*in general, altogether, moreover*); unterwegs (*on the way*); heutzutage (*now-a-days*); beizeiten (*in time, betimes*); bisweilen (*at times*); einmal (*once*); zweimal (*twice*); bergauf (*uphill*); kopfüber (*head over heels*), etc.

2. **With Nouns used in Verbal-Combinations,** in which, by the by, they are strongly accented, and treated as separable particles, i.e. are separated from the verb and placed at the end of the clause when used in a principal sentence and in a simple tense.   Such Verbal-Combinations are:—recht haben

(*to be right*); u'nrecht haben (*to be wrong*); lei'd thun (*to be sorry*); we'h thun (*to hurt*);—schu'lb haben or sein (*to be in fault*);—fei'nd sein (*to be hostile*); mir ist a'ngst, we'hl (*I am afraid, well*); mir ist ne't (*it is necessary to me, I require*); mir ist we'he (*I am grieved*); das ist scha'de (*that is a pity*); ich bin wi'llens (*I have a mind, I intend*);—sta'ttfinden, sta'tthaben (*to take place*); wa'hrnehmen (*to perceive*); tei'lnehmen (*to take part in, to sympathise with*); ü'berhandnehmen (*to increase*); hau'shalten (*to keep house, to manage*); a'chtgeben (*to pay attention*); prei'sgeben (*to abandon, to expose*); bra'chliegen (*to lie fallow*); zusta'tten kommen (*to be of use, to come in usefully*); insta'nd setzen (*to repair, to restore*); zusta'nde kommen (*to accomplish*); imsti'ch lassen (*to leave in the lurch*), etc.—Er hält haus; es ist mir zustatten gekommen; es hat überhandgenommen; es ist mir zuteil geworden. **But:** Er hat keinen Teil an mir, etc.

3. With Pronouns and Numerals, as:—jemand, niemand, jeder, keiner, einer, der eine, der andere, man;—etliche (*some*), einige, einzelne, manche, viele, alle, alles, etwas, nichts, beide;—die (alle) andern, das (alles) andre, die (alle) übrigen, das (alles) übrige, das meiste, der (das) nämliche, der erste, der letzte, der zweite, der nächste, der erste beste, ein jeglicher, etc.

But:—Use Capital Initials (as before):—

(*a*) with Ordinal Numerals and Adjectives preceded by the definite article and used in apposition to a proper noun, as: Friedrich der Zweite; Karl der Große, etc.

(*b*) With Pronouns and Adjectives in titles, as:—Se. Majestät der König; das Kaiserliche Zollamt (*the Imperial Custom-House*); der Wirkliche Geheimrat von Humboldt (*the Privy Councillor von Humboldt*).

(*c*) With Pronouns used in addressing persons, more especially in letters, as:—Sie genießen mein volles Vertrauen; wir glauben Ihnen alles; das Haus Ihrer Eltern war mir stets geöffnet; ich will Dir bald mehr davon erzählen; stets bleibe ich Dein Dich liebender Sohn Heinrich, etc.

4. In Adjectival and Adverbial Clauses, as:—groß und klein (*grown up people and children*); arm und reich (*poor and rich people*); alt und jung, durch dick und dünn;—am besten, fürs erste, bei weitem (*by far*); aufs deutlichste, im allgemeinen, im ganzen, im folgenden, im wesentlichen (*essentially, in all essential points*); von neuem, vor kurzem, im voraus (*beforehand*); von vorne, ohne weiteres, um ein beträchtliches, etc.—and also in idiomatic phrases, such as:—Er zieht den kürzern dabei (*he is the loser by it*); ich will Ihnen Ihre Unarten zugute halten (*I will bear with your rudeness; I will excuse your incivilities*); der Junge hat Sie zum besten (*the boy amuses himself at your expense*); ich will es Ihnen zuliebe thun (*I will do it to please you*), etc.

E. Zerlegung der Wörter in Silben.

(Division of Words into Syllables.)

1. When part of a German word has to be separated from the rest in order to be carried on to the next line, the division into Syllables is made as we would naturally deliver them whilst pronouncing the word very slowly and

distinctly.　The compound letters: *ch, ck, dt, pf, ph, sch, sp, st, ß, th,* and *tz,* should, as a rule, not be separated. [For exceptions see § 2 of this chapter.] Examples:—ru-hen, die-ſer, Son-ne, Mut-ter, Mit-tag, den-noch, Flüſ-ſe, Wet-ter-glas, fünf-te, An-ker, Wech-ſel, Hoff-nung, Hoff-nun-gen, Fin-ger, Lang-ſam-keit, —Brü-ſche, ha-cken, Stä-dte, Klo-pfen, Or-tho-gra-phie, lö-ſchen, aus-ſpre-chen, lä-ſtig, ſchie-ßen, Lo-thar, fra-tzen, He-re.

2. The syllables forming the constituent parts of Compound Words should not be broken up, and the principal rule, as expressed above, cannot always be applied to them.　Examples: hin-ein, hier-auf, her-ein, dar-um, war-um, ver-aus, voll-en-den, Inter-eſ-ſe, Miſ-tro-ſter, At-mo-ſphä-re, Schiff-fahrt*, Schwimm-mei-ſter*, ge-müt-lich, Dis-pens, dis-pu-tie-ren, Dis-po-ſi-ti-on, be-ob-ach-ten, auf-er-ſte-hen, Ge-burts-tag, Früh-lings-tag.

* But write '*Schiffahrt*' and '*Schwimmeiſter*' when no separation takes place.

F. Der Apoſtroph. (The Apostrophe.)

1. The Apostrophe is more especially used for indicating the suppression of certain letters in poetry and in the language of every-day life, as in English. Examples: Ich lieb' dich; Steh' auf! Wie geht 's? So iſt 's recht; Geld hab' ich nicht.

2. Contractions of prepositions and articles are used **without the Apo-**strophe, as: am, beim, unterm, ans, ins, zum.

3. The Apostrophe is abolished before the inflections indicating the Genitive relation of proper names, as: Ciceros Briefe; Schillers Gedichte; Homers Ilias; Fritzens Geburtstag; Hamburgs Handel; Sophiens Mutter; die Einwohner Breslaus.

4. Family names, however, terminating in *s* or *z,* the genitive of which cannot be formed by adding *s,* require an Apostrophe to be placed after them for indicating the Genitive relation, as: Demoſthenes' Reden; Voß' Luiſe.

INDEX

THE END.

Clarendon Press Series

LANGE'S GERMAN COURSE

CONSISTS OF THE FOLLOWING WORKS:—

THIRD EDITION, with the German spelling revised to meet the requirements of the German Government Regulations of 1880.

THE GERMANS AT HOME; A Practical Introduction to German Conversation, with an *Appendix*, containing *the Essentials of German Grammar*, and a Synopsis of the changes the German spelling has undergone through the Government Regulations of 1880.

[Price 2*s*. 6*d*.

SECOND EDITION, carefully revised.

THE GERMAN MANUAL; *A German Grammar, A Reading-book,* and *A Handbook of Conversation in German.* [Price 7*s*. 6*d*.

'The German Manual' is intended to follow 'The Germans At Home.' It contains, besides a complete Grammar, a series of interesting anecdotes, stories, fables, letters, and conversations arranged in progressive order, and finishes with a German Play, and Franz Hoffman's well written and highly interesting story of 'BEETHOVEN,' especially adapted for this work. It offers great advantages for self-instruction, and will be very useful to persons who, having a certain knowledge of German, desire to obtain fluency in speaking and writing the language.

A GRAMMAR OF THE GERMAN LANGUAGE, in two Parts. Part I, Accidence; Part II, Syntax. With an *Appendix*, comprehending:—

I. The Declension of German Nouns.
II. Essentials of Construction.
III. Essentials of Word-building.
IV. The Use and Signification of the Auxiliary Verbs of Mood.
V. On Punctuation. [Price 3*s*. 6*d*.

The 'Grammar' forms the first part of the 'German Manual' and, in this separate form, is intended for the use of students who wish to make themselves acquainted with German Grammar chiefly for the purpose of being able to read German books. It is divided into paragraphs, and will commend itself as a text-book to the notice of teachers who, in pursuing the study of German Literature with their pupils, require a Grammar in a concise form for reference and study.

THIRD EDITION, with the German spelling revised to meet the requirements of the German Government Regulations of 1880.

GERMAN COMPOSITION; A Theoretical and Practical Guide to the art of Translating English Prose into German; with an Appendix containing, among other matters, a Synopsis of the changes the German spelling has undergone through the Government Regulations of 1880. [Price 4*s*. 6*d*.

[*A Key to the above, price* 5*s*.]

The book has been arranged so that it may be used with advantage by students who do not possess the author's other works.

SYNOPSIS OF THE CHANGES THE GERMAN SPELLING HAS UNDERGONE THROUGH THE GOVERNMENT REGULATIONS OF 1880; a concise and easy Guide for English students of German desirous of adopting the new official German spelling. Reprinted from 'German Composition.'

[Price 6*d*.

[**Any one of the preceding books, being complete in itself, may be used independently of any other book in the Series, according to the requirements of the student.**]

EXTRACTS FROM OPINIONS
ON H. LANGE'S GERMAN COURSE.

'The works bear evidence of remarkable painstaking, great teaching power, and a thorough understanding of the art of teaching.—DR. KARL DAMMANN, *Lecturer on the German Language and Literature at the Mason Science College, Queen's College, and the Midland Institute, Birmingham.*

'The Germans at Home.'

' The author is a practical teacher, and we are glad to recommend his work as likely to reduce, as far as possible, the inevitable difficulties to be encountered in the first study of a foreign language. Happy boys and girls of the present day, if they only knew their own blessings ! '

Journal of Education.

'"The Germans at Home" consists of forty conversations, intended to illustrate one day out of the life of a German family at home, as its name implies. The result is a decided improvement upon the run of books of this class. The interest of the student is sustained throughout, and everything is done in fact, which can be done to create a royal road to a knowledge of German.' *Manchester Courier.*

'"The Germans at Home" is an excellent book, and is likely to be extensively used.' *Schoolmaster.*

'The traits called "new" in this Course are thus defined by the author. "First the Facts, and then the Theory, the Laws and the Inferences." "The Germans at Home" (printed in Roman characters) contains forty conversations, all connected, so as "to illustrate one day out of the life of a German family at home." The themes are German, the idioms are modern, and the "variations" that follow the conversations seem likely to be useful.' *Athenæum.*

'A Grammar of the German Language.'

' The author has obviously studied to make as clear as possible the arrangement of his materials, and the printer has aided that endeavour.'

Athenæum.

' The Grammar is a good one.' *Schoolmaster.*

'The Germans at Home' and 'The German Manual.'

'Instead of wearying the unhappy student with learning a lot of dry and elaborate technicalities of accidence and syntax at the outset, Mr. Lange starts him with conversations—forty in number, each illustrative of one day out of the life of a German family at home—and very soon lands him "in medias res" by the aid of interlinear translation, by the means of which he can gain a knowledge of the idioms and peculiarities of structure of the language, while he is at the same time acquiring a knowledge of the theory of the language, i.e. of its accidence and syntax. Thus we get in Mr. Lange's system the facts first, and then proceed to the theory, laws, and inferences—first the life and spirit, then the form and body in which they are clothed. Only those who have themselves learnt and taught (or tried to learn and teach) German, can thoroughly appreciate the advantages of this plan, which avails itself of the two leading principles which underlie all learning, and ought to form the basis of all teaching, viz. the principles of imitation and of variation. When we remember the long and weary hours spent by ourselves in learning German, we envy Mr. Lange's pupils, and those who have the chance of using his books.'   *Manchester Critic.*

'Mr. Lange's "German Course" is thoroughly trustworthy and useful.'
Glasgow News.

'Herr Lange has worked out his principle most successfully.'
Edinburgh Daily Review.

'The German Manual.'

'This is a very elaborate work. It contains an amount of matter unusually great, and of unquestionable excellence. If not *multum in parvo*, it is at least *multum in uno.* The bigness of the book is largely due to the fact that the author has amalgamated with this volume the entire grammar, which is also published in a separate form. The grammar is a good one; but the special feature of the "German Manual" consists in its comprehensiveness, which will be apparent from the following summary of its contents:—Part I. Accidence. Part II. Syntax. Part III. Interlinear Translation. Part IV. German for Translation into English. Part V. Notes and Helpful Hints. Part VI. English Version of Part IV. for Re-translation. By an ingenious system of adaptation, the six parts are to be proceeded with simultaneously. Thus every part throwing light upon the rest, and the student having to deal with the same passages over and over again, the process of mental assimilation is likely to be rendered more real and rapid. When we add that the book contains a humorous comedy and an excellent life of Beethoven, our readers will acknowledge that Herr Lange has provided that variety which is proverbially charming. From the conspicuous absence of the namby-pamby element—unfortunately too common in translation exercises—as well as from the general excellence of the work, it may be confidently recommended, especially for the use of adult students.'   *Schoolmaster.*

'Herr Lange's method is excellent for simplicity and clearness.'

Saturday Review.

'German Composition.'

'Having used H. Lange's Composition for about a couple of years with my advanced pupils, I am in a position to state that it has more than answered the very favourable expectations I had formed on a first perusal of the work. To my mind its chief recommendations are :—

1st. It may safely be put into the hands of learners at an earlier stage than most works of this class.

2nd. The judicious manner in which the exercises have been graduated, and the careful elucidation of all grammatical difficulties.

3rd. The admirable rendering of English idioms into their German equivalents.'—JOHN J. T. JACKSON, *Lecturer on Modern Languages and Philology at the Lancashire Independent College, and the Wesleyan College, Didsbury.*

'After a very careful perusal of "Hermann Lange's German Composition," I have no hesitation to say that it seems to me to be the best book of that kind,—not only with regard to the choice of good extracts from modern English authors, but also in respect to the thoroughness and correctness of the Notes. I shall find it exceedingly useful with my pupils for the Army and Civil Service Examinations.'—THEODORE H. DITTEL, *London, Tutor to Students preparing for the Army and Civil Service Examinations.*

'I prefer the book to all others on German Composition.'—ERNEST R. MORGAN, *London.*

'We begin with simple stories of two or three sentences each, and so fully annotated that they may be read off into German by a pupil who knows his first accidence, and ascend by easy gradients to Sir Walter Scott and Macaulay.

It is throughout a careful, accurate, and scholarly piece of work.'

Journal of Education.

Oxford:

AT THE CLARENDON PRESS.

LONDON: HENRY FROWDE,

OXFORD UNIVERSITY PRESS WAREHOUSE, AMEN CORNER, E.C.

CLARENDON PRESS, OXFORD.
SELECT LIST OF STANDARD WORKS

1. DICTIONARIES.

A NEW ENGLISH DICTIONARY
ON HISTORICAL PRINCIPLES,

Founded mainly on the materials collected by the Philological Society.

Imperial 4to.

EDITED BY DR. MURRAY.

PRESENT STATE OF THE WORK.

				£	s.	d.
Vol. I.	A, B	By Dr. Murray	Half-morocco	2	12	6
Vol. II.	C	By Dr. Murray	Half-morocco	2	12	6
Vol. III.	D, E	By Dr. Murray and Dr. Bradley	Half-morocco	2	12	6
Vol. IV.	F, G	By Dr. Bradley	Half-morocco	2	12	6
Vol. V.	H—K	By Dr. Murray	Half-morocco	2	12	6

				£	s.	d.
			L-Lap	0	2	6
			Lap-Leisurely	0	5	0
			Leisureness-Lief	0	2	6
Vol. VI.	L—N	By Dr. Bradley	Lief-Lock	0	5	0
			Lock-Lyyn	0	5	0
			M-Mandragon	0	5	0
			O-Onomastic	0	5	0
			Onomastical Outing	0	5	0
Vol. VII.	O, P	By Dr. Murray	Outjet-Ozyat	0	2	6
			P-Pargeted	0	5	0
			Pargeter-Pennached	0	5	0
			Q	0	2	6
Vol. VIII.	Q–S	By Mr. Craigie	R-Reactive	0	5	0
			Reactively-Ree	0	5	0
			Ree-Reign	0	2	6

The remainder of the work is in active preparation.

Vols. IX, X will contain S–Z with some supplemental matter.

Orders can be given through any bookseller for the delivery of the remainder of the work in complete *Volumes* or in *Half-volumes* or in *Sections* or in *Parts*.

HALF-VOLUMES. The price of half-volumes, bound, with straight-grained persian leather back, cloth sides, gilt top, is £1 7s. 6d. each, or £13 15s. for the ten now ready, namely, A, B, C-Comm., Comm.-Czech, D, E, F, G, H, I-K.

SECTIONS. A single Section of 64 pages at 2s. 6d. or a double Section of 128 pages at 5s. is issued quarterly.

PARTS. A Part (which is generally the equivalent of five single Sections and is priced at 12s. 6d.) is issued whenever ready.

Nearly all the Parts and Sections in which Volumes I–V were first issued are still obtainable in the original covers.

FORTHCOMING ISSUE, 1905. A portion continuing R, by Mr. Craigie.

Oxford: Clarendon Press. London: Henry Frowde, Amen Corner, E.C.

A Hebrew and English Lexicon of the Old Testament, with an Appendix containing the Biblical Aramaic, based on the Thesaurus and Lexicon of Gesenius, by Francis Brown, D.D., S. R. Driver, D.D., and C. A. Briggs, D.D.   Parts I–XI.   Small 4to, 2s. 6d. each.

Thesaurus Syriacus : collegerunt Quatremère, Bernstein, Lorsbach, Arnoldi, Agrell, Field, Roediger : edidit R. Payne Smith, S.T.P.
Vol. I, containing Fasciculi I–V, sm. fol., 5l. 5s.
Vol. II, completing the work, containing Fasciculi VI–X, 8l. 8s.

A Compendious Syriac Dictionary, founded upon the above. Edited by Mrs. Margoliouth.   Small 4to, complete, 63s. net.   Part IV, 15s. net.   *Parts I–III can no longer be supplied.*

A Dictionary of the Dialects of Vernacular Syriac as spoken by the Eastern Syrians of Kurdistan, North-West Persia, and the Plain of Mosul.   By A. J. Maclean, M.A., F.R.G.S.   Small 4to, 15s.

An English-Swahili Dictionary.   By A. C. Madan, M.A.   *Second Edition, Revised.*   Extra fcap. 8vo, 7s. 6d. net.

Swahili-English Dictionary.   By A. C. Madan, M.A.   Extra fcap. 8vo.   7s. 6d. net.

A Sanskrit-English Dictionary.   Etymologically and Philologically arranged, with special reference to cognate Indo-European Languages. By Sir M. Monier-Williams, M.A., K.C.I.E. ; with the collaboration of Prof. E. Leumann, Ph.D. ; Prof. C. Cappeller, Ph.D. ; and other scholars. *New Edition, greatly Enlarged and Improved.*   Cloth, bevelled edges, 3l. 13s. 6d. ; half-morocco, 4l. 4s.

A Greek-English Lexicon.   By H. G. Liddell, D.D., and Robert Scott, D.D.   *Eighth Edition, Revised.*   4to.   1l. 16s.

An Etymological Dictionary of the English Language, arranged on an Historical Basis.   By W. W. Skeat, Litt.D.   *Third Edition.*   4to.   2l. 4s.

A Middle-English Dictionary.   By F. H. Stratmann.   A new edition, by H. Bradley, M.A., Ph.D.   4to, half-morocco.   1l. 11s. 6d.

The Student's Dictionary of Anglo-Saxon.   By H. Sweet, M.A., Ph.D., LL.D.   Small 4to.   8s. 6d. net.

An Anglo-Saxon Dictionary, based on the MS. collections of the late Joseph Bosworth, D.D.   Edited and enlarged by Prof. T. N. Toller, M.A.   Parts I–III. A–SÁR.   4to, stiff covers, 15s. each.   Part IV, § 1, SÁR–SWÍÐRIAN.   Stiff covers, 8s. 6d.   Part IV, § 2, SWÍÞ-SNEL-ÝTMEST, 18s. 6d.

An Icelandic-English Dictionary, based on the MS. collections of the late Richard Cleasby.   Enlarged and completed by G. Vigfússon, M.A.   4to.   3l. 7s.

2. LAW.

Anson.   *Principles of the English Law of Contract, and of Agency in its Relation to Contract.*   By Sir W. R. Anson, D.C.L.   *Tenth Edition.*   8vo.   10s. 6d.

Anson.   *Law and Custom of the Constitution.*   2 vols.   8vo.
Part I. Parliament.   *Third Edition.*   12s. 6d.
Part II. The Crown.   *Second Ed.*   14s.

Bryce. *Studies in History and* Jurisprudence. 2 Vols. 8vo. By the Right Hon. J. Bryce, M.P. 25s. net.

Goudy. *Von Jhering's Law* in Daily Life. Translated by H. Goudy, D.C.L. Crown 8vo. 3s.6d.net.

Digby. *An Introduction to* the History of the Law of Real Property. By Sir Kenelm E. Digby, M.A. Fifth Edition. 8vo. 12s. 6d.

Grueber. *Lex Aquilia.* By Erwin Grueber. 8vo. 10s. 6d.

Hall. *International Law.* By W.E.Hall,M.A. Fifth Edit. Revised by J. B. Atlay, M.A. 8vo. 21s. net.

—— *A Treatise on the Foreign* Powers and Jurisdiction of the British Crown. 8vo. 10s. 6d.

Holland. *Elements of Juris-* prudence. By T. E. Holland, D.C.L. Ninth Edition. 8vo. 10s. 6d.

—— *Studies in International* Law. 8vo. 10s. 6d.

—— *Gentilis, Alberici, De* Iure Belli Libri Tres. Small 4to, half-morocco. 21s.

—— *The Institutes of Jus-* tinian, edited as a recension of the Institutes of Gaius. Second Edition. Extra fcap. 8vo. 5s.

—— *The European Concert* in the Eastern Question, a collection of treaties and other public acts. 8vo. 12s. 6d.

Holland and Shadwell. *Select* Titles from the Digest of Justinian. By T. E. Holland, D.C.L., and C. L. Shadwell, D.C.L. 8vo. 14s.

Also sold in Parts, in paper covers—
Part I. Introductory Titles. 2s. 6d.
Part II. Family Law. 1s.
Part III. Property Law. 2s. 6d.
Part IV. Law of Obligations (No. 1),
3s. 6d. (No. 2), 4s. 6d.

Ilbert. *The Government of* India. Being a Digest of the Statute Law relating thereto. With Historical Introduction and Illustrative Documents. By Sir Courtenay Ilbert, K.C.S.I. 8vo, half-roan. 21s.

Ilbert. *Legislative Forms and* Methods. 8vo, half-roan. 16s.

Jenks. *Modern Land Law.* By Edward Jenks, M.A. 8vo. 15s.

Jenkyns. *British Rule and* Jurisdiction beyond the Seas. By the late Sir Henry Jenkyns, K.C.B. 8vo, half-roan. 16s. net.

Markby. *Elements of Law* considered with reference to Principles of General Jurisprudence. By Sir William Markby. Fifth Edition. 8vo. 12s. 6d.

Moyle. *Imperatoris Ius-* tiniani Institutionum Libri Quattuor, with Introductions, Commentary, Excursus and Translation. By J. B. Moyle, D.C.L. Fourth Edition. 2 vols. 8vo. Vol. I. 16s. Vol. II. 6s.

—— *Contract of Sale in the* Civil Law. 8vo. 10s. 6d.

Pollock and Wright. *An* Essay on Possession in the Common Law. By Sir F. Pollock, Bart., M.A., and Sir R. S. Wright, B.C.L. 8vo. 8s.6d.

Poste. *Gaii Institutionum* Juris Civilis Commentarii Quattuor; or, Elements of Roman Law by Gaius. With a Translation and Commentary by Edward Poste, M.A. Fourth Edition, revised and enlarged, by E. A. Whittuck, M.A., B.C.L. With an Historical Introduction by A. H. J. Greenidge, D.Litt. 8vo. 16s. net.

Radcliffe and Miles. *Cases* Illustrating the Principles of the Law of Torts. By F. R. Y. Radcliffe. K.C., and J.C.Miles, M.A. 8vo. 12s.6d. net.

Sohm. *The Institutes.* A Text-book of the History and System of Roman Private Law. By Rudolph Sohm. Translated by J. C. Ledlie, B.C.L. Second Edition, revised and enlarged. 8vo. 18s.

Stokes. *The Anglo-Indian* Codes. By Whitley Stokes, LL.D. Vol. I. Substantive Law. 8vo. 30s. Vol. II. Adjective Law. 8vo. 35s. First and Second Supplements to the above, 1887–1891. 8vo. 6s. 6d. Separately, No. 1, 2s. 6d.; No. 2, 4s. 6d.

London : HENRY FROWDE, Amen Corner, E.C.

3. HISTORY, BIOGRAPHY, ETC.

Asser. *Life of King Alfred,* together with the Annals of St. Noets, erroneously ascribed to Asser. Edited with Introduction and Commentary by W. H. Stevenson, M.A. 2 vols. Crown 8vo. 12s. *net.*

Aubrey. '*Brief Lives,' chiefly of Contemporaries, set down by John Aubrey, between the Years 1669 and 1696.* Edited from the Author's MSS., by Andrew Clark, M.A., LL.D. With Facsimiles. 2 vols. 8vo. 25s.

Ballard. *The Domesday Boroughs.* By ADOLPHUS BALLARD, B.A., LL.B. 8vo. With four Plans. 6s. 6d. *net.*

Barnard. *Companion to English History (Middle Ages).* With 97 Illustrations. By F. P. Barnard, M.A. Crown 8vo. 8s. 6d. *net.*

Boswell's *Life of Samuel Johnson, LL.D.* Edited by G. Birkbeck Hill, D.C.L. In six volumes, medium 8vo. With Portraits and Facsimiles. Half-bound. 3l. 3s.

Bright. *Chapters of Early English Church History.* By W. Bright, D.D. *Third Edition. Revised and Enlarged.* With a Map. 8vo. 12s.

Bryce. *Studies in History and Jurisprudence.* By J. Bryce, M.P. 2 vols. 8vo. 25s. *net.*

Butler. *The Arab Conquest of Egypt and the last thirty years of the Roman Dominion.* By A. J. Butler, D.Litt., F.S.A. With Maps and Plans. 8vo. 16s. *net.*

Chambers. *The Mediaeval Stage.* By E. K. Chambers. With two illustrations. 2 vols. 8vo. 25s. *net.*

Clarendon's *History of the Rebellion and Civil Wars in England.* Re-edited by W. Dunn Macray, M.A., F.S.A. 6 vols. Crown 8vo. 2l. 5s.

Earle and Plummer. *Two of the Saxon Chronicles, Parallel, with Supplementary Extracts from the others.* A Revised Text, edited, with Introduction, Notes, Appendices, and

Glossary, by C. Plummer, M.A., on the basis of an edition by J. Earle, M.A. 2 vols. Cr. 8vo, half-roan.
Vol. I. Text, Appendices, and Glossary. 10s. 6d.
Vol. II. Introduction, Notes, and Index. 12s. 6d.

Fisher. *Studies in Napoleonic Statesmanship.— Germany.* By H. A. L. Fisher, M.A. With four Maps. 8vo. 12s. 6d. *net.*

Freeman. *The History of Sicily from the Earliest Times.*
Vols. I and II. 8vo, cloth. 2l. 2s.
Vol. III. The Athenian and Carthaginian Invasions. 24s.
Vol. IV. From the Tyranny of Dionysios to the Death of Agathoklès. Edited by Arthur J. Evans, M.A. 21s.

Freeman. *The Reign of William Rufus and the Accession of Henry the First.* By E. A. Freeman, D.C.L. 2 vols. 8vo. 1l. 16s.

Gardiner. *The Constitutional Documents of the Puritan Revolution,* 1628–1660. By S. R. Gardiner, D.C.L. *Second Edition.* Crown 8vo. 10s. 6d.

Gross. *The Gild Merchant;* a Contribution to British Municipal History. By Charles Gross, Ph.D. 2 vols. 8vo. 24s.

Hill. *Sources for Greek History between the Persian and Peloponnesian Wars.* Collected and arranged by G. F. Hill, M.A. 8vo. 10s. 6d.

Hodgkin. *Italy and her Invaders.* With Plates & Maps. 8 vols. 8vo. By T. Hodgkin, D.C.L.
Vols. I–II. *Second Edition.* 42s.
Vols. III–IV. *Second Edition.* 36s.
Vols. V–VI. 36s.
Vols. VII–VIII (*completing the work*). 24s.

Johnson. *Letters of Samuel Johnson, LL.D.* Collected and Edited by G. Birkbeck Hill, D.C.L. 2 vols. half-roan. 28s.

——*Johnsonian Miscellanies.* 2 vols. Medium 8vo, half-roan. 28s.

Oxford : Clarendon Press.

Kitchin. *A History of France.* By G. W. Kitchin, D.D. In three Volumes. Crown 8vo, each 10s. 6d. Vol. I. to 1453. Vol. II. 1453-1624. Vol. III. 1624-1793.

Kyd. *The Works of Thomas Kyd.* Edited from the original Texts, with Introduction, Notes, and Facsimiles, by F. S. Boas, M.A. 8vo. 15s. net.

Lewis (*Sir G. Cornewall*). *An Essay on the Government of Dependencies.* Edited by C. P. Lucas, B.A. 8vo, half-roan. 14s.

Lucas. *Historical Geography of the British Colonies.* By C. P. Lucas, B.A. With Maps. Cr. 8vo.

The Origin and Growth of the English Colonies and of their System of Government (an Introduction to Mr. C. P. Lucas's Historical Geography of the Colonies). By H. E. Egerton. 2s. 6d. Also in binding uniform with the Series. 3s. 6d.

Vol. I. The Mediterranean and Eastern Colonies (exclusive of India). 5s.
Vol. II. The West Indian Colonies. 7s. 6d.
Vol. III. West Africa. Second Edition, revised to the end of 1899, by H. E. Egerton. 7s. 6d.
Vol. IV. South and East Africa. Historical and Geographical. 9s. 6d.

Also Vol. IV in two Parts—
Part I. Historical, 6s. 6d.
Part II. Geographical, 3s. 6d.
Vol. V. The History of Canada (Part I, New France). 6s.

Ludlow. *The Memoirs of Edmund Ludlow, Lieutenant-General of the Horse in the Army of the Commonwealth of England,* 1625-1672. Edited by C. H. Firth, M.A. 2 vols. 36s.

Lyly. *The Works of John Lyly.* Collected and edited, with facsimiles, by R. W. Bond, M.A. In 3 vols. 8vo, uniform with *Kyd*. 42s. net.

Machiavelli. *Il Principe.* Edited by L. Arthur Burd, M.A. With an Introduction by Lord Acton. 8vo. 14s.

Merriman. *Life and Letters of Thomas Cromwell.* With a Portrait and Facsimile. By R. B. Merriman, B.Litt. 2 vols. 8vo. 18s. net.

Morris. *The Welsh Wars of Edward I.* With a Map. By J. E. Morris, M.A. 8vo. 9s. 6d. net.

Oman. *A History of the Peninsular War.* 6 vols. 8vo. With Maps, Plans, and Portraits. By C. Oman, M.A. Vol. I. 1807-1809. 14s. net. Vol. II. Jan.-Sept., 1809 (from the Battle of Corunna to the end of the Talavera Campaign). 14s. net.

Payne. *History of the New World called America.* By E. J. Payne, M.A. 8vo.
Vol. I, containing The Discovery and Aboriginal America, 18s.
Vol. II, Aboriginal America (concluded), 14s.

Plummer. *The Life and Times of Alfred the Great.* By Charles Plummer, M.A. Crown 8vo. 5s. net.

Poole. *Historical Atlas of Modern Europe from the decline of the Roman Empire.* Edited by R. L. Poole, M.A. 5l. 15s. 6d. net. Each Map can now be bought separately for 1s. 6d. net.

Prothero. *Select Statutes and other Constitutional Documents, illustrative of the Reigns of Elizabeth and James I.* Edited by G. W. Prothero, M.A. Cr. 8vo. Edition 2. 10s. 6d.

Ramsay (*Sir J. H.*). *Lancaster and York.* (A.D. 1399-1485). 2 vols. 8vo. With Index. 37s. 6d.

Ramsay (*W. M.*). *The Cities and Bishoprics of Phrygia.*
Vol. I. Part I. The Lycos Valley and South-Western Phrygia. Royal 8vo. 18s. net.
Vol. I. Part II. West and West-Central Phrygia. 21s. net.

Ranke. *A History of Eng-land, principally in the Seventeenth Century.* By L. von Ranke. Translated under the superintendence of G. W. Kitchin, D.D., and C. W. Boase, M.A. 6 vols. 8vo. 63s. Revised Index, separately, 1s.

Rashdall. *The Universities of Europe in the Middle Ages.* By Hastings Rashdall, M.A. 2 vols. (in 3 Parts) 8vo. With Maps. 2l. 5s. net.

Rhŷs. *Studies in the Arthurian Legend.* By John Rhŷs, M.A. 8vo. 12s. 6d.

—— *Celtic Folklore:* Welsh and Manx. By the same. 2 vols. 8vo. 21s.

Rogers. *History of Agriculture and Prices in England,* A.D. 1259–1793. By J. E. T. Rogers, M.A. 8vo. Vols. I, II (1259–1400), 42s. Vols. III, IV (1401–1582), 50s. Vols. V, VI (1583 1702), 50s. Vol. VII, 2 Parts (1703–1793).

Sanday. *Sacred Sites of the Gospels.* By W. Sanday, D.D. With many illustrations, including drawings of the Temple by Paul Waterhouse. 8vo. 13s. 6d. net.

Scaccario. *De Necessariis Observantiis Scaccarii Dialogus.* Commonly called Dialogus de Scaccario. Edited by A. Hughes, C. G. Crump, and C. Johnson. 8vo, 12s. 6d. net.

Smith's *Lectures on Justice, Police, Revenue and Arms.* Edited, with Introduction and Notes, by Edwin Cannan. 8vo. 10s. 6d. net.

—— *Wealth of Nations.* With Notes, by J. E. Thorold Rogers, M.A. 2 vols. 8vo. 21s.

Smith (V. A.). *The Early History of India, from 600 B.C. to the Muhammadan Conquest, including the Invasion of Alexander the Great.* By Vincent A. Smith, M.A. 8vo, with Maps and other Illustrations. 14s. net.

Stubbs. *Select Charters and other Illustrations of English Constitutional History, from the Earliest Times to the Reign of Edward I.* Arranged and edited by W. Stubbs, D.D. *Eighth Edition.* Crown 8vo. 8s. 6d.

—— *The Constitutional History of England, in its Origin and Development. Library Edition.* 3 vols. Demy 8vo. 2l. 8s. Also in 3 vols. crown 8vo. 12s. each.

—— *Seventeen Lectures on the Study of Mediaeval and Modern History and kindred subjects.* Crown 8vo. *Third Edition.* 8s. 6d.

—— *Registrum Sacrum Anglicanum.* Sm. 4to. Ed. 2. 10s. 6d.

Vinogradoff. *Villainage in England.* Essays in English Mediaeval History. By Paul Vinogradoff. 8vo, half-bound. 16s.

4. PHILOSOPHY, LOGIC, ETC.

Bacon. *Novum Organum.* Edited, with Introduction, Notes, &c., by T. Fowler, D.D. *Second Edition.* 8vo. 15s.

Berkeley. *The Works of George Berkeley, D.D., formerly Bishop of Cloyne; including many of his writings hitherto unpublished.* With Prefaces, Annotations, Appendices, and an Account of his Life, by A. Campbell Fraser, Hon. D.C.L., LL.D. New Edition in 4 vols., cr. 8vo. 24s.

—— *The Life and Letters, with an account of his Philosophy.* By A. Campbell Fraser. 8vo. 16s.

Bosanquet. *Logic; or, the Morphology of Knowledge.* By B. Bosanquet, M.A. 8vo. 21s.

Butler. *The Works of Joseph Butler, D.C.L., sometime Lord Bishop of Durham.* Edited by the Right Hon. W. E. Gladstone. 2 vols. Medium 8vo. 14s. each.

Campagnac. *The Cambridge Platonists:* being Selections from the writings of Benjamin Whichcote, John Smith, and Nathanael Culverwel, with Introduction by E. T. Campagnac, M.A. Cr. 8vo. 6s. 6d. net.

Fowler. *Logic;* Deductive and Inductive, combined in a single volume. Extra fcap. 8vo. 7s. 6d.

Fowler and Wilson. *The Principles of Morals.* By T. Fowler, D.D., and J. M. Wilson, B.D. 8vo, cloth. 14s.

Green. *Prolegomena to Ethics.* By T. H. Green, M.A. Edited by A. C. Bradley, M.A. *Fourth Edition.* Crown 8vo. 7s. 6d.

Hegel. *The Logic of Hegel.* Translated from the Encyclopaedia of the Philosophical Sciences. With Prolegomena to the Study of Hegel's Logic and Philosophy. By W. Wallace, M.A. *Second Edition, Revised and Augmented.* 2 vols. Crown 8vo. 10s. 6d. each.

Hegel's *Philosophy of Mind.* Translated from the Encyclopaedia of the Philosophical Sciences. With Five Introductory Essays. By William Wallace, M.A., LL.D. Crown 8vo. 10s. 6d.

Hume's *Treatise of Human Nature.* Edited, with Analytical Index, by L. A. Selby-Bigge, M.A. *Second Edition.* Crown 8vo. 6s. net.

—— *Enquiry concerning the Human Understanding.* Edited by L. A. Selby-Bigge, M.A. *Second Edition.* Crown 8vo. 6s. net.

Leibniz. *The Monadology and other Philosophical Writings.* Translated, with Introduction and Notes, by Robert Latta, M.A., D.Phil. Crown 8vo. 8s. 6d.

Locke. *An Essay Concerning Human Understanding.* By John Locke. Collated and Annotated by A. Campbell Fraser, Hon. D.C.L., LL.D. 2 vols. 8vo. 1l. 12s.

Lotze's *Logic,* in Three Books—of Thought, of Investigation, and of Knowledge. English Translation; edited by B. Bosanquet, M.A. *Second Edition.* 2 vols. Cr. 8vo. 12s.

—— *Metaphysic,* in Three Books—Ontology, Cosmology, and Psychology. English Translation; edited by B. Bosanquet, M.A. *Second Edition.* 2 vols. Cr. 8vo. 12s.

Martineau. *Types of Ethical Theory.* By James Martineau, D.D. *Third Edition.* 2 vols. Cr. 8vo. 15s.

—— *A Study of Religion:* its Sources and Contents. Second Edition. 2 vols. Cr. 8vo. 15s.

Selby-Bigge. *British Moralists.* Selections from Writers principally of the Eighteenth Century. Edited by L. A. Selby-Bigge, M.A. 2 vols. Crown 8vo. 12s. net, uniform with Hume's *Treatise* and *Enquiry* and the 4 vol. crown 8vo edition of *Berkeley.*

Spinoza. *A Study in the Ethics of Spinoza.* By Harold H Joachim. 8vo. 10s. 6d. net.

Wallace. *Lectures and Essays on Natural Theology and Ethics.* By William Wallace, M.A., LL.D. Edited, with a Biographical Introduction, by Edward Caird, M.A. 8vo, with a Portrait. 12s. 6d.

5. PHYSICAL SCIENCE, ETC.

Chambers. *A Handbook of Descriptive and Practical Astronomy.* By G. F. Chambers, F.R.A.S. *Fourth Edition,* in 3 vols. Demy 8vo.

Vol. I. The Sun, Planets, and Comets. 21s.

Vol. II. Instruments and Practical Astronomy. 21s.

Vol. III. The Starry Heavens. 14s.

De Bary. *Comparative Anatomy of the Vegetative Organs of the Phanerogams and Ferns.* By Dr. A. de Bary. Translated by F. O. Bower, M.A., and D. H. Scott, M.A. Royal 8vo, half-morocco, 24s. net; cloth, 21s. net.

—— *Comparative Morphology and Biology of Fungi, Mycetozoa*

and Bacteria. By Dr. A. de Bary. Translated by H. E. F. Garnsey, M.A. Revised by Isaac Bayley Balfour, M.A., M.D., F.R.S. Royal 8vo, half-morocco, 24s. *net;* cloth, 21s. *net.*

—— *Lectures on Bacteria.* By Dr. A. de Bary. *Second Improved Edition.* Translated and revised by the same. Crown 8vo. 5s. *net.*

Ewart. *On the Physics and Physiology of Protoplasmic Streaming in Plants.* By A. J. Ewart, D.Sc., Ph.D.,F.L.S. With seventeen illustrations. Royal 8vo. 8s. 6d. net.

Fischer. *The Structure and Functions of Bacteria.* By Alfred Fischer. Translated into English by A. C. Jones. Royal 8vo. With Twenty-nine Woodcuts. 7s. 6d. *net.*

Goebel. *Outlines of Classification and Special Morphology of Plants.* By Dr. K. Goebel. Translated by H. E. F. Garnsey, M.A. Revised by I. B. Balfour, M.A., M.D., F.R.S. Royal 8vo, half-morocco, 22s. 6d. *net;* cloth, 20s. *net.*

—— *Organography of Plants,* *especially of the Archegoniatae and Spermophyta.* By Dr. K. Goebel. Authorized English Edition, by I. B. Balfour, M.A., M.D., F.R.S. Part I, General Organography. Royal 8vo, half-morocco, 12s. *net;* cloth, 10s.*net.* Pt. II, half-morocco, 24s. *net;* cloth, 21s. *net.*

Miall and Hammond. *The Structure and Life-History of the Harlequin Fly (Chironomus).* By L. C. Miall, F.R.S., and A. R. Hammond, F.L.S. 8vo. With 130 Illustrations. 7s. 6d.

Pfeffer. *The Physiology of Plants. A Treatise upon the Metabolism and Sources of Energy in Plants.* By Prof. Dr. W. Pfeffer. Second fully Revised Edition, translated and edited by A. J. Ewart, D.Sc., Ph.D.,

F.L.S. Royal 8vo. Vol. I, half-morocco, 26s. *net;* cloth, 23s. *net.* Vol. II, 16s. *net;* cloth, 14s. *net.*

Prestwich. *Geology—Chemical, Physical, and Stratigraphical.* By Sir Joseph Prestwich, M.A., F.R.S. In two Volumes. Royal 8vo. 61s.

Sachs. *A History of Botany.* Translated by H. E. F. Garnsey, M.A. Revised by I. B. Balfour, M.A., M.D., F.R.S. Cr. 8vo. 10s. *net.*

Schimper. *Plant Geography upon a Physiological Basis.* By Dr. A. F. W. Schimper. The Authorized English Translation, by W. R. Fisher, M.A. Revised and edited by Percy Groom, M.A., and I. B. Balfour, M.A., M.D., F.R.S. Royal 8vo. With a photogravure portrait of Dr. Schimper, five collotypes, four maps, and four hundred and ninety-seven other illustrations. Half-morocco, 42s. *net.*

Solms-Laubach. *Fossil Botany. Being an Introduction to Palaeophytology from the Standpoint of the Botanist.* By H. Graf zu Solms-Laubach. Translated and revised by the same. Royal 8vo, half-morocco, 17s. *net;* cloth, 15s. *net.*

OXFORD HISTORY OF MUSIC.

8vo. Edited by W. H. Hadow, M.A. *The Polyphonic Period.* Part I (Method of Musical Art, 330–1330). By H. E. Wooldridge, M.A. 15s. net.

The Seventeenth Century. By Sir C. H. H. Parry, M.A., D.Mus. 15s.*net.*

The Age of Bach and Handel. By J. A. Fuller Maitland, M.A. 15s. *net.*

The Viennese School. By W. H. Hadow, M.A.

IN PREPARATION.

The Polyphonic Period. Part II. By H. E. Wooldridge, M.A.

The Romantic Period. By E. Dannreuther, M.A.

OXFORD

AT THE CLARENDON PRESS

LONDON, EDINBURGH, NEW YORK, AND TORONTO

HENRY FROWDE